Bouwman

The Complete World of

Thames & Hudson

the Dead Sea Scrolls

Philip R. Davies, George J. Brooke and Phillip R. Callaway

With 216 illustrations, 84 in color

Contents

Introduction 6
Chronologies and Map 10

I THE SCROLLS REVEALED

Early Dead Sea Discoveries 16
The Damascus Document 18
Editing the Scrolls: The First Fifty Years 22
The First Editors 30

II THE ANCIENT WORLD OF THE SCROLLS

The Historical Framework: From Babylon
to Bar Kokhba 38
Jewish Religious Life 46
Jewish Parties and Sects 54

III INSIDE THE SCROLLS

Making a Scroll 66
Scripts and Writing Styles 68
Carbon-14 Dating 74
Reconstructing a Scroll 76

Cave 1 82
The Rules Scroll 82
The Community Rule 82
The Rule of the Congregation 89
The Rule of Blessings 90

© 2002 Thames & Hudson Ltd, London

First published in hardcover in the United States of
America in 2002 by Thames & Hudson Inc.,
500 Fifth Avenue, New York, New York 10110

thamesandhudsonusa.com

Library of Congress Catalog Card Number
2001094766
ISBN 0-500-05111-9

Printed and bound in Italy by Officine Graphiche
DeAgostini

Half-title: *The first scrolls to be discovered were found wrapped and deposited in large sealed jars, as shown here.*
Title-page: *The Psalms Scroll from Qumran Cave 11.*

The War Scroll 92

The Thanksgiving Hymns 94

The Biblical Commentaries 96

The Genesis Apocryphon 100

The Book of Jubilees 102

Cave 2 106

New Jerusalem 106

Cave 3 108

The Copper Scroll 108

Cave 4 114

The Commentaries on Genesis 116

Targums to Leviticus and Job 118

The 'Reworked Pentateuch' 120

Apocryphon of Joshua 122

Tobit 124

The Books of Enoch 126

Other Ancient Works Preserved in Cave 4 128

The Florilegium 129

The Testimonia 130

Ordinances 132

The Calendar Texts 133

The Halakhic Letter 136

The Wisdom Texts 140

Poetry, Psalms and Prayers 144

The Songs of the Sabbath Sacrifice 146

Fragments of the Damascus Document 149

Documentary Texts 151

Caves 5 to 10 152

Cave 11 154

The Temple Scroll 156

The Psalms Scroll 160

Melchizedek 162

Biblical Manuscripts from the Qumran Caves 164

IV   THE QUMRAN SETTLEMENT

The Qumran Settlement 168

Recently Discovered Ostraca from Qumran 186

Scrolls, Caves and Ruins: Are They Connected? 188

V   THE MEANING OF THE SCROLLS

The Dead Sea Scrolls and Judaism 194

The Dead Sea Scrolls and Early Christianity 200

Who Wrote the Scrolls? 204

Epilogue 206

Where to See the Scrolls 208

Further Reading 208

Illustration Credits 210

Index 211

Introduction

(Right) Two of the three Bedouin who discovered the Cave 1 scrolls: Jum'a Muhammad, left, and Muhammad ed-Dib, on the right.

(Below) Ten of these scroll jars were found lying in Cave 1. One of them contained seven ancient scrolls.

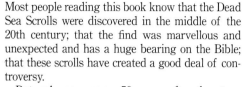

Most people reading this book know that the Dead Sea Scrolls were discovered in the middle of the 20th century; that the find was marvellous and unexpected and has a huge bearing on the Bible; that these scrolls have created a good deal of controversy.

But only now, some 50 years after the story began, have the scrolls been made accessible to all, and published in English. Yet translation is not enough. What, amid the speculation, sensation and genuine disagreement, do the texts *mean*? The aim of this book is not only to present the contents of these scrolls, but to go behind them: to describe the ancient world in which they were created, their possible authors and their hiding place in the Judaean wilderness. It also tells the story of how and what we have learnt from them, with the aid of not just historical knowledge but scientific and technical methods. And perhaps it can also explain the fascination and the mystery of these 2,000-year-old writings.

The modern discovery of the Dead Sea Scrolls could almost come from a script for an *Indiana Jones* film, although the details vary in the numerous tellings. Sometime in 1946–47 (we shall never know exactly when), three young Bedouin were herding goats (or were they sheep?) along the narrow strip that lies between the western shore of what is locally called the 'Salt Sea' and the cliffs leading to the hills of the Judaean wilderness and up towards sea-level, 400 m (1,200 ft) above. Following a wandering goat to the foot of the cliffs, one of the boys climbed to the entrance of one of the many caves that dot the cliff face. His story goes that he threw a stone into the cave and heard the sound of something breaking. Looking inside, he saw several large jars. One version of the story has it that he fled in fear of desert *jinn*. But at any rate, he returned with a companion (or two) and rummaged in what turned out to be 10 jars until they found inside one of them three bundles, two of them wrapped in linen. Then two more. The find is generally credited to Muhammad ed-Dib ('the Wolf'), though whether he was the real thrower of the stone we shall never know.

Back in their camp, the herdsmen opened one of the bundles, and unravelled a long strip of leather covered with strange writing. Of no obvious use to them except as a curiosity, these bundles accompanied them on their travels for some weeks. At last they reached the market town of Bethlehem and took their bundles to their usual dealer, called Khalil Iskander Shahin, or 'Kando'. He took the rolls of leather, and since he also ran a cobbler's shop he may have considered using them for repairs. But one day, curious about the writing, Kando and his intermediary, George Isaiah, took them to St Mark's monastery, belonging to the Syrian church in Jerusalem.

Kando's activities at this point are cloaked in secrecy, but it seems that he organized a raid to find more scrolls in the cave. The Syrian Metropolitan of the monastery, Mar Athanasius Yeshua Samuel, may also have participated in the hunt. As a result the total number of scrolls retrieved rose to seven, of which the Metropolitan bought four for the sum of £24 (then about $100). Yet he had no more idea than did Kando of the script. At some point a contact was arranged with a Jewish scholar from the Hebrew University, something that in the final days of the strife-ridden British Mandate was dangerous to both sides. Whether prompted by this, or by news of scrolls for sale in Bethlehem, Professor Eleazar Sukenik travelled to Bethlehem in November 1947 where he was shown the remaining three manuscripts. He bought them, and later bid unsuccessfully for Mar Samuel's as well. For he recognized the writing, and can probably claim to be the first to appreciate their age and value.

But now Palestine was partitioned between the new State of Israel and the rest (including Bethlehem and the Dead Sea) which was annexed by Jordan. Mar Samuel therefore turned to the American Schools of Archaeological Research (ASOR) in Jordanian Jerusalem, where the scrolls were photographed by John Trever. Trever, with William Brownlee and the School's Director, Millar Burrows, identified these texts and guessed that they were extremely old. It was the famous archaeologist and epigrapher W.F. Albright in Baltimore, consulted by Trever, who confirmed the enormity of the find; scrolls from the time of Judas Maccabee, the time of Herod, of Jesus. The news broke worldwide on 12 April 1948.

In the ongoing warfare that followed the partition of Palestine, Mar Samuel took his scrolls to the United States, where he offered them for sale. In 1954 an advertisement appeared in the *Wall Street Journal* for 'Four Dead Sea Scrolls', which were anonymously purchased for $250,000 by the State of Israel and reunited with Sukenik's three. Thus the scrolls from this first Qumran cave found a Jewish home. Meanwhile, the ASOR published its four, and Sukenik, with others after his death, published his three. The scrolls from Cave 1 (or excellent replicas) can now be seen in the Shrine of the Book, a specially-built annex to the Israel Museum in West Jerusalem. Most of the other scrolls cannot be publicly viewed, except on a CD-Rom.

Once the war following Israel's independence had ended, the hunt for the scroll cave, now in Jordanian territory, resumed. In January 1949 it was identified and the Jordanian Director of Antiquities, Gerald Lankester Harding, together with Roland de Vaux of the École Biblique et Archéologique Française in Jerusalem, examined it. The cave was located a kilometre north of a ruin beside the Wadi Qumran, which Harding and de Vaux also looked at and dismissed as the remains of a Roman fort. Two years later, having been persuaded of a close link between the scrolls and this site, they looked again and the excavations of Qumran began. As this was going on, more manuscripts were being found in other caves nearby. Eleven such caves were found in all, and that number still stands.

No one could have imagined the revolution in the study of ancient Judaism and early Christianity that these scrolls would spark off. Muhammad ed-Dib certainly had no idea that the leather bundles he took to sell in Bethlehem would soon be joined by hundreds more rolls and fragments. Within less than 10 years the remains of over 800 manuscripts in Hebrew, Aramaic and Greek would be removed from 11 caves in the area.

These caves all lie within a few kilometres of the ruin of an ancient settlement known as Qumran, where it is thought that the owners (and, according to many experts, some of the authors) of these scrolls once lived. One cave alone (Cave 4), in which over 500 manuscripts had lain for 2,000 years, reduced over time to thousands of fragments, lies on the very edge of this site. Who its ancient inhabitants were, and why they came to live in such a place, is still being discussed, and the answers are thought to lie mainly in the scrolls themselves.

Yet it is rather unlikely that the entire archive could have come from one tiny community, despite what many scholars initially thought. The contents of the scrolls in fact reflect a great variety of issues facing Jews in the period of the Second Temple (6th century BCE–1st century CE): public worship, private piety, the problem of evil, the future of the world, the divine will, human nature, the meaning of sacred scripture and, not least, the identity of the true 'Israel'. Almost the whole spectrum of religious ideas that have exercised the minds of later Jewish and Christian believers are to be found here. In these writings lie the seeds of 2,000 years of Western civilization.

The scrolls have been the subject of battles over ownership and proper interpretation that have

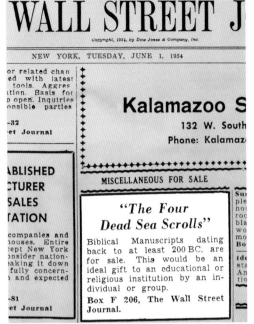

(Above) The Wall Street Journal *of 1 June 1954 contained an advertisement placed by Mar Athanasius Samuel for his scrolls. The scrolls were anonymously purchased by the State of Israel for $250,000.*

(Below) The Bethlehem antiquities dealer Khalil Iskander Shahin, known as 'Kando', with John Allegro.

raged for decades. The scholars who initially studied the scrolls from the first cave, driven by excitement and a strong sense of responsibility, hastened to publish photographs, transcriptions and translations. These initial scrolls from the first cave (Cave 1) turned out to include – apart from two scrolls of the biblical book of Isaiah – a guidebook for communal life, a paraphrase of part of Genesis, a commentary on the prophetic book of Habakkuk, a dramatic rule book for a final war between the 'children of light' and the 'children of darkness', and a collection of individual and communal hymns. The distinctive nature of most of these writings gave the impression that this library belonged to a radical group that had settled in the Judaean desert in order to escape the evils of the world and await God's judgment on humanity. But subsequent finds from other caves have turned up as well many writings without sectarian characteristics, and also fragmentary copies of every book in the Hebrew Bible except Esther and, possibly, Nehemiah.

The editors appointed to publish the huge number of texts from Cave 4 did not feel it necessary to publish as rapidly, and the impressions gained from the Cave 1 scrolls were not quickly modified. But thanks to continuing pressure from many sides (including scholars, the media and the State of Israel) all the scrolls became accessible between 1988 and 1991, and since 1994 have been available in English translation. With the total picture now visible, different theories about the authors of the scrolls, and how the scrolls came to be at Qumran, vie with one another, and whether any general consensus will be reached remains to be seen.

But at all events, the Dead Sea Scrolls must be considered the basis on which we now understand the many versions of ancient Judaism that existed before two major religious systems, rabbinic Judaism and Christianity, came into being. The scrolls reflect the world of religious beliefs and practices in which Jesus, his followers, his hearers and opponents all grew up, as did the great Rabbi Hillel. Through them we can visit a world of religious and political debate where idealism and pragmatism, hope and despair, nationalism and individualism, intense love and intense hatred all jostled together, in a ferment that was to end in the destruction of the Temple of Jerusalem and the birth of new religions.

How to use this book

A number of scholarly conventions used in this book require some explanation. One, the use of BCE ('Before the Common Era') for BC and CE ('Common Era') for AD, has become standard where Jews and Christians work together.

The large number of scrolls and fragments have, over time, been known by different names. We have adopted the most common, but ensured that each manuscript is also identified by the number that it has been officially allotted. Both of the major translations of the scrolls into English contain lists of the scrolls and their numbers.

A 'manuscript' is defined as a physical scroll, and a 'text' as the composition that it contains. These can be identified in three different ways:
• By their colloquial name, for example the Community Rule.
• By a number, which is made up of the cave number in which the manuscript was found, location (in this case, Qumran, or Q), and the manuscript number. Often several different manuscripts contain the same text. In this case, they are usually denoted by consecutive numbers. For example, the ten manuscripts of the Community Rule from Cave 4 are known as 4Q255–64 (they were found in Cave 4 at Qumran, and the different manuscripts are numbered 255–64). Manuscripts of the same text have often been found in different caves.
• Some of the manuscripts are also known by a code name, for example the Community Rule is frequently referred to as 1QS. Within this system, different manuscripts of the same text are distinguished by consecutive superscript letters. So the ten manuscripts of the Community Rule from Cave 4, or 4Q255–64, are also referred to as 4QS[a-j].

Manuscripts are assigned to the same text even in cases where they represent a different edition (as in the case of the manuscripts of the Community Rule from Cave 4). It must be realized that many of the writings from Qumran were compiled from other writings, and revised from time to time. Whether we can speak of 'recensions' or 'editions' of a single 'document' is sometimes questionable;

The man-made Cave 4 as seen from the promontory on which the Qumran site stands.

we may have simply one text used as a source by another. Where only a small fragment of a manuscript exists and identification is difficult or disputed, scholars now generally prefer to use numbers rather than names. Thus, 4Q285 is preferable to 4QM^g, since the connection of this fragment with the War Scroll (M) is uncertain.

In addition, an Aramaic text has 'ar' added to its name (for example, the Aramaic Apocalyptic text from Cave 6 is known as 6QApoc ar). Similarly, a *pesher* ('commentary') is denoted by the letter 'p' and a papyrus manuscript by 'pap' (for example Benedictions, from Cave 6, is known as pap6Q16).

Citations from a manuscript are normally by column and line (e.g. 1QS 3:10), but where the manuscript has deteriorated and is now in several fragments, each of which has its own column and line numbering, the fragment number sometimes has to be specified as well, for example 4Q225 frag. 22, col. 3, line 16. This is often abbreviated to 4Q225 22 iii 16, where the fragment and line numbers are indicated by Arabic numerals and the column number by Roman numerals. However, for the sake of clarity in this book, we have usually used the former system.

The vast majority of the Qumran manuscripts are in tiny fragments and not large scrolls, and even larger fragments or scrolls often either miss the tops or bottoms, or beginnings or ends, and contain holes. Therefore, no presentation of the contents of the Qumran caves can be complete, and no translation entirely reliable. The task of reading, let alone understanding, these manuscripts will go on for a long time.

Trever's Great Discovery

The young John Trever was residing at the American Schools of Oriental Research, studying plants and animals of the Bible, when the Dead Sea Scrolls story broke. In the absence of the School's Director, he had an appointment with members of the Syrian Orthodox Church to see their recent acquisition. Once inside Trever's room, a satchel containing four leather scrolls wrapped in newspaper was opened. Trever unrolled the largest and laid it on the bed. The Hebrew script was strange, and he fetched a set of slides illustrating the history of the Biblical text. One slide showed the Nash Papyrus, dated to the 2nd or 1st century BCE and containing the Ten Commandments and the *Shema* (Deuteronomy 6:4). His eyes wandered from the slide magnifier to the scroll and back: 'My heart began to pound. Could this manuscript, so beautifully preserved, be as old as the Nash

Papyrus? Such a thought appeared too incredible. … Restraining my enthusiasm, I calmly asked the Syrians if they would permit me to take a picture of a column of the larger scroll. They agreed, but then I recalled that the camera I needed was at the Museum, where I had left it the day before, intending to return that morning. All I could do was to copy by hand a few lines from a well-preserved section.'

Once the Syrians had left, Trever and his colleague at the School, William Brownlee, studied the transcription. To save time, they first tried a long shot: perhaps this was a biblical text. Pulling down a Hebrew dictionary, they quickly arrived at this very passage. Trever had just copied from the oldest scroll of the book of Isaiah ever seen.

From left to right: George Isaiah, Mar Samuel and John Trever with the Isaiah Scroll.

Chronology
Jewish history from Babylon to Bar Kokhba

596 and 586 BCE	Judaean upper class deported to Babylonia by Nebuchadnezzar (see 2 Kings 24:1–25:21)
539–538 BCE	Cyrus conquers Babylon and permits Jews and other deportees to return home and build the Temple (see 2 Chronicles 36:22–23 and Ezra 1:1–4)
?520–515 BCE	Temple rebuilding in the time of Haggai and Zechariah (see Haggai 1:1–15)
445 BCE	Nehemiah sent to Jerusalem under Artaxerxes II to rebuild Jerusalem (see Nehemiah 2:1–8)
334 BCE	Alexander the Great (356–323) begins invasion of Persian Empire
312 BCE	Ptolemy, ruler of Egypt, annexes Palestine
198 BCE	Antiochus III, ruler of Syria, captures Palestine from the Ptolemies
c. 175 BCE	Struggle in Jerusalem over the High Priesthood, leading to assassination of Onias III (see 2 Maccabees 4:1–34)
168–167 BCE	Antiochus IV proscribes traditional Jewish practices and builds an altar to Zeus in the Jerusalem Temple (see Daniel 11:30–35)
164 BCE	Rededication of Temple under Judas Maccabee (see 2 Maccabees 10:1–8)
152 BCE	Jonathan (Maccabee) becomes the first Hasmonaean ruler of Judaea and assumes the High Priesthood
Mid-2nd century BCE	Possible emergence of parties within Palestinian Judaism, including the Essenes
142 BCE	Jonathan is murdered; succeeded by brother Simon
134 BCE	Simon murdered; succeeded by John Hyrcanus
107 BCE	Hyrcanus destroys Samaritan temple on Mt Gerizim
104 BCE	Aristobulus succeeds Hyrcanus
103 BCE	Alexander Jannaeus succeeds Aristobulus. Qumran probably constructed and occupied about this time
76 BCE	Shelamzion (Salome) Alexandra, widow of Alexander, succeeds her husband
68–67 BCE	War between Salome's sons Hyrcanus II and Aristobulus II
63 BCE	Roman general M. Aemilius Scaurus governor of Syria (see 4Q333). Intervention by Romans in Judaea. Pompey enters Jerusalem
40 BCE	Herod made king of Judaea by Romans
31 BCE	Major earthquake damage at Qumran (?)
19 BCE	Herod begins rebuilding of Temple
4 BCE	Herod dies; kingdom divided between Archelaus, Antipas and Philip
6 CE	Judaea comes under direct Roman rule
26–36 CE	Pontius Pilate governor of Judaea (see Matthew 27:2)
41 CE	Agrippa I king of Judaea and Samaria
44 CE	Agrippa II succeeds his father as king of Jews, but Judaea reverts to direct Roman rule (see Acts 25–26)
66 CE	Outbreak of First Jewish Revolt against Rome
68 CE	Roman destruction of Qumran
70 CE	Fall of Jerusalem and destruction of Temple
73/4 CE	Fall of Masada
132–35 CE	Second Jewish revolt led by Simon Bar Kokhba. Jerusalem reconstructed under Hadrian as Aelia Capitolina

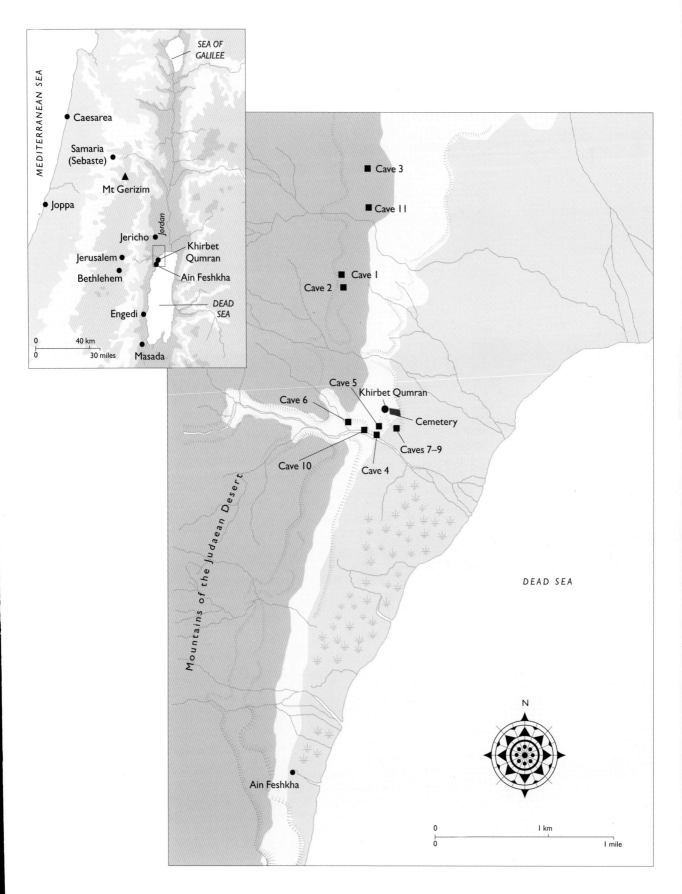

SEA OF
GALILEE

MEDITERRANEAN SEA

Caesarea

Samaria
(Sebaste)

Mt Gerizim

Joppa

Jericho

Jordan

Jerusalem

Khirbet
Qumran

Bethlehem

Ain Feshkha

Engedi

DEAD
SEA

0   40 km
0   30 miles

Masada

Cave 3

Cave 11

Cave 1

Cave 2

Cave 5

Khirbet Qumran

Cave 6

Cemetery

Caves 7–9

Cave 10

Cave 4

Mountains of the Judaean Desert

DEAD SEA

Ain Feshkha

N

0   1 km
0   1 mile

11

Chronology of Discoveries and Publications

Fall **1946**/Winter **1947**	Muhammad ed-Dib finds Cave 1 and its scrolls
March **1947**	Muhammad brings scrolls to Kando in Bethlehem
July **1947**	Kando sells 4 scrolls to Mar Athanasius Samuel; Feidi Salahi offers 2 scrolls to E. L. Sukenik of the Hebrew University
29 Nov **1947**	United Nations votes in favour of Partition Plan for Palestine; Sukenik purchases 2 scrolls – the Hymns (1QH), the War Scroll (1QM)
Dec **1947**	Sukenik buys third scroll – the second Isaiah scroll
1948	Mar Samuel takes 4 scrolls to Lebanon
Jan **1948**	Anton Kiraz shows Sukenik 4 more scrolls
Feb **1948**	Mar Samuel shows 3 scrolls to members of the American Schools of Oriental Research in Jerusalem
12 April **1948**	*The Times* of London releases the ASOR announcement of the discovery
26 April **1948**	Sukenik announces his purchase of scrolls
14 May **1948**	Israel becomes an independent state
1948–49	Yigael Yadin was General Chief of Staff of Israeli Army in the War of Independence
1949	Father Roland de Vaux appointed Director of the École Biblique
28 Jan **1949**	Captain Philippe Lippens, Belgian soldier with the United Nations Armistice Observer Corps, and others locate Cave 1
15 Feb–5 March **1949**	G. Lankester Harding, Director of the Jordanian Antiquities Authority, and de Vaux excavate Cave 1
1950–51	Linen from Cave 1 scrolls tested by Carbon-14; ASOR publish Isaiah[a], the commentary on Habakkuk (1QpHab) and Community Rule (1QS)
24 Nov–Dec **1951**	Archaeological work begins at Khirbet Qumran
Feb **1952**	Bedouin find Cave 2
10–29 March **1952**	Expedition of the ASOR finds 225 caves, including Qumran Cave 2
14 March **1952**	Cave 3 found
Aug–Sept **1952**	Bedouin find Caves 4 and 6
1952	Cave 5 found by archaeologists
Sept 22–29 **1952**	De Vaux and J.T. Milik excavate Cave 4
1953	Heidelberg Professor Karl Georg Kuhn identifies the Copper Scroll as list of treasures
9 Feb–4 April **1953**	Second season of excavations at Khirbet Qumran
Spring **1953**	International team of text editors formed: Roland de Vaux, Jozef T. Milik, Jean Starcky, Patrick Skehan, Frank M. Cross, Jr., John Strugnell, John Marco Allegro, and Claus-Hunno Hunzinger (later replaced by Maurice Baillet)
Autumn **1953**	Milik and Cross begin major work on Cave 4 texts
1954–59	Manuscripts sold to various institutions
1954	John D. Rockefeller funds publication of scrolls for six years
15 Feb–15 April **1954**	Third archaeological campaign at Khirbet Qumran
1 June **1954**	Mar Samuel's advertisement in the *Wall Street Journal*
1 July **1954**	Israel purchases Cave 1 scrolls; money available for erection of the Shrine of the Book to house them
1955	German state, Baden-Württemberg, participates in purchase of scrolls; Sukenik publishes the Isaiah[b] scroll, the Thanksgiving Hymns (1QH[a]) and the War Scroll (1QM); other Cave 1 materials published; Vatican purchases some scroll material
2 Feb–6 April **1955**	Fourth archaeological campaign at Khirbet Qumran; Bedouin find Caves 7–10 in marl terrace
13 Feb **1955**	Israel's Prime Minister, Ben Gurion, announces purchases of scrolls for $250,000 (provided by Samuel Gottesman of New York)
March **1955**	First season of excavations at Masada
Jan **1956**	Bedouin find Cave 11
18 Feb–28 March **1956**	Fifth archaeological campaign at Khirbet Qumran
1956	De Vaux and others investigate Ain Feshkha
1 June **1956**	Copper Scroll is revealed to public
Autumn **1956**	Yadin and Nahman Avigad, palaeographer, publish Genesis Apocryphon (1QapGen)
July **1957**	Joseph Fitzmyer and others begin work on scrolls concordance (continued until Rockefeller funding ended in 1960)
1958	Father Jean Carmignac starts the journal *Revue de Qumrân* (remains editor until his death in 1986)
1958	Cross's palaeographical study of scrolls appears; official excavation of Ain Feshkha
25 Jan–21 March **1958**	Sixth and final archaeological season at Khirbet Qumran and Ain Feshkha
July **1958**	Kando sells last Cave 4 texts to Jordanian authorities
1960	Allegro publishes his edition of the Copper Scroll

June **1960**	Rockefeller funding for Cave 4 editors ends
27 July **1960**	Jordanian government reimburses institutions for purchase of scrolls
June **1961**	500 Cave 4 manuscripts already identified
1962	Texts from Caves 2, 3, 5–10 published
1965	James A. Sanders publishes Psalms Scroll from Cave 11
Nov **1966**	Jordanian government nationalizes Palestine Archaeological Museum
1967	Six-Day War; Yadin acquires Temple Scroll (presumably from Cave 11) from Kando
1968	Allegro publishes volume of Cave 4 manuscripts
1971	Pierre Benoit succeeds de Vaux as editor-in-chief of the international team and of the series *Discoveries in the Judaean Desert*; J.P.M. van der Ploeg, A.S. van der Woude and B. Jongeling publish Cave 11's Targum to Job
1973	De Vaux's *Archaeology and the Dead Sea Scrolls* appears in English
Oct **1973**	Yom Kippur/Ramadan War
1976	J.T. Milik publishes fragments of the books of Enoch
1977	Yadin publishes Temple Scroll; tefillin and mezuzot published
1980	Cross and Strugnell begin to distribute scrolls to graduate students for publication
1982	Maurice Baillet publishes a batch of Cave 4 manuscripts
Spring **1984**	Elisha Qimron previews the so-called Halakhic Letter (4QMMT) at conference on biblical archaeology in Jerusalem
June **1984**	Yigael Yadin dies
1985	Carol Newsom publishes Songs of the Sabbath Sacrifice from Caves 4, 11 and Masada; David N. Freedman and K.A. Mathews publish *The Palaeo-Hebrew Leviticus Scroll*
1986	Father Jean Carmignac dies; Émile Puech of the École Biblique becomes editor of *Revue de Qumrân*; Eileen M. Schuller publishes *Non-Canonical Psalms* from Cave 4
1987	Benoit dies, having been replaced by John Strugnell of Harvard University in 1984
1990	Stephen A. Reed comes to Jerusalem to catalogue scrolls
Nov **1990**	Strugnell removed as editor-in-chief and replaced by Emanuel Tov of the Hebrew University in Jerusalem; editorial team increased to approximately 60 members
1990	14 manuscripts tested by Carbon-14 (AMS)
1991	Following conference in Madrid, controversy over restricted access to unpublished scrolls intensifies
Sept **1991**	Ben Zion Wacholder and Martin Abegg publish computer-assisted reconstruction of scrolls
22 Sept **1991**	Huntington Library in San Marino, California, announces release of photographic negatives of scrolls
15 Oct **1991**	NOVA documentary, 'Secrets of the Dead Sea Scrolls', shown in USA
1992	Robert Eisenman and Michael Wise publish *The Dead Sea Scrolls Uncovered*; Patrick.W. Skehan, Eugene Ulrich and Judith E. Sanderson publish palaeo-Hebrew and Greek biblical manuscripts from Cave 4
1993	Publication of microfiches of scrolls under auspices of Israel Antiquities Authority
April **1994**	Launch of *Dead Sea Discoveries*, a second journal devoted exclusively to the scrolls
1994	Some of the Works of the Law (4QMMT) published; Genesis–Numbers manuscripts published by Ulrich, Cross and others; second Carbon-14 (AMS) tests administered on 18 texts and 2 pieces of linen
1995	2 volumes of parabiblical texts published by Harold Attridge, Magen Broshi and others
1996	2 ostraca discovered at Khirbet Qumran published; manuscripts of Deuteronomy, Joshua, Judges and Kings published by Ulrich and Cross; Joseph M. Baumgarten published manuscripts of the Damascus Document; George J. Brooke and others publish a second volume of parabiblical manuscripts
1997	To commemorate the fiftieth anniversary of the discovery of the first scrolls, conferences held in Jerusalem and San Francisco (among other places) and several collections of scholarly essays published
1998	The centenary of the rediscovery of the Damascus Document manuscripts in Cairo marked by a conference at the Hebrew University, Jerusalem
1999	As the official publication series (*DJD*) speeds towards its conclusion, the editor-in-chief, Emanuel Tov, announces his impending retirement from that post.
2000	Publication of the *Encyclopedia of the Dead Sea Scrolls*
2001	By the end of the year 28 volumes of *DJD* published under Tov's editorship. Only 4 volumes outstanding

Despite the drama of the find in 1947, the story of the Dead Sea Scrolls does not properly begin there. Manuscripts from this region, scholars believe, have been found and forgotten several times. In one of the most curious yet important cases, a composition that clearly originated from the Qumran collection had been copied in two manuscripts in the 10th–11th centuries and hidden away in a Cairo synagogue, to be found at the end of the 19th century. And even after the initial discovery of Cave 1, the scrolls were not destined for an easier passage. As we described in the Introduction, they could hardly have been found in a worse time or place – in the midst of Jewish-Arab hostility, on the eve of a partition of Palestine that would separate the Cave 1 scrolls from their caves, and separate Jewish scholarship from access to the scrolls that were later to be found in the other caves.

The story in the following pages shows that the finding of manuscripts is merely the starting point in their 'discovery'. It remains for them to be carefully preserved, properly conserved, and efficiently edited and published so that the knowledge they have to impart can be shared. The Cave 1 scrolls survived their journey with the Bedouin, their lodging in the Bethlehem shop and, in some cases, their transportation to the United States. They were promptly published, too, enabling a wide public debate to take place on their origin and meaning. The scrolls from the other 10 caves have on the whole fared less well. They were also acquired in many cases from the Bedouin, and thus possibly suffered damage after their discovery. But the number of manuscripts that came to light, and the fact that so many of them were in small pieces, defied the resources available. A small team of editors worked to put them together, transcribe and translate, and identify their contents. After 50 years, their work, often substantially achieved decades earlier, is now reaching completion, after years of controversy and accusations of conspiracy. Now all the texts can be read in translation and viewed on CD-Rom.

Cave 4, overlooking the Wadi Qumran.

1 The Scrolls Revealed

Early Dead Sea Discoveries

Discoveries of scrolls near the Dead Sea have been made before. In the 3rd century CE the Christian theologian and scholar Origen (185–284 CE), who collected Hebrew and Greek manuscripts of the Hebrew scriptures in his search for the original texts of the Bible, reproduced a Greek version of the book of Psalms that came from a scroll discovered in a jar, near Jericho (which lies a few kilometres north of the Dead Sea). Not long afterwards, Eusebius of Caesarea, the church historian (260–340 CE), passed on a similar story about a Psalms scroll from the Jericho area, and added that other Hebrew and Greek manuscripts had also been discovered in the reign of the Roman emperor Caracalla (211–217 CE) in a jar near Jericho.

In the 8th century, Timotheus I, the patriarch of Seleucia (in modern Iraq), wrote this in a letter to a fellow-bishop:

'We have learned … that some books were found ten years ago in a rock-dwelling near Jericho. The story was that the dog of an Arab out hunting, while in pursuit of game, went into a cave and did not come out again; its owner went in after it and found a chamber, in which there were many books, in the rock. The hunter went off to Jerusalem and told his story to the Jews, who came out in great numbers and found books of the Old Testament and others in the Hebrew scripts.'

Qumran lies only about 12 km (7.5 miles) from Jericho, and the mention of caves and scrolls in jars (not to mention the Arab and his dog!) makes one think of Muhammad ed-Dib's discovery in 1947 (see p. 6). Hartmut Stegemann of the University of Göttingen has suggested that the cave mentioned by Timotheus was actually Qumran Cave 3, since it is the only Qumran cave large enough for a dog to wander about in. He goes on to speculate that this cave (originally containing 35 jars of scrolls) had been discovered by Qaraites, a medieval anti-rabbinic Jewish sect, who removed between 70 and 140 scrolls. Origen's Psalms Scroll, however, Stegemann traces to Cave 7, which, he says, resembles an open room rather than a cave.

The connection between the Qaraites and Qumran is intriguing. The Qaraites flourished from the 10th to the 13th centuries CE. One of their leading writers (al-Qirqisani) referred to people called the 'cave men' and their writings. Indeed, it has been claimed that Anan, the founder of the Qaraites, possessed a copy of the document later known as the 'Zadokite Fragments' or 'Damascus Document'. Two medieval manuscripts of this work, found at the end of the 19th century in the store-room of an ancient Qaraite synagogue in Cairo, are definitely copies of texts later found at Qumran. While we can only guess about the Qumran connection with earlier scroll finds, there seems to be at least a likelihood that the Qaraites did recover some Qumran scrolls, and were influenced by the doctrines found in them.

Much more recent is the case of Moses William Shapira, an antiques dealer who in the years 1878–84 purchased some biblical fragments through his shop in Jerusalem, again purportedly discovered by the Dead Sea, but this time near the eastern shore. These fragments (principally of the book of Deuteronomy) were brought to London amid great media coverage, but finally dismissed as forgeries. In the ensuing disgrace, yet still confident of their authenticity, Shapira committed suicide in Rotterdam. His fragments were purchased, but their present where-

(Right) The first 'Dead Sea Scrolls' may have been discovered as early as the reign of the emperor Caracalla at the beginning of the 3rd century CE.

(Below right) Cave 3, the possible site of an earlier scroll discovery.

(Below) A version of Deuteronomy 19 in a 10th- or 11th-century Bible belonging to the Qaraite sect.

abouts are unknown. John Allegro, a modern scroll editor who told Shapira's story, believed Shapira may have possessed a genuine Qumran scroll.

All these incidents suggest that the Qumran archive may once have been larger than at present; but if it is indeed true that earlier visitors to these caves removed scrolls, we must be thankful that no systematic hunt took place, and that a large number were left in their original hiding place to be recovered, preserved and edited together in our own day.

The Shapira Affair

Moses William Shapira was an antiques dealer in Jerusalem who regularly supplied the British Museum with Hebrew manuscripts in the years 1878–84. In 1883 he acquired an item inscribed in what he described as the ancient 'Moabite' script. Shapira claimed that the manuscript came from a site on the east bank of the Jordan river.

Shapira apparently thought he possessed pieces of the oldest manuscript of the Bible in the world. The remains consisted of 15 dark strips of parchment containing sections of the books of Deuteronomy, Numbers and Exodus.

The find was widely reported in the newspapers, and the British Museum called in experts to judge its authenticity. Within a record-setting 90 minutes Dr Christian David Ginsburg, apparently doubting its genuineness from the start, rendered a verdict. It was a forgery! Not only was the use of the 'Moabite' script unusual, but the strips were folded and not rolled up as if belonging to a scroll. Ginsburg also noticed one smooth edge of the leather, the result, he said, of a knife. He deduced that the parchment had been cut from the bottom margin of synagogue scrolls not more than 200 years old. Some substance had been used to blacken the material and make it look more ancient. The script looked to him like an imitation of the script on the Moabite stone. Vertical margins were clearly marked, but the writer had occasionally written well beyond them.

The text also exhibited a curiosity, containing the injunction 'you shall not kill the person of your brother'.

Shapira sent Ginsburg a letter expressing his embarrassment at being accused of deceit. On 9 March 1884, he shot himself in his Rotterdam hotel room. The disgrace had been too much.

The Shapira manuscript has since disappeared. No one was concerned to preserve this, as a fake. But was it so obviously a forgery? Or was Shapira the victim of an academic conspiracy or incompetence? Before the discovery of the Qumran scrolls, few scholars dared to believe that manuscripts as ancient as this were still in existence. But now we know they were. Moreover, some Dead Sea Scrolls biblical manuscripts are inscribed in the ancient Hebrew/Phoenician script (regularly used in Palestine before the 6th century). Even more important, the scrolls include several manuscripts that juxtapose passages from the Mosaic Torah and preserve different readings, in ways that the Shapira manuscript apparently did.

Thanks to John Allegro's interest, published in *The Shapira Affair* (1964), Shapira's case has been reopened. But without the manuscript we shall never know whether this man, who was known to have sold other forgeries, told the truth.

'You have made a fool of me' wrote Moses Shapira to Christian Ginsburg on 23 August 1883, not long before he committed suicide.

The Damascus Document

Factfile

Name: Damascus
Document, Zadokite
Work, Zadokite
Fragments, CD
('Cairo Damascus')
Editors: Solomon
Schechter, J.T. Milik, Joseph
Baumgarten
Commentaries: Rabin,
Ginzberg, Davies,
Baumgarten and
Schwarz, Baumgarten
and Davis
Manuscripts: Two from
Cairo: A=16 pages,
B=2 pages
Fragments from Qumran
Caves 4 (4Q266–73), 5
(5Q12) and 6 (6Q15)
Script: Cairo version:
Medieval; Fragments
from Qumran:
Hasmonaean and
Herodian

*(Opposite) Page two from
Manuscript A of the Cairo
Damascus Document
(now in the Cambridge
University Library).*

*(Following pages) Solomon
Schechter, Reader in
Rabbinics at Cambridge
University, in his study
surrounded by tea-chests
full of fragments from the
Cairo Genizah in 1896.*

'Now listen, all you who know justice, and understand the
actions of God; for he has a dispute with all of humanity
and will condemn all who reject him…'

(CD 1:1–2)

'All the men who entered the new covenant in the land of
Damascus and turned back and betrayed…shall not be
counted in the assembly of the people…'

(CD 19:33–35)

'This is the rule of the Inspector of the camp. He shall
instruct the members in the deeds of God… he shall have
pity on them as a father his sons…'

(CD 13:7–9)

'No man shall sleep with his wife in the city of the
sanctuary, defiling the city of the sanctuary…'

(CD 12:1–2)

In 1896, half a century before the discovery of the
Dead Sea Scrolls, Solomon Schechter of Cambridge
University retrieved a collection of medieval manuscripts from a synagogue in the old city of Cairo in
Egypt. Among these manuscripts were two that
described the organization and ideology of a Jewish
sect. Schechter named these 'Fragments of a Zadokite
Work', but they were later known as the 'Damascus
Document'. Both titles have some justification: the
manuscripts mention the priestly caste of 'Zadokites'
and name Damascus as a place of exile of the sect – a
sect which has been identified with almost every con-
ceivable grouping in Jewish antiquity.

The Cairo manuscripts derive from the 10th and
11th centuries CE, but it is now certain that the document existed at Qumran, for fragments of ten different copies of it have been found in Caves 4, 5 and
6, enabling the work to be traced back to at least
the 1st century BCE. The Damascus Document (the
Cairo and Qumran forms are very similar) was
compiled from various sources, and includes sermons and interpretations of biblical texts and
laws.

Contents

The actual structure of the whole is not entirely
understood, but it has two distinct parts. First
comes what is commonly called the 'Admonition'
(ms A pp. 1–8; ms B pp. 19–20). This is a kind of
extended sermon explaining the 'actions of God' in
rejecting Israel at the time of the Babylonian exile
(6th century BCE: see 2 Kings 25) and making with a
particular group a 'new covenant' in the (real or

symbolic) 'land of Damascus'. The 'Admonition'
describes the history of that covenant group and
its *raison d'être*, to obey God's laws exactly until
the 'end of days'. It reminds the reader of the basis
of that covenant, and utters threats against defec-
tors from its ranks.

The second part, named the 'Laws' (ms A pp.
9–16), comprises several collections of rules for the
community, or rather communities, of this sectarian
covenant group in their 'cities' and 'camps'. These
reflect the sect's belief that it was living according
to the proper interpretation of the Law of Moses,
and they cover such things as the use of the divine
name in swearing oaths (compare Matthew 5:37),
the fulfilment of vows and free-will offerings, leprosy and contagion, permitted and forbidden sexual
intercourse, relations with Gentiles, and careful
observance of the sabbath. Also noteworthy is the
regulation that members are to give up two days'
monthly wages for the support of the less fortunate.

The Damascus Document thus gives us the earliest and most complete description of a Jewish
sectarian community, separated by both its beliefs
and its lifestyle from other Jews. Many scholars read
in it an account of the origins and structure of the
community at Qumran, but this is improbable, since
it is clear that the 'Damascus' sect had many settlements, not just one, and its organization differs from
that of the community described in the Community
Rule (the 'Union', Hebrew *yahad* – we will be using
this term throughout the book) which is the more
likely to have lived at Qumran. A further crucial
difference is that while the 'Damascus' communities
had clearly broken off most of their contact with
the Jerusalem Temple, believing its priests to be in
error, it held the Temple itself in high regard and
maintained some degree of participation in the cult.
The 'Union' had abandoned all connections with the
Temple and saw its own organization and practices
as fulfilling many of the Temple's cultic functions.

However, there is obviously a relationship
between the two sects. Whether the Damascus sect
is a parent movement to the 'Union' or an extension
of it remains disputed. The claim in the Damascus
Document that the sect had already existed for a
long time is hard to evaluate. On the one hand, it is
likely that its legal traditions, even its calendar, go
back a long time. On the other hand, its transforma-
tion into a sect presupposes a radical break with
other forms of Judaism which probably took place
in the 2nd or early 1st century BCE, when their practices were banned under one or other king of the
native Hasmonaean dynasty that ruled from
Jerusalem between the 160s and 60s BCE. The Damascus Document is full of biblical language and
allusions, and part of its purpose seems to be to
present the sect as the true heir of the biblical Israel
and to demonstrate that its fortunes are anticipated
in scriptural texts.

אל בצרתם להשם את כל המונם ומעשיהם לנדיא לפנו

ועתד שמע אלי כל באי ברות ואבלח אונכם בדרכו

רשעים   אל אהב דעת חכמה זתושייה זיעוב לפנו

ערמה זדעת זם ישרתו דך ארך אפום עמו ורזב כלי חות

לכפר בעד שבו פשע ובוח וגבורה זחמה גזולד בלהבי אש

בו בל מלאכו חבל על סרדו דרך זמעשו חק לאין שארות

ופליטד למו כו לא סחר אלבחם מקדם עולם ובטום נסרן ירע

את מעשיהם ויתעבאת דורות מדם זיסתר אתפנו מן זארץ

מי עד תנומם וידע את שנו מעמד ומספר זפרוש קצידך לבל

חזו עולמים ונדיות עד כמד יבא בקציהם לכל שנו עולם

ובכולו דקום לו קריאו שם למען התור פליטד לשו ולמלא

פנו תבל מזרעם   ויודיעם ביד משרחן דורתקדשו וחו

אבות ובפדש שמו שמרחיידם ואתאשר שנא זתלעד

ועתזבום שמע לו ואבלח עונכם לו אות ולאבון במ ו

אל ולסחור אתאשר דיעד ולמאום כאשר שוטא לזתזדלך תמס

בכלידכיר ולאלתור במדשבות יצר אשמזד ועצו זנת כירתם

זמע תם זגבורו חול נבשלו בת מלעום ועד זנגד בלב בשריות

לבם נפלו עדיו השמום בה נאזחו אשו לא שמרו מצות אל

ובנחום אשר כרום ארוים לזבחם וכחדן גרוחזים כו נפלו

כל כשד אשר זוו בחרבה כינוע וידיו מלאוח בעשורום את

רעונם ולאשמרו את מצות עשיהם על אשר זהזד אבנום

Editing the Scrolls: The First Fifty Years

As described earlier (p. 7), the scrolls from Cave 1 were quickly separated into two lots, one in the possession of Professor Sukenik of the Hebrew University, the other owned by Mar Samuel, the Syrian Metropolitan of St Mark's Monastery, who entrusted their publication to the American Schools of Oriental Research (ASOR). Sukenik's editions of the War Scroll and the Thanksgiving Hymns appeared in Hebrew between 1948 and 1950; during

John Strugnell examines fragments from Cave 4 in the 'scrollery' at the Palestine Archaeological Museum.

1950–51 the ASOR published photographs and transcriptions of the Isaiah Scroll, the Community Rule, and the Commentary on Habakkuk. In 1954, Sukenik's edition of the second Isaiah Scroll, the War Scroll, and the Thanksgiving Hymns appeared posthumously. The remaining fragments, recovered from Cave 1 when it was rediscovered by an official party, also appeared in 1955 in the first volume of the official series, known as *Discoveries in the Judaean Desert of Jordan* (the 'of Jordan' was dropped later in the series). Then, finally, in 1956, Sukenik's son Yigael Yadin and Nahman Avigad published the Genesis Apocryphon. The contents of Cave 1 were thus quickly issued and scholars

and public alike responded with immense interest to this 'greatest manuscript find of all time', as it was acclaimed.

In 1949, meanwhile, Cave 1 had been successfully located and the rest of its contents removed by an official expedition. It was then that the site of Qumran itself drew their attention, and excavations began in 1951 under Gerald Lankester Harding (in charge of the Jordanian Department of Antiquities) and Fr. Roland de Vaux (of the École Biblique in Jerusalem). From 1952 manuscripts from other caves began to turn up, in most cases discovered by the Bedouin. The most important of these was Cave 4, located next to the edge of the Qumran settlement. The huge number of tiny fragments that Cave 4 yielded necessitated not only a campaign to raise funds to buy them from their finders, but also a team of editors to assemble and publish them.

The editorial team

In 1953–54 de Vaux assembled his team of editors (see p. 30). Each member was assigned a specific group of manuscripts. Thus, Jozef Milik was assigned non-biblical manuscripts, targums (Aramaic translations of biblical books), apocrypha, pseudepigrapha, and known sectarian writings. These also included tefillin (phylacteries) and mezuzot. (Following the rule of Deuteronomy 6:8–9, tefillin and mezuzot are strips of leather inscribed with certain passages from the Bible – Exodus 12:43–13:16, Deuteronomy 5:1–6:9 and 10:12–11:21. Tefillin are placed in small boxes and tied to the head or left arm; mezuzot are attached to the doorpost.) Frank Cross was given the task of publishing 61 biblical manuscripts and John Allegro 24 parabiblical texts, commentaries, and other exegetical works. Jean Starcky was called upon to edit 30 plates of non-biblical Aramaic fragments and 12 plates of Hebrew, and Patrick Skehan was allotted 32 biblical manuscripts. John Strugnell took responsibility for 80 non-biblical manuscripts and Claus-Hunno Hunzinger took charge of the War Scroll fragments from Cave 4 and liturgical texts. Hunzinger left the team after a short while and was replaced by Maurice Baillet of the École Biblique in 1958.

Why and how were these editors chosen? What were their qualifications for the job of editing ancient Hebrew, Aramaic and Greek manuscripts? How was de Vaux appointed as editor-in-chief by Harding? What programme had de Vaux established for his editorial staff? What methods were they to follow? How were they made accountable? If the answers to these questions are not entirely clear

– and sometimes unsatisfactory – it is to be remembered that the flood of manuscript fragments, numbering 15,000 or so, was entirely unexpected; there were few resources at hand, and no mechanism available for carrying out such a task. The team members were a mixed bunch, including some very gifted young people. But the editorial team was somewhat *ad hoc*, and their task greatly underestimated. That their remit was even by the end of the 20th century still incomplete was due to the fact that this small team was allowed to continue for so long when it was clear that they could not, or would not, finish the job.

At any rate, to begin with, a 'scrollery' was set up in the basement of the Palestine Archaeological Museum, later known as the Rockefeller Museum, for steady work on the fragments from Cave 4. There was no atmospheric control to help preserve these fragile treasures: windows were open. Clear adhesive tape was used to connect and repair fragments, and some editors were photographed with lit cigarettes dangling from their lips and fingers while inspecting scroll fragments. Some of the already decaying material must have been lost or deteriorated under the uncontrolled conditions. But the fragments were photographed, and placed under glass. And they were sorted with surprising speed. By the end of the 1950s the vast majority of fragments were grouped with others from the same original manuscript. To help the process, two young scholars, later to become eminent professors (Raymond Brown and Joseph Fitzmyer) were recruited between 1957 and 1960 to produce a card-index concordance of the fragments. The last of the Cave 4 fragments were purchased from the Bedouin in 1958. By 1960, when the Rockefeller funding ended, about 511 manuscripts had been sorted out and lay under 620 museum plates.

How was the editorial task funded? Milik and Starcky were paid for by the National Centre for Scientific Research in Paris, Baillet by the École Biblique. Cross, Strugnell and Skehan were supported from 1954 to 1960 by John D. Rockefeller subsidies. In the course of this work all these men received other institutional support. Hunzinger's work was underwritten by the Deutsche Forschungsgemeinschaft. Allegro received support from various British sources (but not Manchester University, where he began to work during his editorship).

Money was also obtained by selling Cave 4 scrolls. In the mid- and late 1950s the Jordanian authorities sold fragments to McGill University in Montreal, the Vatican, the University of Manchester, the University of Heidelberg, McCormick Theological Seminary in Chicago, Oxford University, and the All Souls Church in New York City. Many of these institutions, of course, were connected to the editors. Some, however, did not in the end receive the manuscripts they had bought.

Early controversy

Unfortunately, not only were the editors collaborating within the scrollery, but also developing animosities that were soon to be made public. Allegro disagreed with most of his colleagues about the publication and interpretation of the scrolls, and, having arranged for the opening and transcription of the Copper Scroll, led a survey to the Judaean desert in search of the lost treasure which it mentioned. Although the publication of this text was assigned to Milik, Allegro grew tired of waiting and published it in 1960. He was also the only editor to believe the treasure was real (rightly, in the eyes of many scholars). Allegro also lectured and wrote about his views on his own assigned texts in advance of their official publication, and at one point his claims provoked a public rebuttal from de Vaux and many other members of the team.

The first official publication of Cave 4 texts came from Allegro in 1968. Two years later

The main entrance to the Rockefeller Museum in Jerusalem, formerly the Palestine Archaeological Museum.

Leading Dead Sea Scroll Scholar Denounces Delay

Dead Sea Scroll Variation on "Show and Tell"— It's Called "Tell, But No Show"

New York Times Endorses BAR's Position

The Dead Sea Scrolls Are Now Available to All!

Who Controls the Scrolls?

(Far right) Hershel Shanks, the editor of of the popular journal Biblical Archaeology Review and a leading figure in the campaign to widen access to unpublished scrolls.

(Above and right) Captions and a cartoon from Biblical Archaeology Review's campaign.

"Let's find a dark place where we can open it."

John Strugnell, instead of completing any of his assigned texts, wrote a 114-page critique of Allegro's work. It is true that Allegro's texts were not edited to the highest possible standards. But there was apparently some pressure from de Vaux. No other editor matched Allegro's alacrity.

De Vaux died in September 1971. It is not clear how much control he actually had over the members of a team which had by now dispersed when their funding ran out. Some of the editors now had university posts. Some recognized practically no obligation to Father de Vaux, nor to his successor, Father Pierre Benoit, also of the École Biblique.

In 1962 the texts from the so-called 'minor caves' (2–3, 5–10) had been officially published by Baillet, Milik and de Vaux. The texts from Cave 11 were disposed of by a deal with ASOR and the Royal Netherlands Academy of Sciences, who each purchased the rights to these scrolls. Thus in 1965 James Sanders, appointed by ASOR, edited the Psalms Scroll from

Cave 11 and J. van der Ploeg and A.S. van der Woude published the Job Targum.

There was already a tendency not to produce the simple editions, with plates and translations, that the Cave 1 texts had had. There was a growing preference to produce authoritative, exhaustive studies, and not always in the official series. This tendency culminated in Milik's long commentary on the Enoch fragments from Cave 4 in 1976. His work was criticized by those scholars who wanted to study the evidence and not a theoretical reconstruction produced after nearly two and half decades of waiting. By contrast, in 1977 Yigael Yadin published a beautiful and nearly exhaustive commentary on the Temple Scroll in Hebrew only 10 years after he had acquired it (the English edition appeared in 1983).

But the Cave 4 texts remained invisible to the public, and to most scholars, since there was an embargo on access: the assigned editors had, and maintained, their right to exclusive access (although their students and certain colleagues were occasionally favoured). After a while (perhaps too long a while), patience began to run out, and in 1977 Geza Vermes, known chiefly for his translations of the scrolls, spoke of 'the academic scandal *par excellence* of the century'. In the same year David Noel Freedman, professor at the University of Michigan, editor of *Biblical Archaeologist* at the time, and close colleague of Frank Cross, made the clearest critique of past procedures as well as offering some suggestions for the future. He questioned:

'...the procedure whereby a single scholar, or a small group, can or should have the exclusive right to study and publish inscriptional materials at their own pleasure or discretion, thus effectively barring the scholarly community and ultimately the public from access to such materials.' (*Biblical Archaeologist,* 1977)

Although Freedman praised the sorting and assembling of fragments, he expressed the view that all the scrolls should have been published by the time of his writing. In part, he blamed the delay on the monopolistic system. He called for a frank discussion of the publication issue. Besides noting that there was no reason for the editors to provide 'official' editions, he made the radical proposal that photographs or facsimiles be published, that the editors themselves would profit from communal wisdom. Working in isolation could only have a negative effect. In the future one should expect texts to be published within a year of their discovery 'at the outside'.

Admitting his own irresponsibility as one of the editors of a Leviticus text from Cave 11 written in palaeo-Hebrew, Freedman confessed: 'I should have either published the scroll or returned it to the team for reassignment.' This confession came after about a 10-year delay, and his basic excuse was the pressure of other obligations. His publication finally

appeared in 1985. Meanwhile, other editors were offering similar explanations, which as time drew on grew less and less acceptable. What greater commitment could any scholar have than to publish the Dead Sea Scrolls?

Death also took its toll. In 1980 Skehan died, bequeathing his (still unpublished) lot to Eugene Ulrich of the University of Notre Dame, who gave some texts to graduate students and retained some for himself. Meanwhile the editorial process remained impervious to outside influence, while editors permitted themselves occasionally to talk

about the materials that their audience could not see. For example, in 1984 Elisha Qimron of Beersheva University, recently co-opted by Strugnell to complete long-overdue work on a so-called Halakhic Letter, gave a speech to a biblical archaeology conference in Jerusalem. He titillated his audience with glimpses of some of the text, and suggested that he had nothing less than a letter from the founder of the 'Qumran Sect', a figure referred to in several Qumran texts as the 'Teacher of Righteousness'. Both scholars were preparing a huge edition of this 'Letter' with commentary. By this means, of course, they deprived the scholarly world of a chance to examine the texts until they had reached their own definitive conclusions. There was much displeasure among the audience.

Jozef Milik at work in the 'scrollery'.

The campaign for publication

The campaign started by Vermes was given momentum in the late 1980s by the editor of the *Biblical Archaeology Review* (*BAR*), Hershel Shanks. His critique of the editorial team amounted to a crusade. In 1985 a scrolls conference was held at New York University, at which many speakers called for the unpublished materials to be made

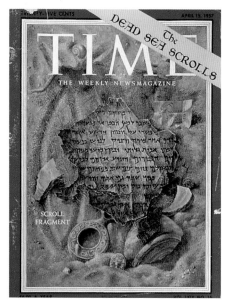

Ever since the 1950s, when this front cover of Time *appeared, public interest and excitement have been generated by many popular magazine articles.*

John Strugnell's dismissal of his critics as 'fleas' was turned against him by Hershel Shanks.

available to a larger group of scholars. When Benoit resigned as editor-in-chief in 1984, the opportunity came for the Israeli Department of Antiquities (which had had oversight of the scrolls since Israel's occupation of East Jerusalem in 1967) to put pressure on the editorial team. They appointed John Strugnell, who had been given the largest assignment but published nothing, though he had recently begun to give some of his texts to other scholars including doctoral students for their dissertations. (Carol A. Newsom published The Angelic Liturgy, which she renamed Songs of the Sabbath Sacrifice; Eileen Schuller produced an edition of non-canonical psalms.) Meanwhile, qualified scholars of the Bible and other graduate students were denied access.

Lawrence Schiffman's opinion is rather direct: 'The editorial team refused anyone else access to the remaining unpublished documents. Like misers, they hoarded the scrolls as currency to enrich their careers and those of their students' (*Reclaiming the Dead Sea Scrolls*, 21). Ironically, Schiffman had by then become an insider of sorts and was permitted to study certain texts. He became one of the current editors, and has since mellowed his criticism.

1987 was an eventful year. Dissatisfaction had reached a high pitch, and even though Strugnell had added Israelis and Jews to the team, his own publishing record underlined the reservations of many scholars. The 40th anniversary of the discovery of the scrolls witnessed a conference in London where Geza Vermes deplored the scandal and pressed for action. 'Suggested' timetables were mentioned (1996, 2000, 2004) but nothing was binding, and accountability had never been built into the project. In fact, *BAR*'s reports left one wondering whether certain members of the team knew they were meant to be meeting regularly to discuss progress and deadlines.

In 1989 a conference in Poland, organized by Z.J. Kapera, editor of the *Qumran Chronicle* and the *Mogilany Papers*, agreed a so-called 'Mogilany Resolution' that essentially demanded the release of all plates of the scrolls' fragments. In the mean-

time Philip R. Davies of Sheffield University and Robert Eisenman of California State University, Long Beach, formally requested to see certain scroll fragments, and were denied permission. Davies sent the reply that he received to *BAR* to refute Strugnell's claim that access was not being denied to genuine scholars.

But then the situation rapidly changed. The Israel Antiquities Authority (IAA) sacked Strugnell and appointed Emanuel Tov as chief editor, with Émile Puech and Eugene Ulrich as associates. Then in 1991 the team was bypassed, though in ways that they had themselves made possible. Strugnell had, some years previously, distributed a small number of copies of the concordance to the Cave 4 texts, and, under his editorship (and external sponsorship), a new set of photographs of the scrolls had been made, for distribution and safe keeping by a few universities across the world. The concordance consisted of photocopies of cards on each of which was written a word, its location (manuscript number and fragment number) and the words preceding and following it. With the aid of a computer, it was thus possible to reconstruct entire texts, and this exercise was carried out by Ben Zion Wacholder and his student Martin Abegg in Cincinnati. The reconstructed texts were quickly published by the Biblical Archaeology Society (BAS, publisher of *BAR*).

Meanwhile the director of the Huntington Library, William Moffett, discovering that it possessed a copy of the recently-made photographs, announced that in accordance with Library policy these would be made available for consultation by 'qualified' scholars. At the same time, Robert Eisenman, and James Robinson of the Claremont Graduate School, also published (again through the BAS) the entire set of Cave 4 plates, though without transcription or translation. The combined force of all these developments broke the embargo; the editors and the IAA admitted defeat.

There was some backlash, however. In 1992 Eisenman and Michael Wise published an edition of 50 texts, based on their unauthorized set of photographs. A number of scrolls scholars, many enjoying a year of research at the Annenberg Research Center in Philadelphia, Pennsylvania, together with members of the IAA's Oversight Committee in Israel, signed a petition accusing Eisenman and Wise of plagiarizing the work of other scholars without acknowledgment. At a conference in New York in December 1992, the two were brought without warning before an *ad hoc* inquisitorial ethics panel. Wise apologized; Eisenman refused. The most balanced and conciliatory member of the ethics panel, James VanderKam of the University of Notre Dame, pardoned Wise. Eisenman remained an outcast. The condemnation was formally retracted but Wise's career suffered. Eisenman and his views continue to enjoy popularity, largely among those outside the 'guild'.

Another unsavoury episode befell Z.J. Kapera of Poland, who had published a text of a widely circulating unofficial copy of the edited 4QMMT (short for the Hebrew *Miqsat Ma'ase ha-Torah*, 'Some Works of the Law', also known as the Halakhic Letter). The scholars responsible for the edition, Elisha Qimron and John Strugnell, were speaking tantalizingly about this text and promising a massive commentary. They were permitting certain scholars to study their working notes and use them in composition conference papers. But Kapera had overstepped the mark (their mark). He was ordered (under pain of some unknown but serious threat) to destroy all copies of his edition. In a further action, Qimron, who claimed copyright of the text of his edition, sued, in Israel, the Biblical Archaeology Society and Hershel Shanks, the editor of the *Biblical Archaeology Review,* for copyright infringement in printing a page from the draft edition. Qimron was successful, receiving a large sum in damages. Shanks and the BAS appealed, but this was rejected at the end of 2000.

In 1994, Strugnell and Qimron's edition of the Halakhic Letter, finished with the help of Ada Yardeni and Jacob Sussman, finally appeared. Including the concordance and the index it ran to 240 pages – the fragments themselves occupying a mere 8 pages! If one dismisses the time elapsed between 1954 and 1980, it took 14 years for at least four scholars plus the publishing staff to complete this task. Even as this edition reached the market, the two editors were not in agreement about their reconstruction or their interpretation. Volume 10 of *Discoveries in the Judaean Desert* (as it was) will probably be remembered as the most notorious of the entire series – and rightly so.

The scandal of the scrolls has now been largely forgiven (in some cases even denied) in the subsequent period of reconciliation. VanderKam has even commented that not many scholars seemed to have minded the delay until the late 1980s and Strugnell's dismissal. He himself had experienced an ethical dilemma after first agreeing to share his photographs of fragments of the book of Jubilees, then retracting the offer under pressure.

Since these difficult times, under the efficient and respected leadership of Emanuel Tov, volumes of biblical and non-biblical manuscripts from Cave 4 have begun to flow from the Clarendon Press in Oxford. This is mainly due to the greatly enlarged team, now at nearly 60 members, to the (sometimes reluctant) relinquishing of texts by older scholars to younger ones, and to Tov's commitment to the task and his resolve to present good editions of the remaining Cave 4 texts. Not least, the present editorial team really *is* a team.

The Secret Concordance of Cave 4 Manuscripts and the Computer Reconstruction of Documents

In the late 1950s and early 1960s after Roland de Vaux set up a team of scholars to edit the manuscripts found in Qumran's Cave 4, a quartet of assistants, Joseph Fitzmyer, Raymond Brown, plus William Oxtoby and Javier Teixidor, began creating an alphabetical list of vocabulary cards for these texts. Each card contained a single word, with its fragment identified and the word preceding and following it (if legible). The purpose of these cards was to assist the editors in their task.

As protest in the 1980s over the snail's pace of publication of the Cave 4 materials reached its height, these vocabulary cards were put in order, photocopied, bound, and about 200 copies were distributed to a few libraries and scholars around the world. In the case of a copy acquired by Sheffield University, some reservations were expressed lest Philip Davies should try to reconstruct whole texts from these cards. Davies laughed at the prospect of this seemingly thankless endeavour.

But the last laugh went to the veteran scholar Ben Zion Wacholder, and his student Martin Abegg, who set about precisely this task, with the aid of this concordance and a computer. By the

Ben Zion Wacholder of Hebrew Union College, Cincinnati, holding the first volume of reconstructed texts.

early 1990s and virtually coterminous with the appointment of a new chief editor of the scrolls, Wacholder and Abegg had reconstructed texts associated with the Damascus Document, the Mishmarot (priestly rotation texts), wisdom, visions, and thanksgiving hymns among others. They were then published by the Biblical Archaeology Society.

At the time, Wacholder and Abegg's achievement represented a major advance, for it provided those who could read ancient Hebrew and Aramaic with a look at previously unknown scrolls in a reconstructed format. That was much more than most of the official editors had done. Wacholder and Abegg's work was characterized by many 'insiders' as a 'bootleg' or 'renegade' version of the texts. Wacholder aptly put the matter in a personal way: 'Now I am an old man. It is a painful thing to have been so close to something so rare. But I realized that if I waited, I would long be dead.'

The accelerated pace of the new editorial team under the leadership of Emanuel Tov may have superseded the work of Wacholder and Abegg, but it is clear that such reforms were partly prompted by the work of these two scholars.

The reconstructed texts, of course, were as reliable as the work of the editorial team. Hartmut Stegemann, who (although never an editor *per se*) has aided members of the editorial team for several decades in reconstructing their texts, commented on the work of Wacholder and Abegg: '[it is] a trustworthy representation of about 98 per cent of the textual evidence'.

DISCOVERIES IN THE JUDAEAN DESERT · VIII

THE GREEK MINOR PROPHETS
SCROLL FROM · NAHAL HEVER
(8HevXIIgr)

(THE SEIYÂL COLLECTION I)

BY
EMANUEL TOV

WITH THE COLLABORATION OF
R. A. KRAFT
AND A CONTRIBUTION BY
P. J. PARSONS

OXFORD · AT THE CLARENDON PRESS

JORDAN DEPARTMENT OF ANTIQUITIES
ÉCOLE BIBLIQUE ET ARCHÉOLOGIQUE FRANÇAISE
PALESTINE ARCHAEOLOGICAL MUSEUM

DISCOVERIES IN THE JUDAEAN DESE
OF JORDAN · V

QUMRÂN CAVE 4
I (4Q158–4Q186)

BY
JOHN M. ALLEGRO

WITH THE COLLABORATION OF
ARNOLD A. ANDERSON

OXFORD · AT THE CLARENDON PRES

DISCOVERIES IN THE JUDAEAN DESERT · XXVI Qumran Cave 4 · XIX

DISCOVERIES IN THE JUDAEAN DESERT · X Qumran Cave 4 · V

Some volumes from the Discoveries in the Judaean Desert *series.*

A Note on Publications

The series *Discoveries in the Judaean Desert* (*DJD*), published by the Clarendon Press, Oxford, will of course be regarded, historically, as the primary edition of all the texts that it contains. But it does not contain the major Cave 1 texts, which were published, some by ASOR, some by Eleazar Sukenik, and one by Yigael Yadin and N. Avigad. Cave 11 texts were also first published outside this series, except for the Psalms Scroll (11QPsª), which James Sanders published as *DJD* 4. There are also provisional (but usually excellent) individual publications of texts by students of Cross and Strugnell.

The quality and the conventions of the *DJD* series are uneven, and its readings have often been improved since, as have the juxtaposition of fragments (often with a corresponding difference in the interpretation of the text). Many volumes have also suffered from a lack of neutrality in interpreting the texts. Cross's palaeographic dating, and the older standard theory of the scrolls' origins, have often been taken as facts. But it is indispensable, and will soon be finished, though it will never contain the complete scrolls.

A new series, *The Dead Sea Scrolls*, edited by James Charlesworth of Princeton Theological Seminary, and published by Mohr of Tübingen and Westminster John Knox Press of Louisville, is providing critical editions, including the Hebrew/Aramaic texts, English translations, introduction and commentary in a more accessible format. It is also rather variable in its quality, but often superior to the *DJD* editions.

Plates of the scrolls have also now been made available in printed form (by James Robinson and Robert Eisenman, published by the Biblical Archaeology Society), in microfiche (by Brill of Leiden), and in two CD-Rom editions, published by Oxford University Press and by Brill of Leiden.

The pendulum has thus swung completely, if belatedly, from restricted access to very open access indeed. The scholar has access to all the original texts, and the layperson can read translations of all manuscripts and fragments large enough to be coherently rendered. With this new availability has come a new enthusiasm, a new generation of scholars and a new range of ideas about the meaning of the scrolls.

The Contents of Discoveries in the Judaean Desert

Volume		Editor	Title	Contents
1	(1955)	Barthélemy, Milik	Qumran Cave 1	1Q1–72
[2	(1960)	Benoit, Milik, de Vaux	Les grottes de Murabba'at]	
3	(1962)	Baillet, Milik, de Vaux	Les 'petites grottes' de Qumrân	2Q1–33; 3Q1–15; 5Q1–25; 6Q1–31; 7Q1–19; 8Q1–5
4	(1966)	Sanders	The Psalms Scroll of Qumran Cave 11	11QPs^a
5	(1968)	Allegro (with Anderson)	Qumran Cave 4: I	4Q158–86
5a	(NYP)	Bernstein, Brooke	Qumran Cave 4: I (revised)	4Q158–86
6	(1977)	de Vaux , Milik	Qumrân grotte 4: II	4Q128–57
7	(1982)	Baillet	Qumrân grotte 4: III	4Q482–520
[8	(1990)	Tov (with Kraft)	The Greek Minor Prophets Scroll from Nahal Hever	8HevXIIgr]
9	(1992)	Skehan, Ulrich, Sanderson	Qumran Cave 4: IV	Palaeo-Hebrew and Greek biblical mss
10	(1994)	Qimron and Strugnell	Qumran Cave 4: V	4QMMT (Halakhic Letter)
11	(1999)	H. Eshel, E. Eshel, Newsom, Nitzan, Schuller & Yardeni	Qumran Cave 4: VI	Poetical and Liturgical Texts, Part 1
12	(1994)	Ulrich, Cross	Qumran Cave 4: VII	Biblical mss: Genesis–Numbers
13	(1995)	Attridge, Elgvin, Milik, Olyan, Strugnell, Tov, VanderKam & White	Qumran Cave 4: VIII	Parabiblical Text, Part 1
14	(1995)	Ulrich, Cross, White, Crawford, Duncan, Skehan, Tov & Barrera	Qumran Cave 4: IX	Biblical mss: Deuteronomy, Joshua, Judges, Kings
15	(1997)	Ulrich, Cross, Fuller, Sanderson, Skehan & Tov	Qumran Cave 4: X	Biblical mss: The Prophets
16	(2000)	Ulrich	Qumran Cave 4: XI	Biblical mss: Writings
17	(NYP)	Cross, Parry	Qumran Cave 4: XII	Biblical mss: Samuel
18	(1996)	Baumgarten	Qumran Cave 4: XIII	Damascus Document
19	(1995)	Broshi, E. Eshel, Fitzmyer, Larson, Newsom, Schiffman, Smith, Stone, Strugnell & Yardeni	Qumran Cave 4: XIV	Parabiblical Texts, Part 2
20	(1997)	Elgvin, Kister, Lim, Nitzan, Pfann, Qimron, Schiffman, Steudel	Qumran Cave 4: XV	Sapiential Texts, Part 1
21	(2001)	Talmon, Ben-Dov, Glessmer	Qumran Cave 4: XVI	Calendrical Texts
22	(1996)	Brooke, Collins, Flint, Greenfield, Larson, Newsom, Puech, Schiffman, Stone & Trebolle Barrera	Qumran Cave 4: XVII	Parabiblical Texts, Part 2
23	(1996)	Garcia Martínez, Tigchelaar, van der Woude	Qumran Cave 11: II	11Q2–18; 11Q20–30
[24	(1997)	Leith	Wadi Daliyeh I	Seal Impressions
25	(1998)	Puech	Qumrân grotte 4: XVIII	4Q521–28, 4Q576–79
26	(1998)	Alexander, Vermes, Brooke	Qumran Cave 4: XIX	Community Rule
[27	(1997)	Cotton, Yardeni	Aramaic, Hebrew and Greek documentary texts from Nahal Hever and other sites	
28	(2001)	Gropp, Schuller	Wadi Daliyeh II	Samaria Papyri; Qumran
29	(1999)	Chazon et al.	Qumran Cave 4: XX	Poetical and Liturgical Texts
30	(2001)	Dimant	Qumran Cave 4: XXI	Misc., Parabiblical Texts, Part 4
31	(2001)	Puech	Qumrân grotte 4: XXII	Textes araméens 4Q529–49
32	(NYP)	Flint, Ulrich	Qumran Cave 1: II	The Isaiah Scrolls
33	(2001)	Pike, Skinner	Qumran Cave 4: XXIII	Unidentified Fragments
34	(1999)	Strugnell, Harrington, Elgvin	Qumran Cave 4: XXIV	Sapiential Texts, Part 2
35	(1999)	Baumgarten et al.	Qumran Cave 4: XXV	Halakhic Texts
36	(2000)	Pfann et al.	Qumran Cave 4: XXVI	Cryptic Texts and Miscellanea
37	(NYP)	Puech	Qumrân grotte 4: XXVII	Textes araméens 4Q550–75, 580–82
[38	(2000)	Charlesworth et al.	Miscellaneous Texts from the Judaean Desert]	
39	(2002)	Tov	Indices and Introduction	

Volumes in square brackets contain material from sites in the Judaean desert other than Qumran

The First Editors

The Original Editorial Team

Members of the original editorial team were appointed between 1952 and 1954.

Gerald Lankester Harding (1901–79, British). Served as Director of the Department of Antiquities of Jordan for 20 years (1936–56). Began his career on the staff of the famous archaeologist Sir Flinders Petrie, then with J.L. Starkey and Olga Tufnell at Lachish (Tell ed-Duweir, 1932–36). At the time of the discovery of the Dead Sea Scrolls, the 'West Bank', as part of the kingdom of Jordan, fell under his jurisdiction. Along with Roland de Vaux, he excavated Qumran Cave 1. He then appointed de Vaux to head the international team responsible for the publication of the Dead Sea Scrolls. A contributor to the early volumes of the series *Discoveries in the Judaean Desert,* he also helped in the construc-

tion of the Archaeological Museum in Amman and in the founding of the *Annual of the Department of Antiquities of Jordan* (1951). In 1956 he retired to Lebanon and wrote on Jordanian sites and the Arabic language.

Roland de Vaux (1903–71, French, Roman Catholic). Editor of the *Revue Biblique* (1938–53) and Head of the Dominican École Biblique in Jerusalem (1945–65). A renowned biblical scholar, he wrote *The Institutions of Ancient Israel* and *The Early History of Israel*; and as an archaeologist he excavated at Tell el-Far'ah in the 1940s before supervising the dig at Khirbet Qumran. His popular work *Archaeology and the Dead Sea Scrolls* still serves as the basic report on the excavations. Between 1953 and 1971 he served as editor-in-chief of the international editorial team. During his term of editorship, the Cave 1 manuscripts, the Copper Scroll, the fragments from the minor caves, and Allegro's assigned texts from Cave 4 were published in the official series *Discoveries in the Judaean Desert of Jordan.*

Jozef T. Milik (1923– , Polish, Roman Catholic). A former priest and one of the key members of the early international team, he was caricatured as 'the fastest man with a scroll' for his reputation as a decipherer of even the most difficult texts. Affiliated with the École Biblique in Jerusalem and the Centre National de la Recherche Scientifique in Paris, his task on the international team was to

From left to right: Lankester Harding, Jozef Milik and Roland de Vaux examining a piece of pottery at Qumran.

publish the sectarian and related texts from Cave 4, such as the fragments of Jubilees, Enoch, the Community Rule, the Damascus Document, lists of priestly rotas and certain cryptic texts. In 1976 his lengthy *The Books of Enoch* appeared. A decade later he began to relinquish his control of some manuscripts (Jubilees, Damascus Document). He also wrote *Ten Years of Discovery in the Judaean Wilderness,* one of the best early accounts of the scrolls. He later left the priesthood, married and settled in Paris.

Frank M. Cross, Jr. (1921– , American, Presbyterian). As Associate Professor of Old Testament at the McCormick Theological Seminary in Chicago, Cross came to Jerusalem to serve as

Annual Professor of the American Schools of Oriental Research (1953–54). In May 1953 he was given the biblical texts from Cave 4 for publication. From 1958 to 1993 he was Hancock Professor of Hebrew and Other Oriental Languages at Harvard University. Like de Vaux, he was a biblical scholar, and used the biblical manuscripts to lay out a textual history of the Jewish Bible, and from the non-biblical manuscripts explored the development of the Jewish scribal hand from the 3rd century BCE to the 1st century CE. He began to share certain biblical scrolls from Qumran with his graduate students, who published them in the form of doctoral dissertations. Not until recent years has he personally been associated with the publication of his assigned lot. Cross's palaeographical typology of Jewish hands and the resultant datings are still widely followed in scrolls editions. His most popular work on the scrolls, recently revised, is *The Ancient Library of Qumran.*

John Marco Allegro (1923–88, British, agnostic). Perhaps the best known of all the original editors, Allegro was sent from Manchester in 1953 and assigned to edit the exegetical texts from Cave 4. Distressed by the lack of progress of official publication, he regularly published his own assignments in a provisional form in journals, and, believing that the scrolls showed Christianity to have been neither original nor the New Testament historically reliable, suspected a cover-up. A prolific writer, lecturer, keen photographer and documentary-maker, with broad interests in religion, Allegro was responsible for having the Copper Scroll opened up, and undertook his own expeditions in the Qumran region. Having published his own assignment in *DJD* in 1968, he resigned his post at Manchester University in 1970 to devote his time to writing. His notorious *The Sacred Mushroom and the Cross* appeared in 1970; he also wrote a fine introduction: *The Dead Sea Scrolls: A Reappraisal.* His many photographs of Qumran have also been published in microfiche.

John Strugnell (1930– , British, Presbyterian, but later converted to Catholicism). Joined the team from Oxford in 1954 and took responsibility for a sizeable lot of non-biblical texts. From 1966 to 1994 he was Professor of New Testament at the Divinity School, Harvard University. From 1984 he succeeded Benoit as editor-in-chief of the scrolls, and quickly expanded the editorial team to include Israeli and other Jewish scholars. Little was published during this time, and he was forced out

(Above left) Jozef Milik, outside Cave 1.

(Above) Frank M. Cross, Jr.

(Left) John Allegro, at Qumran.

(Below) John Strugnell.

(Right) A famous picture of the members of the editorial team gathered around a table at the Palestine Archaeological Museum. From left to right: Benoit, Hunzinger, Saad (curator of the Museum), Milik, de Vaux, Allegro, Starcky and Fitzmyer.

of his position in 1990 after a controversial interview about Judaism. Notorious for attention to detail, in 1970 he issued a scathing attack on the official edition of Cave 4 texts edited by his colleague John M. Allegro and in 1994 took an independent view on the document Some of the Works of the Law (or Halakhic Letter), of which he was one of the editors.

Pierre Benoit (1906–87, French, Roman Catholic). A Dominican priest who worked at the École Biblique from 1932 on the New Testament and the topography of Jerusalem. He emphasized the importance of the Septuagint (Greek version of the Jewish scriptures) in biblical studies, and contributed to the *DJD* 2 volume on Greek texts from Murabba'at (1961). In 1971, he succeeded de Vaux as editor-in-chief of the scrolls team. During his

tenure two volumes of Cave 4 manuscripts were published in *DJD*, one by de Vaux (archaeology) and Milik (texts) in 1977 and another by Baillet in 1982. In declining health, he had his editorial responsibilities transferred to John Strugnell of Harvard University in 1984.

(Far right) Pierre Benoit (on the left) and Maurice Baillet at the École Biblique.

Dominique Barthélemy (1921–, French, Roman Catholic). A Dominican priest at the École Biblique and specialist in the textual criticism of the Old Testament, he assisted in the publication of Cave 1 fragments and took a leading part in the editing and publication of an ancient scroll of the Minor Prophets in Greek found at Nahal Hever in the Judaean desert. He later returned to Europe to teach at the University of Fribourg in Switzerland.

expertise in Palmyrene and Nabataean, he was assigned the Aramaic texts from Qumran, none of which he published, though his preliminary observations appeared in the *Revue Biblique* in 1956. Overwhelmed by a variety of obligations, in June 1958 he engaged Maurice Baillet to complete some of his editorial responsibilities (*DJD* 7, 1982), while other texts were entrusted to another École colleague, Émile Puech.

(Far left) Claus-Hunno Hunzinger.

(Left) Patrick Skehan.

Claus-Hunno Hunzinger (1929–, German, Lutheran) was seconded by the Deutsche Forschungsgemeinschaft from the University of Göttingen as the German representative on the team. However, after a few years, having published a little material in a provisional form, he left the team and his work was largely taken over by Maurice Baillet.

Maurice Baillet (1923–98, French, Roman Catholic) joined the editorial team in 1958 and took over the materials previously assigned to Hunzinger. He was a co-editor of *DJD* 3, published in 1962, which contained material from the so-called 'Minor Caves' (2–3 and 5–10). He later also published a set of texts from Cave 4 in *DJD* 7, including the so-called 'War Scroll' fragments.

J. Starcky (1909–88, French, Roman Catholic). Once a student at the École Biblique, he first taught in Paris but after World War II he taught New Testament and Aramaic at the École and thereafter spent most of his life in Jerusalem. Noted for his

Patrick J. Skehan (1909–80, American, Roman Catholic). A member of the Catholic University of America in Washington, D.C., Skehan was assigned the biblical texts written in palaeo-Hebrew scripts. Unable to complete this task in his lifetime, it was left to Judith Sanderson and others to bring it to a conclusion.

Other Editors

James A. Sanders (1927–, American) of the Claremont School of Theology, who later directed the Ancient Bible Manuscript Center there, was not a member of the Cave 4 team, but was entrusted with editing and publishing the Psalms Scroll found in Cave 11, which included texts unknown in the biblical Hebrew book of Psalms. This partial scroll included psalm texts known in the Syriac and Greek as well as some ancient but hitherto unknown Hebrew traditions.

(Far left) From left to right: Strugnell, Cross, Milik, Allegro and Starcky.

(Left) From left to right: James A. Sanders, William H. Brownlee and John C. Trever.

Eleazar Sukenik, who published the scrolls of Isaiah[b], the Thanksgiving Hymns and the War of the Sons of Light against the Sons of Darkness.

Eleazar Lipa Sukenik (1889–1953, Israeli). Sukenik founded the Institute of Archaeology at the Hebrew University in Jerusalem. An expert epigrapher, his work on late Jewish tomb inscriptions enabled him to recognize that the scrolls which came into his hand were indeed ancient. He acquired (at some personal risk) and published the Cave 1 scrolls of Isaiah[b], the Thanksgiving Hymns, and the War of the Sons of Light against the Sons of Darkness, the last appearing posthumously in 1955.

Yigael Yadin (1917–83, Israeli). Son of Sukenik, had a brilliant career as underground fighter, statesman (once Deputy Prime Minister of Israel), general and archaeologist. Excavated at Hazor, Megiddo and Masada. Along with Avigad, he wrote a commentary on the Genesis Apocryphon; in 1967 he acquired the Temple Scroll (from Cave 11), and within 10 years had completed his edition with commentary in Hebrew. Put his military knowledge to use in *The Art of Warfare in Biblical Lands* and his edition of the War of the Sons of Light against the Sons of Darkness.

Emanuel Tov (1941– , Israeli). Professor at the Hebrew University in Jerusalem and respected textual critic who has published widely on the Qumran biblical texts and their history as well as ancient scribal techniques and conventions. After six years on the editorial team, he replaced Strugnell as the editor-in-chief in 1990. Under his leadership the team expanded to over 50, ensuring that the remaining Qumran texts are being rapidly published in the official editions. Among his best-known works is *Textual Criticism of the Hebrew Bible.*

Emanuel Tov, who became editor-in-chief in 1990 and announced his impending retirement from the post in 1999.

Editors of Cave 4 Texts

The majority of these editors (listed in alphabetical order) were appointed under the editorship of Emanuel Tov, though the impetus to enlarge the team had already begun under Strugnell.

Philip Alexander (UK)
John M. Allegro (UK – died 1988)
Harold W. Attridge (USA)
Maurice Baillet (France – died 1998)
Joseph M. Baumgarten (USA)
Jonathan Ben-Dov (Israel)
Moshe Bernstein (USA)
George J. Brooke (UK)
Magen Broshi (Israel)
Esther Chazon (Israel)
John J. Collins (USA)
Hannah M. Cotton (Israel)
James Davila (USA)
Devorah Dimant (Israel)
Julie Duncan (USA)
Frank M. Cross (USA)
Torleif Elgvin (Norway)
Esther Eshel (Israel)
Hanan Eshel (Israel)
Dorothee Ernst (Germany)
Daniel Falk (USA)
Joseph A. Fitzmyer (USA)
Peter Flint (South Africa)
Russell Fuller (USA)
Florentino García Martínez (Spain)
Uwe Glessmer (Germany)
Jonas Greenfield (Israel – died 1995)
Daniel Harrington (USA)
Jesper Høgenhaven (Denmark)
Nathan Jastram (USA)
Stephen Kaufman (USA)
Menahem Kister (Israel)
Israel Knohl (Israel)
Armin Lange (Germany)
Erik Larson (USA)
Manfred Lehmann (USA – died 1999)
André Lemaire (France)
Timothy Lim (UK)
Sarianna Metso (Finland)
Jacob Milgrom (USA)
Jozef T. Milik (Poland)
Catherine M. Murphy (USA)
Joseph Naveh (Israel)
Carol Newsom (USA)
Curt Niccum (USA)
Maren Niehoff (Israel)
Bilhah Nitzan (Israel)
Saul Olyan (USA)
Donald Parry (USA)
Stephen Pfann (USA)
Dana Pike (USA)
Émile Puech (France)

Yigael Yadin published an edition of the War Scroll and, even more importantly, recovered and published the Temple Scroll from Cave 11.

Elisha Qimron (Israel)
Judith E. Sanderson (USA)
Lawrence H. Schiffman (USA)
Eileen Schuller (Canada)
David Seely (USA)
Patrick W. Skehan (USA – died 1980)
Andrew C. Skinner (USA)
Mark S. Smith (USA)
Michael Sokoloff (Israel)
Hartmut Stegemann (Germany)
Annette Steudel (Germany)
Michael Stone (Israel)
John Strugnell (UK)
Loren Stuckenbruck (USA)
Shemaryahu Talmon (Israel)
Sarah Tanzer (USA)
Eibert Tigchelaar (Netherlands)
Emanuel Tov (Israel)
Julio Trebolle Barrera (Spain)
Eugene Ulrich (USA)

James C. VanderKam (USA)
Geza Vermes (UK)
Moshe Weinfeld (Israel)
Sidnie A. White Crawford (USA)
Ada Yardeni (Israel)

Editors of Cave 11 Texts

These editors are listed in alphabetical order.

David N. Freedman (USA)
Florentino García Martínez (Spain)
Edward Herbert (UK)
K.A. Mathews (USA)
Carol Newsom (USA)
James A. Sanders (USA)
J.P.M. van der Ploeg (Netherlands)
A.S. van der Woude (Netherlands – died 2001)
Yigael Yadin (Israel – died 1983)

The period in which the scrolls were written was turbulent. After centuries of existence as a province of the Persian empire, then of the Hellenistic kingdoms of Egypt (under the Ptolemies) and Syria (under the Seleucids), Judaea gained a century of independence before again succumbing to an external power, Rome. The Roman yoke was unpopular with many Judaeans and a war in 66–73 CE led to the destruction of the Jerusalem Temple. A second war (132–35 CE) led to the banishment of Jews from Jerusalem and the reconstruction of the city on Roman lines. Thereafter Judaism knew no priesthood, no sanctuary and no sacrificial cult, while Christianity turned all these into symbols as it gradually gained the religious allegiance of the Roman empire.

Religious life was in turmoil during this period. The Temple and priesthood had long dominated the religious (and political) activity of Judaeans, and the high priesthood remained the most powerful office. But the challenge of the new Hellenistic culture, permeating the whole of the classical and Near Eastern world, and the increased power of a non-priestly aristocracy, led to struggles over the high priesthood which triggered a civil war and then a war of independence. The success of that war under the Hasmonaeans did not heal the religious divisions; it may have made them worse. Perhaps there had never been a single 'Judaism'; but now a number of different parties or groups defined their own version of their ancestral religion.

The Qumran scrolls demonstrate one or perhaps more of such versions of Judaism in which the Temple, the priesthood, the Mosaic law and the destiny of Israel are the dominant themes. Whether the writers of these scrolls can be identified with already-known Jewish groups is still undecided. Also unclear are the origins and history of these groups, of which the scrolls give only faint clues. What they do underline, nevertheless, is the variety and vitality of religious life and thought on the eve of both Christianity and rabbinic Judaism.

An aerial view of the Old City of Jerusalem and the Kidron Valley, looking southeast.

II The Ancient World of the Scrolls

The Historical Framework: From Babylon to Bar Kokhba

From Nebuchadnezzar to the end of the Persian empire

The destruction of Jerusalem by the Babylonian king Nebuchadrezzar (the proper spelling: but he is better known from the Bible as Nebuchadnezzar) is a central episode in biblical history. According to 2 Kings 24–25 the Judaean king Jehoiachin yielded to him (in 597 BCE) and all but the poorest of the land were deported, with the Temple also being looted. Eleven years later, his successor Zedekiah rebelled and Nebuchadnezzar had him executed, destroyed the city and its Temple and deported more of the population. The event is presented as an exiling of 'Israel' in punishment for its disobedience against the divine law, a fate that the prophets had foretold (and Solomon, at the building of the Temple, reputedly some 400 years earlier, had anticipated – see 1 Kings 13).

It was about 60 years (the book of Jeremiah makes it around 70) before Cyrus of Persia reversed the policy of deportation and allowed deportees to return to their ancestral lands.

Alexander the Great, shown here, defeated the Persians in the 4th century BCE. Josephus claimed that he visited Jerusalem and the Samaritan temple on Mt Gerizim.

Judaeans living in Babylon began to travel to Judah with money, gifts and the looted Temple vessels, to reoccupy the land and rebuild Jerusalem and the Temple. (The names 'Judah' and 'Judaea' derive respectively from Hebrew (Yehudah) and Greek/Latin (Ioudaia, Judaea) names for the Jewish homeland, and so reflect the political and linguistic transitions of the Second Temple period. 'Judaea' is generally used for the Roman period – 64 BCE onwards.) The books of Ezra and Nehemiah tell of two leaders under whom Jerusalem was, after some delay, rebuilt and repopulated, the Temple rededicated, the Law of Moses read out and religious reforms instituted. From the biblical perspective this was a divinely decreed restoration of the true Israel, even if under an imperial regime, for the Jewish god had inspired Cyrus. The return of these people, and their desire to reclaim and rebuild the tiny province of Judah, must have been a shock to those then inhabiting the land, who for two or three generations had regarded it as theirs. Many would have taken over property left behind. People from across the Jordan river and from Samaria had settled in Judah, and south of Bethlehem nearly all the territory had become Edomite. Thus, the population of the province was made up of groups with different interests, of whom the most influential were immigrants from Babylonia who enjoyed the political support of the Persian regime and claimed to be the only rightful occupants of the Promised Land. It is unlikely, then, that from this time there was a single agreed 'Judaism'. There may well have been disputes between local and immigrant priestly families as to who should officiate in the Temple, for traces of competing genealogies and dynasties (for instance, descendants of Aaron versus descendants of Zadok) can be detected in the Bible. To such circumstances the roots of the religious plurality and sectarianism that underlie the Dead Sea Scrolls may well be traced. Certainly the Damascus Document treats the religious leadership from this time onwards as being in error, and, together with several other Jewish writings (including the books of Enoch and the biblical book of Daniel), it regards the exile as having effectively continued to its own day.

Even before the advent of Nebuchadnezzar the kingdom of Judah had been independent only nominally, having been subject to Assyria for over a century. But under the Persians there was no monarchy to symbolize the political identity of 'Israel'. Instead the Temple began to fulfil that role, and the priesthood assumed an increased authority over the life of the city of Jerusalem and the province of Judah. This was probably encouraged by the Persians. In return, the Persians were regarded as patrons, not as oppressors. The Bible itself makes no criticism of Persian religion, and indeed, the Zoroastrianism that became the official religion of the Persian kings probably exercised a strong

Judaea at the beginning of the Maccabean revolt
conquests of Jonathan
conquests of Simon
conquests of Hyrcanus I
conquests of Aristobulus I
conquests of Alexander Jannaeus

PHOENICIA
ITURAEA
GALILEE
SEA OF GALILEE
SAMARIA
Jordan
GILEAD
MEDITERRANEAN SEA
Jericho
JUDAEA
Jerusalem
Qumran
PHILISTIA
Machaerus
DEAD SEA
Engedi
IDUMAEA
Masada
NABATAEA

0   40 km
0   30 miles

A map showing the growth of Jewish territory under the Hasmonaeans during the 2nd and 1st centuries BCE.

two cities and their temples grew, rather than having been present from the beginning. By the time the scrolls were written, however, Jews and Samaritans were probably quite distinct and mutually hostile.

During the 3rd century BCE the rulers of Jerusalem and Judah maintained a largely pro-Ptolemaic policy, but Palestine had long been regarded by the neighbouring Greek kingdom of the Seleucids, based in Syria (and at first, in Babylonia too), as its own, and after the Battle of Panion in 200 BCE Judah became part of that kingdom. The changeover was accompanied by conflicts between Jews who took different sides. It must be remembered that large Jewish communities also existed in the territories of the Seleucids (especially Babylonia) and Ptolemies. While the descendants of many Judaeans deported by Nebuchadnezzar remained in Babylonia, many others had at the time fled to Egypt (including the prophet Jeremiah). These and other communities were probably swollen by voluntary emigrants, traders and mercenaries. Thus, most of the population of Judah probably had relatives or friends in one of these two regions, and would tend to favour belonging to one or the other kingdom.

Although the victorious Seleucid king Antiochus III reaffirmed the rights of Jews to live according to their traditional ways, a serious crisis built up under his successor, Antiochus IV. A struggle broke out for political control in Jerusalem between the traditional priestly class (and most of the rural population) and a prosperous and powerful lay class (allied to junior priestly families) in favour of

The Seleucid king Antiochus III reaffirmed the rights of Jews to live according to their traditional ways.

influence on the religion of Judah. Its dualistic doctrine, in which there are two equal and competing spirits, and its belief in a fiery end to the cycle of world history, are two of many Zoroastrian ideas that are especially influential in some of the Dead Sea Scrolls. Certainly speculation about the origin and nature of evil, and the calculation of calendars of world history, characterize a great deal of Jewish literature from what is called the 'Second Temple' period.

The arrival of the Greeks

After the demise of the Persian empire and the arrival of Alexander the Great, Judah fell for over a century under the control of the Greek kingdom of the Ptolemies, comprising Egypt and Palestine. This period witnessed an intensification of economic development and an increased presence of Greek culture: language, education, Greek-style cities, and increased contact with the Mediterranean world. The Jewish historian Josephus (1st century CE) claimed that Alexander the Great visited both Jerusalem and the Samaritan temple on Mt Gerizim, near Shechem (see p. 61). The existence of a separate Samaritan temple highlights how little we really know of the development of the Jewish religion. It is likely that the rift between the

This obverse of a silver coin shows Antiochus IV, who was less successful than his predecessor at controlling political factions in Jerusalem.

a more cosmopolitan definition of Judaism (and a desire for control of the Temple, the treasury of the Jewish people, is not to be overlooked). Each side began bidding to Antiochus for the office of high priesthood, and among the bribes offered was the establishment in Jerusalem of a Greek-type city, with its typical institutions, such as gymnasium and school. (To this ferment one may add external difficulties faced by the Seleucids in the challenge from Rome for supremacy in the region.) In the process, one high priest (Onias III) was killed and his son fled to Egypt with his supporters where he founded a temple.

A combination of factors led to Antiochus banning traditional Jewish religious practices and installing an altar to Zeus on the Temple hill. A war

began that was both a civil war and a war of resistance against the Seleucids. Each side was composed of an alliance of parties and interests, and the victors were led by a minor priestly family who achieved by stages an independence for their traditional religion (as they saw it) and then a political independence. This family, the Hasmonaeans (also called the Maccabees, after the nickname of their first leader, Judas), assumed first the high priesthood and then also the kingship.

The rise and fall of the Hasmonaean dynasty, from the middle of the 2nd century to the middle of the 1st century BCE, provides the context in which the majority of the Dead Sea Scrolls were written, and probably for the formation of the sects that inspired, produced, copied and owned them. The

rule of this dynasty saw the territory of Judah gradually expand under successive rulers into the whole of Palestine, including Galilee, parts of Transjordan, Edom and Samaria. The Samaritan temple was destroyed by John Hyrcanus who, having largely annexed the territory once ascribed to King David, plundered the alleged 'King David's tomb'. Military success was accompanied by internal religious conflict, as Jewish parties vied for the patronage of the Hasmonaeans, which moved from one to the other. Hyrcanus' successor, Alexander Jannaeus (note that the Hasmonaeans took Greek and Semitic names), had on one occasion as many as 800 of his opponents crucified (an event alluded to in the Qumran Cave 4 commentary on the book of Nahum).

The Roman period

Internal rivalries between Hasmonaean claimants to the throne eventually contributed to the downfall of this dynasty as the Roman general Pompey arrived in Jerusalem in 63 BCE to arbitrate. During his visit, he is said to have entered the Holy of Holies in the Temple, the place reserved only for the high priest once a year. Jews were already divided in their attitudes towards the Romans, and this act was never forgotten. (The role of one of the envoys, M. Aemilius Scaurus, in the Roman intervention is actually referred to in a Qumran text, 4Q324.)

Under the Romans Jewish territory was again limited to Judaea, a portion of Idumaea, east Jordanian Peraea, and Galilee. A Roman governor was set up in Jerusalem and Judaea was forced to

The aqueduct at Caesarea, the harbour city built by Herod the Great.

pay an indemnity. But when Caesar succeeded Pompey, having been helped by the Idumaean (Edomite) Antipater, he repaid the debt by appointing Antipater as governor of Judah (alongside a high priest of Hasmonaean descent). Antipater made his son Phasael governor of Jerusalem and his other son Herod governor of Galilee. Several years of renewed civil war ensued, and an invasion from the Parthians, a Persian race who now controlled Babylonia and much territory east of the Jordan. During all this, Herod escaped to Rome where he was made king of Judaea in 40 BCE. Three years later he claimed his throne, and for 34 years

reigned peacefully and successfully, though not with great popularity among all his people, since he remained a loyal ally of Rome and, despite his efforts to marry successfully into the Hasmonaean family, in the end he had many of his family executed. Roman land grants increased his territory to embrace Judaea, all of Idumaea, Samaria, Galilee, Peraea and territories to the east and north of the Sea of Galilee. Herod was probably the greatest builder of his age. He constructed the harbour city of Caesarea and built numerous fortresses and residences for himself, such as Masada, Herodium, Machaerus and Jericho. He also had the Jerusalem

Maccabees, Hasmonaeans and Herodians (166 BCE–100 CE)

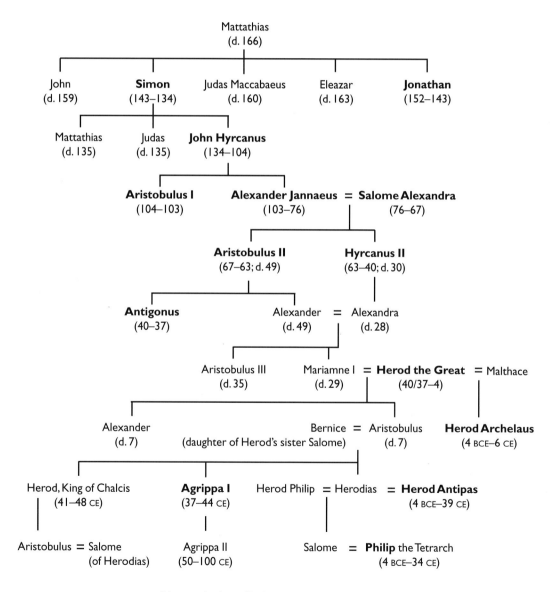

Names of rulers of Judaea are in bold

Extent of Herod's kingdom

0   40 km
0   30 miles

PHOENICIA

ITURAEA

GALILEE

GAULANITIS

TRACHONITIS

SEA OF
GALILEE

Caesarea

SAMARIA

MEDITERRANEAN SEA

Sebaste

Jordan

Qumran

PERAEA

Philadelphia
(Amman)

Jericho

Jerusalem

JUDAEA

Herodium

Engedi

Machaerus

IDUMAEA

DEAD
SEA

Masada

NABATAEA

(Left) Map showing the
extent of the kingdom
of Herod the Great.

(Below) The Arch of Titus in
Rome celebrates the defeat
of the Jews and destruction
of Jerusalem in 70 CE.

Temple massively renovated and enlarged. How
devout a Jew this Idumaean was remains disputed:
his own residences have nothing that would offend
a Jew, but he did install an eagle over the entrance
to the Jerusalem Temple. He restored the Temple,
provided water for Jerusalem and food in times of
famine. But he also patronized Greek cities,
including their athletic contests. Most Jews outside
Palestine probably admired him and recognized his
Judaism as valid. But Judaea itself had long been a
nest of religious zealotry and hatred, at least
among certain sects and parties.

The scrolls say little if anything about Herod. No
doubt most of their writers disliked him as much
as they disliked the Hasmonaeans. But they disliked anyone who was not of their own beliefs.
Towards the Romans the attitude of the scrolls var-
ies. In the Habakkuk commentary (1QpHab) they
are feared, but seen as agents of divine punishments on a wicked Jewish nation. In the War Scroll
(1QM), they are the main element of the Final
Enemy, the 'Kittim' (a word applied in the
Bible mostly to the Greeks, but in Daniel to
the Romans). While some Jews no doubt

(Right) Model of the
Inner Court, containing
the sanctuary of Herod's
Temple, looking west
across Jerusalem.

admired the Romans (as did Josephus), most of the preserved Jewish literature from Palestine criticizes them, longing for salvation for the holy people, pondering the mystery of the course of history and awaiting the calendar of world history to reach its expected end with the destruction of this last human empire.

With the death of Herod, direct Roman administration took over, and relations between Jews and Romans steadily deteriorated during the 1st century CE until, for a variety of reasons, the Jews finally took to war, a war which lost them their Temple and ruined Jerusalem, a city already run by warring extremist religious groups. During this war, according to the archaeological evidence, the Romans also attacked the settlement at Qumran and occupied the site for a number of years. It was in the region of the Judaean desert, in fact, that the resistance to Rome lingered. The last defiant band of fighters retreated to Masada and

was overcome in 74 CE. The connection between this group, the scrolls and the occupants of Qumran is tantalizing. One text known from the caves was found at Masada (the Songs of the Sabbath Sacrifice) and there may have been other 'Qumran' scrolls too, encouraging some scholars to think that the inhabitants of Qumran participated in this final stand. Whether or not this was the case, the final episode of the 'war of the children of light against the children of darkness' staged in Herod's Idumaean fortress could be said to have ended here, and not as foreseen in the Qumran War Scroll. By this time the scrolls were already in the caves, perhaps hidden to protect them from the ravages of the Romans or in the hope of later retrieval. But in the wake of this war, and the destruction of the Jerusalem Temple, new religious systems were to emerge, including rabbinic Judaism and Christianity, and the heritage preserved in the Qumran scrolls was to be submerged for 2,000 years.

The story of the Jewish struggle against the Romans – and indeed of the occupation of Qumran – was not quite over, however. In 132 CE another revolt occurred, led by Simon Bar Kosiba, who took the name Bar Kokhba (son of the star). He too issued coins, and traces of his occupation exist in the Judaean wilderness. We even have letters written by him or on his behalf. But after three years of fighting he too was defeated, and Jerusalem rebuilt as a Roman city, and Jews expelled from it.

(Right) A bronze coin
issued by Bar Kokhba and
in circulation around 132–35
CE, depicting a lyre.

(Opposite) Aerial view of
Masada, showing the tiered
Herodian palace on the
northern end.

44

Jewish Religious Life

The Temple

During the five centuries from the reconstitution of Judaea under the Persians to the destruction of Herod's Temple, the Jews had continually shown their devotion to the city of Jerusalem and its Temple, which, according to its rulers and probably the inhabitants of the city, was the only true place of worship. Only when and where the Temple was not accessible, too distant, or accessible on a limited basis to certain groups, did private or small group worship take place elsewhere. It was certainly such individual worship that provided the catalyst for the development of the Pharisees (p. 59) and Essenes (p. 54), while among Jews living outside Palestine, communal prayer and study were perhaps taking place already during the Ptolemaic period.

The Jerusalem Temple was not merely a house of public worship; it was a place where wealth could be deposited (and was accumulated from gifts and taxes), a major market for exchangeable goods, the chief location for the practice of priestly duties, and the site of private devotions, including the offering of sacrifices and vows, priestly consultation and purification rites. The Temple cult stimulated the local economy, since it demanded wood, animals, incense, oil, implements and much else to sustain its practices. During periods of rebuilding (and even for maintenance), masons, carpenters, smiths, perfumers, caterers and priests would have been needed. There is also evidence of a huge priestly and administrative caste attached to the Temple. The priestly service was conducted in shifts of a week, each shift ('family') officiating twice a year. Increasingly the three major festivals – Passover, Weeks (Pentecost) and Booths (Tabernacles) – became the object of pilgrimage not only from Judaea itself but from the Hellenized world and the Roman empire.

It is usually assumed that the Temple cult remained substantially unchanged throughout the Second Temple period. But since the Temple Scroll (p. 156), for example, describes a different liturgical cycle, and many of the scrolls a different calendar, from that known from other sources, it may be that either different groups shared the Temple, each observing its own rules, or the regime changed as different groups were accorded control of it.

Certainly, it is difficult to explain otherwise how deviant Temple calendars and regimes could have developed. The imposition of a single Temple regime and calendar, and the prohibition of access to those following any other system, may help to explain why at least one group reflected in the scrolls felt it necessary to secede from Temple worship and form themselves into a sect.

However, it has to be acknowledged that we have little information about the regular activities in the Temple. What is clear is the public devotion that increasingly came to be attached to it. Nevertheless, while the *idea* of the Temple as a holy site at the centre of Judaism (of the world, even!) was universally accepted, the differences over the manner of the cult could lead to estrangement. If the cult was not, in the eyes of one group, being correctly carried out, then God was not being worshipped, holiness not imparted, and indeed the Temple itself, the land, and the people of Israel, defiled. And since the Temple was the place at which Israel became holy, and from which divine forgiveness emanated, any threat to its efficacy was momentous.

There were other ways in which the Temple impinged on daily life. All Jews in the 'Land of Israel' were expected to offer first-fruits and tithes of their produce, the proceeds of which went to the Temple. Thus the entire land participated in the Temple cult. Jews everywhere also sent an annual Temple tax of a half-shekel. The temple represented the most holy divine dwelling, and every Jew entering it had to be in a state of ritual purity. For the priests, who alone could approach the altar, an even higher degree was required. This cult of holiness was largely applicable to the Temple, but there were occasions when Jews were required to purify themselves (such as after touching a corpse or contracting a skin disease). Water was the usual means of such purification, and at Qumran, as in many large houses from the Second Temple period, baths were provided for such purposes. These are called *miqva'ot* (singular: *miqveh*). Some groups, perhaps including those living at Qumran, may have aspired to a higher degree of ritual purity; many of the water installations there are interpreted as ritual baths. Meals were occasions on which some devout Jews also tried to preserve their pure status (for example, by not sharing unclean food with unclean persons). Whether the inhabitants at Qumran did the same is not known, but if they were the people to whom the Community Rule applied, they probably tried to be in a state of ritual purity as much as possible.

Sacred scriptures

During the Persian period the scribes of Jerusalem (and perhaps also from elsewhere) wrote and edited a number of writings in Hebrew that began to form a canon of literature. Among these were narratives

A reconstruction of Herod's Temple from the southwest. Herod undertook massive rebuilding work on what was also known as the 'Second Temple', but it was destroyed in 70 CE before it was even finished.

about the past forming a history of the nation, from the beginning of the world itself up to the eve of the Persian period, scrolls of prophetic sayings, three containing oracles, speeches and stories associated with the names of three prophets (Isaiah, Jeremiah, Ezekiel) and another comprising a sequence of prophets (finally totalling 12). There were also collections of religious poetry (Psalms) and wise sayings (Proverbs). During the Hellenistic period this body of literature grew to include more popular, 'unofficial' writings that catered for the wider readership that increased literacy created – such as the books of Ruth, Esther and Jonah. It was possibly the struggle to preserve some cultural independence from the Greek-dominated civilization of the Mediterranean and the Levant that led

to these writings being given a very high value as expressions of the essence and character of long-standing Jewish identity, and the Hasmonaeans were probably responsible for promoting them, encouraging their study and introducing them into the curriculum of Judaean schools (to replace the study of the Greek classics?). By the 1st century CE there was already a fixed or almost fixed 'canon' of Jewish 'writings' (as the word 'scriptures' means). Among the Dead Sea Scrolls are copies of all these books (with one or two exceptions), alongside others that may also have been regarded as belonging to this 'canon'. The authority of such books for regulating Jewish life was increasingly accepted by certain individuals and groups, including the writers of the scrolls and the Pharisees. They came

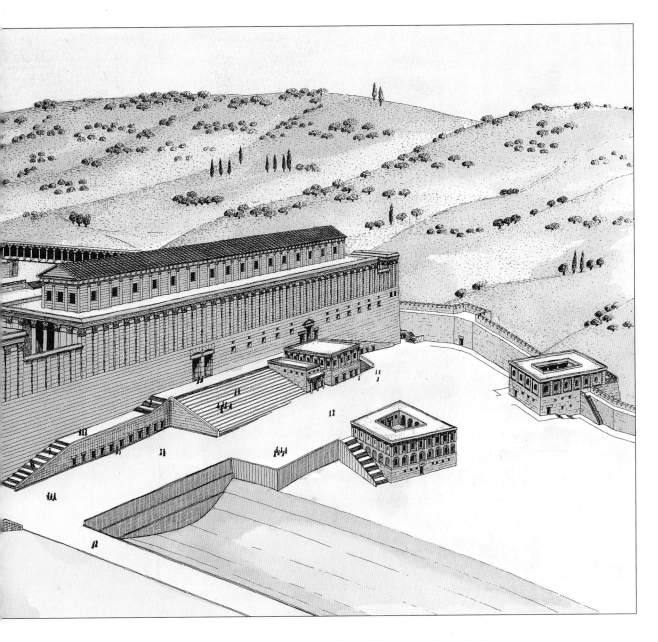

to be seen as exclusively religious texts, since it was as a religion (in the ancient world that term would include both cult and philosophy) that Jews tended to see Judaism.

These writings were also translated into Greek for the benefit of non-Hebrew-speaking Jews, but the collection was larger than the Hebrew canon, including such works as Tobit, Judith, the Wisdom of Jesus Ben Sira, Baruch and 1–2 Maccabees. Some of these have also been found (in Hebrew or Aramaic) among the scrolls. Both in Hebrew and in Greek, however, different texts of these scriptural books existed. The attempt to establish a fixed text of classic works that had been constantly (and not always accurately) copied was a universal problem in the Hellenistic world and it became necessary to

fix one standard text. Signs of such standardization can be detected in the Qumran scrolls, even though they exhibit a great variety of texts.

The scriptures were thought to contain divine wisdom and as such were carefully studied as to their laws, predictions and indeed their hidden secrets. They generated in turn other writings, such as commentaries, paraphrases and rearrangements. They also stimulated the writings of other psalms and wise sayings. Great scriptural figures were the subject of legends, and new writings were attributed to them, often in the form of death-bed advice or revelations about the future. The Dead Sea Scrolls include these, too. The scriptures seem, indeed, to have comprised the intellectual horizon of many Jewish writers of the period.

Private religious practices

Most private religious behaviour was directed towards either Temple or scriptures. The common practices of circumcision, dietary regulation and sabbath worship were regarded as fundamental parts of the divine law revealed in scripture, while prayer and the celebration of holy days were orientated towards the Temple. Study of the scriptures was certainly paramount, either individually or (as we learn from the Qumran scrolls and the New Testament) in a group. Both the 'house of prayer' and the 'house of study', major institutions of rabbinic Judaism, existed already in the Second Temple period, though how widely we cannot know.

One of the means by which the Law (the most important part of the scriptures) was brought close to the individual was by following the command in Deuteronomy 6:4–8:

'Hear, O Israel: The Lord our God is one Lord.
You shall love the Lord your God with all your heart,
and all your soul, and all your strength.
These words, which I command you today, shall be in your heart… and you shall bind them as a sign on your hand, and they shall be like symbols between your eyes.
You shall write them upon the doorposts of your house…'

The opening words were therefore written and placed inside small containers. These were then put on doorposts, in which case they were called 'mezuzot', or bound around the arm when praying, and called 'tefillin' (Hebrew for 'prayers'). The more common English name for the latter is 'phylacteries'. Both mezuzot and phylacteries were found among the Qumran scrolls.

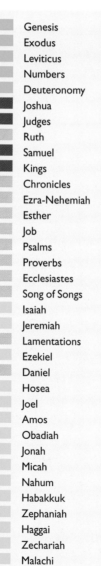

Finally, we should not forget fasting and the making of vows. The former would normally be a communal event on certain solemn days or in times of crisis. The making of vows was private and could involve either a gift to the Temple or a pledge to carry out some service. Giving to the poor also seems to have been an important religious duty (as the book of Tobit makes clear), since it was regarded as a divine commandment. Both in the scrolls and in the New Testament the practice of redistributing community goods among the poor is mentioned.

Beyond these activities, we can suspect that a number of what we might call 'superstitious' practices attached to Judaism, as to any other religion. There was a wide use of amulets to ward off evil spirits; charms and spells were employed; and the claimed magical properties of various substances were exploited. How much (apart from the use of the distinctive names of God) these activities were particularly Jewish is unclear. But the scrolls contain both brontologia (predictions based on the sound of thunder) and horoscopes (divining character from birth date and physical characteristics).

With the destruction of the Jerusalem Temple in 70 CE, cult and priesthood vanished and a new form of Judaism emerged. But it had antecedents. For many Jews, the Temple was too distant, or in the wrong hands, and substitutes were needed, without the idea of the Temple itself being abandoned. Good deeds and private devotion took centre stage. The so-called sectarian scrolls mostly assume the necessity in principle of worship at the Jerusalem Temple, including bloody sacrifices, and the observance of purity rituals, but often state

The Old Testament

All the books of the Old Testament (or Hebrew Bible) were found in the Qumran caves with the exception of Esther. The books of Moses (the 'Torah', the Law, Pentateuch, Genesis-Deuteronomy) were especially important, representing the divine law. The books of the Prophets (Isaiah-Malachi) were also venerated, especially as predicting the future and in particular the 'last days' in which the scroll writers thought that they were living. The book of Psalms (of which there were several editions at Qumran) was also regarded as a prophetic work, written by King David. But we cannot say whether the writers of the scrolls shared the fixed canon of scriptures, the 'Bible', that was already being defined by the Jewish authorities of their day. There are also no New Testament writings at Qumran.

The key below shows how the books are ordered in the Jewish Bible; the list on the right follows the different order in most Christian Old Testaments.

Key

- The Law
- The Former Prophets
- The Latter Prophets
- The Writings

Genesis
Exodus
Leviticus
Numbers
Deuteronomy
Joshua
Judges
Ruth
Samuel
Kings
Chronicles
Ezra-Nehemiah
Esther
Job
Psalms
Proverbs
Ecclesiastes
Song of Songs
Isaiah
Jeremiah
Lamentations
Ezekiel
Daniel
Hosea
Joel
Amos
Obadiah
Jonah
Micah
Nahum
Habakkuk
Zephaniah
Haggai
Zechariah
Malachi

(Below left, and right) Two parts of a phylactery from Murabba'at, in the Judaean desert (1st or 2nd century CE).

that God accepts sincere prayer just as readily as he does sacrifices. One important liturgical text (the 'Songs of the Sabbath Sacrifice') suggests that the writers saw themselves as participating in the angelic worship in the heavenly Temple. The belief in a heavenly counterpart to the earth's high priesthood, Temple, and even city of Jerusalem, is echoed in the New Testament, especially the book of Revelation. In important ways, then, these scrolls anticipate ways in which both Judaism and Christianity transcended the need for the Jerusalem Temple, although the writers of the scrolls would never have dreamed of such a future.

(Following pages) Aerial view of the Western Wall adjacent to the Temple Mount.

(Below) 'A sign on your hand and … like symbols between your eyes': a Jew at prayer with phylacteries.

51

Jewish Parties and Sects

The historian Josephus (c. 38–93 CE) divides the Jews into four parties: Essenes, Pharisees, Sadducees and a 'Fourth Philosophy'. He uses the Greek word *hairesis* ('sect'), from which comes the English word 'heresy'; but a better translation is 'party', for these groups were not necessarily all tightly-knit or exclusive. They can best be understood perhaps as a combination of a modern political party and a church denomination. The Qumran scrolls, however, do give us a picture of groups living a quite separated lifestyle, with highly formal rules of entry and participation, and to which the word 'sect' might be more accurately applied. While most scholars suspect that Josephus' account is an oversimplification, and that there were many other Jewish groups (as well as many Jews in no group at all), other sources do mention at least the first of Josephus' 'parties'. It is worthwhile, then, to review what we know of them, because scholars have at various times sought to identify the writers of the scrolls with all four of these.

Essenes

The Essenes are mentioned by the Alexandrian Jewish philosopher and Bible interpreter, Philo; by the Roman traveller and statesman, Pliny; by the Jewish historian Flavius Josephus; and by some later church historians (based largely if not wholly on the earlier accounts). Philo of Alexandria (c. 30 BCE–45 CE) offers two notes on the Essenes. In his treatise *Every Good Person is Free* (75–91), he says they numbered about 4,000 and that their name derives from the Greek word for holiness, as holiness of the mind was of the utmost importance to them. The Essenes, he says, fled the ungodly cities and dwelt in villages, contenting themselves with farm work and crafts, ignoring commerce and without slaves. They did not hoard silver, gold or land, but lived in common, sharing meals, clothing and a single purse. Unlike other Jews they offered no animal sacrifice, but studied their ancestral laws, especially in synagogues on the sabbath day. Their teaching emphasized the love of God, of virtue, and of humanity. They cared for the sick, aged and weak, and rejected the notion that God caused evil and suffering. In another writing, *Defence of the Jews*, Philo adds that the Essenes were farmers, shepherds, beekeepers and craftsmen, that they banned marriage, practised continence and had no children, adolescents or young men in their community.

In Book V of his *Natural History*, Pliny (23/24–79 CE) locates the Essenes at a spot somewhere above Engedi, a town on the northwestern shore of the Dead Sea. Like Philo, Pliny says there

Did the Essenes Marry?

Josephus states that the Essenes were divided into those who married and those who did not. Those who did, did not greatly approve of it:

'They avoid pleaures as a vice and regard continence and the control of the desires as a special virtue. They disdain marriage…They do not actually on principle reject wedlock and the propagation thereby of humanity, but they want to protect themselves from promiscuous women, since they are convinced that none of them preserves her fidelity to one man.' (*War* 2, 120–21)

'They believe that those who refuse to marry negate the chief purpose of life – the propagation of humanity – and that furthermore, if everyone were to adopt the same approach, the entire race would very quickly become extinct. But they subject their wives to three years' probation and marry them only after they have by three periods of ritual purification demonstrated proof of fertility. They do not have sexual relations with them during pregnancy, thus showing that their

purpose in marriage is not pleasure but the assurance of posterity.' (*War* 2, 160–61)

Likewise, the Damascus Document (6:11) implies a marrying and non-marrying kind of membership. There is, accordingly, a tradition of celibacy reflected in the scrolls, though several manuscripts from the Qumran caves certainly reflect married life. Wives and children are members of the Damascus community; there are laws in the Temple Scroll about women's vows; according to the Rule of the Congregation (1QSa) women may testify against their husbands; and wisdom texts refer to the dangers of certain kinds of women.

For a long time most scholars felt that the Community Rule legislated for an ascetic, monastic type of community that practised celibacy. Some continue to advocate this view. Others have suggested that the communities of the scrolls were varied and celibacy after marriage may have been an option for those desiring to study the Law and draw nearer to their discipline of righteousness. The presence of women's and children's skeletons in the Qumran cemetery does not necessarily answer the question, though it is a problem that for some time was conveniently ignored.

(Following pages) An artist's impression of an assembly of the community members at Qumran.

Joining the Essenes

The Jewish historian Josephus gives a full account of Essene practices, which afford several parallels to the regulations included in the Community Rule (1QS; see p. 82).

'Those desiring to enter the sect do not obtain immediate admittance. This person waits outside for one year. The same way of life is taught to him and he is given a hatchet, the loin-cloth which I have mentioned, and a white garment. Having proven his continence during this time, he comes closer to the(ir) way of life and participates in the purificatory baths at a higher level, but he is not yet completely integrated. But after he has demonstrated his constancy, his character is tested for two more years, and if he appears holy he is accepted into the group. But before touching the common food he makes solemn vows before his brothers.' (*War* 2, 137–39)

'These oaths included swearing to worship properly, be fair, be loyal to those in authority, be modest in duty and appearance, be honest, conceal nothing from members of the group and reveal nothing to outsiders. The member swore also to take care not to share the group's writings, doctrines, and the names of angels with non-members.' (*War* 2, 140–42)

The Community Rule is quite similar:

'Every man, born of Israel, who pledges to join the council of the community shall be examined by the man appointed to the head of the 'Many' concerning his understanding and his deeds. If he is fit for the discipline, he shall admit him into the covenant that he may be converted to the truth and depart from all injustice. And he shall teach him all the rules of the community. And later, when he appears before the congregation, they shall all deliberate his case, and according to the decision of the council of the congregation he shall either enter or depart. After he has entered the council of the

community he shall not touch the pure meal of the congregation until one year is complete, and until he has been examined concerning his spirit and deeds.' (1QS 6:13–18)

Elsewhere Josephus refers to their shared property:

'They put their property into a common stock, and the rich man enjoys no more of his fortune than does the man with absolutely nothing. And there are more than 4,000 men who behave this way.' (*War* 2, 122–23)

Compare the Community Rule:

'Nor shall he have any share of the property of the congregation. Then when he has completed one year within the community, and if it be his destiny, according to the judgment of the priests and the multitude of the men of their covenant, to enter the company of the community, his property and his earnings shall be handed over to the bursar of the congregation who shall register it to his account and shall not spend it for the congregation. He shall not touch the drink of the congregation until he has completed a second year among the men of the community. But when the second year has passed, he shall be examined, and if it is his destiny, he shall be inscribed, and his property shall be merged.' (1QS 6:17–22)

There are also differences in detail between Josephus' account and 1QS, but the similarities are striking.

A view over the ruins of Qumran looking south: the room on the right has been suggested as a possible 'council chamber'.

At Qumran, looking east: the dining room or community meeting room.

was neither money nor women among them, but that throngs of new members came to this community because the fluctuations of fortune had wearied them. (It is this description that largely prompted the original identification of Qumran with an Essene settlement.)

But it is Josephus, who was born and lived in Judaea before moving to Rome, and who participated in the early years of the First Jewish Revolt (66–74 CE), who provides the richest account of Judaism and the Jewish people, including a description of the Essenes. He also incorporates brief anecdotes about individual Essenes, who were, it seems, famous for their predictions. For example, an Essene called Judas predicted the death of Antigonus, a member of the Hasmonaean royal family; a certain Simon predicted the trial of Archelaus (another Hasmonaean); and another, Menahem, predicted to the young Herod that he would be a ruler. Yet another individual Essene, John, was a general in charge of Tamna, Lydda, Joppa and Emmaus during the revolt against Rome. Josephus claims to have known the Essene party from personal experience, having (he says) studied with them for three years. He confirms that the Essenes renounced pleasure and followed a path of continence, adding that they were concerned about the behaviour of women, and, though they did not prohibit marriage, either preferred celibacy or obliged their intended wives to demonstrate their ability to conceive. They despised riches, dressed in white, avoided oaths and the use of oil, lived an egalitarian lifestyle, and carried weapons only when travelling. Every morning they offered prayers towards the sun, assembling at the fifth hour of the day for prayer and studying the ancients. Josephus also maintains that they were experts in medicinal herbs.

Particularly interesting is Josephus' description of the Essene hierarchy. There were four levels, representing different degrees of purity, and long periods of probation for new entrants, with strict initiation ceremonies. The prospective member is tested for a year, and, if he is acceptable, his property and earnings are deposited with the bursar who records this. For the next year he may eat with the community. After this second year, his possessions are merged with those of the community and he may then drink with its members. An Essene could be banished if he revealed the secrets of the group, or the names of the angels, or questioned the authority of the leadership (*War* 2:141–44). The Essenes, he also tells us, practised their own distinctive purification rites and performed their sacrifices separately (whether in the Temple or elsewhere he does not say).

These features resemble many in the Community Rule (6:13–24), and so most scholars have identified the community at Khirbet Qumran with the Essenes. However, Josephus never associates the Essenes with a specific location like Qumran, but says that they settled throughout Palestine. He elsewhere mentions an 'Essene gate' on the south side of Jerusalem, which has recently been discovered, and which is generally thought to have belonged to an 'Essene quarter' in that city.

As for the Essene love of peace hailed by Philo, Josephus notes that they were tortured by the Romans during the Jewish revolt (and, as we have seen, mentions an Essene military leader). His chief distinction between the Essenes, the Pharisees and the Sadducees lies in their views on fate, human will and the afterlife, philosophical issues that would have charmed his Roman audience. According to him, Essenes believed in the immortality of souls that reside beyond the Ocean, and that humans are free but their destiny foreknown.

Despite all these ancient (and not entirely consistent) reports about the Essenes, they remain a fairly obscure group, since neither the New Testament nor the rabbinic writings refer to them – unless, perhaps, under a different name.

Josephus on the Sadducees

The Sadducees on the Soul and the Human Will (according to Josephus):

'The Sadducees believe that the soul perishes along with the body.' (*Antiquities* 18:16)

'[…] do away with fate altogether and separate God not only from the commission of evil but even from the very sight of it. They maintain that man has the free choice of good and evil and that it rests with each man's will whether he will follow the one or the other. As for the survival of the soul after death, penalties in the underworld, and rewards, they will have none of them.' (*War* 2:164–65)

'…the Pharisees had passed on to the people certain regulations handed down by former generations and not recorded in the Law of Moses, for which reason they are rejected by the Sadducean group, who say that only those regulations should be considered obligatory which were written down and that those which had been handed down by the fathers should not be observed. And regarding these matters the two parties came to have disputes and serious differences.' (*Antiquities* 13:297–98)

Sadducees

According to Josephus, again our main source, the Sadducees were the Pharisees' main rivals for political influence. Their power base lay with the priesthood and the aristocracy (their name might derive from the priestly dynasty of Zadok, or, alternatively, from the Hebrew word for 'righteous', *zaddiq*). According to Josephus, they rejected the ideas of fate, resurrection and rewards and punishments after death, and adhered only to laws written in the Bible (*Jewish Antiquities* 13:297; 18:17). They seem to have been religiously and politically conservative, holding power in the Temple and co-operating with, even supporting, Roman rule. They are mentioned in the New Testament also, though the only point of interest is their disbelief in resurrection (e.g. Matthew 22:23; Acts 23:6). Acts 4:14–18 also refers to Ananias, the Sadducee, as the current high priest.

Are the Sadducees mentioned in the scrolls? A great deal of interest centres on the term 'sons of Zadok' ('Zadokites' and 'Sadducees' *might* be the same word in Hebrew) used in the Damascus Document and the Community Rule in connection with their own group (*not* with opponents). This has led to recent suggestions (e.g. by Lawrence Schiffman) that the writers of the scrolls had connections with the Sadducees, an idea supported by identifying some legal opinions expressed in the scrolls with those attributed to *Zadduqim* in the Mishnah and Talmud. One example of such an opinion, found in the Halakhic Letter (4QMMT), is that a liquid stream can convey impurity from one vessel to another; the Sadducean position (mentioned in the Mishnah tractate *Yadayim* 4:6–7) agrees; the rabbis (and implicitly the Pharisees) do not.

It has also been suggested that the calendar of the Temple Scroll (11QT), which differed from the Jewish calendar in force then (and ever since), is also Sadducean. The problem here (and in other cases) is that the Sadducees we know from Josephus and the New Testament look rather

unlike the authors of the sectarian scrolls. The Sadducees must have observed a different calendar from those and their co-operative attitude towards the Romans is hardly endorsed in the Qumran writings. If these writings are Sadducee, we have to suppose a fairly violent rift among this group of which we otherwise know nothing. Moreover, the Qumran texts nowhere simply call their community 'sons of Zadok'; they use the term of their priests only. On the whole, it seems unlikely that we can identify the scrolls writers with Sadducees, though perhaps we can conclude that both groups were opposed to the Pharisees.

Pharisees

Our chief informant about the Pharisees is once again Josephus, who himself claimed to belong to them. According to him, they were a politically and religiously active group, numbering 6,000, who had enjoyed mixed fortunes under a succession of rulers. The Hasmonaean king John Hyrcanus (134–104 BCE)

Solomon is anointed king by the priest Zadok in this painting by Johann Schönfeld of the 1650s. The Sadducees' name may derive from that of the Zadokite dynasty.

had first favoured them, then moved over to the Sadducees; but some Pharisees encouraged the Seleucid king of Syria, Demetrius III, to overthrow his son and successor Alexander Jannaeus, who then turned on them. Just before his death, he advised his queen, Alexandra, to reinstate them. Herod the Great favoured some of them, and later, during the war against Rome, the Pharisees, with other leading groups, attempted to dissuade the Jews from rebelling (*War* 2:409–17).

Josephus says that the Pharisees were the most popular and influential of the Jewish parties, and especially favoured by women in the royal houses; that they were the most learned of Jews in respect to the Law, and believed in life after death and resurrection.

The Pharisees are also mentioned in the New Testament, where they appear as the watchdogs of proper ritual piety, with their own legal traditions centring on observance of purity laws, ritual preparation of foods, tithing and sabbath observances. They usually serve as opponents of Jesus, who condemns them as hypocrites, concerned with details of outward legal observance without the proper inward attitudes (e.g. Matthew 23:23). Paul claimed he had been a Pharisee; perhaps this explains his obsession with the Jewish law.

But despite the hostility of most of the New Testament to Pharisees, the truth seems to have been that they did not necessarily regard Judaism as merely a matter of outward observance. The rabbinic writings certainly present the 1st-century Pharisees as advocates of a strict purity regime, which extended from public life to the home and from the sabbath to other festivals, but reflect also a certain humility, a sense of proportion and a recognition of the importance of love of God and fellow humans. Even in the book of Acts, one of the most famous Pharisees, Gamaliel, is portrayed as advocating a tolerant attitude towards the views of the early followers of Jesus (Acts 5:33–40; 22:3). One doctrine on which Pharisees, early Christians and, possibly, the community of the scrolls would have agreed was the resurrection of the dead.

The Dead Sea Scrolls never refer to Pharisees explicitly. But many scholars regard them as the main targets of criticism in the sectarian writings. Quite contrary to the Gospels, here they are criticized for their laxity towards the law – if by Pharisees are meant the 'smooth-talking interpreters' in, for example, the Habakkuk commentary (1QpHab) and the Damascus Document (CD) – where the Hebrew word translated 'smooth' (*halaqot*) may be a pun on *halakot*, meaning Pharisaic, later rabbinic, legal traditions and rulings. There seems to be a high degree of correspondence between the legal positions of these 'smooth-talkers' and those of the rabbis, who may be regarded as the Pharisees' successors.

Samaritans

One Jewish sect not mentioned with the other four by Josephus is the Samaritans. According to the Bible (2 Kings 17) the Samaritans were descendants of foreigners transplanted to Samaria by the Assyrians in the late 7th century BCE (similar traditions can be found in Genesis 34, Jubilees 30 and Judith 9). The books of Ezra and Nehemiah show them opposing the rebuilding of the Jerusalem Temple and the city walls. But when the antagonism between Jerusalem and Samaria began is hard to know for certain. Both regard the Pentateuch as their scripture, though the Samaritans had their own temple on Mt Gerizim, near Shechem.

In 331 BCE Alexander destroyed the city of Samaria and garrisoned 600 troops there. Many Samaritans then fled to Shechem. Nearly two centuries later, when John Hyrcanus came to power in Jerusalem, he annexed the territory of Samaria and destroyed the Samaritan temple. Herod the Great

(Opposite) The story in Luke 2:41–50 of Jesus sitting in the midst of the 'teachers' and amazing them with his knowledge probably reflects disputes between Jesus with his followers and Pharisees over matters of the law, shown in this painting by Holman Hunt of 1854–60.

(Below) A Samaritan priest displaying a scroll of the Law.

carried out extensive building programmes there, naming the city Sebaste. The Samaritans were later also involved in anti-Roman uprisings and in 68 CE the Roman general (later emperor) Vespasian slaughtered 10,000 of them at Mt Gerizim. But the Samaritans have survived to this day.

Readers of the New Testament will be aware that 'the Jews have no dealings with the Samaritans' (John 4:9). And, given the reverence accorded to the Jerusalem Temple in the scrolls, one would expect their writers to have been anti-Samaritan. However, some apparently 'Samaritan' features of the scrolls have been noted. Some of the biblical manuscripts have texts that are closer to the Samaritan Pentateuch than to the traditional Jewish Bible. The Temple Scroll and the Book of Jubilees, too, both found among the Qumran scrolls and sharing their distinctive calendar, seem to give some prominence to Jacob (who was particularly connected to the north rather than the south) and to Shechem. Some of the sectarian Dead Sea Scrolls also reflect ideas and beliefs similar to those attributed to the Samaritans.

Other possible similarities include the sharing of messianic expectations based on Deuteronomy 18:18; the use of the imagery of 'children of light'; and the absence of the celebration of the Jewish festivals of Purim (mentioned in the book of Esther, which was not found at Qumran) and Hanukkah (which celebrated the rededication of the Jerusalem Temple by Judas Maccabee). But, as is often the case with features of the Dead Sea Scrolls, a scattering of individual similarities is to be expected among different Jewish groups sharing a common scriptural and cultural background. There seems no sign of a systematic relationship between Samaritans and Qumran groups.

Zealots

Josephus speaks of a 'Fourth Philosophy' among the Jews, whose members were in most respects like the Pharisees, but had a passion for liberty and recognized no ruler besides God. They had been founded in Galilee by a political rebel called Judas who was associated with a Pharisee named Zadok, just after the death of Herod the Great. From then onwards, to the fall of Jerusalem in 70 CE, a great number of uprisings against the Roman occupiers and their Jewish supporters occurred. In a rough and ready way these rebels are often designated as Zealots, as if belonging to a single party, but Josephus does not use the term until the last decade before the outbreak of the revolt (in 66 CE). We should not, then, refer to the fourth party within Judaism as 'The Zealots', though this is often done, even by some scholars.

However, the family of Judas seems to have continued to play a role in political insurgency, since the leader of the Zealots at Masada in 74 CE, Eleazar Ben Jair, was a descendant of Judas. There may have been some strong ideological bond among those who struggled against Roman rule, but the picture painted by Josephus reveals a rather broadly-based resistance force, not a single organized group. Indeed, there seem to have been deep antagonisms between the resisting factions, at least in the closing years of the revolt.

As far as the scrolls are concerned, the important point is that this 'Fourth Philosophy' does not seem to have developed any distinctive practices or beliefs beyond resistance to Rome, and thus it is not plausible to assign the scrolls, which clearly reflect distinctive religious sects, to such a movement. Whether or not those who wrote the scrolls would have sympathized with either the Fourth Philosophy or the Zealots, or have participated in rebellion against Rome, is another matter. There is ample evidence, for instance in the War Scroll (1QM), that they could well have done so. Certainly, the destruction of Qumran itself through a military assault, and the presence of what may well be a Qumran text among the ruins at Masada, can be used as evidence that the inhabitants were active in the war against Rome. The lodging of a list of Temple treasures in Cave 3 (the Copper Scroll) may even show that the inhabitants of Qumran were sympathetic to the group(s) who had seized control of the Temple during the revolt.

Early Christians

It may seem strange to consider 'early Christians' as a Jewish sect, but the book of Acts certainly portrays the followers of Jesus as such. They were not the only group to hail a messiah, eat alone and proclaim the imminent coming of the kingdom of God. Christianity as defined by Paul, proclaiming an end to the power of the Jewish law and to the exclusivity of Judaism, and declaring Jesus as the source of liberation from sin and death, was not that of the followers of Jesus, led by his brother James, who were based in Jerusalem until the war with Rome. This 'Jerusalem church', as it is called, awaited the coming of God, and perhaps the return of Jesus, while adhering to the Jewish law.

Jesus and his disciples were Jews who believed that the scriptures foretold the future and that the fulfilment of history was coming in their time; perhaps that the renewing holy spirit of God was about to be poured out on Israel and that Jews should repent and accept God's mercy on them. It is likely that the earliest Christians worshipped in the Temple and lived according to the Law of Moses. What their attitude towards Rome was is unclear: the Christian gospel would later reflect positive attitudes to Rome as the religion spread among non-Jews in the empire. But Jesus had, after all, been crucified under Roman law as a political agitator.

Both resemblances and differences between the early Christians and the writers of the scrolls are numerous. The 'Teacher of Righteousness' of some of the scrolls seems to have been seen, at least initially, as a messianic figure; both the scrolls and the New Testament interpret the scriptures in similar ways, and both found a way of dispensing with the Temple cult as a means to personal holiness and divine favour; Jesus' teaching against divorce looks identical to that in the Damascus Document. The New Testament uses the term 'children of light'; the figure of Melchizedek as a heavenly high priest is used in an important Cave 11 text and in the Letter to the Hebrews; and the scrolls and the Gospels are both antagonistic to Pharisees.

But for these and other parallels that have been suggested between Christians and Qumran – including John the Baptist, thought by many scholars to have been an Essene himself – the common scriptural and

cultural background furnishes an adequate explanation. What is often cited as the most striking parallel, baptism, is probably misleading. The scrolls do not speak of any baptism of repentance, and used water, like most Jews, for purposes of ritual purification – about which Jesus himself does not seem to have been concerned. More basically, the stringent attitude in the scrolls towards the Mosaic law, and obedience as the only road to divine favour, seem at odds with the teaching of Jesus. And the Qumran sectarian scrolls advocate avoidance of other Jews, let alone the sinners whose company Jesus kept. In short, while there are important parallels, there is too wide a gulf between some of the main principles of the scrolls and those of the New Testament for any direct connection between Qumran sectarians and early Christians to be entertained.

Jesus was baptised with water, as shown in this painting by Piero della Francesca (c. 1500). But the scrolls writers only speak of using water for ritual purification or initiation. This draws a clear distinction between the early Christians and the writers of the scrolls.

If the dating and background of the Qumran scrolls have become fairly clear, there remain several unanswered questions. Why and when were they placed in caves? What exactly is the relationship between the caves and the ruins of Qumran? To many scholars the answers are obvious: the sectarian inhabitants of Qumran concealed their library in nearby caves when their settlement was in danger of destruction (see p. 178).

If that is so, why were some scrolls, like those in Cave 1, carefully wrapped in linen and stored in sealed jars, while the contents of Cave 4 seem to have been stored on shelves, leaving only fragments to be discovered in our own time? While there are numerous natural caves close to the settlement, and other caves on the edge of the Qumran plateau, why are some of the scroll caves, like Caves 3 and 11, 2 km (over a mile) away? And why is there a list of Temple treasures (the Copper Scroll from Cave 3) among a collection of sectarian texts?

Another puzzle is the degree of consistency between the contents of the scrolls. It is becoming more widely accepted that not all the scrolls (perhaps even none) were written at Qumran, though most scholars still accept that they belonged to the inhabitants of the settlement. Indeed, among the scrolls can be found a number of shared characteristics: devotion to a calendar of 364 days instead of the 354 maintained by the Temple authorities at the time; criticism of the religious authorities and detailed attention to laws of purity; keen interest in what was thought to be the imminent end of the present world order; and a fascination with the names and functions of heavenly beings. At the same time, there is undoubted variety among the scrolls on other matters: some express a strictly dualistic theology, but many do not; there is no single doctrine of a messiah (and sometimes no messiah figure at all); and at least two clearly distinct (though related) sectarian organizations are described.

Any scholar theorizing on the origin of the scrolls has to bear all these problems in mind, examining each text on its own terms as well as looking carefully for its similarities to, and differences from, other Qumran texts.

The War Scroll from Cave 1.

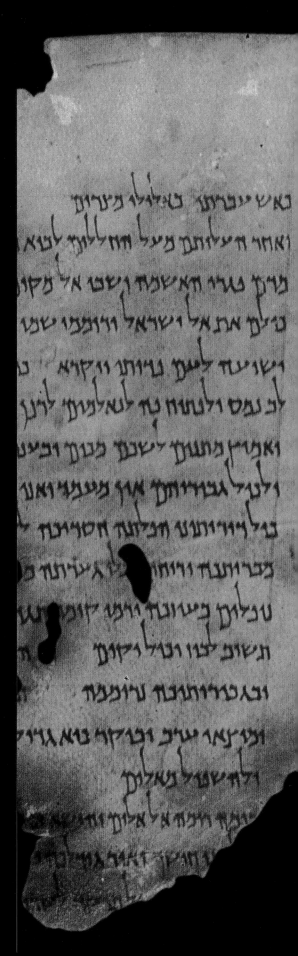

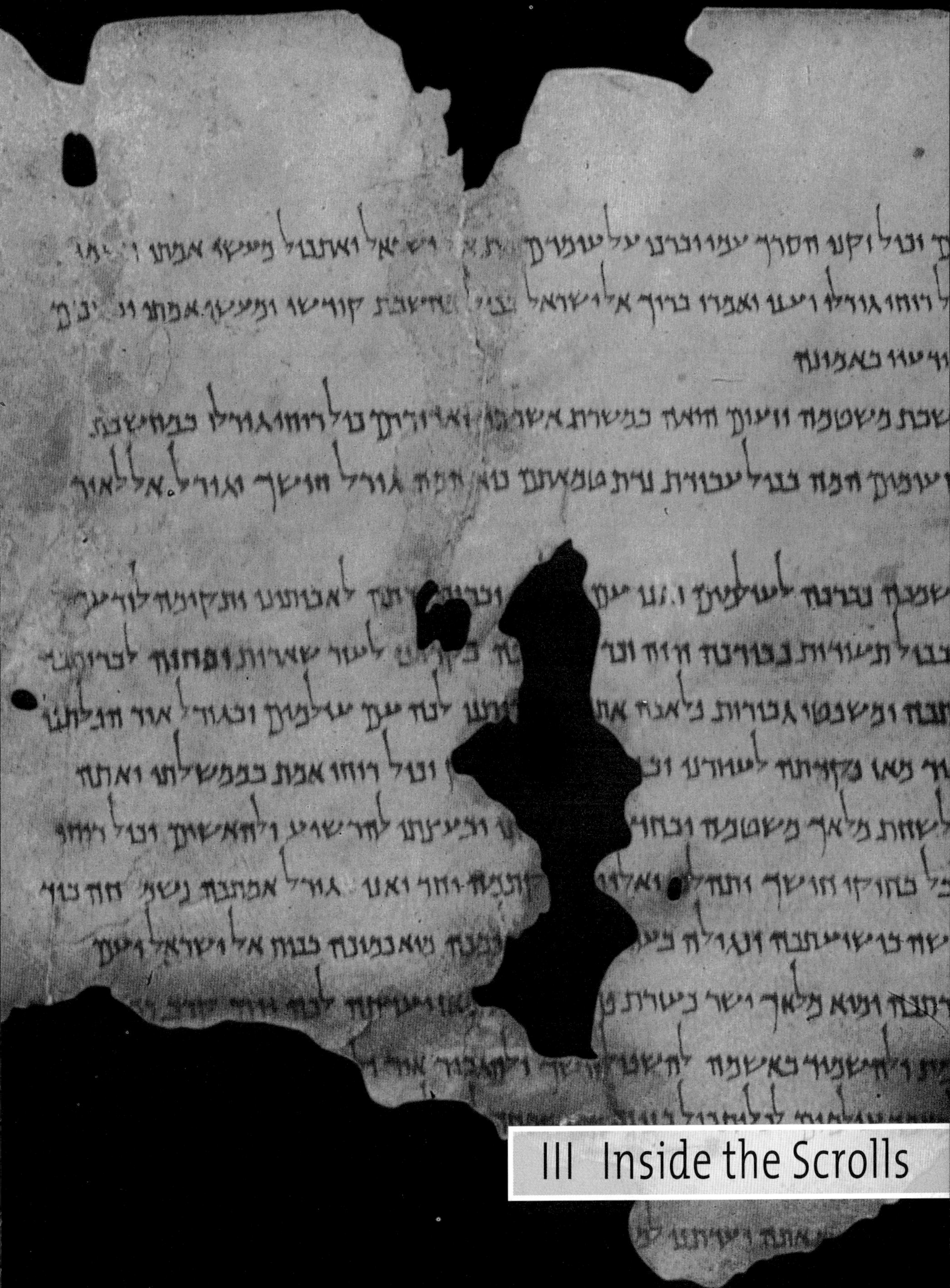

III Inside the Scrolls

Making a Scroll

In the 1st or 2nd century CE, the book was invented. It was called a codex, and consisted of pages bound together in a volume. Because of this invention, it became possible to produce a Bible, and indeed it is thought that the codex was especially favoured by Christians for the purpose of containing several books of scriptures in one small bundle. But until the Middle Ages, Jews continued to write their scriptures on scrolls, as they still do in Orthodox circles for liturgical use. The advent of paper and the invention of printing further revolutionized the production of reading-matter and gave us our modern book. Previously, books had been copied by hand onto parchment, which is animal skin that has been depilated, scrubbed and bleached. This is the material on which the great majority of Qumran scrolls were also written, though about 50 have survived on papyrus, made from strips of reed gummed together in layers.

The length of a scroll varied; scrolls were possibly in some cases prepared in advance for the particular work that was to be written on them. Whether the scribe himself stitched the pieces together to his required length we do not know. The longest Qumran biblical scroll, containing the book of Isaiah (1QIsa^a) is about 7.5 m (24.6 ft) long. The lengthiest non-biblical scroll, the Temple Scroll, is almost 9 m (29.5 ft) long. It has been speculated that another scroll, preserved only in fragments, that contains a paraphrase of the Pentateuch (4Q394–95) may have been as much as 30 m (98.4 ft) in length, if the work was indeed confined to a single scroll. It has been suggested that the books from Joshua–2 Kings were also written on a single scroll, whose length would have been about 20 m (65 ft).

The production of such a huge number of scrolls involved a variety of skills, tools and materials. First, sheep, goats, cows or deer had to be killed and skinned. The skins were then washed, soaked and cleaned of all flesh and hair (some fragments still preserve bristles). If the hides were to be tanned, as some of the scroll fragments may have been, they had to be treated with some form of vegetable or organic matter. Another approach involved dressing the hide with alum and dusting it with powdered chalk. The treated hide then had to be softened by beating so that it would become pliable.

Reed pens such as these, and the bronze inkwell, probably found at Qumran, were used by scribes there.

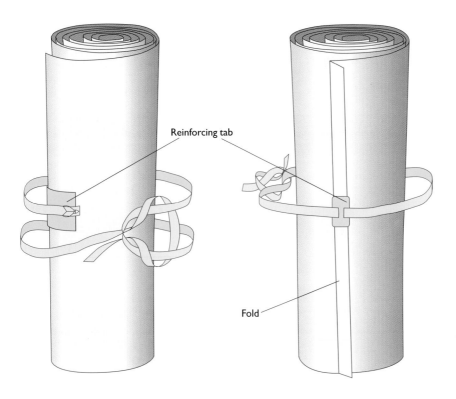

Reinforcing tab

Fold

(Left) Reconstructions of finished scrolls, showing two types of tabs and fastenings.

(Below) Part of 4Q448, showing the original tab in place.

All this work would have involved skins, knives, materials for cleaning and depilation, hammers or mallets, measuring tools, pointed instruments, pens, ink, inkwells, needles and thread. In the case of papyrus, supplies of papyrus reed, pumice stones and some sort of paste were required. The production of papyrus for writing entailed cross-layering strips of papyrus reed at right angles, beating or pressing the strips together, polishing the dried sheets with pumice and cutting it to standard size. Nothing short of a highly skilled cottage industry was involved in the making of scrolls.

Once the treatment process was completed, the parchment was cut into sheets and sewn together to form a scroll. Usually a handle sheet was attached to one end, namely the beginning of the text, which would be on the outside. The scroll was then ready for the scribe. He would first mark the edges of the columns by scoring margins, and then he would rule the lines. The size and availability of parchment dictated the number of columns to a sheet, the number of lines to a column, and the size of the margins at the top and bottom and between the columns.

The scrolls were inscribed using a pen and ink made from a carbon-based dye. The standard and style of writing varied considerably. Both formal and cursive scripts were used, and some manuscripts were carefully penned in an orderly fashion, others untidily. Some scrolls have been corrected by another scribe, and the Cave 1 scrolls of the Community Rule were actually written by two different persons (one of whom corrected the work of the other).

How much of this process of preparing and inscribing scrolls could have occurred at Qumran? It was long thought that the inhabitants of Qumran carried out the entire process. Nearby Ain Feshkha includes some installations that the excavator, Roland de Vaux, interpreted as a tannery. More recently, Hartmut Stegemann has suggested that Qumran itself was purpose-built as a book production centre. Both suggestions are speculative. Many scholars continue to believe that some or all of the scrolls were at least written at Qumran, in a room identified as a 'scriptorium', and, even if this identification is uncertain, the three or four inkwells retrieved from the ruins show that for whatever purposes, writing was carried out at the settlement. But the variety of styles of writing and of content suggest a variety of origins, and the claim that 95 per cent of the Qumran scrolls were written by different people, if true, makes it unlikely that they all come from a small community at Qumran, where one would have expected to find several cases of manscripts written by the same scribe, and a greater uniformity of writing styles.

Scripts and Writing Styles

The study of ancient Hebrew and Aramaic scripts was still in its infancy when Cave 1 was discovered. Eleazar Sukenik, the first editor of the Thanksgiving Hymns, recognized the similarity of the Qumran scripts he was seeing here to the 1st-century CE funeral inscriptions he had recorded in and around Jerusalem. John Trever, who had examined the long Isaiah scroll at the American School, also suspected an ancient script, and thought of the Nash Papyrus. The Nash Papyrus, containing the Ten Commandments and the *Shema* (Deuteronomy 6:4), had been dated by William F. Albright to the time of the Maccabees (2nd century BCE). Thus, even by the 1950s the writing on the scrolls had been dated between the 2nd century BCE and the 1st century CE, supporting deductions from external sources and internal allusions.

The Nash Papyrus enabled John Trever to estimate the antiquity of the Isaiah Scroll.

Qumran palaeographers, of whom the most influential is Frank M. Cross, Jr, have claimed to be able to date manuscripts very precisely on the basis of their script, placing them in a sequence running from the 4th century BCE to the 1st century CE. External comparisons include the Elephantine Papyri, written in Aramaic in a cursive hand in the 5th century BCE, and the Edfu Papyri from the 3rd century BCE. At the other end are fragments discovered at Masada and Wadi Murabba'at, which can be fairly precisely dated. A letter from Murabba'at is dated to the second year of Nero (55/56 CE) and a letter from the Jewish rebel leader Bar Kokhba to 134 CE. The dating of the Nash Papyrus to 150 BCE is another key. But stress has also been laid upon the typologies of Qumran scripts, which have been converted into a scheme of uniform development that has been translated by Cross into a neat chronological sequence that prompts him to date each document to within 25 years.

What do Cross and other palaeographers look for? Above all, they are concerned with changes in the physical appearance of letters of the alphabet: variation in a) size or stance, b) roundness or angularity (curl, slant), c) length of base strokes, d) length of legs, e) faithfulness to line, f) ligatures, and g) ornamental ticks. Generally such features define a script as belonging to the Archaic, Hasmonaean or Herodian periods (type), and as formal, semiformal or cursive (style). The Archaic script is characterized by broad, squat letters, varying sizes of letters, and slight, if any, distinction between the medial and final forms of certain letters. It bears a close resemblance to the Aramaic scripts on the

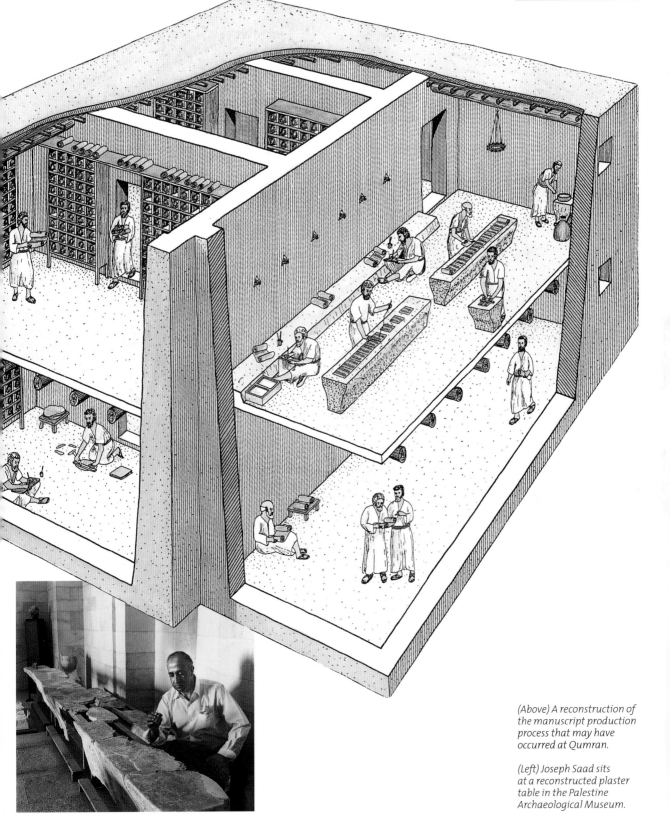

(Above) A reconstruction of
the manuscript production
process that may have
occurred at Qumran.

(Left) Joseph Saad sits
at a reconstructed plaster
table in the Palestine
Archaeological Museum.

Palaeography of the Dead Sea Scrolls

Palaeography is the study of ancient scripts. In the case of the Qumran scrolls, palaeography is used to classify the various kinds of handwriting styles, though it can also determine manuscripts written by the same scribe.

From his study of the scrolls and other texts from the Second Temple period (6th century BCE–1st century CE), Frank M. Cross has developed a typology of Qumran Hebrew scripts which is followed by many if not most Qumran editors:

Archaic   *c.* 250–150 BCE
            (mostly biblical texts)
Hasmonaean   *c.* 150–50 BCE
Herodian   *c.* 50 BCE–70 CE
            (This period far exceeds the reign of Herod the Great, but covers his dynasty, down to Agrippa II)

Because letter forms constantly evolve, it is possible to be more precise, for example in assigning texts to the early or late Hasmonaean or Herodian, or even to a transitional Hasmonaean-Herodian. Within the Hasmonaean and Herodian scripts one can also distinguish between formal, semiformal and cursive.

But the major problem with Cross's system is already evident in these names, because he believes that typological differences can be precisely converted into dates – so precisely that he and his followers believe they can assign any manuscript, on the basis of its script, to within 25 years. This view implies that a scribe, over a 30- or 40-year career, would change his own script uniformly. It also assumes that all scribes belonged to the same school (at Qumran) and were taught to write the same way.

While Cross's typology is excellent, it does not automatically yield chronology. The margin in dating needs to be at least 25 years *in each direction* (the lifetime of a scribe). Recent Carbon-14 (AMS) datings, claimed to support Cross's datings, actually do not support the precision he claims, though this method of dating is not sufficiently close to determine the matter.

How does the palaeographer examine scripts? The analysis is largely based on the shape of individual letters. The features of these letters include 'arms', 'roofs', downstrokes, 'legs', angles, curves, the number of strokes, base strokes, location of a crossbar, serifs, and ligatures. These features can be convex, concave, long, short, rounded, curved, hooked, open, closed, and triangular. Ada Yardeni, perhaps the leading Israeli palaeographer, notes that scribes regularly used differing executions of a single letter within a single manuscript.

1	2	3	4	
				aleph
				bet
				gimmel
				dalet
				he
				waw
				zayin
				het
				tet
				yod
				kaph
				final kaph
				lamed
				mem
				final mem
				nun
				final nun
				samech
				ayin
				peh
				final peh (feh)
				zade
				final zade
				qof
				resh
				shin
				tav

Additionally, one can observe whether a script is erect or slanting to the right or left, the size of the script, its width, and the length of certain letter forms. The broad classifications of formal, cursive, mixed, semicursive and rounded also enable scholars to distinguish generally different styles.

Yardeni studied a number of manuscripts not considered by Cross, including the six Cave 4 Damascus Document manuscripts. She classifies 4Q271 as 'early Herodian or Late Herodian', while 4Q266 is roughly contemporary with 4Q271 and other manuscripts that are also designated as 'Herodian'. 4Q268, a magnificently penned script, is simply called 'calligraphic Herodian'. Yet Yardeni also designates one manuscript as 'late 1st century BCE', and another to the first half of the 1st century CE, confusingly exchanging a typological for a chronological classification.

How does a palaeographer get from the study of a scribe's individual style to a relative dating? Some manuscripts are penned much more tidily than others, and some scribes are more conservative in their habits. Two contemporary scribes, especially working in different communities, may employ different scripts.

A clear example of the differences in how palaeographers see things is the case of an ostracon found in the late 1990s at Khirbet Qumran. Cross and Esther Eshel called it 'late Herodian' and read a single line as referring to the community (*yahad*) at Qumran. But Ada Yardeni read it as 'early Herodian' and argued that it referred to types of trees (see p. 186). Palaeographical analysis is scientific and also helpful – unless it claims more than it can deliver.

papyri from Elephantine (5th century BCE) and Edfu (3rd century BCE), both from Egypt. The earliest formal Archaic hand among the scrolls is represented by biblical manuscripts: 4QSam[b] dates to the late 3rd century BCE, 4QJer[a] is a little younger and 4QExod[f] comes from the late 3rd or early 2nd century BCE. From the second quarter of the 2nd century are 4QQoh[a] and 4QDeut[a]. There are no non-biblical manuscripts assigned paleographically to the 3rd century BCE.

In scripts designated Hasmonaean, Cross sees a tendency towards uniformity in size and idiosyncrasy in shape. By the Herodian period, letters have become uniform. There is a feeling for a base line and the use of ligatures and serifs (ornamentation). These are perhaps the easiest to identify. The earliest Herodian formal hand is that of 1QM and the latest 4QDeut[j], 4QDan[b], and 4QPsalms[s]?, which Cross compares with the scripts of biblical manuscripts at Murabba'at.

According to Cross's typology, sectarian works begin in the Hasmonaean period. The oldest manuscripts of the Community Rule date to the middle or late Hasmonaean period as do the fragments of the Damascus Document. The majority of manuscripts, however, are clearly Herodian, such as

'The Gezer Calendar' is one of the earliest inscriptions (10th century BCE) discovered in Palestine, written in the 'Palaeo-Hebrew' script. By comparing dated inscriptions, palaeographers can construct a history of writing styles, and this scheme can in turn help to date otherwise undatable texts.

The diagram shows the characteristic letter forms of:

1 Palaeo-Hebrew
2 Hasmonaean (125–50 BCE)
3 Herodian (50 BCE–70 CE)
4 Medieval

the biblical commentaries (or *pesharim*) and the War Scroll (1QM). One manuscript of the Song of the Sabbath Sacrifice is Late Herodian. But some of the last scrolls to be inscribed are again books of the Bible – 4QDeut[j], 4QDan[b], 4QPsalms? and 11QPs.

Finally, several manuscripts were written in archaizing palaeo-Hebrew scripts. This ancient alphabet, replaced in the Persian period by the now familiar 'square script', was revived on Hasmonaean Jewish coins, perhaps to recall the Judaean monarchs of antiquity in the last age of political independence. At any rate, this script was also used for a small number of biblical manuscripts at Qumran as well as part of a Horoscope text (4Q186). In some writings that use the 'square script', the divine names, Yahweh and El, are inscribed in archaic letters.

But can Qumran manuscripts be accurately dated, as palaeographers claim, to within 50 years? The rigidity and certainty of Cross and his disciples is now being replaced by a more flexible attitude. Quite apart from whether a single scribe in a 30-year (or more) career would steadily change his writing (or teach a pupil a newer style than his own), crucial to the question is whether or not all the scrolls were written at Qumran, within a single scribal school or tradition. If not, can a strict and measurable evolution of script be determined?

Palaeography has achieved some useful results in the identification of individual scribes' handwriting. The editors of Cave 4 texts, used to long hours poring over these scrolls, developed an ability to identify the handwriting of certain individuals. But although this can never be as reliable as typological analysis, this technique suggests that extremely few of the Qumran scrolls can be assigned to the same scribe as another. (Two that can are the Community Rule and the Testimonia; see p. 130.) The implication of this conclusion is that the 800 Qumran manuscripts were written by a large number of scribes – perhaps as many as 750! If this deduction is correct, the likelihood that these texts were all produced in the rather small community at Qumran is small. Current scholarship, while accepting the principle of typology of scripts, is rightly less certain about precise chronology than it once was.

A modern Jewish scribe working on a Torah scroll.

Spelling in the Scrolls

The study of spelling is known as orthography or 'correct writing'. Since Hebrew does not have proper vowel letters, reading was sometimes helped by the use of consonants to indicate these. The technical word for these letters is *matres lectionis* (literally, 'mothers of reading'), and the most common are *w* (waw) and *y* (yod), to indicate o/u and i respectively. The letters *h* (he) and the glottal stop (aleph, represented in transliteration by ') were also used to indicate an 'a' vowel. Some Qumran manuscripts exhibit the use of a 'full' (the technical word is *plene*) spelling, while others retain the 'defective' (few *matres lectionis*) convention (which is also found in the traditional Hebrew biblical text). The *plene* spelling is used for, among others, the major 'sectarian' scrolls, such as the Community Rule (1QS), War Scroll (1QM), Hodayoth (1QH) and *pesharim*, and Emanuel Tov has suggested that a particular kind of *plene* orthography is distinctive of a Qumran 'scribal school'. But it is also used in some biblical manuscripts. Whether or not this is true, the differences in spelling furnish a strong argument that the scrolls did not all originate from the same place.

Common and distinctive cases of a Qumran *plene* spelling include *kwl* for *kl* ('all'); *hw'h* and *hy'h* for *hw'* and *hy'* ('he' and 'she'); and *ky'* for *ky* ('that'). Curiously, added *matres lectionis* sometimes do not seem to provide clues to the current pronunciation, but represent an archaic pronunciation that the scribes (often wrongly) assumed.

There is no satisfactory explanation for this practice. There was no such thing as a dictionary with 'official' spelling, and fuller spellings were generally more common at this time (e.g. in the rabbinic literature) – though not as full as the Qumran usage. The use in the scrolls of such letters can hardly have been intended to facilitate pronunciation, since the scribes were presumably quite familiar with biblical Hebrew. For whatever reason it was developed, it presumably became conventional in at least one scribal tradition.

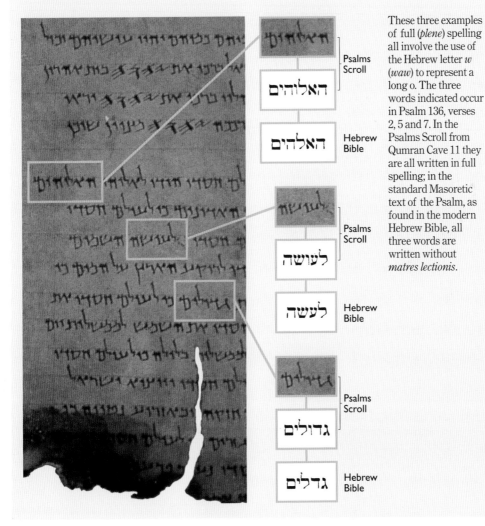

Psalms Scroll

Hebrew Bible

Psalms Scroll

Hebrew Bible

Psalms Scroll

Hebrew Bible

These three examples of full (*plene*) spelling all involve the use of the Hebrew letter *w* (*waw*) to represent a long o. The three words indicated occur in Psalm 136, verses 2, 5 and 7. In the Psalms Scroll from Qumran Cave 11 they are all written in full spelling; in the standard Masoretic text of the Psalm, as found in the modern Hebrew Bible, all three words are written without *matres lectionis*.

Carbon-14 Dating

Recent Carbon-14 testing (more precisely referred to as Accelerator Mass Spectrometry) of the parchment of a selection of Dead Sea Scrolls has been interpreted as confirming accepted palaeographical datings. This is largely true in broad terms. But AMS cannot date these materials within a 50-year range, much less in terms of quarter centuries and thirds of centuries, or even to a specific year such as 'c. 50 BCE', as is sometimes done on the basis of palaeography. The practitioners of C-14 (AMS) science speak of a range based on probability. For example, with a 68 per cent probability a specific parchment can typically be dated to within about a century. If the probability is raised to 95 per cent the range exceeds a century. Moreover, there remains a possibility of a rare 'rogue' result, such as in cases where the material has been contaminated. Again, it must be remembered that C-14 (AMS) dates the material, not the text. In most cases we can assume that the scroll was inscribed soon after the animals that provided the skin were killed. But that may not always be so. Finally, of the thousands of Qumran fragments, only a relatively small number of samples have been analyzed in different laboratories. Though Carbon-14 analysis has certainly been refined in recent years, it is unlikely ever to be able to give us dates as precise as we would like for any scrolls as ancient as these. It can certainly confirm (barring the occasional erratic result) the verdict of palaeography in general, though not the very precise palaeographical dates sometimes cited.

Carbon-14 Dating Chart

Description of Scroll	Number of Samples	Calibrated Age Range(s)	Palaeographic or Specified Age
Testament of Kohath	4	388–353 BCE 295–220 BCE	100–75 BCE
Reworked Pentateuch	3	339–324 BCE, 209–117 BCE	125–100 BCE
Book of Isaiah	4	335–327 BCE, 202–107 BCE	125–100 BCE
Testament of Levi	5	191–155 BCE, 146–120 BCE	Late 2nd century –early 1st century BCE
Book of Samuel	2	192–63 BCE	100–75 BCE
Temple Scroll	5	97 BCE–1 CE	Late 1st century BCE –early 1st century CE
Genesis Apocryphon	4	73 BCE–14 CE	Late 1st century BCE –early 1st century CE
Thanksgiving Hymns	5	21 BCE–61 CE	50 BCE–70 CE

Laying Out an Ancient Scroll

Always attentive to the physical layout of the scrolls he studied, Yigael Yadin made observations on the number of text columns on each leather sheet and the sizes of the sheets and columns. The extant portions of the War Scroll (1QM, see diagram) included 19 or 20 columns. These were spread out rather unevenly over five sheets. Sheet 1 had four columns; sheet 2 six; sheet 3 five; sheet 4 three and sheet 5 one, perhaps two. A sheet in the Temple Scroll typically contained three or four columns of text, except for the first sheet, which had 5 columns, and the last, which was incomplete with one column, but sized in such a way as to have accommodated four.

Yadin cited a Talmudic scribal tradition stipulating the minimal and maximal number of columns per sheet: 'No sheet should have less than three columns or more than eight' (from the Talmudic tractate *Soferim* 2:10). The War Scroll and the Temple Scroll clearly conform to this requirement.

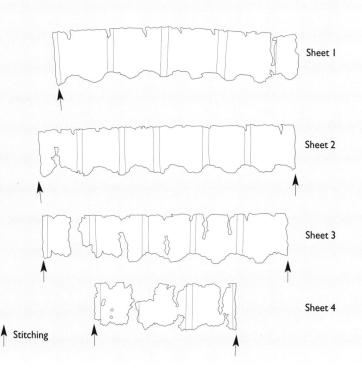

Sheet 1

Sheet 2

Sheet 3

Sheet 4

▲ Stitching

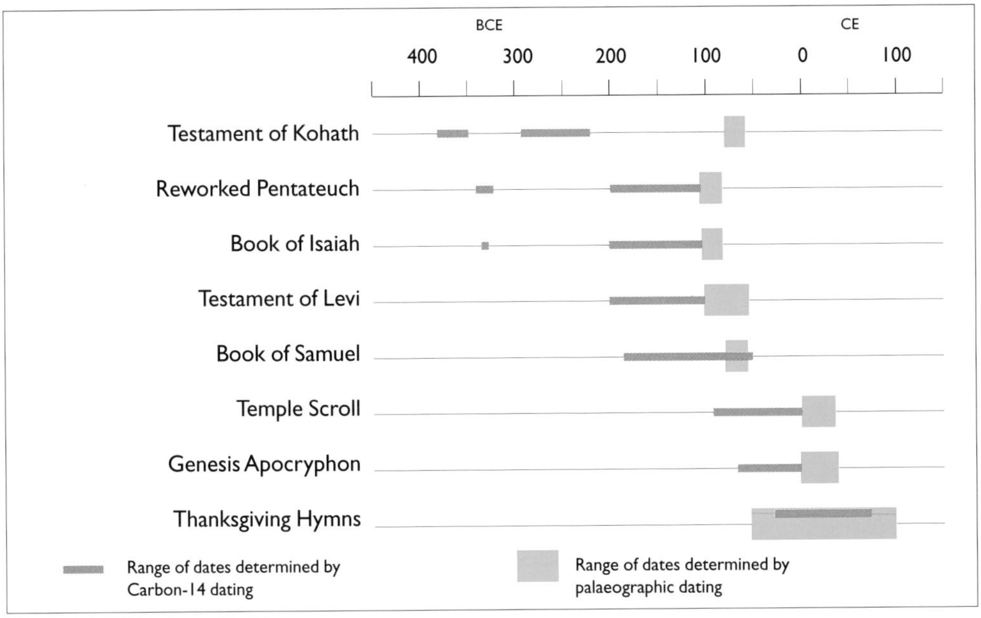

This chart compares the range of dates determined by Carbon-14 dating with those cited by palaeographers.

Reconstructing a Manuscript from Fragments

How do you reconstruct a document from fragments of different manuscripts of that document – when you don't even know what that document is about? First, you have to identify the fragments that belong to the same manuscript, using for clues the script and handwriting, colour and condition of the leather and similar damage patterns. Different manuscripts of the same document then have to be identified from the similarity of their contents. In some fortunate cases (such as that illustrated below), fragments of the same manuscript lie on top of each other in more or less the same relative position as they did when the scroll was intact

Next, to reconstruct the original document means putting together the fragments of several manuscripts, in the right order, and building a text from these. Pieces of the text that overlap in different manuscripts can provide helpful clues.

Altogether, eight manuscripts of the Songs of the Sabbath Sacrifice were available to Carol Newsom: six from Cave 4, one from Cave 11 and one from Masada. The illustration below shows how Newsom put together part of one of these manuscripts, 4Q405. The edges of the columns are the starting points for this exercise, rather like the edge pieces in a jigsaw; and other pieces are then fitted in according to the sense in the text. The columns represented here are 14–17, running from right to left, and the fragments of 4Q405 used here are those numbered 8–16.

From the total reconstruction of the document, Newsom determined that col. 14 begins with the opening of the eighth Sabbath Song, while col. 17, with less certainty, probably ends somewhere in Song 10.

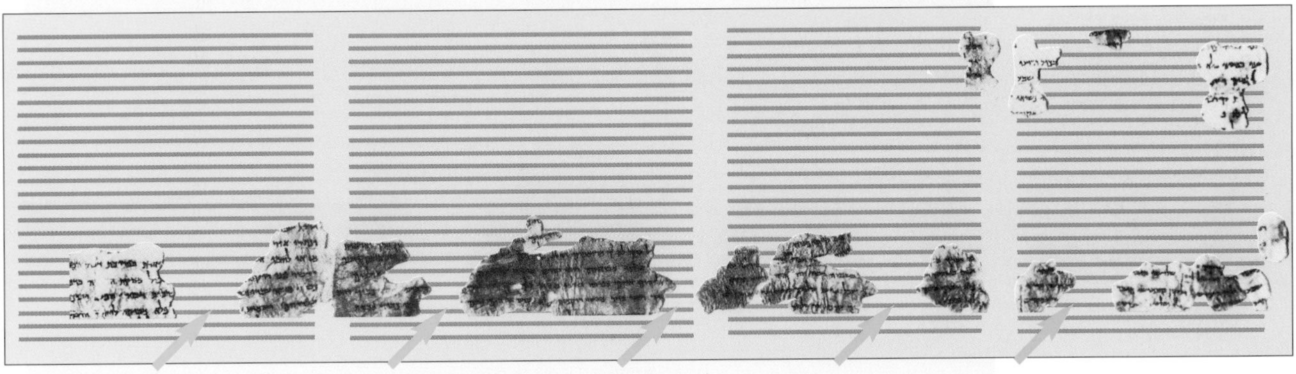

Reconstructing a Scroll

'…the reward is, instead of a list of hypothetical suggestions, an accurate, methodologically well-established new edition of a text formerly unknown to the scholarly world.'

(Hartmut Stegemann)

Émile Puech illustrates the value of damage patterns for his reconstruction of the Thanksgiving Hymns (1QHᵃ), which independently confirmed Stegemann's main conclusions.

As thousands of dislocated fragments discovered in the Qumran caves, especially Cave 4, arrived at the Rockefeller Museum during the 1950s, the editorial team sorted them out by looking for similar physical features of the leather or papyrus, such as thickness and coloration, and their handwriting. Then the fragments thought to belong to the same original manuscript were grouped together for publication in the official edition. But large sections of the manuscripts were already destroyed, and where the fragments were tiny (in the majority of cases), it was impossible to place these fragments in the right order – unless the contents belonged to a work already known (such as a biblical book). In dozens of cases the original work could not be reconstructed.

In 1963 Hartmut Stegemann wrote a doctoral dissertation at the University of Heidelberg on the scroll of Thanksgiving Hymns (1QHᵃ), which contains many small fragments. As earlier editors had done, Stegemann first collected the fragments according to materials, scripts and contents. But then he looked at the *shapes* of the fragments and, where he could find them, pieces of margins, edges of columns and empty lines or spaces. Comparing all these data, he estimated the column height and width. But the most ingenious feature of Stegemann's approach was his careful attention to the *damage pattern* of fragments. Many ancient scrolls were greatly damaged by moisture seeping through one layer after another, or by insects eating their way into parts of a scroll. These ravages show up as regular patterns in the unravelled scroll, decreasing toward the end (middle) of the scroll. So fragments that preserved any recognizable part of the damage pattern were placed on a horizontal axis. Then, comparing the scale of the damage pattern, it was possible to work out which fragment was nearer to the outside of the scroll, and thus came earlier or later in the work, depending on whether a scroll had been rolled up with its beginning on the inside or the outside.

Almost two decades after first applying his method of reconstruction, Stegemann shared it with Carol Newsom, who had been assigned the task of editing The Angelic Liturgy, later renamed Songs of the Sabbath Sacrifice (4Q400–05). Roughly 100 fragments from one manuscript (4Q405) were pieced together, using Stegemann's advice, to reconstruct 14 columns of the original. The physical reconstruction could then be confirmed by noting the literary features of the songs themselves, since they are assigned to 13 consecutive sabbaths. Eileen Schuller has also used Stegemann's method in editing the non-canonical psalms, establishing six columns out of the 79 fragments. Stegemann believes he has been successful in reconstructing 4Q511, the Songs of the Sage, helped by the use of introductory and concluding formulae.

But there are pitfalls for over-ambitious material reconstructions. Fragments may seem to be thematically and semantically compatible, but different in their scripts. Physical misalignment of fragments can also occur, if the distances between lines, line lengths, and letter heights are not very carefully calculated. Here, too, greater precision is

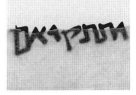

*(Above left and above)
With the aid of computer
enhancement Bruce
Zuckerman of West Semitic
Research can turn possible
readings into probable ones.*

being aimed for by calculating average widths of individual letters and spaces between them in a particular manuscript.

A further complication is combining fragments of several manuscripts of the same work into a single text. This can frequently be done quite successfully, but different manuscripts often contain different editions of that work, and combining them can produce a totally false outcome. Fragments of six manuscripts were combined to reconstruct Some of the Works of the Law (4Q394–99). For years they were advertised as a letter written by the Teacher of Righteousness or some leader of the Qumran community to the Wicked Priest. The official edition, however, also provides a calendrical section at the front, quite unrelated to the rest. Have we really a letter here? A single work, even? This reconstructed 'document' has no clear beginning to help

us; analysis of the scripts suggests that certain fragments may not belong to the same manuscript as the others; and the spelling between fragments differs. Certain fragment joins are also unmistakably misaligned. The editors' desire to reconstruct a valuable historical document reveals many of the dangers of attempting to reconstruct original scrolls too exactly.

The availability of images of the fragments in CD-Rom has taken this work further. It is now possible, with the aid of graphic software, to move fragments around on the screen to achieve new alignments, or even to copy a letter or word from one part of a fragment into a gap elsewhere to see if it fits exactly. This 'virtual reconstruction' does not entirely replace work with the original fragments themselves, but in some respects offers better possibilities for reconstruction.

Classifying the Scrolls

Before listing the Qumran scrolls, it may be helpful to explain that they fall into three categories (see pie chart). A quarter of them are copies of scriptural texts (from the Old Testament or Hebrew Bible). In this category we could include tefillin and mezuzoth (which contain only scriptural texts), and targums (translations of scriptural texts). A second category, also about a quarter of the manuscripts, is usually called for convenience 'sectarian texts', compositions associated with the Qumran community and the wider Essene movement of which it was a part. The third category contains non-biblical, non-sectarian Jewish literature. Some of this was previously known to us, largely through its preservation by the Christian churches (such as Enoch, Jubilees, Tobit and Ben Sira), but most of it has been lost since antiquity.

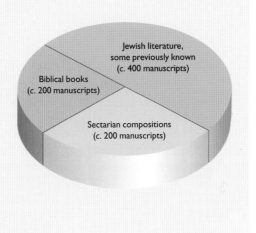

Jewish literature, some previously known (c. 400 manuscripts)

Biblical books (c. 200 manuscripts)

Sectarian compositions (c. 200 manuscripts)

List of Scrolls by Cave

The following is a list of the texts found in the caves. In some cases, texts are represented by different editions found in different caves (thus, the Community Rule and War Scroll are represented in both Caves 1 and 4). Because of the fragmentary state of most of the manuscripts, often a text can only be reconstructed by using the fragments of different manscripts of the same text (which may not have been identical, of course!). So the following list is not necessarily definitive. A question mark following the name of a text means that this identification is not certain.

Because of the large number of texts found, it is not possible to give in this book an account, however brief, of every single one. In this section we have covered all the major texts, excluding the biblical manuscripts (in italics) and those texts which are so fragmentary that little useful can be said about them.

Texts that were recovered by the official team are all numbered; those unnumbered are from the original discoveries in Cave 1 and were published outside the *DJD* series. Manuscripts of biblical books are in italics and an asterisk indicates that major preliminary studies have already been carried out.

The complete list can also be found in F. García Martínez, *The Dead Sea Scrolls Translated*, pp. 467–519; in the Brill microfiche catalogue; in Vermes, *The Complete Dead Sea Scrolls in English*, pp. 601–609; and in *DJD* 39.

Cave 1

(The scrolls originally found by the Bedouin were not, and have not been, accorded a number)

Genesis (1QGen=1Q1)
Exodus (1QExod=1Q2)
Leviticus (1QpalaeoLev=1Q3)
Deuteronomy (1QDeut^a,b=1Q4, 1Q5)
Judges (1QJudg=1Q6)
Samuel (1QSam=1Q7)
Isaiah (1QIsa^a (unnumbered), 1QIsa^b=1Q8)
Ezekiel (1QEzek=1Q9)
Psalms (1QPs^a-c=1Q10–12)
Daniel (1QDan^a,b=1Q71, 1Q72)
Phylactery (1Qphyl=1Q13)
*Community Rule (1QS; see p. 00)
*Rule of the Congregation (1QSa=1Q28a; see p. 00)
*The Rule of Blessings (1QSb=1Q28b; see p. 00)
*War Scroll (1QM, unnumbered; but some fragments=1Q30–33; see p. 00)
*Thanksgiving Hymns (1QH, unnumbered, but some fragments=1Q35; see p. 00)
*Genesis Apocryphon (1QApGen, unnumbered; but some fragments=1Q20; see p. 00)
Testament of Levi (1QTLevi ar=1Q21)
Liturgy of Three Tongues of Fire (1Q29)
Sayings of Moses (1QDM=1Q22)
Book of Giants (1QEnGiants=1Q23–24; see p. 00)
Liturgical texts (1Q30–31)
Hymns (1Q36–40)
Jubilees (1Q17–18; see p. 00)
Book of Noah (1QNoah=1Q19)
Apocryphal Prophecy? (1Q25)
Sapiential text (1Q26)
Mysteries (1QMyst=1Q27)

*Commentary on Habakkuk (1QpHabakkuk; see p. 00)
Commentary on Micah (1QpMic=1Q14; see p. 00)
Commentary on Zephaniah (1QpZeph=1Q15; see p. 00)
Commentary on Psalms (1QpPs=1Q16; see p. 00)
New Jerusalem (1QNJ ar=1Q32; see p. 00)
Priestly liturgy (1QLitPr^a, 1QLitPr^b=1Q34)
Unidentified fragments (1Q41–70 (70 is papyrus)

Cave 2

Genesis (2QGen=2Q1)
Exodus (2QExod^a-c=2Q2–4)
Leviticus (2QpalaeoLev=2Q5)
Numbers (2QNum^a-d=2Q6–9)
Deuteronomy (2QDeut^a-c=2Q10–12)
Jeremiah (2QJer=2Q13)
Psalms (2QPs=2Q14)
Job (2QJob=2Q15)
Ruth (2QRuth^a,b=2Q16–17)
Ecclesiasticus/Sirach (2QSir=2Q18)
Jubilees (2QJub a,b=2Q19–20)
Moses Apocryphon (2QapMoses=2Q21)
David Apocryphon (2QapDavid=2Q22)
A Prophetic Apocryphon (2QapProph=2Q23)
New Jerusalem (2QJN ar=2Q24; see p. 00)
Judicial text (2Q25)
Book of Giants (2QEnGiants=2Q26; see p. 00)
Unidentified fragments (2Q27–33)

Cave 3

Ezekiel (3QEzek=3Q1)
Psalms (3QPs=3Q2)
Lamentations (3QLam=3Q3)
Commentary on Isaiah (3QpIsa=3Q4)
Jubilees (3QJub=3Q5)
Hymn of Praise (3QHym=3Q6)
Testament of Judah? (3QTJud=3Q7)
Texts mentioning the Angel of the Presence and the Angel of Peace (3Q8)
Unknown sectarian text (3Q9)
Copper Scroll (3QTreasure=3Q15; p. 00)
Unidentified fragments (3Q10–14)

Cave 4

The largest number of scrolls by far come from Cave 4. They are mostly very fragmentary and it has taken 50 years to publish them all. They are listed here roughly in the order of their official catalogue numbers, but the fragments of some manuscripts which appear to contain the same or similar works have been grouped together. The catalogue numbers are arranged approximately in the following order: biblical manuscripts (4Q1–155), sectarian and other texts closely related to biblical texts (4Q156–248), sectarian rules (4Q249–78), and other compositions, some of which may have been sectarian in origin (4Q279–528) and which are sometimes arranged in sub-groups (e.g., calendrical texts 4Q317–30, rewritten Bible 4Q364–91, wisdom texts 4Q411–26, liturgical texts 4Q427–57). Most of the Aramaic texts (indicated by ar) are grouped at the end (4Q529–75). There is some doubt about whether some or all of the documentary texts actually come from Qumran Cave 4 (4Q342–59) (see p. 151).

Genesis-Exodus *(4QGen-Exod^a=4Q1)*

Genesis *(4QGen$^{b-k,m-n}$=4Q2–10, 4Q576)*

Palaeo-Hebrew Genesis-Exodus *(4QpaleoGen-Exod^l=4Q11)*

Palaeo-Hebrew Genesis *(4QpaleoGen^m=4Q12)*

Exodus *(4QExod$^{b-e,g-k}$=4Q13–16; 4Q18–21)*

Exodus-Leviticus *(4QExod-Lev^f=4Q17)*

Palaeo-Hebrew Exodus *(4QpaleoExod^m=4Q22)*

Leviticus-Numbers *(4QLev-Num^a=4Q23)*

Leviticus*(4QLev^{b-g}=4Q24–26, 4QcryptA Lev^h=4Q249j)*

Numbers *(4QNum^b=4Q27)*

Deuteronomy *(4QDeut^{a-q}=4Q28–44)*

Palaeo-Hebrew Deuteronomy *(4QDeut^{r-s}=4Q45–46)*

Joshua *(4QJosh^{a-b}=4Q47–48)*

Judges *(4QJudg^{a-b}=4Q49–50)*

Samuel *(4QSam^{a-c}=4Q51–53)*

Kings *(4QKgs=4Q54)*

Isaiah *(4QIsa^{a-r}=4Q55–69b)*

Jeremiah *(4QJer^{a-e}=4Q70–72b)*

Ezekiel *(4QEzek^{a-c}=4Q73–75)*

Twelve Minor Prophets *(4QXII^{a-g}=4Q76–82)*

Psalms *(4QPs^{a-x}=4Q83–98g)*

Job *(4QJob^{a-b}=4Q99–100)*

Palaeo-Hebrew Job *(4QpaleoJob^c=4Q101)*

Proverbs *(4QProv^{a-b}=4Q102–103)*

Ruth *(4QRuth^{a-b}=4Q104–105)*

Canticles *(4QCant^{a-c}=4Q106–108)*

Qohelet *(4QQoh^{a-b}=4Q109–10)*

Lamentations *(4QLam=4Q111)*

Daniel *(4QDan^{a-e}=4Q112–16)*

Ezra *(4QEzra=4Q117)*

Chronicles *(4QChr=4Q118)*

Greek Leviticus *(4QLXXLev^{a-b}=4Q119–20)*

Greek Numbers *(4QLXXNum=4Q121)*

Greek Deuteronomy *(4QLXXDeut=4Q122)*

Palaeo-Hebrew Paraphrase of Joshua *(4Qpaleo paraJosh=4Q123)*

Palaeo-Hebrew Unidentified *(4QpaleoUnident 1–2=4Q124–25)*

Greek Unidentified Text *(4QUnident gr=4Q126)*

Greek Paraphrase of Exodus *(4QparaExod gr=4Q127)*

Phylacteries *(4QPhyl A–U=4Q128–48)*

Mezuzot *(4QMez A–G=4Q149–55)*

Leviticus Targum (4QtgLev=4Q156)

Job Targum (4QtgJob=4Q157)

Reworked Pentateuchs(4QRP A–E=4Q158, 4Q364–67)

Ordinances (4QOrdinances^{a-c}=4Q159, 4Q513–14)

Vision of Samuel (4QVisSam=4Q160)

Commentaries on Isaiah (4QpIsa^{a-e}=4Q161–65)

Commentaries on Hosea (4QpHos^{a-b}=4Q166–67)

Commentary on Micah (4QpMic=4Q168)

Commentary on Nahum (4QpNah=4Q169)

Commentary on Zephaniah (4QpZeph=4Q170)

Commentaries on Psalms (4QpPs^{a-b}=4Q171, 173)

Unidentified Commentary (4QpUnid=4Q172)

Thematic Commentary A(Florilegium)(4QFlor=4Q174)

Testimonia (4QTest=4Q175)

Tanhumim (4QTanh=4Q176)

Thematic Commentaries B–E (4QCatena A–B=4Q177, 4Q182; 4Q178, 4Q183)

Apocryphal Lamentations (4QapocrLam A–B=4Q179, 4Q501)

Ages of Creation (4QAgesCreat A–B=4Q180–81)

Wiles of the Wicked Woman (4Q184) (also known as 'The Seductress' or 'Lady Folly')

Sapiential Work(4QSapiential Work A–B=4Q185, 4Q419)

Horoscope (4QcryptA Horoscope=4Q186)

Tobit (4QTob^{a-d} ar=4Q196–99; 4QTob^e=4Q200)

Enoch (4QEn^{a-g} ar=4Q201, 203–207, 212)

Book of Giants (4QEnGiants^{a-f}=4Q203, 4Q206 frags, 4Q530–33)

Enoch Astronomical Book (4QEnastr^{a-d} =4Q208–11)

Aramaic Levi Document (4QLevi^{a-f}=4Q213–14b)

Testament of Naphtali (4QTNaph=4Q215)

Time of Righteousness (4Q215a)

Jubilees (4QJub^{a-j}=4Q176a, 4Q216–24, 4Q482–83)

Pseudo-Jubilees (4QpsJub^{a-c}=4Q225–27)

Text with Citation of Jubilees (4Q228)

Pseudepigraphon in Mishnaic Hebrew (4Q229; not locatable)

Catalogue of Spirits (4QCatalogue of Spirits^{a-b} =4Q230–31; not locatable)

New Jerusalem (4QNJ=4Q232; not locatable; 4QNJ^{a-b} ar=4Q554–55)

Fragments with Place Names (4Q233; not locatable)

Exercitium Calami A–C (4Q234, 4Q341, 4Q360)

Unidentified Text (4QUnid.Text nab=4Q235)

Part of Habakkuk 3 (4Q238; not locatable)

Pesher on the True Israel (4Q239; not locatable)

Commentary on Canticles (4Q240; not locatable)

Prayer of Nabonidus (4QPrNab ar=4Q242)

Pseudo-Daniel (4QpsDan^{a-c} ar=4Q243–45)

Apocryphon of Daniel (4QapocrDan ar=4Q246)

Pesher on the Apocalypse of Weeks (4Q247)

Historical Texts (4QHistorical Text A–G=4Q248, 4Q331–33, 4Q468e–f, 4Q578)

Midrash Sefer Moshe (4QcryptA Midrash Sefer Moshe=4Q249)

Rule of the Congregation (4QcryptA Serekh ha-Edah^{a-i}=4Q249a–i)

Text Quoting Leviticus A–B (4QcryptA Text Quoting Lev A–B=4Q249k–l)

Hodayot-like Text (4QcryptA Hodayot-like Text D=4Q249m)

Liturgical Works (4QcryptA Liturgical Work E–F=4Q249n–o; 4QLiturgical Work A–D=4Q409, 4Q476–76a, 4Q527)

Prophecy (4QcryptA Prophecy=4Q249p)

Fragment Mentioning Planting (4QcryptA Planting=4Q249q)

Unidentified (4QcryptA Unidentified A–R=4Q249r–y, 4Q250c–i, 4Q313b–c)

Miscellaneous Fragments (4QcryptA Miscellaneous=4Q249z)

Text Concerning Cultic Service (4QcryptA Text Concerning Cultic Service A–B=4Q250–50a)

Text Related to Isaiah 11 (4QcryptA Text related to Isa 11=4Q250b)

Halakhic Texts (4QHalakha A–C=4Q251, 4Q264a, 4Q472a)

Commentaries on Genesis (4QCommGen A–D=4Q252–54a)

Commentary on Malachi (4QCommMal=4Q253a)

Community Rule (4QS^{a-j}=4Q255–64)

Miscellaneous Rules (4QMiscellaneous Rules=4Q265)

Damascus Document (4QD^{a-h}=4Q266–73)

Tohorot (4QTohorot A–C=4Q274, 4Q276–78)

Communal Ceremony (4Q275)

Four Lots (4Q279)

Curses (4Q280)
Unidentified Fragments (4Q281–82)
Purification Liturgy (4Q284)
Harvesting (4Q284a)
Blessings/Berakhot (4QBer$^{a–e}$=4Q286–90)
Work Containing Prayers (4QWork Containing
    Prayers A–C=4Q291–93)
Sapiential-Didactic Work (4QSapiential-Didactic
    Work A–C=4Q294, 4Q412, 4Q425)
Words of the Maskil to All Sons of Dawn (4Qcrypt
    A Words of the Maskil=4Q298)
Mysteries (4QMyst$^{a–c}$=4Q299–301)
Admonitory Parable (4Q302)
Meditation on Creation (4QMeditation on Creation
    A–B=4Q303–305)
Men of People who Err (4Q307)
Phases of the Moon (4QcryptA Phases of the
    Moon=4Q317)
Zodiology and Brontology (4QZodiology and
    Brontology ar=4Q318)
Otot (4QOtot=4Q319)
Calendrical Document Mishmarot
    (4QCal.Doc.Mishmarot A–D=4Q320–21a, 4Q325)
Mishmarot (4QMishmarot A–I=4Q322–24a, 4Q324d,
    4Q328–30)
Calendrical Document (4QCal.Doc. A–F=4Q324b–c,
    4Q326, 4Q337, 4Q394)
Ordo (4Q334)
Astronomical Fragments (4Q335–36)
Genealogical List (4Q338)
List of False Prophets (4QList of False Prophets
    ar=4Q339)
List of Netinim (4Q340)
List of Proper Names ('4QTherapeia') (4Q341)
Letters (4Q342–43)
Debt Acknowledgment (4Q344)
Deeds (4QDeed A–F=4Q345, 4Q347–48, 4Q359)
Deed of Sale (4Q346)
Accounts (4QAccount A–F=4Q350, 4Q352a, 4Q354–58)
Account of Cereal (4QAccount of Cereal
    A–B=4Q351–52)
Account of Cereal or Liquid (4Q353)
Unidentified Fragments (4Q360–61)
Undeciphered Fragments (4QcryptB undeciphered
    frags A–B=4Q362–63)
Cryptic C Text (4QcryptC Text=4Q363a)
Temple Scroll? (4QT$^{a–b}$=4Q365a, 4Q524)
Apocryphal Pentateuch (4QApocryphal Pentateuch
    A–B=4Q368, 4Q377)
Prayer of Enosh (4Q369)
Admonition on the Flood (4QAdmonFlood=4Q370)
Apocryphon of Joseph (4QapocrJoseph$^{a–c}$
    =4Q371–73)
Discourse on the Exodus/Conquest Tradition (4Q374)
Apocryphon of Moses (4QapocrMoses$^{a–c}$=4Q375–76,
    4Q408)
Apocryphon of Joshua (4QapocrJosh$^{a–b}$=4Q378–79)
Non-Canonical Psalms (4QNon-Canonical Psalms
    A–B=4Q380–81)
Paraphrase of Kings (4Q paraKings=4Q382)
Apocryphon of Jeremiah (4QapocrJer
    A–C$^{a–f}$=4Q383–84, 4Q385a, 4Q387–87a, 4Q388–90)
Pseudo-Ezekiel (4QpsEzek$^{a–e}$=4Q385, 4Q385b, 4Q386,
    4Q388, 4Q391)
Works of God (4Q392)

Communal Confession (4Q393)
Miqsat Ma'ase ha-Torah (Halakhic Letter)
    (4QMMT$^{a–f}$=4Q394–399; 4QcryptA MMT^g=4Q313)
Songs of the Sabbath Sacrifice
    (4QShirShabb$^{a–h}$=4Q400–407)
Vision and Interpretation (4Q410)
Sapiential Hymn (4Q411)
Composition Concerning Divine Providence (4Q413)
Rituals of Purification (4QRitPur A–B=4Q414,
    4Q512)
Instruction (4QInstruction$^{a–g}$=4Q415–18a, 4Q418c,
    4Q423)
Text with Quotation from Psalm 107 (4Q418b)
Ways of Righteousness (4QWays of
    Righteousness$^{a–b}$=4Q420–21)
Paraphrase of Genesis and Exodus (4Q422)
Instruction-like Work (4Q424)
Sapiential-Hymnic Works (4Q426, 4Q528)
Hodayoth (Thanksgiving Hymns) (4QH$^{a–f}$=4Q427–32)
Hodayoth-like Text (4QHodayoth-like Text
    A–D=4Q433–433a, 4Q440–40a)
Barkhi Nafshi (4QBarkhi Nafshi$^{a–e}$=4Q434–38)
Lament by a Leader (4Q439)
Fragment Mentioning a Court (4Q440b)
Individual Thanksgivings (4QIndividual
    Thanksgiving A–B=4Q441–42)
Personal Prayer (4Q443)
Incantation (4Q444)
Laments (4QLament A–B=4Q445, 4Q453)
Poetic Texts (4QPoetic Text A–B=4Q446–47)
Apocryphal Psalm and Prayer Mentioning King
    Jonathan (4Q448)
Prayers (4QPrayer A–E=4Q449–52, 4Q454)
Didactic Works (4QDidactic Work A–C=4Q455)
Hallelujah (4Q456)
Creation (4Q457a)
Eschatological Hymn (4Q457b)
Narratives (4QNarrative A–I=4Q458, 4Q461–63,
    4Q464a, 4Q469, 4Q480, 4Q481b, 4Q481e)
Narrative Work Mentioning Lebanon (4Q459)
Narrative Work and Prayer (4Q460)
Exposition on the Patriarchs (4Q464)
Unclassified Fragments (4Q464b, 4Q468j)
Text Mentioning Samson? (4Q465)
Text Mentioning Light to Jacob (4Q466)
Unidentified Fragments (4Q468a–c, 4Q468m–bb)
Eschatological Work (4QEschatological Work
    A–B=4Q468g, 4Q472)
Hymnic Texts (4QHymnic Texts A–B=4Q468h,
    4Q468k)
Sectarian Text (4Q468i)
Fragment Mentioning Qohelet 1:8–9 (4Q468l)
Text Mentioning Zedekiah (4Q470)
War Scroll-like Texts (4Q471)
Polemical Text (4Q471a)
Self-Glorification Hymn (4Q471b)
Prayer Concerning God and Israel (4Q471c)
The Two Ways (4Q473)
Text Concerning Rachel and Joseph (4Q474)
Renewed Earth (4Q475)
Rebukes Reported by the Overseer (4Q377)
Fragment Mentioning Festivals (4Q478)
Text Mentioning Descendants of David (4Q479)
Text Mentioning Mixed Kinds (4Q481)
Apocryphon of Elisha (4Q481a)

Prayer for Mercy (4Q481c)
Fragments with Red Ink (4Q481d)
Unclassified Fragments (4Q481f)
Testament of Judah (4Q484)
Prophetic or Sapiential Text (4Q485)
Sapiential Works (4QSap A–B=4Q486–87)
Apocryphon (4QApocryphon ar=4Q488)
Apocalypse (4QApocalypse ar=4Q489)
Fragmentary Apocalypse (4QFrags. ar=4Q490)
War Scroll (4QSefer ha-Milhamah=4Q285;
    4QM^a–f=4Q491–96)
War Scroll-like Text (4Q497)
Hymnic or Sapiential Fragments (4Q498)
Hymns or Prayers (4Q499)
Benediction (4Q500)
Marriage Ritual (4Q502)
Daily Prayers (4QPrQuot=4Q503)
Words of the Luminaries (4QDibHam^a–c=4Q504–506)
Festival Prayers (4QPrFêtes^a–c=4Q507–509)
Songs of the Maskil (Songs of the Sage)
    (4QShir^a–b=4Q510–11)
Unclassified Fragments (4Q515–20)
Messianic Apocalypse (4Q521)
Prophecy of Joshua (4Q522)
Jonathan (4Q523)
Beatitudes (4Q525)
Testament? (4Q526)
Words of Michael (4QWords of Michael ar=4Q529)
Noah (4QNoah^a–c ar=4Q534–36)
Testament of Jacob (4QTJacob ar=4Q537)
Testament of Judah (4QTJud ar=4Q538)
Testament of Joseph (4QTJoseph ar=4Q539)
Apocryphon of Levi (4QapocrLevi^a–b ar=4Q540–41)
Testament of Qahat (4QTQahat ar=4Q542)
Visions of Amram (4QVisions of Amram^a–g
    ar=4Q543–49)
Proto-Esther (4QPrEsther^a–f ar=4Q550–50e)
Daniel-Susanna? (4QDanSuz? ar=4Q551)
Four Kingdoms (4QFour Kingdoms^a–b ar=4Q552–53)
Visions (4QVision^a–c ar=4Q556–58)
Biblical Chronology (4QBibChronology ar=4Q559)
Exorcism (4QExorcism ar=4Q560)
Physiognomy or Horoscope
    (4QPhysiognomy/Horoscope ar=4Q561)
Aramaic Texts (4QAramaic D–Z=4Q562–75)
Text Mentioning the Flood (4Q577)
Hymnic Work? (4Q579)

Cave 5

Deuteronomy (5QDeut=5Q10)
1 Kings (5QKgs=5Q2)
Isaiah (5Qisa=5Q3)
Amos (5QAmos=5Q4)
Psalms (5QPs=5Q5)
Lamentations (5QLam^a,b=5Q6–7)
Phylactery (5Qphyl=5Q8)
Work with Place Names (5Q9)
Work with Citations from Malachi (5QapMal=5Q10)
Community Rule (5QS=5Q11)
Damascus Document (5QD=5Q12; see p. 00)
A Rule of the Sect (5QRègle=5Q13)
Curses (5QCurses=5Q14)
New Jerusalem (5QNJ ar=5Q15; see p. 00)
Unidentified fragments (5Q16–24)

Cave 6

Genesis (6QpalaeoGen=5Q1)
Leviticus (6QpalaeoLev=5Q2)
Deuteronomy (6QDeut=6Q3)
Kings (6QKgs=6Q4)
Psalms (6QPs=6Q5)
Song of Songs (6QCant=6Q6)
Daniel (pap6QDan=6Q7)
Book of Giants (6QEnGiants=6Q8; see p. 00)
Samuel-Kings Apocryphon (6QapSam/
    Kgs=6Q9)
Prophecy (6QProph=pap6Q10)
Allegory (6QAllegory=6Q11)
Apocryphal Prophecy (6QapProph=6Q12)
Priestly prophecy (6QPriestProph=6Q13)
Apocalyptic text (6QApoc ar=6Q14)
Damascus Document (6QD=6Q15; see p. 00)
Benedictions (6QBen=pap6Q16)
Calendar (6QCal=6Q17)
Hymns (6QHym=pap6Q18)
Aramaic text related to Genesis (6QGen ar?=6Q19)
Text related to Deuteronomy? (6QDeut?=6Q20)
Prophetic fragment (6QfrgProph=6Q21)
Unidentifed fragments (6Q22-31)

Cave 7

Exodus (Greek) (7QLXXExod=7Q1)
Letter of Jeremiah (Greek) (7QLXXEpJer=7Q2)
Unidentified Greek fragments (7Q3–19)

Cave 8

Genesis (8QGen=8Q1)
Psalms (8QPs=8Q2)
Phylactery (8Qphyl=8Q3)
Mezuzah (8Qmez=8Q4)
Hymn (8QHym=8Q5)

Cave 9

Unidentified Papyrus Fragment

Cave 10

Undeciphered Ostracon

Cave 11

Leviticus (11Q1–2)
Deuteronomy (11Q3)
Ezekiel (11Q4)
Psalms (11Q5–9; see p. 00)
Job Targum (11Q10)
Apocryphal Psalms (11Q11)
Jubilees (11Q12; see p. 00)
Melchizedek (11QMelch=11Q13; see p. 00)
Fragment of War Scroll? (11Q14)
Hymns (11Q15–16)
Songs of the Sacrifice (11Q17; see p. 00)
New Jerusalem (11Q18)
Temple Scroll? (11QT=11Q20–21; see p. 00)
Unidentified texts (11Q23–28)
Fragment related to Commuity Rule (11Q29)
Unclassified fragments (11Q30)
Unidentified (11Q31)
*Leviticus Targum (see p. 00)

*Major editions not yet
published in the *DJD* series
and therefore sometimes
unnumbered

81

Cave 1

Cave 1, a little over 1 km (about ¾ mile) north of the Qumran settlement (see map, p. 11), is a natural cave fairly high in the cliff face. It is 8 m (26 ft) long and 4 m (13 ft) high, varying in breadth between 0.75 m (27 in) and 2 m (6 ft). The Bedouin found 10 jars here, one containing three scrolls (Isaiahᵃ, 1QS and 1QpHab), and later four more scrolls. The official Jordanian Antiquities exploration team rediscovered Cave 1 in 1949 and retrieved some further scraps of manuscript, pottery and leather phylactery holders. The contents of this cave found by the Bedouin were published by the American Schools of Oriental Research and by the Hebrew University; the findings of the Jordanian Antiquities team were published in *DJD* 1.

The entrance to Qumran Cave 1 (the original entrance is the small upper hole).

THE 'RULES SCROLL'

One manuscript from Cave 1 contains three texts. Why this is so, and what their relationship is, remains unclear. The texts are known as 1QS, 1QSa and 1QSb. 1QS has the heading 'Rule (Hebrew: *serekh*) of the *yahad*', and the words 'for the *maskil*' ('wise teacher', the name of a community leader); 1QSa opens: 'this is the rule of the congregation of Israel'; and 1QSb is entitled: 'Words of Blessing. For the *maskil*'. Hence it is possible that the three were collected because they were all regarded as 'rules' or because they were 'for the *maskil*' or both.

The three are conventionally treated as three separate texts, and we shall follow that convention. Originally, the major text (1QS) was published by ASOR, while the others appeared in *DJD* 1.

The Community Rule

'All those who embrace the Rule of the *yahad* shall enter into the Covenant before God to keep all his commandments so that they do not abandon him during the dominion of Belial out of fear or terror or affliction.' (1QS 1:16–17)

Contents

The Cave 1 manuscript of the Community Rule, which is written on the same manuscript as the Rule of the Congregation and the Rule of Blessings, opens with a reminder of the principles that every member of that community must cherish, and describes the procedure for an annual covenant ceremony, including a prayer and a cursing of Belial (Satan) (cols 1–3:12). It is followed by a treatise on the ways of light and darkness, an exposition of a dualistic theology (3:13–4:26). Columns 5–7 deal with disciplinary matters, including the admission of new members and behaviour during meetings. Columns 8–9 may contain a kind of foundation document, perhaps the original core of the Rule, and cols 10–11 contain a hymn of praise to the Creator. Many of these sections have their own headings, and, like the heading to the whole work itself, identify what follows as 'for the *maskil*'. A *maskil* is a spiritual instructor, and the term may indicate a senior grade within the community, which called itself the *yahad*, or 'Union'. Some scholars, however, believe there was only one *maskil*, a leader of the *yahad*.

This document has always been regarded by scholars as providing the essential definition of the 'Qumran community' or 'Qumran sect'. A reference in 8:13 to separating from wicked people and a quotation of the famous scriptural text 'In the desert prepare the way of the Lord' (Isaiah 40:3) have often been taken as a direct allusion to Qumran

Two groups of fragments of a Community Rule scroll from Cave 4. (Above) 4QS^d cols 7–8; (left) 4QS^d col. 9.

Which Rule is the Earliest?

It is now obvious that the Community Rule went through various editorial stages. The ten Cave 4 manuscripts are generally shorter, though even they do not have an identical arrangement. In at least two, 1QS cols 1–5 are missing, as is the final hymn of 1QS 10–11. There are also some significant alterations in wording. The divergences are quite instructive:

1QS 5:1 'This is the Rule for the men of the community (*yahad*) who have volunteered themselves to be converted from all evil and adhere to all his comm andments according to his will.'

4QS^e 1:1 'Instruction for the *maskil* about the men of the law (Torah) who have volunteered to convert from all evil and hold fast to all that he has commanded.'

1QS 5:2 'They shall separate from the congregation of unjust people and shall unite, with respect to the Law and their possessions, under the authority of the sons of Zadok, the priests who maintain the covenant, and of the group of the men of the community who hold fast to the covenant. All decisions regarding doctrine, property, and justice shall be determined by them.'

4QS^e 1:2 'They shall separate from the congregation of unjust people and shall unite, with respect to doctrine and property. They shall be under the authority of the congregation in dealing with all doctrine and property.'

From these parallel passages one can posit the existence of a community in quite different stages of its history. The authority of the group in 1QS is a combination of Zadokite priests and lay leaders. The Cave 4 text speaks only of the authority of the congregation. Which is the earlier stage, a Zadokite-led one or a more democratic one? Was the community originally called a *yahad*, or known as a group of 'men of the law'?

While 1QS is deemed to be the earlier manuscript on palaeographical grounds, most scholars think the 4Q manuscripts represent earlier versions. In either case, it is clear that the character and structure of this community evolved over time, its changes reflected in the altered texts.

Factfile

THE 'RULES SCROLL'
Length (1QS, 1QSa and 1QSb): 2 m (6.5 ft)
Script: Late Hasmonaean to Herodian

Community Rule
Manuscripts: 1QS, fragments of manuscripts 4QS^a-j (4Q255–64), 5Q11
Editors: M. Burrows, J.C. Trever, W.H. Brownlee; P.S. Alexander, G. Vermes
Commentary: P. Wernberg-Møller, A.R.C. Leaney, J. Pouilly, J.H. Charlesworth, S. Metso

Metso's Community Rule Theory

Multiple manuscripts of several Qumran works illustrate the literary history of those compositions. Of these, the Community Rule is perhaps the most important because its history might also illuminate the history of the *yahad* itself. The most detailed analysis of the textual history of the Community Rule is by Sarianna Metso.

According to Metso, the earliest form of the Rule has not been preserved in any one manuscript. She deduces that the original form contained a blueprint for a new community and some disciplinary rules (1QS 5–9). After this, the work was expanded in two parallel processes. One of these two developments culminated in the addition of what is now 1QS 1–4, dealing with membership requirements, the covenant renewal ceremony, and the dualistic doctrine of the two spirits, all intended 'for the *maskil*', and a final hymn was also added.

It is strictly incorrect, then, to call 1QS '*the* Community Rule' – it is only one edition, and not necessarily the definitive one, though it seems the longest. Metso also regards it as the latest; but Philip Alexander, who has co-edited the Cave 4 manuscripts of the Rule for *DJD*, regards 1QS as the oldest version (because it exhibits the oldest handwriting). Until there is a consensus on the history of the Community Rule, there can be no agreed framework for the evolution of the *yahad* itself. And can we be sure that the Rule was always an entirely practical document, functioning in a real community, or was it perhaps revised in some part as an idealized description? The diagram below shows Metso's interpretation of the evolution of the Community Rule.

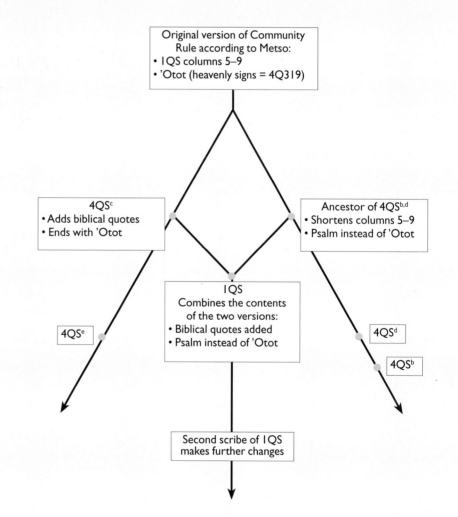

Original version of Community Rule according to Metso:
- 1QS columns 5–9
- 'Otot (heavenly signs = 4Q319)

4QSᶜ
- Adds biblical quotes
- Ends with 'Otot

Ancestor of 4QSᵇ,ᵈ
- Shortens columns 5–9
- Psalm instead of 'Otot

1QS
Combines the contents of the two versions:
- Biblical quotes added
- Psalm instead of 'Otot

4QSᵉ

4QSᵈ

4QSᵇ

Second scribe of 1QS makes further changes

itself. One of the earliest questions to be asked was: what community was this? Quite apart from the possible association of Qumran with a settlement of Essenes (see p. 55), there are strong resemblances between some of the practices of the *yahad* (including entrance procedures) and what Josephus says of the Essenes in his *Jewish War* (5:128–32; 7:137–43).

The community's beliefs

It is clear, not only from differences in subject matter and in terminology, that this Rule evolved, and different parts reflect different stages in its development. In recent years, further manuscripts of this composition from Cave 4 have been published, and these confirm such a conclusion, since they are not identical in all respects, but display a different arrangement and wording. But how to construct from these clues a history of the *yahad* has proved to be difficult, for there are no explicit historical statements at all. In general, however, it seems that the earliest stages suppose a small community that saw its role as atoning for the sins of Israel, probably because it regarded the Temple as defiled, and thus introducing the notion of a 'spiritual Temple' (cols 8–9). The later stages reflect a larger group, controlled by disciplinary laws and committed to a sectarian self-definition that saw the *yahad* as composed of 'children of light', as contrasted with the 'children of darkness' beyond their boundaries.

The strongly dualistic passage in columns 3–4 (which some of the Cave 4 editions do not contain) is the most explicit statement in any ancient Jewish text of a doctrine that almost certainly derives from Zoroastrianism. According to the community's teaching, God has appointed two spirits, of light and darkness or truth and falsehood, and assigned all humans to one or the other. These 'spirits', however, appear sometimes as external personifications, such as the 'prince of light' and 'angel of darkness'; and sometimes as lying inside each person. Indeed, towards the end of this teaching, it is explained that no one is truly all light or all darkness, but each person has elements of both. In another document found in Cave 4 (4Q186, popularly but perhaps mistakenly known as a Horoscope), a description of certain kinds of individual is given, in which the proportion of 'light' and 'darkness' in their character is correlated with physical characteristics and with their birth sign. It is therefore not impossible that membership of the community was dependent upon such factors. But despite the strong predestinarianism of this doctrine, the Rule clearly envisages the possibility of disobedience within its ranks and even defection from them.

(Following pages) The Community Rule – 1QS cols 5–6.

(Below) William H. Brownlee displays the Cave 1 'Rules Scroll' showing the text of the Community Rule.

A Covenant Renewal Ritual Calendar

This Greek coin from the 2nd century CE shows the symbol of the tribe of Levi – grape clusters.

1QS 2:19–24 describes an annual covenant ritual, where members begin or renew their membership, pledging 'to obey all his [God's] commandments so that they may not abandon him during the dominion of Belial because of fear or terror or affliction.' It is a solemn ceremony, inspired in part by Deuteronomy 27–28.

The priests and the Levites bless God and those entering the covenant say 'amen, amen.' Then the priests recount God's blessings and deeds favouring Israel, while the Levites recite the evil deeds, rebellions and sinful actions of Israel during the reign of Belial. This is followed by a communal confession: 'We have strayed. We have [disobeyed]. We and our ancestors before us have sinned and done wickedly in going [against…] of truth and righteousness. [God has] judged us and our ancestors also, but blessed us with his mercy forever.' The priests then pronounce a blessing, and the Levites curse those who follow Belial. This section is closed by a double 'amen'.

Cave 4 manuscripts probably connected with the Damascus Document show that this covenant ceremony was also practised in the 'Damascus' communities and took place on the 15th day of the third month, i.e. at the feast of Weeks, or Pentecost. 'And all the inhabitants of the camps shall assemble in the third month and curse him who turns aside to the right [or to the left] of the Law' (4Q266, frag. 11). This ceremony is one example of how the sectarian communities replaced Temple festivals with their own – and, of course, according to their own calendar.

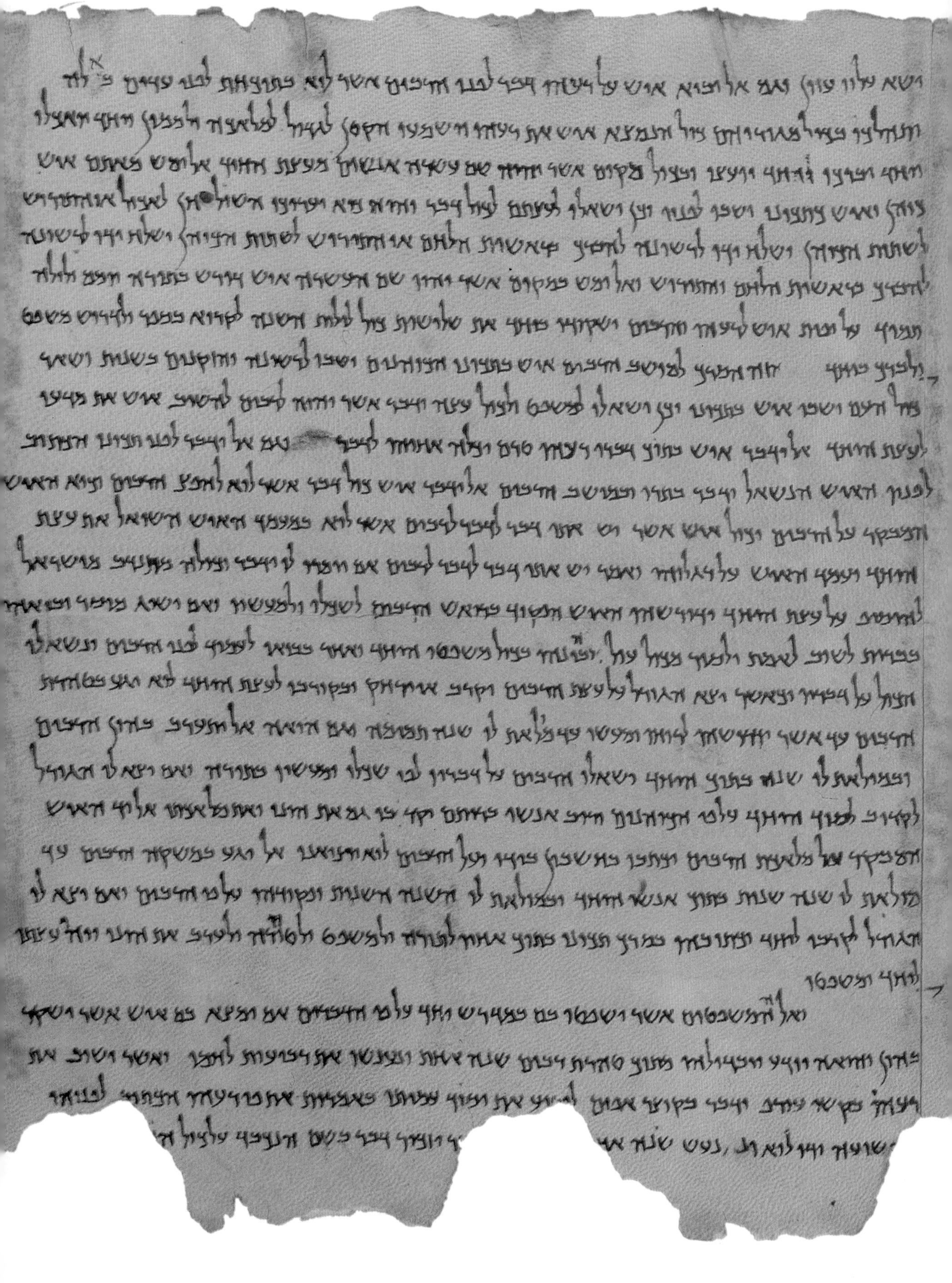

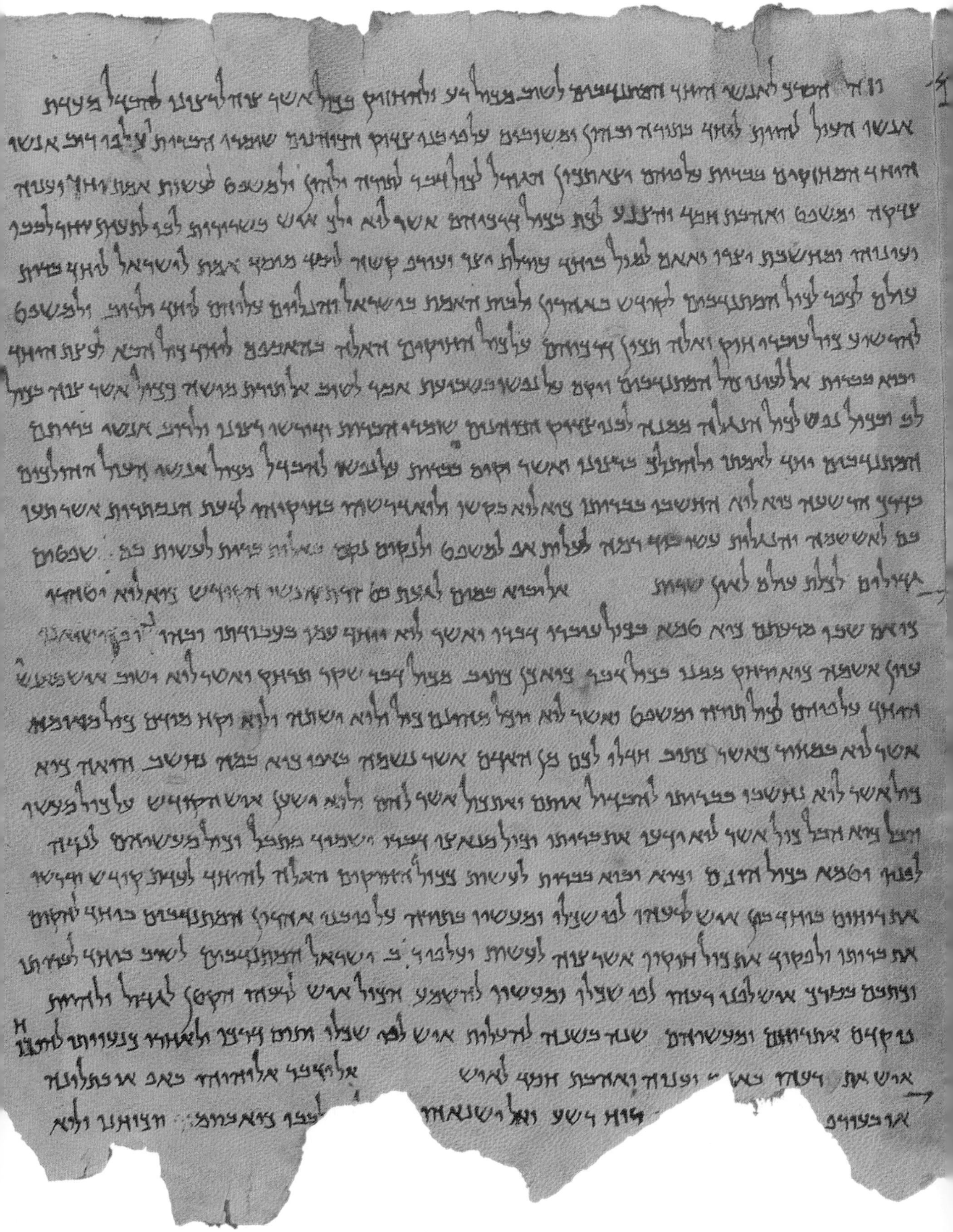

Zoroastrianism and the Scrolls

Where does the dualism of some of the Qumran texts come from? It seems to many scholars to be influenced by Zoroastrianism, the religion of the ancient Persians. For two centuries the people of Judah lived under the Persians, from whose patronage they seem to have benefited. At all events, Persian kings are never condemned, and their religion never attacked, in the Jewish scriptures. The influence of their religion upon the emerging Judaism of the province of Judah has long been debated, and the Dead Sea Scrolls have renewed that debate.

A relief of Ahura Mazda, from the east door of the Tripylon of the palace at Persepolis, Iran.

Although most Persian religious sources are from a much later period, Zoroaster (or Zarathustra, dates unknown) is held to have developed a dualistic religion, in which two uncreated beings, the wise and benign Ahura Mazda and his adversary Angra Mainyu, were locked in struggle. The similarity to the God of Israel and the satanic figure of Belial in the Community Rule and the War Scroll is quite striking, since such dualism is not encountered elsewhere in the Jewish scriptures

(in Job, Satan is one of God's servants). And just as Ahura Mazda was believed to send out lesser deities or angels, the scrolls mention hosts of angels and spirits attached to the 'angel of light' and to Belial, the 'angel of darkness'.

Zoroaster also envisioned that the battle between good and evil would end in a state of 'making wonderful', a restoration and removal of evil, similar to the 'renewal' mentioned in the scrolls. Zoroaster appealed to humans to become redeemers of the world; and in the Community Rule those who join the *yahad* are viewed as an atoning sacrifice for the sins and evil within Israel.

The need for physical purity pervades both Zoroastrian thought and religious law in the scrolls. The Temple Scroll and the Damascus Document in particular legislate for a community governed by the principle of purity. Menstruating women and the dead are both strictly to be avoided. Certain scrolls that speak of 'the end of days' display a belief in the present age as the last epoch. Apparently some Persian seers writing in Greek predicted that a redeemer figure would defeat the Macedonians, the world's last political and military powerhouse. Both Daniel and some of the scrolls seem to have a similar view. Other scrolls apparently saw Rome as the last foreign ruler of Israel. Israel would produce its own messianic figure to end the course of history.

If these parallels are significant (coincidence is not a likely explanation), then either (a) Zoroastrian beliefs permeated the scrolls from inherited ideas in Judaean religion, which have elsewhere in the literature been partly obliterated, or (b) there are unique links between the writers of the scrolls and the religion of the Persians, or their successors the Parthians – who for a while controlled the territory across the Dead Sea from Qumran and even invaded Judah in the days of Herod the Great. But how would such a unique connection between Zoroastrianism and the Jewish groups behind the scrolls be explained?

The language of 'children of light' so characteristic of the *yahad* is also reflected a few times in the New Testament. In Luke 16:8 Jesus says that the 'children of this world' are wiser in their generation than the 'children of light', and the Gospel according to John (3:19–21; 12:35–36) also employs this terminology. The rabbis, too, developed the notion of a 'good inclination' and a 'bad inclination' in each person, which in some sense resembles the community's doctrine, but it is not at all predestinarian, and these 'inclinations' are not personified.

The community's organization

The organization and discipline of this *yahad* were tight. The document *appears* to be referring to a

male celibate group, though with this theory the presence of some female and infant skeletons at Qumran needs explaining. The 'children of light' who joined the *yahad* are expected to follow God's commandments during the reign of Belial (the 'angel of darkness'). At the community's annual covenant renewal assembly, which we now know probably took place at the festival of Weeks/Pentecost, the priests recounted the saving deeds of Israel's God. The members publicly confessed their guilt and the guilt of their forefathers. The Levites cursed and damned those who continued to resist a genuine conversion of their lives, beliefs and behaviour. Also cursed were any members who entered the community under false pretences. There was thus a very strong feeling of separation from the evil world outside their boundaries, as well as a tight disciplinary regime:

'They shall separate from the congregation of false people and unite, as far as the Law and possessions are concerned, under the authority of the sons of Zadok, the priests who guard the covenant, and of the multitude of the men of the community who cling firmly to the covenant.' (1QS 5:1–3)

For new entrants, there was a trial period of two years (6:13–23). Only after a year could a prospective member consume the communal 'pure meal', but he could still not share any of the community's property. His property and wages were given to the community's treasurer but could not be used for communal purposes. After a second year and further successful evaluation, he was permitted to enjoy the 'drink of the congregation', and his property was incorporated into that of the community. So closely was this 'Union' conceived by its members that each person and his possessions were physically part of a single entity, though whether possessions were commonly *owned* or just commonly *used* is uncertain. Drinking together was the highest expression of this unity, because liquids are highly susceptible to impurity and one impure member could defile the entire community.

The rules governing members' behaviour were also strict: no lying about property, slandering of a fellow-member, uttering of the divine name nor speaking against the priests. No nakedness, no speaking nor gesturing foolishly, no sleeping, leaving too frequently nor spitting during an assembly. Penalties ranged from reduction of rations to outright expulsion, as in the case of sharing food or property with a former member who had been banished (6:24–7:27). The impression given by the Community Rule is thus of a group founded on a vision of atonement by righteous living, which became a well-organized community with a developed sectarian ideology and disciplinary structures.

The Rule of the Congregation

'This is the Rule for all the congregation of Israel in the last days, when they assemble…to walk according to the regulations of the Zadokite priests and the men of their covenant.' (1QSa 1:1–2)

The two columns of this document describe a congregation (Hebrew: *'edah*), including women and children, which was presumably joined to the *yahad* (there is damage to the manuscript at the crucial point). Its members will first attend a reading of the Law (see Deuteronomy 31:9–13). Under a new heading, 'Rule for all the hosts of the Congregation, for every person born in Israel' (1:6), the text legislates for the education of every young male Israelite, and his responsibilities at various stages of life, under the authority of the priests. Councils of this congregation are made up of leaders of its various subdivisions (as enumerated in the biblical books of Exodus and Numbers): tribes, thousands, hundreds, fifties, tens, with elders and Levites – all under priestly authority. No one with any mental or physical defect may hold office. Finally, there is a description of an assembly at which all are seated according to rank, and the chief priest (the messiah of Aaron?) shall preside, with the messiah of Israel, a lay leader, alongside him. At communal meals, the priestly messiah first blesses the bread and wine, then partakes, followed by the priestly messiah and then the rest of the people. The concluding sentence reads: 'And this is how they shall proceed at every meal where at least ten men are present'.

Like the Community Rule, this document may also be composed from several sources. In its present form, it looks like a draft for the future Israel that will emerge from the *yahad*, constituted along the lines of the biblical 'congregation of Israel' (e.g. in the book of Numbers), but with some elements of the disciplinary regime of the *yahad* incorporated. Much attention has been given to

Factfile
Manuscript: 1QSa
Editor: D. Barthélemy (*DJD* 1)
Commentary: L.H. Schiffman, J.H. Charlesworth

Bruce Zuckerman examines the Rule of the Congregation.

the roles of the two 'messiahs' in the communal meal. Priority clearly lies with the priest, not his lay counterpart. But is this some kind of 'messianic banquet', or, as the final sentence of the text seems to say, a regular occurrence, perhaps anticipating the ideal state of affairs at the end of history?

It has recently been suggested that this Rule reflects the organization of the Damascus community (see p. 18) and was later adapted by the *yahad*, and turned into a future vision. The congregation reappears in the War Scroll, and indeed, in this Rule, there is mention (1:21) of the 'war of conquest of the nations'.

(Opposite) The Rule of the Congregation, one of a small number of scrolls held in the National Archaeological Museum, Amman.

Factfile
Manuscript: 1QSb
Editor: J.T. Milik

The Rule of Blessings

'The *maskil* shall bless the Prince of the Congregation…and renew for him the covenant of the Community, so that he may establish the kingdom of his people for ever… "May he make you horns of iron and your horseshoes of bronze; may you cavort like a young bull [and trample the nations] like the dust of the street!"' (1QSb 5:20, 26)

The ending of the scroll containing 1QS, 1QSa and 1QSb lay on the outside, and thus received the most damage. Hence this document, headed 'Words of Blessing', is very fragmentary. Like 1QS, its contents are designated for the *maskil*, which is the term used of a spiritual and disciplinary leader (possibly *the* leader) within the community. He asks God from his heavenly abode to bless in turn the members of the community (the 'faithful', those who 'hold fast to the Covenant'), the high priest, the Zadokite priesthood (see Numbers 6:24–26), and the Prince of the Congregation.

Of the priests it is said, 'May you participate in the service of the Temple of the Kingdom…in company with the angels of the Presence', referring to the heavenly temple cult administered by divine beings (as described in the Songs of the Sabbath Sacrifice, see p. 146), while the Prince of the Congregation will crush the nations and rule them. The high priest and Prince of the Congregation must correspond to the 'messiah of Aaron' and 'messiah of Israel' who appear at the end of the preceding text, 1QSa, which may explain why the two texts have been copied together. Whether the blessings themselves were intended to be recited in the present or in the glorious days to come is unclear, but probably the latter: there are very similar eschatological prayers elsewhere in the Qumran collection (see p. 144). The reference to the *maskil* also furnishes a connection with 1QS, and perhaps the manuscript represents a collection of texts for use by a leader in the *yahad*.

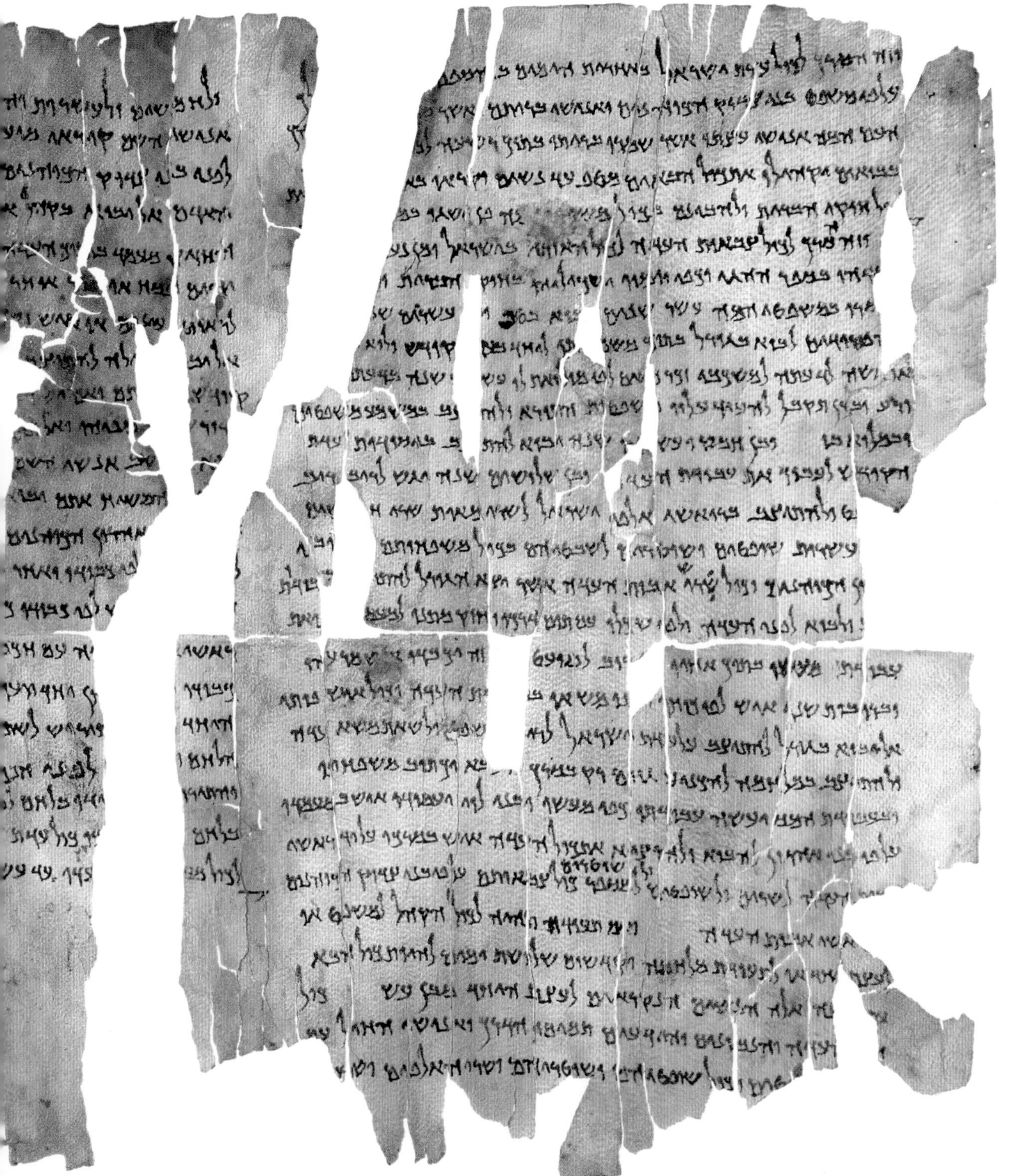

Factfile

Manuscript: 1QM, fragments of manuscripts 4QM^a-f (4Q491–96), 5Q11
Editors: E.L. Sukenik, M. Baillet (*DJD* 7)
Commentary: Y. Yadin, P.R. Davies, J. Duhaime
Length (1QM): 2.9 m (9 ft 6 in)
Script: Herodian (1QM); Hasmonaean and Herodian (4QM)

The War Scroll

'For it is a time of trouble for Israe[l, a moment pre-ordained] for war with all the nations. And the party of God will be in eternal redemption, but there will be annihilation for all wicked nations. Those [prepared] for war shall set up camp opposite the king of the Kittim and the whole army of Belial that has gathered to him – for a day [of vengeance] by the sword of God.' (1QM 15:1–3)

Visions of the final victory over evil are not uncommon in ancient Jewish literature (including the New Testament), but only in this scroll do we find an explicit description of a war between the powers of good and darkness. This opens with a seven-stage battle with the Roman empire, here disguised

found also in the Community Rule and in some other Qumran texts. Like many other Qumran scrolls, 1QM assumes a 52-week, 364-day calendar, not a 354-day lunar one, when it describes the restored Temple cult (col. 2). It has obviously been compiled from several kinds of sources, including hymns and prayers for wartime, military manuals and descriptions of Roman weaponry and manoeuvres. It may well bear traces of traditions stemming from the successful guerrilla exploits of the Maccabean warriors of the mid-2nd century BCE. One curiosity is that although there is a mention of the 'shield of the Prince of the Congregation' he is nowhere described as leading any fighting. This is done entirely by priests, who nevertheless keep well out of range of the polluting blood!

There are also fragments of this work (or at least of versions of it) in Cave 4.

Columns 12–14 of the Cave 1 War Scroll.

under the name 'Kittim' (which the book of Daniel also uses for 'Romans', 11:30), in which the Romans are annihilated for ever. This is followed by 33 years of war between Israel and the nations.

The Cave 1 scroll, which with 19 columns seems to be nearly complete, is relatively well preserved and written in a neat formal script. It was among the first batch to be discovered, and came into the possession of Eleazar Sukenik of the Hebrew University. The first and best commentary was aptly written by Sukenik's son, the scholar, general and politician Yigael Yadin.

There are clear links between this scroll and some other writings from Qumran. In particular, 1QM (*Milhamah* is Hebrew for 'war') represents a dualistic view of humanity, divided between the good and the evil, each with its patron spirits,

Contents of the Cave 1 War Scroll

Col. 1 gives an overview of war between the 'children of light' and the 'children of darkness': an initial phase of seven years ridding the Promised Land of non-Israelite occupants (Ammonites, Moabites, Edomites, Philistines) and especially the 'Kittim' (Romans). Wicked Jews were also destroyed, and the ten lost tribes restored.

'And this is the scroll of the organization of the war. The first engagement of the children of light is to attack the company of the children of darkness, the army of Belial, the troops of Edom and Moab and the Ammonites, the army of the inhabitants of Philistia, and the troops of the Kittim of Assyria, together with their allies, the breakers of the covenant. The children of Levi, Judah and Benjamin, the "exiles of the wilderness" shall war with them…' (1:1–2)

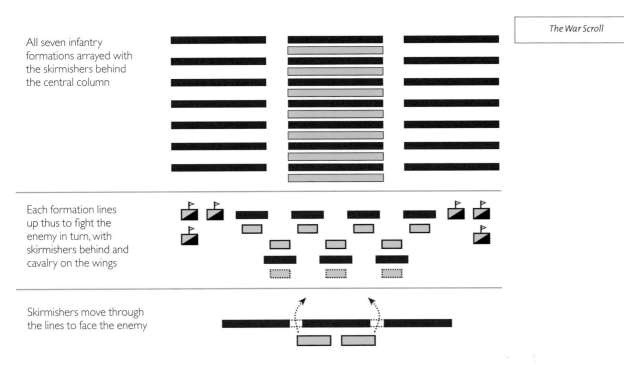

All seven infantry formations arrayed with the skirmishers behind the central column

Each formation lines up thus to fight the enemy in turn, with skirmishers behind and cavalry on the wings

Skirmishers move through the lines to face the enemy

Cols 2–9, probably from an older collection of texts about a protracted war between Israel and the nations, enumerate further campaigns until 40 years are over and the entire world is vanquished. Every seventh year will be a sabbatical, in which Israel (and its enemies!) will desist from hostility. Various battle manoeuvres to be used, signals on banners and trumpets, armoury, age limits and other incidental details are listed. An important feature here is that the 12 tribes are organized as were the Israelites in the wilderness (Numbers 1–10, where the entire nation is always specified). Many prayers are offered by the chief priest:

'Blessed be the God of Israel for all his holy plan and his true deeds. Blessed be all those who serve him in justice, who know him in faith. But cursed be Belial for the plan of hatred and cursed for his guilty power. Cursed be all the spirits of his party for their wicked plan, and cursed for all their words of filthy uncleanness, for they are of the party of darkness, but the army of God is for eternal light…' (13:3–5)

Cols 15–19 contain an account of a seven-stage battle in which the 'children of light' and 'children of darkness' achieve alternating success. But finally,

'…in the seventh stage, when the great hand of God shall be raised up against Belial and against all the army of his dominion for eternal confusion…then shall the sons of Japheth fall, never to rise, and the Kittim shall be destroyed without remnant or survivor, and there shall be raising of the hand of the God of Israel against the whole

multitude of Belial. At that time, the priests shall sound a trumpet-call…and all the battle formations shall follow this signal and spread out against the entire Kittim army, to annihilate them…' (18:1–5)

But did the authors *really* believe in a final war with Rome, with God intervening to give them victory? Or is this description just a fantasy? And who are the 'children of light' – the Jewish people, or just a sect? The Jews of Palestine did indeed wage war on the Romans in 66 CE, a war which ended in defeat with the destruction of the Temple in 70 CE and the fall of the last stronghold at Masada four years later, with the death of those fanatical zealots who believed, as this scroll describes, that God would fight for them. But the conduct of the battle depicted in this scroll is nevertheless more like a liturgy or a ballet. On cue, the trumpets sound, the weapons are used, the enemy falls (and conveniently rests in the seventh year as well?). It is a strange text to modern eyes, but it may give us an insight into Jewish feelings and hopes that soon proved to be so tragically misguided.

(Above left) The War Scroll (1QM)'s pitched battle plan, according to Yigael Yadin.

(Below) The War Scroll describes battle traditions that may well stem from the Maccabean wars of the mid-2nd century BCE, as depicted by the 10th-century Book of Maccabees.

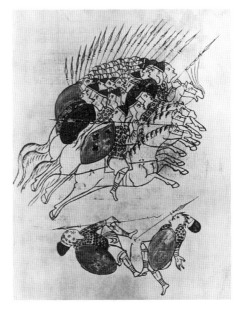

Factfile

Manuscripts: 1QHᵃ, fragments of manuscripts 1QHᵇ, 4QHᵃ⁻ᵉ (4Q428–31), 5Q11
Editors: E. L. Sukenik, E.M. Schuller
Commentary: S. Holm-Nielsen, J. Licht
Length (1QH): 4.3 m (14 ft 1 in)
Script: Herodian (1QH); Hasmonaean and Herodian (4QH)

The Thanksgiving Hymns

'[I thank you, O Lord]
because of the spirits you have placed within me
I shall find a reply on my tongue
to narrate your righteous deeds
and your patience…
the deeds of your mighty hand.
To confess my former sins,
prostrate myself and beg your indulgence
for my [wicked] deeds
and the perversity of my heart
because I wallowed in filth
and cut myself off from the spring of truth.'
(1QH 4:17–19)

though the scroll would have contained many more, as its first three columns are lost.

There is no pattern discernible in the arrangement of the Hymns. Thanks to the work of Stegemann and especially Puech, it has been established that the original arrangement by Sukenik was wrong. His placement of the many fragments that had detached from the manuscript has also been corrected and extended by Puech (using the methods described on p. 76).

Many of these poems stress the lowliness of the human condition and contrast it with the power of God. The human body is a sinful vessel shaped out of clay, whose fates have already been decided by divine decree:

Columns 9–12 of the Thanksgiving Hymns (1QHᵃ).

Sometimes also called the 'Hymns Scroll' this was among the Cave 1 scrolls acquired and published by Eleazar Sukenik.

Contents

Because most of these hymns or prayers express gratitude to God for having delivered the poet from some dangerous situation, they begin with the words *'odekah* ('I thank you'), and the scroll has appropriately been dubbed 'The Thanksgiving Hymns' (Hebrew *Hodayoth*) (1QHᵃ). This opening formula enables at least 24 hymns to be identified,

'I, a shape of clay kneaded in water
a ground of shame and a source of pollution
a melting pot of wickedness and an edifice of sin
a straying and perverted spirit of no understanding…
Everything has been inscribed in your presence
with a recording pen
for all periods of eternity
the numbers of the everlasting years…'
(1QH 9:21–24)

The poet often thanks God for having given him the knowledge to understand the divine mysteries, despite his weakness and ignorance. However, there are also more specific recollections, such as experiences of persecution at the hands of others. In much of the writing of these Hymns one finds strong echoes of the biblical Psalms, and indeed the Hymns abound with phraseology taken from them. One example is this phrase from 1QH 10:29: 'The net which they spread for me has entangled their feet; into the trap they set for my life they have fallen.' The words can be traced to Psalm 9:15: 'The nations have sunk down in the pit that they made: in the net that they hid has their own foot been snared', as well as Psalm 35:7: 'For without reason they hid their net for me; without reason they dug a pit for my life', and Psalm 142:3: 'In the path where I walk, they have hidden a trap for me.' Because of the influence of biblical language, and because the personal details given are often stereotypical, it has been doubted whether one can reconstruct with confidence from these allusions the experiences of one particular individual.

But on the other hand, there are certain passages suggesting the poet is the pillar of a community of people who rely on him as a source of strength. He also speaks of exile, of being transplanted to a place where there are water and trees in a dry land. He speaks of severe diseases and great physical weariness. Not surprisingly, perhaps, many scholars seized on these items as evidence that the poet is none other than the founder of the *yahad*, the 'Teacher of Righteousness', who, according to the Habakkuk Commentary, was persecuted, led a community, and had the gift of understanding divine secrets. Even the descriptions of dry places and streams could suggest Qumran, to which the Teacher might be thought to have brought his followers.

It is less common now to be so confident of the authorship of these Hymns. Quite possibly they were composed for or by a sectarian leader (a *maskil*?) and, as in all ancient Hebrew poetry, the line between literalness and metaphor is sometimes invisible. It is the powerful religious sentiment, rather than possible historical clues, that makes these poems worth reading.

History or Hagiography?

Scholars have long treated the Hymns and the *pesharim* (p. 96) as historical sources for the life and times of the Teacher of Righteousness, the presumed founder of the *yahad*. A number of the individual hymns in this scroll describe in the first person the feelings and experiences of a religious leader who went into exile and founded a community, and it is thus tempting to assign these compositions to the Teacher himself. But not once does the poet call himself by this title.

Although the language of the Hymns is often quite general and stereotypical, the *pesher* commentaries offer a more explicit (though still frustratingly indirect) account of certain episodes in the life of the 'Teacher of Righteousness' (exile, founding a community). Particularly striking are the terms used to describe the enemies: 'teachers of smooth things,' and 'lying persons'. The question is: are these allusions in the Commentaries based on independent memory or are they derived from reading the Hymns as autobiography? The following is a striking illustration.

1QH 12:8–12:
'They have banished me from my land like a bird from its nest; all my friends and brothers are driven far from me and view me as a broken pot. But these lying teachers and false diviners have made devilish plots against me to exchange Your law, engraved in my heart, for smooth things for Your people, from those who thirst for the drink of knowledge they withhold it and assuage their thirst with vinegar, in order to gaze on their straying, on their folly over feast days, on their fall into the trap.'

1QpHab 11:
'*Woe to him who causes his neighbours to drink, who pours out his venom to make them drunk, so that he may gaze upon their feasts.* (Habakkuk 2:15). This concerns the Wicked Priest who pursued the Teacher of Righteousness to destroy him in his furious rage, in the place of his exile, on the day of fasting, the sabbath of rest.'

One might well think of the Hymn and the Commentary as referring to the same event. But while the *pesharim* attach the nicknames to specific groups and persons, the Hymns use them generically, as descriptions of enemies, not ciphers. They know no persecuting priest and no individual Liar, as do the *pesharim*. For this reason, it is possible that the writer of the Habakkuk Commentary has used the Hymns, reading them as autobiographical, constructing from them a life of the Teacher to be read into the scriptural text, and furnishing colourful but fictional figures as opponents for him. If this has occurred, how much do we really know about this Teacher?

Factfile

Manuscripts:
Commentaries on
Habakkuk (1QpHab),
Micah (1Q14, 4Q168),
Psalms (4Q171 and 173,
1Q16), Nahum (4Q169),
Isaiah (4QpIsa 161–65,
3Q4), Hosea (4Q166–67),
Zephaniah (1Q15, 4Q170),
Malachi (5Q10)
Editors: W.H. Brownlee
(1QpHab), J.M. Allegro
(4Q166–73), D.
Bathélemy and J.T. Milik
(*DJD* 1) (1Q14–15); M.
Baillet, J.T. Milik and R. de
Vaux (*DJD* 3) (5QpMal)
Commentary: W.H.
Brownlee, M.P. Horgan,
G. Doudna
Script: Herodian

The Biblical Commentaries

*'There is still another vision concerning the appointed
time. It shall tell of the end and shall not lie* (Habakkuk 2,
3a). Interpreted this means that the last age shall be
prolonged and shall exceed all that the prophets said,
for the mysteries of God are marvellous. *If it tarries,
wait for it, for it shall surely come and shall not be late*
(Habakkuk 2, 3b). Interpreted this concerns the men of
truth, those who keep the Law, whose hands do not tire
in the service of truth when the final age stretches out
over them. For all the ages of God reach their appointed
end as he decided for them in the mysteries of his
wisdom.' (1QpHab 7:5–14)

The purpose of the Commentary

Pesher is a name given to a kind of biblical commentary found only at Qumran, in which individual texts are taken in sequence and given precise
predictive meanings, relating to the recent history
of the authors' community, which thought itself to
be living at the 'end of days'. They deal only with
prophetic books, but these include Psalms, which
was also thought to be prophetic. (Some other
Qumran texts, however, do contain passages of
this kind of commentary.)

Each of these *pesharim* follows the order of the
biblical book being interpreted, citing a verse or
small number of verses before offering the interpretation. The interpretations of successive verses
are not necessarily related at all. The technique is
atomistic, with the scriptural passages treated as a
sequence of individual ciphers. The Psalms *pesher*
from Cave 4 was originally thought to deal only
with Psalm 37, but the fragmentary ending now
suggests that other psalms may be cited. The scope
of the scriptural text addressed by this *pesher* is
therefore unclear.

The Habakkuk Commentary

Of these commentaries, the longest and best-
known (and the first to be discovered and published) is the Habakkuk *pesher* from Cave 1.
According to this text, God told the prophet what
would happen at the 'end', but not when this 'end'
would be. However, he later revealed to the
'Teacher of Righteousness' the identity of the
events alluded to:

*'And the Lord answered [and said to me, "Write down
the vision and make it plain] upon the tablets, that [he who
reads] may read it speedily"* (Habakkuk 2:1–2). Its meaning: and God told Habakkuk to write down that which
would happen to the final generation, but He did not

*The crucifixion of Jesus by
the Romans. But the scrolls
reveal that this was also
practised by Jewish leaders.*

Crucifixion

Compared with a quick stoning at the village gate,
public crucifixion was extraordinarily shameful
and cruel. This form of punishment has often been
associated with the Romans, but was widely
practised before them. The reliefs (in the British
Museum) of Sennacherib invading Judah in 701
BCE show men impaled on sharpened beams.

Crucifixion involved stretching the body on
a vertical piece of wood. The onset of death was
protracted, and the purpose was as much public
humiliation as it was the administration of pain.
Hence it was often carried out on large numbers
at a time, and in public places, such as roadsides
or outside city walls near a gate.

The commentary on Nahum refers to someone
nicknamed the 'Wrathful Lion' (1:6–8) who hanged
his opponents alive in Jerusalem. This lion is
usually identified as the Jewish leader Alexander
Jannaeus (see Josephus, *War* 1:92–97; *Antiquities*
13:376–83) who crucified 800 of his opponents 'in
the middle of the city [Jerusalem]'. (However, it has
also been argued that the 'Lion' is actually a foreign
ruler.) Scholars have usually
interpreted a Jewish ruler's
use of crucifixion itself as
something that had never
before happened in Israel.
But with the publication of
the Temple Scroll this view
has been modified. The
Temple Scroll 64:6–13
presents several cases
of treason. The stated
punishment is, in accord
with Deuteronomy 21:22–23,
'hanging on the tree' (or
'wood'). It required that
death be the outcome of
the hanging. But the text
stipulates that the body is not
to stay up overnight. It must
be taken down and buried so
as not to defile the land. Neither of the Qumran
texts appears to criticize the practice, and the hymn
preserved in 4Q448 contains a blessing, possibly
for Jannaeus, whom it addresses as 'King Jonathan'.

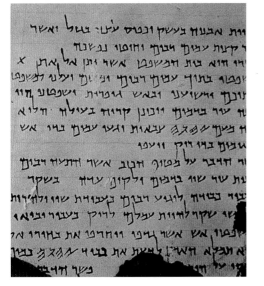

inform him of the completion of the last time. And as for that which he said, that he who reads may read it speedily. Interpreted this concerns the Teacher of Righteousness, to whom God made known all the mysteries of the words of his servants the prophets.' (1QpHab 6:13–7:5)

A *pesher* thus turns out to be the revealed answer to an obscure oracle, a 'mystery'. A similar device can be found in the stories of Joseph and Daniel, both of whom interpret dreams, though Daniel 9 deals with a hidden meaning of a scriptural text. In the Qumran texts, the exercise as a whole was meant to affirm that the scriptures did indeed speak about the writers' community and that the end-time was already present.

The prophecies of Habakkuk are set in the 6th century BCE, when Judah was threatened by the 'Chaldeans', the neo-Babylonians. The prophet describes their warlike character, but also comments on the persecution of the righteous by the wicked in Jerusalem. The commentator equates the Chaldeans with the 'Kittim', who are to be identified with the Romans; and he personifies the righteous and wicked in Habakkuk as the 'Teacher of Righteousness' and the 'Wicked Priest', though he also introduces a third main character as the 'Liar'. He refers to events that involved these characters, chiefly attacks on the Teacher by the Wicked Priest and the arrival of the 'Kittim' in many lands.

(Above left) Column 10 of the Habakkuk Commentary (1QpHab). Note the use of palaeo-Hebrew characters for the divine name in the scriptural quotations, lines 7 and 14.

(Above right) This 13th-century mosaic of the prophet Habakkuk can be seen in the Basilica di San Marco, Venice.

Ancient historical events are transformed into contemporary ones through pesher *interpretations: this is a detail from the Assyrian relief of the capture.*

But nowhere are any real names used: the persons identified from the biblical text are always given nicknames. For this reason, a good deal of scholarly effort has been expended in trying to unravel the identity of the 'Wicked Priest' and the 'Teacher of Righteousness', but without any consensus. Much of what is said about the 'Wicked Priest' (he became wealthy, connived with Gentiles, inflicted violence, and suffered a nasty end) could apply to several candidates, or may in any case be stereotypical. And while the advent of the Romans in the Levant can easily be read off from the Commentary, most of the events described as fulfilling the prophecy are unknown to us. Nevertheless, in the first 40 years of Dead Sea Scrolls study, it was usual for the early history of the Qumran community to be reconstructed out of the clues in this text. Thus the 'Wicked Priest' has been variously identified with several high priests of Jerusalem, and the statement in the *pesher* that the Wicked Priest pursued the Teacher (who is also called a priest) to his 'house of exile' on their fast day (1QpHab 11:2–8) is taken to refer to a pursuit to Qumran, where the Teacher and his followers observed a different calendar. Nowadays, other texts, such as the Damascus Document (CD) and the Halakhic Letter (4QMMT), have generated alternative theories. It is no longer universally agreed even that the details preserved in the commentaries can be entirely relied upon as factual.

Certain groups are also mentioned in the Habakkuk Commentary, including the 'Seekers of Smooth Things' and the 'House of Absalom'. There is widespread agreement that the 'Seekers' are the Pharisees, and it has been suggested that their nickname in Hebrew (*dorshey halaqot*) is a deliberate pun on *halakot*, the name given by Pharisees (and rabbis) to their interpretations and elaborations of biblical law. By contrast, the 'poor' and 'simple' represent the righteous, probably members of the sect founded by the Teacher. 'Poor' was in fact used in both the Old Testament Psalms and the New Testament to convey virtue as well as (or even instead of) economic deprivation.

More clues from other commentaries

The Psalms Commentary, represented in fragments of three manuscripts from Caves 1 and 4, and covering Psalms 37 and 38, adds that the 'Wicked Priest' sought to kill the 'Teacher' 'because of a law which he had sent him' (4QpPs 4:5–12). Scholars have speculated that this law was perhaps the Temple Scroll or its 'law for the king' (which stipulates that the monarch be instructed by the priests, be monogamous, avoid amassing personal wealth, and be of Jewish ancestry) – or even the 'Halakhic Letter'.

In 4QpNahum the commentator actually names historical figures, Seleucid kings (who were of Greek descent and culture):

'*The lion has entered there, the female lion, the baby lion, [but no one was frightened* (Nahum 2:11). Its interpretation concerns De]metrius, a Greek king [lit: 'king of Yawan'] who desired to come to Jerusalem on the counsel of those who seek smooth things (1:1–2). [...] Greek kings from Antiochus until the appearance of the rulers of the Kittim.' (4QpNah fragments 3–4, col. 1:1–3)

The Demetrius referred to is probably the Seleucid king Demetrius III, who, with the help of certain Pharisees, attempted to take control of Jerusalem

c. 90 BCE. Another character mentioned, but by his nickname, is the 'Furious Lion Cub' who avenged himself on the 'Seekers of Smooth Things' by hanging men alive, that is, crucifying them. Most scholars identify this character as the Hasmonaean king Alexander Jannaeus, who crucified 800 of the Pharisees for attempting to betray him to the Seleucid Demetrius. This reference, together with mention of the 'Kittim', suggesting a strong Roman military presence, points to a date in the middle of the 1st century BCE as the earliest time of composition. Since there are no clear references to later events in any of the *pesharim*, it seems very possible that they were all composed then. The similarity of genre, style, and of historical allusions in these commentaries shows, as far as we can tell from what is left, a fairly coherent set of writings that may well have been written at about the same time. The palaeography of the manuscripts fits such a dating well.

Fragments of six manuscripts of a commentary on Isaiah (five from Cave 4, one from Cave 3) have also given us the figure of the 'Prince of the Congregation' and the 'Sprout of David', which are names applied elsewhere in the scrolls to a non-priestly (kingly) messiah.

The fragments of *pesharim* on Hosea (4QpHos[a-b]), Micah (1QpMic, 4QpMic?), Zephaniah (1QpZeph, 4QpZeph), and Malachi (5QpMal) add little to what we know from the others: they all seem to apply prophetic announcements of doom to the immediate future of the writers. What remains of the Psalms Commentary covers mostly Psalm 37, but a citation of Psalm 45 afterwards shows that this was not a sequential commentary on the entire collection. Like 1QpMicah, it also mentions the 'Teacher of Righteousness' and the 'Liar' (5QpMal: 'Spouter of Lies'), one of his enemies. The commentaries on Zephaniah and Malachi amount only to a few lines.

(Left) John Allegro pores over the fragments of the Nahum Commentary.

(Below) Fragments 3 and 4, which offer the bulk of the Nahum Commentary.

Factfile

Manuscript: 1QapGen
ar (1Q20)
Editors: N. Avigad and
Y. Yadin
Commentary: J. Fitzmyer
Length: c. 2 m (6–7 ft)
Script: Herodian

The Genesis Apocryphon

'Then I decided that the conception was through the agency of the [angelic] Watchers, that the seed had been planted by the holy ones or fallen ones […] I was confused because of the child.' (1QapGen 2:1–2)

'Then my wife Bathenosh answered me very emotionally, cry[ing…]. She said, "O my brother, my lord, remember the pleasure…the moment of intercourse and my ardent response."' (2:8–10)

This least well-preserved of the major scrolls from Cave 1, and the only one in Aramaic, was originally entitled the Apocalypse of Lamech, since this

spring who became giants. In Genesis 4 Lamech took two wives, Adah and Zillah, neither of whom bore Noah. In the next chapter he becomes the father of Noah at the age of 182, but nowhere is a mother named. Although Bathenosh maintains her innocence, Lamech goes to his father Methuselah to have his case investigated. The son, whose legitimacy is confirmed by Methuselah, is born with miraculous appearance and powers. In the next recognizable section Noah's ark has landed on the mountains of Hurarat (Genesis has 'Ararat'), where he erects an altar, burns incense, and atones for the entire earth. Then he relates the names of his sons' sons and additionally four daughters of Japheth. Noah plants a vineyard (on Mount Lubar) but instead of the biblical story about Noah's drunkenness we have Noah's celebration of the first wine

Columns 18–22 of the Genesis Apocryphon.

figure, the son of Methuselah and father of Noah, is the speaker in the portions preserved. The language and handwriting suggest a date around the turn of the era. The scroll consists of four sheets of leather (22 columns), with the beginning and end damaged. In recent years, advanced image enhancement techniques have revealed more readable text. But how extensive this manuscript was originally is unknown.

Contents

The contents seem to have comprised a loose paraphrase (with a good deal of addition) of Genesis, though whether the entire book was covered is unknown. In what is preserved of cols 2–3 (of col. 1 only part of one line can be read), Lamech speaks of his fear that his wife, Bathenosh, has been impregnated by one of the holy 'watchers', a class of angels who, Genesis 6 tells us, became enamoured of earthly women, came to earth and had intercourse with them. The women bore them off-

feast on the first day of the fifth year after planting. On this occasion Noah and his family bless the Lord of Heaven for deliverance from the deluge.

Thus, while the author's tale is based on Genesis, his concern to vindicate Noah, name the location of Noah's vineyard and express harmonious worship and thanksgiving in the early years after the flood show him anxious to provide a few additional details and to have proper cultic behaviour from the patriarch. But from col. 17 onwards the story expands considerably. The then-known world is apparently apportioned among Noah's progeny and then, in the best-preserved section of the scroll, occurs a retelling of the journeys and adventures of Abraham, or Abram as he was then (Genesis 12:8–15:4). The first deals with Sarah (or Sarai)'s abduction: Abraham dreams of men hewing down a cedar and letting a palm remain. The palm cries out not to cut down the cedar, saying they are of the same family. Abraham explains to Sarah that they are the two trees, and she must call him 'brother' before strangers. Three Egyptian princes come, and one, Hyrcanus, encourages Pharaoh to summon Sarah. But God sends chastising spirits against the Pharaoh to prevent cohabitation. After Abraham prays for, and heals, the Pharaoh, Sarah is given wealth and the handmaid Hagar. This version obviously combines the two stories of Genesis 12 and 20. The narrator also adds names: a river Carmon, a pharaoh Zoan, a prince Hyrcanus.

Cols 21–22 parallel Genesis 13:3–15:4, with some noticeable differences: Lot buys a house in Sodom; Abraham actually walks around the Promised Land. Thus, this rewritten biblical narrative illustrates how some ancient Jews read and interpreted Genesis, introducing details and patriarchal piety. It is also effusive about Sarah's beauty.

Significance

Several other examples of rewritten biblical stories, especially from Genesis, have been found at Qumran. In many cases there is a clear theological intention. Here, although theological issues are addressed, there seems a strong element of folkloristic expansion, perhaps reflecting already popular versions of the Genesis tales. Genesis was so much written about in Jewish literature of the period probably because it contains an account of the origins of the world and mankind, and thus also clues to the end of the world. The flood and Noah's rescue, for example, were seen as a prefiguration of the punishment on the wicked world that the writers expected soon, and deliverance of the small band of the righteous (namely, themselves).

Sarah leads Hagar to Abraham in this painting by Adriaen van der Werff (1659–1722).

Factfile

Manuscripts: 1Q17–18, 2QJub, 3QJub, pap4QJub, 4Q216–28, 11Q12
Editors: J.C. VanderKam (*DJD* 13: 4Q), van der Woude et al (DJD 23: 11Q)
Commentary: J.C. VanderKam, R.H. Charles
Length: fragmentary
Script: Late Hasmonaean to Herodian (4Q); Late Herodian (11Q)

The Book of Jubilees

'And Moses was on the mountain forty days and forty nights, and God taught him the earlier and the later history of the division of all the days of the Law and the testimony.' (1:4–5)

'There are forty-nine jubilees from the days of Adam until this day, and one week and two years: and there are yet forty years to come for learning the commandments of the Lord.' (50:4)

The Book of Jubilees was known to Western scholars before the Qumran discoveries. In the late 18th and 19th centuries Western scholars learned about the Book of Jubilees as part of the scriptural canon of the Abyssinian (Ethiopic) church. Portions of the same book were also discovered in Latin, and it was assumed that these had been translated from Greek. Qumran Caves 1–4 and 11 have now delivered 15 fragmentary manuscripts of the book in its original Hebrew. Only parts of eight of the 50 chapters (about 38–40 verses in all) have survived.

This work covers the contents of the books of Genesis and Exodus, up to the giving of the Law on Mt Sinai. It claims to be the heavenly written counterpart to the Torah (Law) revealed to all Israel. It may have been held in great esteem by the groups represented at Qumran, since the Damascus Document (16:2–3) seems to cite it authoritatively (and give us its original title), and the calendar which forms the basis of the book's structure and presentation is reflected and supported in many of the Qumran scrolls.

A major feature of Jubilees is its systematic dating of events from creation to Sinai in relation to 49-year periods or 'jubilees'. Jubilees stresses both Israel's misbehaviour and the obedience

The 'Book of Time's Divisions'

Was the Book of Jubilees regarded as a highly authoritative text for the writers of the scrolls? Many scholars think so. Column 16:1–5 of the Damascus Document seems to refer to it:

'As for the determination of their times to which Israel turns a blind eye, behold it is strictly defined in the *scroll of the divisions of the times into their jubilees and weeks*. And on the day when a man swears to return to the Law of Moses, the angel of persecution shall cease to follow him – provided that he keeps his promise.'

While Jubilees itself does not seem to be a sectarian writing, its authors may have belonged to those Jewish groups from whom the 'Damascus' sect and then the *yahad* (community) formed: the concerns of Jubilees with strict observance of the 364-day calendar and with scrupulous obedience to the Law of Moses are certainly shared by the scrolls.

towards the law of the patriarchs, even before the Law had been given. In this respect it resembles several other Qumran scrolls.

Scholars believe that Jubilees was composed between 170 and 140 BCE, since Jacob's battle in 34:1–10 and 37:1–38:4 perhaps alludes to victories of Judas Maccabee against the Seleucids in the late 160s BCE. Whether or not this is the case, palaeographers have dated some Cave 4 manuscripts to *c.* 100 BCE.

Contents

Jubilees begins with Moses on Mt Sinai receiving a divine revelation, and claims to be the text of that

The battle of the Maccabees, from the 13th-century Arsenal Bible. Jubilees perhaps alludes to the victories of Judas Maccabaeus.

revelation, given by God and written down for Moses by the 'angel of the Presence'. It stresses, like many of the other scrolls, the observance of sabbaths and a 364-day calendar, but also avoidance of any Gentile customs. It also claims that certain festivals are celebrated by angels in heaven (who are, of course, also circumcised), so that earthly practice must conform.

The narrative then traces the early history of humanity and the ancestors of the Israelites, from the creation of the world up to Moses' own time, and devotes a great deal of space to the life of Jacob. Although, according to the instructions given to the angel, the book is supposed to reveal the future 'until My sanctuary is built in their midst for ever and ever', its narrative does not go beyond the arrival of the Israelites at Mt Sinai.

The book stresses the piety and conformity to the Law (yet to be revealed!) of the patriarchs, with emphasis on the proper observance of sabbaths and feast days. It also attributes (as do several other scrolls) the wickedness of humanity to 'the spirit of Beliar' (more usually in the scrolls, Belial) (1:20) and the belief in an eschatological punishment of the wicked. It does not betray any signs of being written within a sectarian community, but more probably reflects a violent dispute among Jews of the Hasmonaean period over the proper calendar and the need for exact observance of the Law. Several other texts found at Qumran (Enoch, perhaps the Halakhic Letter) may also reflect these pre-sectarian conflicts, from which the Qumran communities of 'Damascus' and the *yahad* later arose.

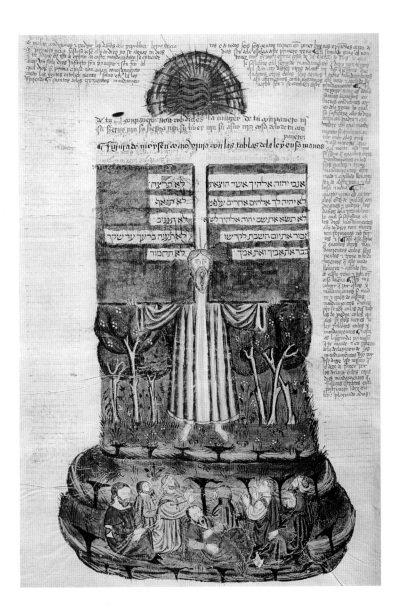

The 15th-century Alba Bible depicts Moses bringing the Tablets of the Law down from Mt Sinai, having received a divine revelation (Jubilees claims to be the text of that revelation).

The World Calendar of Jubilees

'This is the account of the division of days of the Law and the testimony for observance according to their Weeks [seven years] and their Jubilees [seven Weeks, or 49 years] throughout all the years of the world just as the Lord told it to Moses on Mt Sinai.' (Opening of Jubilees)

First Jubilee	*Week 1*	Creation, including of Adam and Eve
		Adam and Eve in Eden
	Week 2	Temptation by the snake, banishment
Second Jubilee	*Week 3*	Birth of Cain
	Week 4	Birth of Abel
	Week 5	Birth of daughter Awan
Third Jubilee	*Week 1*	Cain kills Abel
	Week 5	Birth of Seth
	Week 6	Birth of daughter Azura
		Cain marries Awan
Fourth Jubilee	*Week 7*	Birth of Enoch to Cain and Awan
Fifth Jubilee	*Week 1*	Cities built. Cain builds city of Enoch
Seventh Jubilee	*Week 3*	Enoch marries Noam
	Week 5	Birth of Kenan to Enoch and Noam
Eighth Jubilee	*Week 7*	Kenan marries Mualeleth
Ninth Jubilee	*Week 1*	Birth of Mahalalel to Kenan and Mualeleth
Tenth Jubilee	*Week 2*	Mahalalel marries Dinah
	Week 3	Birth of Jared to Mahalalel and Dinah
Eleventh Jubilee	*Week 4*	Jared marries Baraka. Birth of Enoch
Twelfth Jubilee	*Week 7*	Enoch marries Edni. Birth of Methuselah

(Enoch is 'taken', spends six jubilees with the angels and ends up in the garden of Eden)

Fourteenth Jubilee	*Week 3*	Methuselah marries Edna. Birth of Lamech
Fifteenth Jubilee	*Week 3*	Lamech marries Batenosh. Birth of Noah
Nineteenth Jubilee	*Week 7*	Death of Adam at 930 years old
		Cain's house falls on him and kills him
Twenty-first?* Jubilee	*Week 5*	Noah marries Emzara. Birth of Shem and Ham
	Week 6	Birth of Japheth to Noah and Emzara
Twenty-second Jubilee	*Week 5*	Noah builds the ark as commanded, and enters
		Flood, Noah's sacrifice. Covenant of Noah
		Inauguration of Feast of Weeks (Pentecost)
	Week 7	Noah plants a vine on the mountains of Ararat
Twenty-eighth Jubilee		Noah gives his grandsons commandments

Noah's sons corrupted the covenant until the days of Abraham, who alone kept it

Twenty-ninth Jubilee	*Week 1*	Arpachshad, son of Shem, marries Rasueya
		Birth of Cainan to Shem and Rasueya
Thirtieth Jubilee	*Week 2*	Cainan marries Melka. Birth of their son Shelah
Thirty-first Jubilee	*Week 5*	Shelah marries Muk. Birth of Eber
Thirty-second Jubilee	*Week 7*	Eber marries Azurad. Birth of Peleg
Thirty-third Jubilee	*Week 1*	The division of the earth among Noah's sons
		Death of Noah.
		Peleg marries Loma. Birth of Reu
	Week 4	Building of the Tower of Babel

Thirty-fourth Jubilee	*Week 4*	Human race dispersed from the land of Shinar
Thirty-fifth Jubilee	*Week 3*	Reu marries Ora. Birth of Seroh/Serug
Thirty-sixth Jubilee	*Week 5*	Serug marries Melka. Birth of Nahor
Thirty-seventh Jubilee	*Week 6*	Nahor marries Iyaska. Birth of Terah
Thirty-ninth Jubilee	*Week 2*	Terah marries Edna. Birth of Abraham
	Week 5	Abraham invents the plough
	Week 6	Abraham rejects idolatry
Fortieth Jubilee	*Week 2*	Abraham marries Sarah
	Week 3	Haran marries. Birth of Lot. Nahor marries
	Week 4	Abraham burns idol temple. Haran dies in the fire
		Terah and his family move to Haran
	Week 6	Abraham blessed by God, and understands Hebrew
		Abraham leaves for Canaan
	Week 7	Abraham builds an altar at Bethel
		Abraham journeys to Hebron and to Egypt
Forty-first Jubilee	*Week 1*	Abraham returns to Bethel. Abraham and Lot part
		Lot goes to Sodom. Capture and rescue of Lot
		Covenant renewed on feast of Weeks
		Birth of Ishmael to Abraham and Hagar
	Week 4	Covenant renewed and circumcision ordained
		Birth of Isaac
	Week 7	Near-sacrifice of Isaac
Forty-second Jubilee	*Week 1*	Sarah dies in Hebron. Rebecca chosen for Isaac
		Abraham marries Keturah
	Week 6	Jacob and Esau born
	Week 7	Abraham commands his sons and dismisses Ishmael
		Abraham instructs Isaac on sacrificial procedure
Forty-fourth Jubilee†	*Week 1*	Abraham blesses Jacob. Death of Abraham
	Week 3	God blesses Isaac. Isaac goes to Beer Lahi-Roi
	Week 4	Esau gives his birthright to Jacob. Isaac visits Gerar
		Isaac blesses Jacob
	Week 2	Jacob dreams at Bethel and serves Laban
	Week 3	Jacob marries Leah, then Rachel
		Birth of Reuben, Simeon, Levi, Judah,
		Dan and Naphtali
	Week 4	Birth of Asher, Issachar, Zebulun and Joseph
	Week 5	Jacob goes across the Jordan
	Week 6	Rape of Dinah and revenge of Levi and Simeon
		Levi chosen for priesthood
		Birth of Benjamin. Death of Rachel
		Sale of Joseph by his brothers
Forty-fifth Jubilee	*Week 1*	Death of Rebecca and Isaac
	Week 2	Death of Leah. Judah and Tamar
	Week 3	Famine brings family of Jacob to Egypt
	Week 5	Death of Jacob
Forty-sixth Jubilee	*Week 6*	Death of Joseph, then his brothers
Forty-seventh Jubilee	*Week 7*	Moses' father comes from Canaan to Egypt
Forty-eighth Jubilee	*Week 4*	Birth of Moses
Forty-ninth Jubilee	*Week 3*	Moses goes to Midian
Fiftieth jubilee	*Week 2*	Moses returns to Egypt. Exodus

'The account of the division of days ends here' (50:13)

*Extant text has 'twenty-fifth'
† the chronology of this Jubilee is disordered in the extant text

Mt Sinai, upon which the Lord told Moses the Law, according to Jubilees.

Cave 2

New Jerusalem

'And he showed me all the measurements of the blocks. Between one block and another runs a street, 6 rods wide, 42 cubits. And in the main street, running from east to west: width of street, two of them 10 rods, 70 cubits. He measured the third, the one that passes to the north of the Temple – 18 rods wide [126 cubits]. The width of the streets running from south [to north]: two of them are 9 rods and 4 cubits each, 67 cubits; the middle one [in the cen]tre of the city, he measured its width: 13 rods and one cubit, 92 cubits. All the streets of the city are paved with white stone…alabaster and onyx.'
(5QNJ frag. 1, 1:2–6)

While the official Jordanian Antiquities team had rediscovered Cave 1 and moved on to excavate the ruins of Qumran, the Bedouin kept searching. In February 1952 they came across another cave with manuscripts, about 150 m south of Cave 1 (see map, p. 11). This disappointingly contained only fragments of scrolls, but these were quicky sold. As with Cave 1, this cave was then visited by an official team and cleared, and a systematic search of all the caves in the cliffs was undertaken.

Cave 2 has an uneven floor, and several small cavities inside on two levels. The archaeologists found only pottery: the remains of several 'scroll jars', a lid and three bowls.

The New Jerusalem text, which is written in Aramaic, is represented by fragmentary manuscripts found in Caves 1, 2 (four tiny fragments only), 4, 5 and 11 dated palaeographically to the late 1st century BCE. It presents a guided tour of an immense city of the imagination. Some call this city the Jerusalem of the last days. Others believe it is only an idealistic layout.

Contents

From the start the writer is concerned with measurements and dimensions. He first provides the measurements for each block of houses: it measures 51 reeds by 51 reeds (1 reed = 7 cubits; a cubit is approximately half a metre, or 1.5 ft.). Surrounding each housing block is a passage 21 reeds wide. Between the blocks are streets six reeds wide. Avenues to the east and west measure 10 reeds. An avenue to the north of the Temple is said to be 18 reeds wide, while those running from south to north measure 9 reeds plus four cubits in width. Through the middle of the city runs an avenue 13 reeds and one cubit (92 cubits, 46 m, 50 yards). The city's streets are paved with white stone, marble and jasper.

Each block has 80 side doors, beside which are 12 main entrances of three reeds with towers 5 reeds square. Measurements for these doors, for the thresholds, stairways and individual houses are also provided. Then their rooms, furniture and windows are described. At this point the preserved text breaks off.

Other fragments of the text suggest that the description may have started with the gates of the Temple and moved outwards to the city. This plan would correspond roughly to that of the Temple Scroll.

Significance

The scroll demonstrates the interest, shown by many of the Qumran texts, in Jerusalem as the holy city of God, to be kept pure and to be restored by God in the near future. The description of this new city is clearly inspired by the account in Ezekiel 40–48 and preserves a tradition reflected also in Revelation 21. It illustrates the obsession of the writers (again, as in many of the scrolls, and particularly in the Temple Scroll, which may be dependent on it) with the imminent end of history and with the city of Jerusalem itself. Jerusalem was the focus of much of the thinking of the writers of the scrolls, many of whom were experiencing a degree of estrangement, physical or ideological, from the city and Temple of their own time.

Factfile

Manuscripts: 1QNJ ar, 2QNJ ar (2Q4), 4QNJ[a-b] ar (4Q554–55), 5QNJ (5Q15), 11QNJ ar (11Q18)
Editors: M. Baillet, J.T. Milik and R. de Vaux (*DJD* 3: 2Q, 5Q); É. Puech (*DJD* 37: 4Q) B. Jongeling (*DJD* 23: 11Q)
Commentary: Licht and M. Chyutin
Script: Late Hasmonaean to Herodian

The Old City of Jerusalem as it is today.

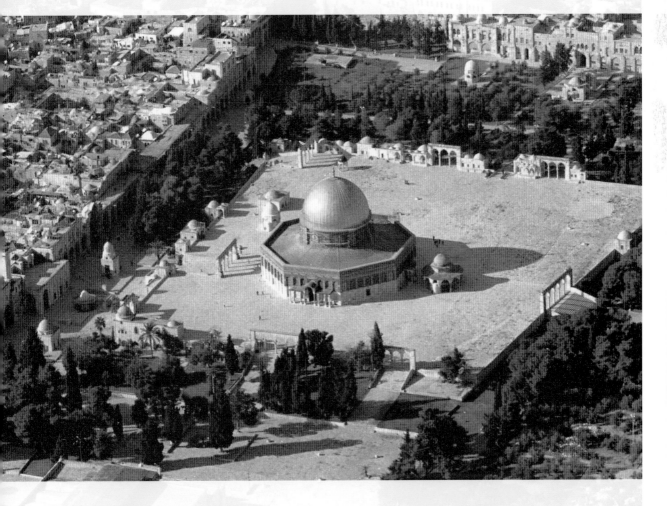

Cave 3

'In the mound of Kokhlit, tithing vessels,...and ephods – the total of the tithe; and the seventh treasure is a second tithe rendered unclean. Its opening is at the edge of the canal on the northern side, six cubits to the immersion bath XAI.' (1:9–11)

Cave 3 was revealed on 14 March 1952, as the result of the systematic search prompted by the Bedouin's discovery of Cave 2 (p. 106). It lies about 600 m (1,970 ft) from Cave 1 (see map, p. 11) and is the most northerly of all the manuscript caves. Its roof had fallen in long ago and the entrance, now narrow and jagged, was covered with debris. Apart from a good deal of pottery (including 40 empty 'scroll jars') and some very small inscribed pieces of leather and papyrus, this cave contained the most enigmatic of all the Qumran texts, written on a scroll of copper that had broken in two. The pieces had been wedged, one on top of the other, against an inner wall. This was the only success achieved by the archaeologists in this particular search along the cliffs near Cave 1.

In 1952, five years after Bedouin first brought their scrolls to Bethlehem and Jerusalem, archaeologists involved in surveying about 250 caves in the Judaean wilderness discovered two inscribed rolls of oxidized copper lying against the wall of Cave 3. These rolls were eventually transported to Manchester, England, where Professor H. Wright Baker of the College of Science and Technology cautiously sliced them into longitudinal sections that could be photographed and studied. Thus it was confirmed that both rolls constituted a single document. Because its language was unlike the literary Hebrew of the other Dead Sea Scrolls, and more like that of the Mishnah (the Jewish lawcode compiled *c.* 200 CE), some have thought it did not derive from the community at Qumran. Its dating is also later than most of the other scrolls: between 50 and 100 CE.

Cave 3, where the Copper Scroll was found, was hard to detect because its roof had collapsed in antiquity.

Factfile
Manuscript: 3Q15
Editors: J.T. Milik and J.M. Allegro
Commentary: A. Wolters, K. P. McCarter and J. Lefkovits
Length: 2.6 m (8 ft 3 in)
Script: Unique

A sheet from the Copper Scroll (3Q15) detailing locations of concealed treasures, probably from the Jerusalem Temple.

In Search of Hidden Treasures

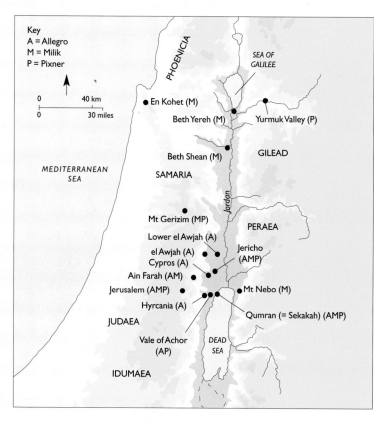

Key
A = Allegro
M = Milik
P = Pixner

0   40 km
0   30 miles

PHOENICIA

SEA OF GALILEE

En Kohet (M)

Beth Yereh (M)

Yurmuk Valley (P)

GILEAD

Beth Shean (M)

SAMARIA

MEDITERRANEAN SEA

Jordan

Mt Gerizim (MP)

PERAEA

Lower el Awjah (A)

el Awjah (A)
Cypros (A)

Jericho (AMP)

Ain Farah (AM)

Jerusalem (AMP)

Mt Nebo (M)

Hyrcania (A)

JUDAEA

Qumran (= Sekakah) (AMP)

Vale of Achor (AP)

DEAD SEA

IDUMAEA

The map shows locations where the treasure may have been hidden according to Allegro, Milik and Pixner.

community's *mebaqqer* or 'inspector' had catalogued its holdings in the Copper Scroll and in a duplicate copy, and hidden them away in case of his death. He wanted any surviving members to be able to recover this treasure. More recently, the view prevails that the treasure must have belonged to the Temple.

J.T. Milik thought the Copper Scroll was 'the work of a crank'. His colleague John M. Allegro, ever interested in sensational finds, took a different view and put together a team to explore around Qumran and Jerusalem in search of the treasures, but nothing came of this venture. In 1983 Bargil Pixner revived the mission to trace the precise hiding places of the ancient writer. Almost a third of the caches he associated with Mt Zion (nos. 1–17). At least four locations he associated with Khirbet Qumran and Jericho (nos. 22, 23, 24, 26). A third area, representing 13 caches, was what had been Batanaea, on the slopes of the Yarmuk river across the Dead Sea (nos. 35–47), and a fourth region was Mt Gerizim near Shechem (Nablus) (no. 60). But it seems unlikely that the treasures would have been so widely scattered.

There have been other treasure hunters. From the late 1960s onwards the American Vendyl Jones has tried to find the ashes of the red heifer (see Numbers 19) based on his reading of the Copper Scroll 6:5, which may refer to a vessel known as a *qalal*. In a twin cave (south of Cave 11) that Jones identified as the scroll's 'Cave of the Column' he claims to have found a reddish substance presumed to be incense. Sceptics remain unconvinced.

The Israeli archaeologist Joseph Patrich was recently successful in discovering a juglet containing what is thought to be balsam oil, not too far from Qumran. But no-one has yet found any of the Copper Scroll treasures. Have they already been found long ago? If Milik was right, and the treasures never existed, why was this piece of very high-grade copper so laboriously inscribed?

When scholars read about the massive quantities of gold and silver presumed hidden in and around Jerusalem, most of them viewed the Copper Scroll from Qumran Cave 3 as nothing more than legend and hyperbole. The German scholar K.G. Kuhn disagreed. He suggested that the Qumran

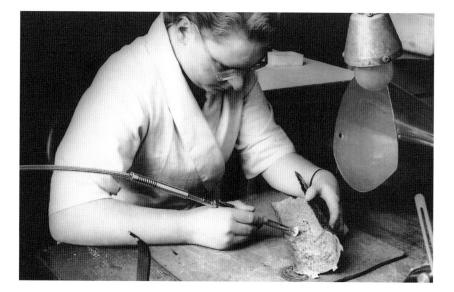

Wright Baker's assistant in Manchester cleans a strip of the freshly-cut Copper Scroll.

Contents

The Copper Scroll enumerates 64 locations where large amounts of gold, silver, coins, vessels, priestly garments, and even scrolls were hidden. These locations are at or under a natural or architectural structure, such as a cistern, courtyard, tomb, cave or monument:

'In the tomb of … the third: one hundred gold bars.' (1:2)

'In the courty[ard of]… in a southerly direction nine cubits: silver and gold vessels of offering, bowls, cups, tubes, libation vessels. In all, six hundred and nine.' (3:13)

'In the tomb which is in the Wadi of Kippah from Jericho to Sekakah, at its entry from Jericho to Sekakah, dig seven cubits, thirty-two talents.' (5:26)

It also mentions, towards the end, the hiding-place of a copy of this list.

Scholars were incredulous after calculating the huge amounts of gold and silver said to be hidden throughout Judaea and its outlying regions. One estimate is that the total exceeds 100 tons of gold and silver combined. Could a small community located at Qumran have possessed such wealth? J.T. Milik, the scroll's official editor, thought he was dealing with an ancient literary fiction. But John Allegro, also on the editorial team and greatly interested in the scroll and responsible for bringing it to Manchester for opening, believed it was genuine, and most scholars today agree with him.

This difference of interpretation is the result of more than scholarly disagreement. Allegro differed from the rest of the editorial team, especially de Vaux, in wishing to publish the newly-deciphered texts as quickly as possible. He was suspicious of the fact that, while he had lobbied hard to get the Copper Scroll opened, and had made the first transcription and translation, he was forbidden to publish this until Milik, who had been assigned this text, had issued his own, official edition. As Milik's edition was delayed further and further, and Allegro's impatience (and suspicions) grew, the Englishman finally released his own edition.

Though there may have been other reasons, the delay with Milik's work and the attempt to prevent Allegro publishing may have been caused by fear that publication of a 'treasure list' would result in a huge Bedouin hunt for loot over the Judaean desert. Is this understandable fear also the reason why Milik, rather implausibly, insisted that this text belonged to a 'well-known' genre of fabled but non-existent treasure trove?

Several features of the scroll make it likely, in fact, to be a realistic and credible historical witness. It is the only document inscribed on copper, a medium of record which would have probably been used for some realistic practical purpose.

Moreover, the copper is of exceptionally high grade. Analysis of the script reveals that at least two engravers were engaged in copying a text that they may not even have been able to read.

Can the hiding places be identified? Although some of the geographical locations mentioned in the scroll are traditional – the Vale of Achor, the Valley of Sekakah, Jericho, Doq, Siloa, Bet-Eshdatain, and Mt Gerizim – many others are probably identified by ancient names not preserved in traditional historical records. The hiding places chosen by the author seem quite prosaic and typical of places where Jews hid themselves and their possessions throughout history. In four cases caves are mentioned, and water conduits or reservoirs in 13 cases. Underground chambers or cavities are listed 14 times. Thus, although the amount of hidden bullion seems fantastic, the types of hiding places seem very realistic.

Scholars pore over a facsimile column of the Copper Scroll at a conference in Manchester.

If the treasure is real, whose was it? While some scholars believe that it may have belonged to the Essenes, the view currently prevails that these caches contained the property of the Jerusalem Temple treasury, hidden on the eve of the city's destruction by the Romans in 70 CE. Seemingly against this view is the fact that the community settled at Qumran had cut itself off from all political and religious interaction with the wicked priesthood and people of Jerusalem. But during the war other priests, perhaps more sympathetic to the

presumably intended to be fixed to a wall: it was not intended to be rolled up, and the rolling actually caused rivets between the plates to fall out *before* it was deposited – hence the existence of *two* rolls. The identity of several place-names in the first four columns of the scroll is also uncertain, as are the Greek letters that conclude some of the treasure entries. These letters have been construed as abbreviations for the Greek names of the presumed owners, or of Greek measurements, or some kind of code.

John Allegro examines the two rolls of the Copper Scroll before having them brought to Manchester.

groups responsible for the scrolls, had taken control of the Temple. Accordingly, it is not at all improbable that, had a sectarian settlement existed at Qumran, a list of the hiding places was deposited in its vicinity.

Doubt has long been expressed in some quarters that this scroll has anything to do with the remaining cave scrolls, and suggestions that it was deposited separately from the other manuscripts in Cave 3. It was even suggested that the treasure, and the scroll, belonged to the time of the Bar Kokhba war (128–35 CE). That view, too, is nowadays less popular.

The scroll is, in any event, a mysterious document. Originally it would have been a long plaque,

The treasures have never been found, despite recent informal searches (many unpublicized). One of these, conducted by the American Vendyl Jones, involved several seasons emptying caves, with the aid of student volunteers and with varying degrees of approval from his Israeli colleagues, in a search for Temple treasure. A search by the Israeli archaeologist Joseph Patrich discovered a jar thought to have contained balsam. In all probability, if the treasures were real, they were either recovered or looted long ago. But if the Copper Scroll was concealed along with the other manuscripts, it could furnish an important clue to their concealment.

Back in Jordan, the newly dissected Copper Scroll is exhibited.

Cave 4

In September 1952 the Ta'amireh Bedouin discovered a cave located only a few hundred feet across the ravine west of Khirbet Qumran. They soon put about 15,000 fragments on the market. It became an urgent matter to find and excavate the cave, and the following month the archaeologists were looking at a large, oval chamber, opening onto two inner chambers, hewn from the side of the Qumran plateau overlooking the Wadi Qumran Valley. In the walls were holes that had been pierced, probably for inserting wooden shelving. About 100 fragmentary manuscripts were salvaged, and several hundred more gradually purchased, by the Jordanian government and by academic and religious institutions. A few items of domestic pottery were also discovered – parts of jars, lids, bowls, jugs, a pot, a juglet and a lamp.

But how could such a huge, unexpected influx be handled? De Vaux set about creating an editorial team. American, French, British and German institutions were invited to send their candidates, each of whom were assigned certain sorts of texts: biblical manuscripts were entrusted to Frank M. Cross, Jr; Jozef T. Milik, John Strugnell and Claus-Hunno. Hunzinger (who joined the team very briefly) were given non-biblical manuscripts and John M. Allegro the biblically-derived texts. Abbé Jean Starcky was assigned several Hebrew and Aramaic manuscripts and Monsignor Patrick W. Skehan some further biblical manuscripts, particularly those written in palaeo-Hebrew script (see p. 70).

The later scandal over non-publication (see p. 22) centred on these editors and their Cave 4 texts. As it turned out, John Allegro published his 29 texts in 1968, which by comparison with his colleagues was fairly quick; but several years later his colleague Strugnell published an extensive critique. De Vaux and Milik published the tefillin (phylacteries), mezuzot and targums in 1977, and M. Baillet published 39 more manuscripts in 1982. In 1985 and 1986 Strugnell's Harvard students Carol Newsom and Eileen Schuller published texts from his batch: the Songs of the Sabbath Sacrifice and Non-Biblical Psalms. In the 1990s, under the leadership of Emanuel Tov, the pace accelerated, and volumes of the official edition appeared. Publication of the Cave 4 manuscripts, in about 27 volumes, will be complete within a few years.

Cave 4 is unique in the number and range of its texts, most of which are preserved in very small scraps. Many of the original manuscripts contain works found in other Qumran caves. Was this specially-hewn cave, lying so close to the ruins, a library for the inhabitants of Qumran? Of all the circumstantial evidence linking the scrolls with the settlement, Cave 4 is by far the strongest.

In the following description of the major texts from Cave 4, we have not followed the chronological order of publication, but begin with those texts based directly on the Bible (commentaries, translations), followed by those linked to the scriptures more indirectly, then finally texts that seem to have a non-exegetical function. Nearly every Qumran text, in fact, is imbued with the language of the Jewish scriptures, but this ordering of the contents will enable to reader to follow the way in which scripture is used, from direct comment to more general interpretation, to liturgy using biblical language, and finally to matters well beyond the orbit of the scriptures.

(Main picture) Looking up from the floor of the Wadi Qumran at Cave 4. (Inset) The interior of the cave, showing holes for shelving.

Factfile

Manuscripts:
4QCommGen
(4Q252–54)
Editors: J.M. Allegro
and G.J. Brooke
Commentary: M.
Bernstein
Script: Late Hasmonaean

The Commentaries on Genesis

'Timnah was the concubine of Eliphaz, son of Esau, and she bore him Amalek (Genesis 36:12). He was the one that Saul ki[lled]. As it was said through Moses concerning the end of time: "I will blot out the memory of Amalek from under the heavens".' (4Q252 4:1–3, quoting Deuteronomy 25:19)

these represent different versions of a commentary, if not different commentaries. The best-preserved of these manuscripts (4Q252) includes both the flood story (Genesis 6) and the 'Blessings of Jacob' (Genesis 49), though it did not cover every biblical episode in between. The Joseph story, for instance, is apparently omitted.

Two of the other manuscripts also refer to the flood or to Noah's ark (4Q253 and 4Q254a – the 'a' referring to the fact that this manuscript turned out

(Right) The largest fragment of 4Q252, the most extensive extant Commentary on Genesis.

The Commentaries on Genesis consist of four manuscripts, comprising 29 fragments. Together they are sometimes called the 'Genesis Pesher', but the word *pesher* occurs only once in one of the commentaries, while much of the text is paraphrase of the biblical story, not the characteristic eschatologically-focused phrase-by-phrase exegesis of the *pesharim* (see p. 96). Originally thought of as a single commentary, it is now believed that

to be a slightly different work from 4Q254, but there was no room to renumber it). 4Q252 enhances the biblical account by synchronizing the day of the month and the day of the week on which each event occurred. There is also a clear statement that the year consisted of 364 days, not 12 lunar months (see p. 133 on the calendar). 4Q252 also offers an explanation of why Noah cursed Canaan and not Ham (God had already blessed all Noah's sons). It

also identifies Esau's grandson as Amalek, the ancestor of the nation that Saul destroyed (1 Samuel 14:48; 15:3–7).

The author of 4Q252 also bolsters his argument by citing other biblical texts, from 2 Chronicles, Deuteronomy, 1 Samuel and Jeremiah. For example, the blessing of Judah (Genesis 49) is read as fulfilled in Jeremiah 33:17, which concerns the longevity of the Davidic line. 4Q254a introduces a note of eschatological warning by having the raven sent out by Noah returning to inform 'latter generations' about the future. Another fragmentary passage suggests that Noah's departure from the ark was commemorated annually (4Q254a). It seems, then, that at least this Commentary is partly intended to present the flood story as relevant for its own time, as a paradigm and warning of God's final judgment on the world.

(Above and left) The flood story is discussed in detail in the Commentaries on Genesis, and is depicted in a 17th-century painting by Giovanni Benedetto Castiglione (above) and in a series of mosaics in the Basilica di San Marco, Venice (left).

Targums to Leviticus and Job

'[He shall sprinkle the blood upon it (the altar) with his finger 7 times], cleansing it and making it holy [from the imp]urities [of the Israelites].' (4QtgLev frag. 2:2–3=Lev. 16:19)

The term *targum* refers to an Aramaic rendering of a biblical book. Plenty of evidence exists for the creation of such targums after the Second Jewish Revolt against Rome (132–35 CE), and there is good evidence (see e.g. Luke 4) that by the 1st century CE it was usual in the synagogues for the scriptural reading to be followed by an oral rendering in Aramaic. The written rabbinic targums, dating

(Above) As well as Hebrew scriptural texts such as Leviticus, pictured here, the caves contained Aramaic translations.

'Gird up your loins like a man, and I will interrogate you. Answer me: where were you when I created the earth? Tell me, if you know. Who determined its shape? – if you know – and who held the measuring-line? Or, upon what are its foundations set? Or who laid its cornerstone?' (11QtgJob 30:1–4 = Job 38:3–6)

from a later time (mostly medieval), range from the fairly literal to the highly fanciful, but these two examples from Qumran are straightforward translations. They also show that written targums

The Missing Song of Miriam?

Philo of Alexandria described a Jewish group called the *Therapeutae*, who led a simple life devoted to dining, philosophizing and worshipping together. After the evening meal, the president (*proedros*) spoke on the holy scriptures, then launched into singing. He was then joined by a choir of men and women:

'They rise up all together and standing in the middle of the dining room form themselves into two choirs, one of men and one of women, the leader and precentor chosen for each being the most honoured amongst them and also the most musical. They sing hymns to God…
…they mix and both become a single choir, a copy of the choir set up of old beside the Red Sea in honour of the wonders there wrought…both men and women forming a single choir that sang hymns of thanksgiving to God their saviour, the men led by the prophet Moses and the women by the prophetess Miriam.' (Philo, *On the Contemplative Life*, 83–87)

In the biblical version, Moses and the Israelites sing the song (Exodus 15:1) and Miriam sings the first two lines later (verse 20). Scholars think the song

may have been originally attributed to Miriam and later transferred to Moses, leaving Miriam only the echo. Philo has his own solution to this curiosity. The 'Reworked Pentateuch' text from Cave 4 has another solution: it restores a possible Song of Miriam in frag. 6a col. 2 and frag. 6c:

'…you have despised…
for pride…
you are great, a saviour…
the hope of the enemy has perished
and…has stopped…
they have perished in the mighty waters,
the enemy…and lifts up to their height.
[You have given a ransom]…
…[he who ac]ts proudly.'

The dance of Miriam, from a 14th-century Spanish illuminated haggadah.

appeared earlier than was previously thought.

The small fragment of the Leviticus targum that is preserved (eight verses) contains a translation of Leviticus 16:12–15 and 18–21, dealing with the Day of Atonement and the purification of the Temple.

Why the writers and readers of the Qumran scrolls would need an Aramaic translation remains a puzzle. For while many Aramaic-speaking Jews sacred writings, as well as perhaps the most difficult Hebrew. So the presence of an Aramaic version is not entirely surprising.

Rabbinic tradition relates that Rabban Gamaliel, who was, according to Acts 22:3, the teacher of Paul of Tarsus, hid a Targum to Job. Two Job Targums were found, in Qumran Caves 4 and 11. The Cave 4 targum of Job (4Q157) preserves very little:

did not know Hebrew (hence the need for targums), the readers of the Qumran scrolls must have been able to understand it quite well, and, indeed, many probably spoke it. But while Leviticus is comparatively easy Hebrew, Job is not, and it contains a large number of words found nowhere else in the bits of an Aramaic translation of Job 3:5–9 and 4:16–5:4. The Cave 11 manuscript is in considerably better condition. Running to over 28 columns, it provides an Aramaic rendering of Job 17:14–42:4. Both manuscripts offer a fairly literal translation, apparently based upon the traditional Hebrew text.

Factfile

Manuscripts: 4Q156 (Leviticus), 4Q157, 11Q10 (Job)

Editors: R. de Vaux and J.T. Milik (*DJD* 6: Leviticus and Job); J.P.M. van der Ploeg and A.S. van der Woude (11QJob)

Commentary: J.P.M. van der Ploeg and A.S. van der Woude

Script: Hasmonaean (Leviticus), Late Herodian (Job)

Bruce Zuckerman (on the right) and Stephen Reed view the unrolled Job Targum from Cave 11 (11Q10).

The 'Reworked Pentateuch'

'And Jacob asked him, saying, "Tell me, I pray, your name". [And he said, "Why do you ask] me [my name]?" Then he blessed him there. And he said to him, "May the Lord make you fruitful and bl[ess] you. [May he fill you with knowledge] and understanding and save you from all violence and…until this day and for everlasting generations."' (4Q158 frags 1–2, 6–9; cf. Genesis 32:29)

Also once known as 'Pentateuchal Paraphrase', the four manuscripts 4Q364–67, consisting of about 186 fragments, are thought to represent the remains of a lengthy composition containing the biblical text from Genesis to Deuteronomy with several additions, omissions and new textual sequences. If they are all copies of the same work, that work, according to Stegemann (see p. 76) would have required a scroll of 25 m (Tov and White settle on 22–27 m). A fifth manuscript, previ-ously published as 'Biblical Paraphrases' (4Q158), is sometimes thought to belong to this 'Reworked Pentateuch'.

The main form of rewriting in the 'Reworked Pentateuch' is topical juxtaposition (the linking of passages that deal with the same subject matter), but free composition is also introduced at times. Both techniques seem to have the aim of making the text easier to understand and more edifying. For example, 4Q364 frag. 3 preserves a 'blessing' before Genesis 28:6 that appears in no version of the Bible. Frag. 4b–c col. ii joins Genesis 30:20–26 with the 'angelic speech' of Genesis 31:11–13. Frag. 23a–b col. 1 brings together Numbers 20:17–18 (but in the version of the Samaritan Pentateuch, not the received Hebrew text) with Deuteronomy 2:8–14. 4Q365 frag. 6a col. ii 6c preserves vestiges of a poetic interlude slightly reminiscent of the Song of the Sea (Exodus 15:1, 7, 10) preceding Exodus 15:22–26 (see p. 118), and frag. 23 preserves an extensive addition to Leviticus 23:42–24:2, which prescribes the tribal order for bringing the wood

A depiction of the Exodus from the 14th-century Golden Haggadah. The story appears in a slightly adjusted form in the 'Reworked Pentateuch'.

offering for sacrifice (some scholars, however, view this fragment as another copy of the Temple Scroll cols 23–24. It may have been an independent work used as a source for such a writing.) Frag. 28 contains a combination of Numbers 4:47–49 and 7:1; both deal with the temple service. Similarly, 4Q366 frag. 4 col. 1 connects two passages about the festival of Booths (Numbers 29:32–30:1 and Deuteronomy 16:13–14).

One aim, then, of this work in its various manuscript forms is to enhance the coherence of the scriptural account by providing links within the biblical story and adding explanations, rather as the Temple Scroll (see p. 156) amplifies and rearranges biblical laws into a more rational sequence. But in this process much has also been left out. It is unlikely that any of the five manuscript versions of this composition contained the whole of the Pentateuch in a reworked form. Indeed, there is no extant evidence in any of the five manuscripts for 53 of the 187 chapters of the Pentateuch.

In fact, it is not entirely clear that 4Q158 is a manuscript of the same work as 4Q364–67, although the editors of the 'Reworked Pentateuch' believed so. John Allegro, the editor of 4Q158, called these fragments a paraphrase only because some of them *resemble* portions of Genesis and Exodus; very little accords with the known text of the Pentateuch. For example, fragment 14 seems to echo a liturgical tradition associated with the escape from Egypt, and fragments 9–12 appear to be an abridgement of the laws related to the 'goring ox' in Exodus 21. But there is also some rearrangement of the scriptural text: fragments 6–8 join Exodus 20 and Deuteronomy 5 and 18, which combine Sinai traditions and the future-orientated 'prophet like Moses' tradition. However, that juxtaposition is also made in the Samaritan Pentateuch, and the author of this Qumran text may well have been working from this version rather than what became the standard, Masoretic text.

One of the concerns of 4Q158 (and perhaps the other manuscripts too), is to link together Moses and Abraham, the two greatest figures of Jewish ancestry. This is also one of the aims of Jubilees (see p. 102) in having the patriarchs anticipate the Mosaic law that would be given later on Sinai. Hence, the promise of land to Abraham and the giving of the Law are presented as two sides of the same coin.

The existence of these fragments shows clearly that Palestinian Jews of the Second Temple period felt it entirely acceptable to handle the biblical text in a variety of ways: to paraphrase, rearrange, omit and supplement it. This did not mean, however, that they were careless of the actual wording when such exegesis was needed – as the *pesharim* demonstrate. There were, in other words, many ways of understanding and using the scriptures.

Where Do These Fragments Belong?

The five manuscript versions of the 'Reworked Pentateuch' (4Q158 and 4Q364–67) were perhaps in their original state the longest of the Dead Sea Scrolls, a rewriting of the entire Pentateuch as much as 25 m (82 ft) long. But one manuscript originally assigned to this work, 4Q365a, has always raised questions. Its fragments do not cite biblical passages.

Yigael Yadin attributed 4Q365a fragments 2, 3 and 23 to a copy of the Temple Scroll, while Michael Wise took them as sources for the Temple Scroll. Sidnie A. White (Crawford), the editor of 4Q365a along with Emanuel Tov, thinks they may represent a different recension or edition of the Temple Scroll, because frag. 2, col. 1, lines 8–10, which overlaps with 11QT 38:12-15, seems to reproduce a shorter version of the passage. Fragments 1 and 3 cover festival materials and building specifications, like the Temple Scroll, but frag. 5, which concerns the visibility of wheels, does not fit at all. So 4Q365a is a real puzzle, its different fragments seeming to belong in different places.

This case exemplifies the kind of problems facing a scroll editor in assigning fragments to their original manuscripts, and in identifying the works that those manuscripts contained. This is not always easy, and especially when the remains are fragmentary the character of the whole work can be elusive. For some scholars the 'Reworked Pentateuch' is more or less a reorganization of older classical materials, or a collection of excerpts with some additional comments here and there. The Temple Scroll (which is much more complete) differs in that it reorganizes biblical material in a systematic way, though it also includes non-biblical materials.

But what the 'Reworked Pentateuch' and other Qumran 'parabiblical' scrolls demonstrate is the variety of ways of handling the sacred text – rearranging, expanding and paraphrasing, as well as interpreting.

The editor's problem: hundreds of tiny fragments to be assembled into documents and manuscripts.

Factfile

Manuscripts: 4Q378–79
Editor: C.A. Newsom
Script: 'Developed Herodian'

(Main picture) Jericho rebuilt: the modern city seen from the ruins of the ancient one.

Apocryphon of Joshua

'…they [cr]ossed (the river) on dry ground in [the fi]rst month of the forty-f[irst] year of their exodus from the lan[d] of Egypt. That was a jubilee year at the beginning of their entry into the land of Canaan. And the Jordan overflows its banks from the f[our]th month until the wheat harvest.' (4Q379 frag. 12, cf. Joshua 4:22,19)

Two manuscripts, in 70 fragments, have been entitled 'Apocryphon of Joshua' (previously 'Psalms of Joshua'). Although many of the 41 fragments of 4Q379 reflect a possible relationship to the biblical book of Joshua, many preserve so little of the original context that reconstruction is difficult. Certain fragments use language from psalms, praise, and prayer (frag. 18, frags 12 and 22, frag. 27), others mention cities connected with Joshua: Aroer (frag. 2; see Joshua 12:2; 13:9, 16; Numbers 32:34) and Bethel (Joshua 8).

Newsom regards the work as a farewell speech by Joshua, and a couple of fragments preserve enough of the original narrative context to enable one to discern its possible outline, but the order of fragments is uncertain. However it does have some text in common with another Qumran composition, 4QTestimonia (4Q175; see p. 130), which includes the curse of Joshua on anyone who would rebuild Jericho.

Contents

4Q379 fragment 12 parallels Joshua 3:13–16, in narrating the crossing of the Jordan river in the first month of the 41st year of the exodus from Egypt. Like the book of Jubilees, it notes that this event occurred in a jubilee year during the wheat harvest. Fragment 22, col. 2 relates to Joshua 6, the capture of Jericho. A passage lacking in the book of Joshua but recurring in Testimonia suggests that this curse would extend to the ramparts of the Daughter of Zion (Jerusalem).

The other manuscript (4Q378), in 29 fragments, is less clearly related to Joshua, and seems more akin to Deuteronomy. Fragment 6 mentions a prayer of intercession, while in frag. 14 the Israelites are mourning the death of Moses. Fragment 22 refers to Moses, Joshua and God's promise to Abraham. Fragments 12 and 22 col. 2 of 4Q379 do illustrate a clear relationship with Joshua; frag. 12 adds chronological information about crossing the Jordan, and frag. 22 seems to quote the text of Joshua but in an expanded form.

A text found at Masada and edited by S. Talmon in *Journal of Jewish Studies* 47 (1996), pp. 128–39, is also entitled 'A Joshua Apocryphon' and, in the opinion of the editor, originated at Qumran. But it bears no obvious relationship to 4Q378 or 379, and its connection with the story of the book of Joshua is in any case uncertain. It relates a battle in which God gives Israel victory.

The Words of Joshua

The Testimonia's last section begins 'When Joshua had finished offering praise and thanks' and goes on to quote his curse on the rebuilder of Jericho. The same words are preserved in the Apocryphon of Joshua (4QapocJosh[b], 4Q379), frag. 22.

Was one text copied from the other? If so, which? Most scholars argue that the Apocryphon of Joshua must have preceded the Testimonia since the latter is a collection of prophecies from authoritative prophetic sources. The Apocryphon of Joshua, although quite fragmentary, seems to be an independent composition. The strongest argument for the priority of the Apocryphon of Joshua comes in 1:7, which reads 'blessed be Yahweh [God of Israel]'. Although the Testimonia begins with an allusion to Joshua's worship, the quote has been extracted from a larger context. The Psalms of Joshua provides such a context.

The editor of the Apocryphon of Joshua, Carol Newsom, suggests that it was written by a scribe in a non-Qumran context. But because of its full Hebrew spelling (see p. 73), she and others believe that Testimonia was copied at the Qumran scribal school. Another scholar, Hans Burgmann, noted that the name Ephraim in the Apocryphon was understood positively. As he understood Qumran thought, the Qumran community despised Ephraim, which was used as a code name for the Pharisees.

Possibly, however, both texts draw from an older source. It is not unlikely that the words of Joshua belonged to an older but superseded edition of the book of Joshua itself.

Joshua's encounter with an angel dressed as a warrior and holding a sword, as shown in the 10th-century Byzantine Joshua Roll.

Tobit

'[The angel said to him, 'Catch and] hold the fish!'. And the young man caught [the fish and held it and brought it] onto dry land. [And the angel said to the young man, "Spl]it it open and take out its [skin, heart and liver, and heap them in your] hand, but [throw away] its intestines, [because its skin, heart] and liver [are good medi-cine]…[The young man cooked part of the] fish and ate it.' (4QTobit^b, frag. 3, lines 8–10 = Tobit 6:4–6)

Tobit has long been known as one of the books of the Apocrypha, and its Greek text was thought to have been a translation, though whether from Hebrew or Aramaic was uncertain. It still is, for Tobit has now been found at Qumran in five manu-scripts and in both languages (four in Hebrew, one in Aramaic). It is fairly fully preserved, and the most complete manuscripts, 4Q196–97, have been dated palaeographically to about the middle of the 1st century BCE.

The book is a tale of piety tinged with humour. Tobit is a truly pious individual living in Nineveh, who interrupts a feast to bury a fellow-Jew. He then falls asleep next to the city wall and bird droppings fall into his eyes, causing immediate blindness. In the following chapters Tobit's son Tobias (or Tobiah) is concerned to retrieve his father's money and to find an appropriate wife from his own fami-ly. He travels to Media, part of the Persian empire lying east and north of the Tigris river, with a cer-tain Raphael (a name meaning 'God heals') who,

A Marriage Ritual

Tobit 8 contains two 'marriage prayers'. From approximately the same date, the 19 fragments of 4Q502, says Maurice Baillet, are a marriage ritual. Joseph Baumgarten, however, says they are a celebration of old age.

Fragments 1–3
'3…his wife for…4…to procreate off-spring…these…5…which…holy ones praising God…6…to be holy…for him, a daughter of truth and who walks…'

Fragments 7–10
'2…praise…3…together…4 […They shall bless the] God of Israel, and beginning to speak, they shall [say] 5 [Blessed is the God of Israel who]…the time of happiness to praise his name 6…adults and youths…'

Fragment 19
'1 And he will sit with him in the assembly of the holy on[es…] 2 seed of blessing, old men and old w[omen…] 5 and virgins, boys and gi[rls…] 4 together with all of us…'

unknown to him, is a guardian angel. On the way Tobias catches a fish, and Raphael counsels him to save its gall, heart and liver. It turns out that smoke from the heart and the liver will prevent him from being killed by the demon Asmodeus on his wed-ding night and the gall will cure his father's blind-ness. Tobias' bride-to-be has the misfortune of having lost seven previous husbands to Asmodeus. On his marriage night the smell of the liver thwarts Asmodeus and, after feasting properly at the home of his bride in Media, Tobias returns home, where the fish gall is applied to his father's eyes. Suddenly Tobit sees again. Not only that, his son has returned with a proper bride.

In this beautiful story, one of the best-crafted in all of biblical literature, instruction, thanksgiving,

(Above left) 4Qpap Tob^a ar is the most extensive of the Qumran Tobit manuscripts.

(Above left) Tobias with the angel who accompanied him on his journey, by Pollaiuolo (c. 1432–98).

(Left) 4QTob^e frag. 6 contains a Hebrew text of Tobit 12:20–13:4.

prayer and almsgiving strike a pleasing balance. Misfortune turns to blessing, if one believes and does good to others.

The story is hardly a product of any Jewish sect, and its presence among the Qumran texts is rather strange: most of the non-scriptural texts are nevertheless closely linked to scriptural characters or values, and this is not. Although taken into the Christian canon, there is no evidence, by way of citation or allusions, that the writers of the scrolls regarded this work as scriptural.

Factfile

Manuscript: 4QEn^a-g, 4QEnastr^a-d (4Q201–12)
Editor: J.T. Milik
Commentary: M. Black and J.C. VanderKam
Script: Hasmonaean to Herodian

The Books of Enoch

'Before these things Enoch was hidden, and no human being knew where he was hidden, and where he abode, and what had become of him. And his activities had to do with the Watchers, and his days were with the holy ones. And I, Enoch, was blessing the Lord of majesty and the King of the ages, and lo, the Watchers called me – Enoch the scribe – and said to me: "Enoch, you scribe of righteousness, go, declare to the Watchers of the heaven who have left the high heaven, the holy eternal place, and have defiled themselves with women…you shall have no peace nor forgiveness of sin…"' (1 Enoch 12:1–6)

Until the discoveries at Qumran, the book of Enoch (1 Enoch) was known as a collection of apocalypses, in Ethiopic, containing the divine wisdom Enoch received from the angelic world during his stay with them. Manuscripts of five component parts of 1 Enoch have now come to light in their original Aramaic. These parts are the Book of Watchers (Ethiopic chs 1–36), the Book of

The myth of the fallen angels is only briefly mentioned in Genesis, but was of great significance to the community at Qumran. Rubens painted this interpretation c. 1619/22.

Astronomical Secrets (chs 72–82), the Dream Book (chs 83–90), and Enoch's Epistle (chs 91–108). The Book of Parables (chs 37–71) is absent. The Book of Astronomical Secrets (represented by fragments of 4 manuscripts, 4QEnastr^a-d), is also longer and more detailed at Qumran. Related to Enoch, but apparently an independent work, is the so-called Book of Giants, which the editor, J.T. Milik, considered an original part of an ancient Enochic Pentateuch, later replaced by the Parables.

In Genesis Enoch lived to be 365 years old, and God suddenly took him away. Nowhere else in the Hebrew Bible is he mentioned, but he was certainly known about. Ben Sira (44:16; 49:14) praises him, and Jubilees claims he was the first mortal to learn

writing. That is, he was the progenitor of literary culture. Jude 14–15 quotes Enoch 1:9 concerning God's judgment against sinners, and Jude 6 is a transparent reference to the punishment of the Watchers in the netherworld (Enoch 10:4–6, 12–16; 12; cf. 2 Peter 2:4–5). The Enochic tradition is now also recognized as an important background to many of the Qumran scrolls.

Cave 4 has preserved fragments, but no extensive portions of the book of Enoch or of any of its parts. Chapters 16–17, much of 24, 72–75, and 80–81 are missing, and only extremely brief passages from about 44 chapters survive containing in many cases not even a complete sentence. The 11 manuscripts date from the early 2nd century BCE to the Herodian period, and at least the Astronomical Book predates the book of Daniel.

As contained in the full Ethiopic form, the Book of Watchers (which comes first) tells of rebellious angels ('Watchers') who descended to earth and impregnated women, who bore them gigantic children; these Watchers taught the secrets of making weapons of war and ornaments, sorcery,

spells, and the cutting of medicinal roots. Violence spread on the earth, and the angels were sentenced to be bound for 70 generations until the day of judgment. Enoch is permitted to intercede, but is ordered to reprimand them. He is whisked away to heaven from where he can see the universe – mountains, trees, the centre of the earth, the paradise of the righteous and even the tree of knowledge.

A central feature of the Enochic corpus is the belief that sin originated in the heavenly world (no mention of Adam or Eve), that the course of human history is pre-ordained, and that the true calendar is determined by the sun, not the moon. All these tenets are also prominent in the non-biblical scrolls from Qumran. The Enoch traditions may well have been considered as authoritative

4QEnoch^a fragment 1, pieces c, d and e, cols 2 and 3, containing parts of 1 Enoch chapters 2–8, from the Book of Watchers.

The Book of Astronomical Secrets describes the courses of the heavenly bodies throughout the year. The Dream Book tells in symbolic form the history of Israel from the fall of the angels to the Maccabean triumph and the final divine judgment. The Epistle consists of ethical admonitions to Enoch's children, embedded in which is the 'Apocalypse of Weeks', measuring the history of the world, like Jubilees, in 50- (or 49)-year epochs.

by the Qumran community and other groups. They directly influenced the Book of Jubilees (see p. 102) and, in turn, the Damascus Document. Whether a form of 'Enochic Judaism' can be separated from 'Mosaic Judaism', with which it merged but by which it was largely supplanted, is an interesting and important question currently under discussion.

Other Ancient Works Preserved in Cave 4

The literature associated with Enoch indicates the willingness of Jewish writers in the Graeco-Roman period to collect or create traditions of wisdom in the form of revelations about the future and with the authority of well-known ancient figures, and the tendency to imbue these characters

tion. The Qumran caves, especially Cave 4, have preserved fragments of portions of testaments ascribed to Naphtali (4Q215) and to Judah (3Q7; 4Q484; 4Q538) – possibly parts of a cycle of 12 Testaments of the Patriarchs, such as later existed in Greek. There are also Testaments of Joseph (4Q539), Amram (4Q543–48) and Qahat (4Q542), and Jacob addresses his priestly son Levi in the so-called Aramaic Levi Document (4Q213–14). Most of these combine ethical instruction with predictions of the future.

(Above right) 4Q386 (4QPseudo-Ezekiel[b]), fragments 1 and 2, which contain a rewritten version of the vision of the dry bones (Ezekiel 37).

(Below) A 6th–7th-century coptic wood relief of Moses holding the Tablets of the Law.

with great piety and foresight. Jubilees consists formally of a revelation to Moses by an angel on Sinai, while Enoch learns from his travels to heaven. The Genesis Apocryphon dwells on the virtues of Noah and Abraham; and Noah himself is the subject of many other fragmentary texts, perhaps because, as the survivor of the last great worldwide devastation, he was a model for those who expected to be saved from the coming judgment.

A popular literary form was the Testament, a farewell speech or death-bed admoni-

Words assigned to Moses are plentiful (1Q22, 29; 2Q21; 4Q374–75, perhaps 4Q376, 4Q377–78, 4Q388a, 4Q389) and there are also apocrypha of Joshua (4Q378–79), Samuel (4Q160), Elisha (4Q481a), Zedekiah (4Q470) and Jeremiah (4Q384–85b), as well as Pseudo-Ezekiel (4Q385–86) and Pseudo-Daniel (4Q243–45; 4Q551?) texts. If not all these can be confidently attributed owing to their fragmentary nature, the cumulative evidence is strong that such attribution was popular.

David traditions are also represented in 11QPs[a] (see p. 160), which presents him as a wise man whose prolific production of psalms and songs came through prophecy. 2Q22, apparently the words of a mighty warrior, is also possibly connected with David. The proliferation of such traditions shows that the scriptures far from exhausted the stock of stories about Israel's past: indeed, they seem to have inspired a great deal of creativity. On the other hand, some of the non-scriptural texts may be as ancient as any scriptural ones and may have originated independently.

The Florilegium

'He has commanded that a sanctuary of men be built for himself, that there they may send up, like the smoke of incense, the works of thanksgiving.' (4Q174 1:7)

This text subtly combines scriptural passages to make points about events and figures of the 'last days' (as the Qumran scrolls usually refer to the end-times). This is also a feature of several Qumran writings, especially the Melchizedek text from Cave 11. The passages used in the Florilegium include 2 Samuel 7:10, Deuteronomy 23:2–3 and 2 Samuel 7:11–14. There are also allusions to Amos 9:11, Psalms 1:1, Isaiah 8:11, Ezekiel 44:10 (cf. 37:24–28), Psalms 2:1 and Daniel 12:10.

2 Samuel 7:10–14 is central to the theme of the work, for it contains God's promise of a house to David. In 2 Samuel, that 'house' means a dynasty; in Chronicles, it means the temple (God's 'house'); in the Qumran text the house is both of these, but also the community. The point of quoting Psalm 1:1 is that God had separated a certain group from following the ways of the people, that is, the Gentiles. Isaiah 8:11 and Ezekiel 44:10 show that an elect group will stand in the trial at the end of days. Finally, Daniel 12:10 confirms that the wise ones, the *maskilim*, are those who understand God's words and plans in the end-time. These are none other than the 'children of light'.

This 'human house' (literally 'sanctuary of Adam') will exist as a symbolic temple, practising 'the whole Law' and thereby offering up sweet scents of incense to God. But a literal sense may persist as well. There is to be a 'branch of David' who, together with the 'Interpreter of the Law', will lead the 'children of light'. Thus, by a mechanism that is very similar to that of the Melchizedek midrash (see p. 162), scripture, through various texts, is made to reveal the sect as the heirs of the divine promise to David.

Annette Steudel has argued that this Florilegium belongs with a text also known as 4QCatena A (4Q177), the two forming a single text that she calls the 'Eschatological Midrash' (midrash means 'interpretation' and is commonly used of a range of Jewish exegetical writings). To support her argument, Steudel not only points to the similarity of script between the two texts and the continuity of content across them, but also uses the physical reconstruction methods of her teacher, Hartmut Stegemann (see p 76).

Factfile
Manuscript: 4QFlor (4Q174)
Editor: J.M. Allegro (*DJD* 5)
Commentary: G.J. Brooke, A. Steudel
Length: 4 columns preserved
Script: Herodian

Daniel and the Dead Sea Scrolls

The book of Daniel, it is generally agreed by biblical scholars, was written in the middle of the 2nd century BCE, not long before the majority of the scrolls. The book appears to stem from a group calling themselves *maskilim* ('wise'), who see their task as instructing the *rabbim* (literally the 'many') (see Daniel 12:3). Both these terms are found in the Community Rule to designate respectively the leaders and the remainder of the members of the *yahad*.

Daniel chapter 9 also contains a calendrical reckoning of Jewish history that appears to be related to Enoch, Jubilees and the Melchidezek fragments, all found at Qumran, while the prayer that precedes this reckoning is very similar to parts of the Words of the Heavenly Lights (4QDibHam, 4Q504–06).

As well as eight manuscripts of the book of Daniel, the Qumran caves also contained small fragments of three manuscripts of a 'Pseudo-Daniel' composition (4Q243–45) and a text in Aramaic containing a prayer of the Babylonian king Nabonidus (4Q242):

'…[I, Nabonidus] was afflicted with a malignant swelling, by the decree of the [Most] High, in Teiman, and was banished far from human society until I prayed to God and an exorcist forgave my sin. He was a Je[w] from [the exiles]…'

This looks remarkably like a version of the story in Daniel 4, which features Nebuchadnezzar, but which scholars long ago suspected of originating as a story about Nabonidus, who retreated from Babylon to Teiman. This king's name, plus the anonymity of the Jew, suggest we have here an older version of the story.

Close connections between those responsible for Daniel and for the scrolls have often been claimed, with some plausibility, though the nature of these connections is still unclear.

Daniel in the lions' den, from an 11th-century Greek mosaic.

Factfile

Manuscript: 4QTest
(4Q175)
Editor: J.M. Allegro
(*DJD* 5)
Length: One sheet
Script: Hasmonaean

The Testimonia

'I will raise up for them a prophet like you from among
their brothers. I will put words into his mouth and he
shall tell them all that I command him. And I shall
demand a reckoning of anyone who does not listen
to the words that the Prophet will speak in My name.

He began to speak, and said, "Oracle of Balaam son of
Beor. Oracle of the man whose eye is discerning. Oracle
of him who has heard the words of God…"' (4QTest 5–9)

Although only one sheet long, the Testimonia preserves a type of religious literature that reflects
systematic and serious study of sacred scripture. It
combines four paragraphs taken from consecutive
biblical works: Exodus 20:21, Numbers 24:15–17,
Deuteronomy 33:8–11, and Joshua 6:26 (the last of
these in a version also found in a previously
unknown apocryphon, p. 122). The Testimonia thus
comprises a collection of proof-texts concerned
with God's activities at the end-time. The first three
texts reflect future blessings deriving from a
prophet like Moses, a messiah like David, and a
teacher like Levi. The quote from an apocryphal
Joshua seems intended to contrast this by cursing

three individuals, apparently a father and two sons,
who shed blood in the vicinity of Jerusalem. While
practically no one has attempted to identify the
three positive figures, many scholars readily associate the father and two sons either with Alexander
Jannaeus and his sons (Allegro), or Simon
Maccabee and his sons, Judas and Mattathias, who
died at Doq near Jericho in 135 BCE (Cross), or with
the Hasmonaean king John Hyrcanus and his two
sons (and successors) Aristobulus and Alexander
Jannaeus (O. Betz). More cautious and sceptical
interpreters admit the difficulty of identifying the
'sons of Belial' with known historical personalities,
but recognize that the ancient writer had clearly
reinterpreted Joshua's curse about Jericho in the
light of more recent events.

Interestingly, scholars believe the person who
copied this text also copied the Community Rule
(1QS) from Cave 1 and a Samuel manuscript from
Cave 4. Both have been dated palaeographically to
the Hasmonaean period. It is rare that different
Qumran scrolls can be assigned to a single scribe in
this way, since the vast majority of scrolls appear
to be written by different persons – casting doubt
on the idea that they were all written within a small
community (see section on palaeography, p. 70).

Testimonia, Messiahs and Samaritans

The Testimonia (4Q175) is a collection of
scriptural quotations apparently connected
by their allusion to a messianic figure. Such
collections are also known from early Christian
literature, where the quotations are often called
'proof-texts'.

It begins with a text that in the Masoretic
tradition is Deuteronomy 5:28–29: 'You [Moses]
have heard all that this people have spoken to
you; all they have said is right. If only their heart
were always like this, always to revere me and
keep my commandments…' followed immediately
by Deuteronomy 18:18–19 (again, in the
Masoretic tradition): 'I will raise up for them a
prophet like you from among their brothers'.

It then moves to the 'oracle of Balaam' in
Numbers 24:15–17, which prophesies that 'a star
shall arise from Jacob and a sceptre from Israel',
then to Deuteronomy 33:8–11, which is a blessing
on the Levites, ending 'Crush the loins of his
enemies, of those who hate him, so that they do
not rise again' – a possible reference to messianic
activity. The three texts together may well be
intended to illustrate the coming of three messianic
figures: a prophet, star/sceptre and priest.

But the collection ends with a quotation of
Joshua 6:26, where the hero pronounces after the
destruction of Jericho, 'Cursed be whoever
rebuilds this city! May he lay its foundation on
his eldest and erect its gate over his youngest!'
But 4QTest then adds an interpretation, also

preserved in 4Q379, the
Apocryphon of Joshua. This
passage does not deal with
messianic figures, but
apparently relates to a recent
perceived fulfilment of the
curse by a 'man of Belial'
who has shed blood in
Jerusalem. The relationship
of this passage to the rest of
the Testimonia is uncertain.

It is striking that a
combination of Deuteronomy
5:28–29 and Deuteronomy
18:18–19 also occurs in the
version of Exodus 20:21
that is contained in the
Samaritan Pentateuch.
There are several instances
of readings in Qumran
biblical manuscripts that
agree with the Samaritan
scriptures, and connections
of some kind between the scrolls and
Samaritans have sometimes been suggested.
If the opening quote here is in fact taken from
a passage that was found, as in the Samaritan
version, in the book of Exodus rather than in
Deuteronomy, the citations in this text would
follow the canonical order: Exodus, Numbers,
Deuteronomy.

*The fall of Jericho is
interpreted by the
Testimonia, and is depicted
here by Jean Fouquet
(c. 1425–80).*

The Testimonia text from Cave 4. Note the four dots in line 1 representing the divine name.

Factfile

Manuscripts:
4QOrdinances[a–c]
(4Q159, 4Q513–14)
Editors: J.M. Allegro (*DJD*
5), M. Baillet (*DJD* 7)
Script: Late Hasmonaean

(Above) The inscription on this Jewish silver shekel reads 'Jerusalem the Holy'. Jews everywhere were expected to pay a 'Temple tax'.

(Right) Fragments of Ordinances (4Q159). The relative positions of the two groups cannot be determined.

'A woman may not wear the clothes of a male; every[one who does so commits an offence. A man may not] put on a woman's robe, nor is he to wear a woman's dress, for it is an abomination.

Whenever a man slanders a virgin of Israel, if he says it at the moment of taking her, they shall examine her, and if it turns out that he has not lied about her, they shall put her to death. If he has testified [false]ly against her, they shall fine him two minas [and he may not] divorce her all her life.' (4QOrd frags 2–4, lines 6–10)

Three fragmentary manuscripts from Cave 4 (4Q159, 4Q513–14) contain interpretations of scriptural laws, rather like those in the Cave 4 manuscripts of the Damascus Document and in the Temple Scroll. The first law of 4Q159 (based on Deuteronomy 23:25–26) permits a destitute Israelite to gather food for himself and his family at a threshing-floor or winepress. He may also eat in a field of corn but not take anything home. The next topic is the 'ransom tax', which, according to Exodus 30:11–16, is half a shekel 'according to the shekel of the sanctuary' and applies to all men over 20. The tax is designated for the upkeep of the sanctuary. According to Jewish usage in the Graeco-Roman period, the tax was annual, but the Ordinances require it only once in a lifetime. This is often interpreted as an attempt to reduce the annual income of the Temple, and if so would presumably have a sectarian bias. There follows a calculation of amounts based on mass contributions, as described in Exodus 38:25–26.

On two other fragments of 4Q159 are found a prohibition against Israelites selling their own people to the Gentiles as slaves (see Leviticus 25:39–46); reference to a 12-member judicial panel that decides cases of rebellion; a prohibition on men and women from wearing each other's clothing (Deuteronomy 22:5); and a rule for the accused virgin. If her husband claims correctly that she is not a virgin, she is put to death. If wrong, he must pay her 2 minahs (=100 shekels) and may never divorce her (Deuteronomy 22:13–21).

4Q513 overlaps with 4Q159 where it calculates the mass contributions to the building of the sanctuary, and continues to calculate other scriptural

units of measurement – the *meah* (24 to a shekel), *zuz* (6 *meahs*), the *bath* and the *ephah* ('a *bath* of wine corresponds to an *ephah* of corn'). 4Q514 deals with states of impurity and how they are to be removed in order to eat. It implies that meals were to be taken in a condition of ritual purity, such as several Jewish groups at this time (including the *yahad*) practised (see e.g. 1QS 6).

The interpretation of scriptural laws was at this time already a matter of disagreement between various Jewish groups. But are there obvious sectarian biases here (the Temple tax is one possibility)? Some have seen a principle of leniency towards the poor (which the Temple tax rule might also support), but from these fragments it is dangerous to generalize. Nevertheless, at least they confirm that the application of scriptural laws to all aspects of contemporary Jewish life (and not just a sectarian community regime) was of concern to the authors of the scrolls.

The Calendar Texts

The Dead Sea Scrolls contain several writings dealing directly with the calendar, as well as many in which it is a major issue. The 'official' Jewish year consisted, as now, of 12 lunar months, 354 days. In this calendar the months also have their own names. But the scrolls endorse a calendar of 364 days, in which all months have 30 days, and four days are inserted (quarterly). In this system, the months are simply numbered (since they do not correspond to the named lunar months). This calendar is strongly advocated in 1 Enoch and Jubilees and can be detected in the biblical flood story (Genesis 6–9). Here the flood lasts one year and ten days – in a lunar calendar reckoning, 364 days. According to 1 Enoch (and the Qumran text 4Q252) it lasted exactly a (solar) year.

The legitimacy of the solar year was a major issue for the authors of the scrolls. Adherence to the 354-day year is regarded as straying from the commandments of God, and following the ways of the Gentiles (see Jubilees 2:9, 17; 6:30–31). One of the implications of calendar use was observance of the sabbath (another key issue in the scrolls), for in a solar calendar the sabbath occurred on the same dates each year, and so conflicts with other festivals could be permanently avoided. Moreover, calendrical concerns extended beyond the year: the chronology of world history was based on 'sabbaths of years' (7-year cycles, each ending with a 'sabbatical year'), and 'jubilees', seven of these units (49 or 50 years). In Enoch, Jubilees, and several Qumran scrolls, the history of Israel from creation (or from exile) to the end was calculated as ten jubilees (490 or 500 years). Apart from Enoch and Jubilees, the Qumran texts that make the calendar an issue include the Temple Scroll, the Songs of the Sabbath Sacrifice, a narrative section in the Psalms Scroll, the Damascus Document and the Genesis Commentary.

Where did this 364-day calendar come from? There is no agreed answer, but it belongs in a context of quite precise astronomical and astrological lore which almost certainly originated (like the Enoch traditions themselves?) in Babylonia. The Book of Astronomical Secrets (which is generally agreed to date no later than the 3rd century BCE) notes, among much else, the phases of the moon, synchronizes the days of the year with the zodiac, and records variation in the sun's path and the length of daylight and darkness. Further astronomical observation was necessary to correlate the two calendars: 4Q317 represents a schedule of moon observations brought in line with the days and months of the 364-day year.

For many centuries, the Babylonians had been correlating astral and meteorological phenomena

Factfile

Manuscripts: 4Q318– 30, 334, 337, 394
Editors: S. Talmon, J. Ben-Dov, U. Glessmer (*DJD* 21), M. Sokoloff and J. Greenfield (*DJD* 36)
Script: Hasmonaean and Herodian

with historical events. 4Q318, sometimes called a 'Brontologion', perpetuates the ancient skill of predicting the future based on the signs of nature (here, thunder). The first section of 4Q318 (technically a selenadromion, charting the phases of the moon), is particularly valuable in attempting to integrate several calendrical and astronomical traditions:

'Adar. On the first and on the second, the ram; on the third and on the fourth, the ox; on the [fifth and on the sixth and on the seventh, the twins].'

Unlike any other Dead Sea text this one names the Jewish month (Adar) and associates days of the month with concrete signs of the zodiac. The ram is what we know as Aries, the ox Taurus, and the twins Gemini. The author wanted to date significant events based on accurate observations of heavenly patterns. This may be the oldest witness to an actual Jewish handbook of astrology. It bears some connection to Enochic traditions, but takes them a step forward by providing omens about imminent events.

'[Should] it thunder […], a siege against […]and adversity for the nation and violence [in the cour]t of the king, and among the nations in[…] shall be. Concerning the Arabs,[…]famine, and they will plunder each oth[er…]Should it thunder in the twins (Gemini), panicand sickness because of foreigners and […]' (4Q318 2:6–9)

From this fragmentary passage it seems that national and international affairs took a turn for the worse when thunder could be heard on days associated with Gemini, probably Taurus, and likely on other occasions.

In some calendrical fragments, the days of the month are synchronized with priestly rotas at the Temple; in others these dates are in turn associated with events of public history. The texts include references to Nabataeans, Shelamzion, Hyrcanus, Aristobulus, Aemilius, and the high priest Johanan. For historians tempted to place the people of the scrolls within known history the references to the last five figures suggest at least that the author was aware of the last Hasmonaean rulers. Shelamzion was Salome, the widow and suc-

Calendar of Priestly Rotas (Mishmarot: 4Q320–22)

The Mishmarot texts from Qumran Cave 4 include, among other things, synchronistic tables that correlate the standard Jewish calendar of 12 lunar months (about 48 weeks) with the 364-day (52-week) calendar of the scrolls and with zodiac signs, feast days and sabbaths. These dates are also matched to the 48 weekly priestly shifts of Temple service by 24 priestly families – see table (right).

The table below shows the first three months of the 364-day year in which the 3rd, 6th, 9th and 12th months each have 31 days and festivals, which never fall on a sabbath, occur on the same date every year.

BY PRIESTLY ROTA	BY DAY/MONTH
YEAR 1	
Yedaiah, day 1	month 7, day 12
Miyamim, day 3	month 8, day 12
Shekaniah, day 4	month 9, day 11
Yeshabab, day 6	month 10, day 10
Petahiah, sabbath (day 7)	month 11, day 9
Delaiah, day 2	month 12, day 9
YEAR 2	
Harim, day 3	month 1, day 7
Hakkoz, day 5	month 2, day 9
Eliashib, day 6	month 3, day 6
Immer, day 1	month 4, day 5
Ezekiel, day 2	month 5, day 4
Maoziah	month 6, day 4

Beginning of Days of Consecration

WEEKDAY	I					II				III			
Wednesday	1	8	15	22	29	6	13	20	27	4	11	18	25
Thursday	2	9	16	23	30	7	14	21	28	5	12	19	26
Friday	3	10	17	24		1	8	15	22	29	6	13	20	27
Saturday	4	11	18	25		2	9	16	23	30	7	14	21	28
Sunday	5	12	19	26		3	10	17	24	1	8	15	22	29
Monday	6	13	20	27		4	11	18	25	2	9	16	23	30
Tuesday	7	14	21	28		5	12	19	26	3	10	17	24	31

Passover

Day of Waving the Sheaf

Feast of First-Fruits of Wheat

(Below and right)
Fragments of 4Q321,
officially designated the
Calendrical Document/
Mishmarot B.

cessor of the Hasmonaean Alexander
Jannaeus and mother of Hyrcanus
(II) and Aristobulus (II). This
author also knew of the civil war that
Hyrcanus and Aristobulus provoked and the role of
the Roman general M. Aemilius Scaurus during the
60s BCE. 4Q333 includes the phrase 'Amelius killed',
and the context suggests the seventh month. 4Q319
is concerned with tabulating the conjunctions of
the sun and the moon during a jubilee, with years
named for priestly families.

The problem with priestly families is as follows.
The solar calendar comprised a year of 52, not 48,
weeks. There was a rota of priestly service in the
Temple, according to which each of 24 priestly
families worked two weekly shifts a year (see 1
Chronicles 24:1–19). Rather than invent two new
families to fit the solar calendar, the Qumran texts
have to accommodate the 'lunar' system. In a series
of texts entitled 'Mishmarot' or priestly temple
schedules, 4Q320 synchronizes lunar and solar
dates within a framework of priestly rotations. The
author of 4Q320 starts with the first year of the
cycle in the service of the family of Gamul, which
in Chronicles was the 22nd family. Another fragment enumerates which families serve at the beginning of the solar, 30- or 31-day months, lists festivals in a six-year cycle, and correlates full moons
with a priestly rotation. 4Q325 preserves the priestly rotation and the festivals within a six-year cycle.

Vigorous adherence to a solar calendar is one of
the strongest arguments that the Qumran scrolls
come, if not from a single group, then from groups
that were closely related, and united in their opposition to a calendar sanctioned in their time by a
priesthood that they regarded as corrupt, in error
and doomed to destruction.

(Right) The ram's horn
was blown to mark the
beginning of each new
year as well as other
solemn occasions.

The Halakhic Letter

'…we have separated ourselves from the multitude of the people…and from being involved with these matters and from participating with [them] in these things.' (C 7–8)

Among the batches of fragments from Cave 4 that reached the Palestine Archaeological Museum, East Jerusalem, in the early 1950s was a group provisionally designated 4QMishn (Mishnah), because some of their vocabulary was, unlike that of the other known scrolls, close to that of the rabbis. But at the time, none of the (non-Jewish) editors could appreciate, or foresee, the importance that these fragments would eventually have in the debate about the origin of the Dead Sea Scrolls. (The new title derives from a Hebrew phrase in the document, meaning 'Some Precepts of the Law'.)

Three decades later a packed audience at the Biblical Archaeology conference in Jerusalem in 1984 sat mesmerised as Elisha Qimron, Strugnell's newly-appointed co-editor, announced

Poured Liquids

4QMMT, the 'Halakhic Letter', raises the issue of the purity of liquid streams. This was also a matter of debate between the Pharisees and the Sadducees in later rabbinic texts. The basic disagreement here is whether or not an unbroken liquid flow connects or insulates the purity or impurity of vessels at each end:

'And concerning liquid streams: we hold that they are not pure, nor do these streams act as a separator between impure and pure. For the liquid of streams and of what receives them are alike, a single liquid.' (4QMMT B:55–58)

What 4QMMT means is that liquid streams have the same status as the vessels into which they fall or are poured. This would mean, for example, that if the receiving vessel and the pouring vessel are pure, the liquid is pure, but if the receiving vessel is not pure, then the act of pouring would connect the two vessels, via the liquid, and so would make even

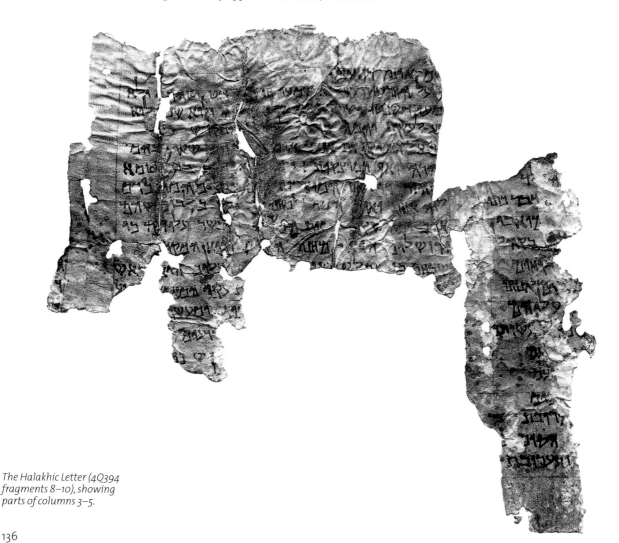

The Halakhic Letter (4Q394 fragments 8–10), showing parts of columns 3–5.

a clean pouring vessel impure. This would, of course, be of serious moment in cases of ritual purity, eating, and drinking. The compiler of 4QMMT disagreed with those who argued that in such cases liquid streams acted as an insulator, and did not conduct impurity in this way.

The editors of 4QMMT quote the Mishnah (the rabbinic law code) to show that 4QMMT's opinion was shared by the Sadducees.

'The Sadducees say: We protest against you, O Pharisees, for you pronounce clean the unbroken stream.' (*Yadayim* 4:7)

The Mishnah upholds the Pharisaic ruling:

'An uninterrupted flow, a current on sloping ground and the dripping of moisture are not considered a connective either for communicating uncleanness or for producing cleanness.' (*Toharot* 8:9)

Can such disputes in early Judaism have led to the formation of sects? Perhaps, among other issues, they did.

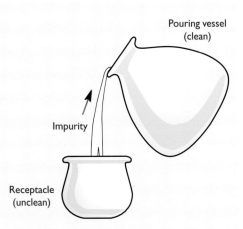

According to 4QMMT if the stream is unbroken the liquid conducts impurity back from the impure receptacle to the (originally pure) pourer.

that 4QMMT represented copies of a 'letter' written by Qumran's 'Teacher of Righteousness' to his rival, the 'Wicked Priest'. This 'letter' proved, they claimed, that the Qumran community had seceded from the Jerusalem establishment around 150 BCE because of major differences in biblical interpretation and cultic practice. Other scholars have pointed out certain legal opinions expressed in 4QMMT that agree with rabbinic descriptions of Sadducean viewpoints. Accordingly, for many scholars 4QMMT is a document about historical origins that allows one to identify its authors as Sadducees.

Since the publication of these views in the official edition, there has been debate on whether the text really is a letter (and on who wrote it); on the Sadducean character of the halakhah (legal practice) and, indeed, on whether the document has been properly reconstructed from the fragments. This text also became the centre of the scandal in the early 1990s about delayed publication of Cave 4 texts.

The editors believe that the fragments come from six manuscripts copied between the early 1st century BCE and the early 1st century CE, which have been combined into a single text. In Qimron's edition (the standard), the reconstructed text is divided into three sections, A–C, and the most convenient way of referring to the text is not by manuscript and fragment but to this reconstructed form, where references are A, B or C followed by a line number. The first of the three sections of this text consists of a list of sabbaths and festivals and is now widely treated as a separate text. The second part comprises a series of legal rulings on which the writers and recipients disagree, and focuses on laws about holiness. It condemns priests serving at the Jerusalem Temple who permit Gentile offerings and sacrifices:

'...the priest[s] should take care concerning this practice so as not to cause the people to bear punishment.' (B 12–13)

The priests are also admonished not to accept any items made of the hide or bones of unclean animals (B 21–26), and it states that those involved in the ceremony of the red heifer (see Numbers 19:1–10) do not become pure until the sun has set. The editors note that this view agrees with one ascribed to *zadduqim* in rabbinic texts. According to the Pharisaic position endorsed by the rabbis, these persons were considered pure *before* the sun went down. Another issue of contention is whether or not impurity can flow in reverse, for example through a liquid, from an impure receptacle to a pure pouring vessel (B 55–58).

Also of concern is the purity of the priesthood. Marriage is forbidden (B39) with certain foreigners, the blind, and the deaf, because they have the potential to endanger the purity of the Temple. The priests must also be especially cautious in observing purity regulations regarding lepers. Certainly, marriage between priests and laity is forbidden:

'They are holy, and the sons of Aaron are[most holy.] But you know that some of the priests and [the laity mingle with each other]...[And they] unite with each other and pollute the [holy] seed [as well as] their own [seed] with women whom they are forbidden to marry.' (B 79–92)

Sabbath observance is one of the strictest principles of the scrolls. Here, a modern Jewish family continues the sabbath tradition.

Opinions of the Sadducees

In contrast to the later rabbis, who followed Pharisaic rulings, the Sadducees seem to have left practically no literary legacy. But in some rabbinic writings, Sadducean points of views are quoted. Several of these opinions agree with those in 4QMMT (the Halakhic Letter).

Apart from the issue of poured liquids (see p. 137), Pharisees and Sadducees apparently disagreed strongly over the time for purifying the priests for the ceremony of the red heifer.

The priest burning the [red] heifer was rendered ritually unclean because of the Sadducees, so they would not say that [the purification ceremony] was performed by [ritually clean] people for whom the sun had [already] set.' (Mishnah *Parah* 3:7)

And also with regard to the purification of the heifer [brought as] a sin-offering, the one who slaughters it and the one who burns it and the one who collects its ashes and the one who sprinkles the water of purification – it is by sunset that all these become clean, and the pure shall sprinkle on the impure.' (4QMMT B 13-17)

A second point of contention involved the impurity of the corpses and bones of animals.

The flesh of animal corpses and forbidden reptiles [is unclean], which is not the case with their bones. (Mishnah *'Eduyot* 6:3)

Even the skins and the bones of unclean animals…and even the skins of the carcasses of clean animals… [are unclean]. (4QMMT B 21-23)

A third issue was whether deaf-mutes might prepare ritually pure food. The rabbinic ruling (from the Toseftah, a compilation of rabbinic laws parallel to the Mishnah) compared with 4QMMT:

All ritually pure food in Jerusalem was prepared relying on them…for ritually pure food does not require intention. (Toseftah *Terumoth*. 1:1)

and concerning the deaf who have not heard the laws and the judgements and the purity regulations, and have not heard the ordinances of Israel, since he who has not seen or heard does not know how to obey [the law].' (4QMMT B 52–55)

The existence of 'Sadducean' opinions in an important manuscript from Qumran Cave 4 led to speculation that the Qumran writings originated in a Sadducean context. Some say at that stage the priestly founders of the sect(s) were in fact Sadducees. But shared opinion on these few matters does not necessarily mean shared identity.

There is also counter-evidence. A number of Qumran texts express an interest in angels, which Josephus says that the Sadducees dismissed. Josephus also identifies the Sadducees closely with the Temple establishment. If Sadducees are also at the roots of the Qumran literature, there must have been (as the supporters of the Sadducee connection have to hypothesize) a split within that movement.

Who Owns the Copyright?

In the late 1970s and early 1980s scholarly frustrations at the delay in publishing the scrolls increased. It was known that most texts had been translated, though were still not publicly available. One such text was claimed to be a letter from the 'Teacher of Righteousness', supposed founder of the *yahad*. Strugnell, originally assigned this text, co-opted Israeli scholar Elisha Qimron to assist him.

As delay in publication continued, a photocopy of an (unsigned) handwritten transcription and translation was unofficially circulating, and the Polish scholar Z.J. Kapera, publisher of *The Qumran Chronicle*, printed and distributed it to his readers. In *A Facsimile Edition of the Dead Sea Scrolls* the Biblical Archaeology Society editor Hershel Shanks included a picture of a page of Kapera's publication.

Qimron (without Strugnell) decided to sue the Biblical Archaeology Society, claiming breach of copyright, on the grounds that he was the author of the text that he had reconstructed (from several fragments). He estimated that his creative work constituted about 40 per cent of the reconstructed text, and on 30 March 1993 Judge Dalia Dorner of the District Court of Jerusalem awarded Qimron 20,000 Israeli shekels ($ 7,407) in damages and a further 80,000 shekels ($29,630) more for 'mental

Elisha Qimron, the holder of copyright to the reconstructed Halakhic Letter.

anguish' – along with costs! Qimron was not the author of the ancient text, ruled Judge Dorner, but rather the author, the creative genius, *of the reconstructions*. Despite the protests of the defendants, Hershel Shanks, and the editors of the volume, Robert Eisenman and James Robinson, Qimron was given the copyright to the composite text he called 4QMMT ('Some of the Works of the Law').

The verdict on the appeal was delivered at the end of 2000 and Qimron's case was upheld. The possessiveness with which scholars treat texts assigned to them partly caused the delay that has bedevilled the official publication process; Qimron's action has merely taken such possessiveness further.

While part of 4QMMT seems to be addressed to priests involved in the cult at the Jerusalem Temple, the third section is addressed to a respected individual. The writer asserts this man's integrity and good reputation and encourages him to study carefully 'the book of Moses and the books of the Prophets and David' (C 9–11) – in other words, books of scripture. He also refers to the blessings and curses on Israelite and Judaean kings and asks his recipient to recall their deeds, leaving the impression that at least this part of the text was addressed to a royal leader of the nation, a Judaean monarch:

'We have (indeed) sent you some of the precepts of the Law according to our decision, for your welfare and the welfare of your people. For we have seen (that) you have wisdom and knowledge of the Law. Consider all these things and ask him that he strengthen your will and remove from you the plans of evil and the device of Belial so that you may rejoice at the end of time.' (C26–30)

Almost certainly, one of the Hasmonaean rulers must be meant. But whoever the writer and the addressee may have been, it is obvious that there is no formal breach between the two, only disagreement. The tone of the address suggests a desire to persuade, not condemn. Does it therefore stem from a period before there was a formal breach between the community/communities of the scrolls and the Judaean political and religious establishment? If so, this text may hold the key to their origins as well as their identity, and show that it was a conflict between priestly views on purity laws that, at least ostensibly, formed the main reason for the secession of some groups. If these differences may have seemed rather incidental, or even trivial, to the first editors of the scrolls (and perhaps to some modern readers), they were vitally important to those Jews of the period who were trying to live a life of obedience to the law based on maintaining a strict distinction between the pure and impure.

The text has generated modern as well as ancient controversy. Elisha Qimron has secured copyright on his reconstructed text; John Strugnell, in an editorial appendix to the official edition, questions whether the text has been properly reassembled; and the Sadducaean identity of the scroll writers remains hotly disputed. In general, too, this text highlights the important question of whether the scrolls, to be properly understood, must be seen from the perspective of rabbinic Judaism, and 'reclaimed', after decades of non-Jewish study, 'for Judaism'.

The Way Things Are – How to Keep Them That Way

'Do not put a matter in the charge of a lazy person, for he will not follow your orders; do not send him to collect anything…do not trust a tax collector to collect money for your needs. Do not trust a man with twisted lips with your trial; he will surely distort with his lips, he will not be partial to the truth…' (Sapiential Work C (4Q424) frag. 1, lines 6–9)

'Open the spring of your lips to bless the holy ones… He has separated you from every spirit of flesh, so keep separate from all that he hates and keep yourselves apart every abomination of the soul.' (4Q418, frag. 81, lines 1–2)

'Blessed is the man who attains wisdom and walks in the law of the Most High, and dedicates his heart to its (sc. wisdom's) ways, and is constrained by its discipline, and always takes pleasure in its admonishments.' (Beatitudes (4Q525), frag. 2, lines 3–4)

The meaning of 'wisdom'

By 'wisdom' is meant proper ethical behaviour, informed by an understanding of the whole cosmos. This may take the form of proverbial instruction on what to do, sermons on the purpose of life, or even speculations on the origins and destiny of the world. The biblical books of Proverbs, Ecclesiastes and Job (along with several Psalms, such as Psalm 1) are examples of this kind of literature. In the late Second Temple period two tendencies are particularly observable: one is a belief in the limits of human knowledge of the mysteries of life, and thus an emphasis on revelation of such secrets (this tendency can be seen in the book of Daniel); the other is an attempt to equate wisdom with the content of Torah, 'the Law', at this time becoming synonymous with the Five Books of Moses (Genesis–Deuteronomy). It was in these writings that the divine will was most pefectly expressed, although their true meaning was, of course, always a matter of interpretation, and in the case of some Qumran writers a meaning revealed to a chosen few.

But alongside the Torah and its correct interpretation, there is other teaching, of a largely ethical nature, dealing with the fate of humans and their proper conduct: in other words, 'wisdom'. Passages of wisdom teaching can be identified in the Two Spirits section in 1QS 3–4 and in the first two pages of the Damascus Document in particular. But only recently have the large number of wisdom texts from

This 4th-century silver casket of Italian origin shows the Judgment of Solomon, who was known for his wisdom.

Among the Wisdom Texts from Cave 4 is one called simply 'Sapiential Work A' (4Q416–18), in which the author repeatedly speaks of the *raz nihyeh*, which has been translated as 'the mystery of existence' or 'approaching mystery' or 'the way things are'. Unlike biblical books of instruction (such as Proverbs, Ecclesiastes and Job), which confine their wisdom to the eternal truths of human earthly existence, the wisdom of the scrolls is tinged with the expectation of an imminent judgment for humans, and with a belief that heavenly mysteries can be deciphered to reveal to the righteous the world beyond human knowledge. And this knowledge brings 'salvation': 'Gaze on the mystery of life and grasp the origins of salvation' (4Q417).

But alongside this grand advice stand hints about mundane matters: money, wealth, luxuries, dealings with neighbours, and daily work:

'If in your need you borrow money from people do not delay…right and do not leave
Do not exchange your holy spirit for any wealth, for no price is worth it…
Do not fill yourself with bread while there is no clothing. Do not drink wine while there is no food. Do not seek luxury when you lack bread.
[If someone entrusts] a deposit to you, do not touch it lest it be burnt, and your body be devoured by its flame.'

Several admonitions advise one to avoid certain types of people, those who hinder one on the path towards acquiring one's inheritance:

'Do not humble yourself to one who is not your equal. Do not strike him who is without your strength, lest you stumble and your shame increase greatly
Do not entrust a sleepy man with something delicate, for he will not treat your work gently…
Do not [send] a grumbler to procure money for your need nor put your trust in a man with twisted lips. Do not put a stingy man in charge of your mone(y)
A man who judges before inquiry…do not put him in charge of those who pursue knowledge.
Do not send a blind man to bring a vision to the upright. Likewise do not send a man who is hard of hearing to inquire into judgment, for he will not smooth out a quarrel between people.'

Finally, here is a parable that sounds familiar:

'Wise men, consider this: A man has a good tree (growing) up to heaven, to the lengths of the lands, yet it (pro)duces thorny fruits.'

As in the New Testament parables, 'the way things are' is sometimes revealed in the form of a 'mystery' expressed in everyday images.

Cave 4 been published. Their presence emphasizes the function of wisdom teaching within the societies lying behind these texts. The *maskil*, for whom several texts are explicitly written, is now perhaps less to be seen as a leader of a community than as a teacher, and perhaps not a single figure, but a rank or title earned by one who has achieved wisdom and, like the 'Solomon' of Proverbs, passes it on to his 'sons'.

What are now referred to as the 'wisdom texts' from Qumran deal with practical and theological instruction on how to live properly. Confusingly, some of them were provisionally labelled 'Sapiential Work' (4Q415–18, 4Q423 (the same work is found in 1Q26)) but are now known as 'Instruction'. They stress that wisdom is knowledge of a 'mystery'. They also hint (where they do not openly declare) that a final judgment is imminent. Wisdom, learnt and practical, saves a person, not from material ruin or an evil reputation, as in Proverbs, but from ultimate destruction. The dualism in Proverbs between wise and foolish, righteous and wicked, used there as a didactic tool, becomes hardened in the Qumran texts so that the terms now identify two different kinds of human being: those inside the sectarian fold and those outside, those chosen by God and those rejected, the 'children of light' and 'children of darkness'.

Wisdom as understanding of 'mysteries'

Among the most fascinating Wisdom Texts recovered from Cave 4 are those entitled 'Mysteries' (4Q299–300). (Two 'Mystery' manuscripts were already known from Cave 1, 1Q26 and 27.) One fragment notes that iniquity is not located in any one people but in every nation, just as are pieces of the truth. In time righteousness and knowledge will conquer the world, wiping out all forms of evil and wickedness in their wake. The 'Mysteries' also speak of God's foreknowledge and predestination of all events and plans in history. True sages are patient and focus on the eternal secrets and the roots of wisdom, in contrast to magicians or soothsayers who speak 'parables without understanding'. The disciples are told that the big mystery is a

sealed vision that is unfathomable. Yet clues to finding this wisdom lie in God's creation and ongoing orchestration of natural events. The disciples are urged not to bear a grudge, a form of evil and disruptive behaviour. One can also learn from meditating on the past and its lessons.

Another manuscript, also designated as a Mystery Text (4Q301), is formulated in the first person and addressed to a group. It deals with God's goodness towards his elect and his willingness to punish the wicked. Thus God will rule and judge from his 'temple of the kingdom' and true justice will prevail. Several other manuscripts are similar to the Mystery Texts (4Q415–18, 4Q423, 1Q26). In addition to speaking about the mystery

that is coming into being, they refer to the poverty of the listeners or readers. The sage advises them not to beg God for food, to pay back loans quickly, and not to be mirthful during a period of mourning. He admonishes them not to humiliate themselves with one not of their status, not to strike a weaker person, nor to hold on to deposits and certainly not to accept goods from a stranger; not to associate with certain types of persons, such as the blind, the deaf, the unjust man, one who hates, or has a 'fat heart'. Perhaps some of these descriptions have a spiritual rather than physical sense. But the (male) audience is told to rule over the spirit of their wives and control their vows and free-will offerings. They are also encouraged to praise God and seek his pleasure.

4Q184, the so-called 'Wiles of the Wicked Woman'.

John Allegro piecing together fragments of a Wisdom Text.

Wisdom as living according to a 'rule of creation'

Three fragmentary texts called Meditations on Creation (4Q303–05) permit the reader to discern wisdom in the creative acts of God. In particular, the author speaks of the heavenly lights that serve as a point of orientation, of human insight into divine wisdom, and of the woman whose purpose is to serve as a man's helpmate. One manuscript (4Q298), penned in an esoteric script, represents instruction within a small school or group setting. It speaks of the fruits of listening well, understanding the design of God's creation, accepting one's status in life and following the rules, leading a life of virtue, and meditation on the ages of the world. The author of this text speaks to the 'children of dawn', a term which may refer to members of the community of 'children of light'.

Another text, entitled simply Composition on Divine Providence (4Q413), recalls the previous instructional text. The writer says: 'let me instruct you in wisdom', then proceeds to urge his listeners to meditate on 'the former years and contemplate the events of past generations as God has revealed'. The modern editor of this text notes similarities with the language of the Damascus Document, the Community Rule 3:13–25, and the epilogue to the Halakhic Letter.

Several other fragments of sapiential hymns and didactic texts, although fragmentary, offer words of advice. One contains a list of liturgical commands: 'place a bond on your lips…for your tongue, doors of protection…ponder…praise…give thanks… day and night' (4Q412). The budding sage is encouraged to practise rightful speech and rightful thoughts in the forms of praise and meditation. A text entitled Ways of Righteousness recalls the language of the Community Rule: 'he shall bring his wisdom, his knowledge, his understanding, and his goodness' (4Q421 frag. 1a, col. 1:2). The same manuscript also describes the virtuous deportment of the sage: he hears before answering, understands before responding. He exhibits patience and a foreknowledge of the consequences of his words.

Wisdom and the feminine

As in the Bible (especially the book of Proverbs), wisdom is represented as a female principle. But so is its opposite, folly. Pursuit of wisdom in both the scriptures and the Qumran texts is often presented as a courtship. (In a male celibate society like the *yahad*, this device would have a certain irony!) One well-known text, called 'The Seductress' or 'Lady Folly' (originally 'Wiles of the Wicked Woman' – 4Q184) describes a harlot who displays her goods within the city gates. Her beauty, clothing, and even her internal organs have one purpose alone, and that is to entice righteous men into her traps. This woman does not seem to represent all women, but the imagery of an attractive and alluring female indicates how easily a good and righteous man can be brought from the proper way and end up in hell. Sages and all others should avoid this wicked woman, whether she appears literally on the streets of Jerusalem or Jericho, or comes in the form of wealth and power. It is possible that this text offers advice pertaining to female company, but it is more likely to be allegorical (see also Proverbs 7), like the Admonitory Parable which says: 'discern, oh wise men, if a man has a good tree…'. (compare Psalm 1).

One of the more puzzling phrases in several wisdom texts is, in Hebrew, *raz nihyeh*, which different translators render in various ways (see p. 140). It is hard to translate, because *nihyeh* is the passive of the verb 'to be'. Suggestions include 'the secret of what is to pass' (with reference to the coming judgment), and 'the secret of the way things are'. Both can be defended from the Qumran texts as a whole, which contain a great deal of apparently esoteric teaching on the nature of humans (e.g. ruled by two spirits) and the threat of impending divine judgment. If study of priestly rules about holiness can help clarify the origin of the sectarians behind the scrolls, the use and development of wisdom teaching can illustrate how universal values of behaviour can be adapted to transmit sectarian ones.

Grace – Or a Lament over Jerusalem?

A number of Cave 4 fragments contain the same opening formula, 'Bless, O my soul…' (Hebrew: *barki nafshi*). One of them (4Q434a) has been interpreted as a 'grace after meals' by Moshe Weinfeld. He has noted that the Qumran text is like later rabbinic graces after meals at a mourner's house. Both mention mourning, the destruction of the Gentiles, the renewal of creation, forgiveness of sin, God's goodness, the eternal throne (of David?), and the land. Weinfeld writes: 'The Qumran fragment contains all of the basic elements of the grace after meals that were also common in rabbinic Pharisaic Judaism' (*Journal of Biblical Literature* 111 (1992), p. 437).

Was 4Q434a used at a funeral meal? The fragment mentions a 'destitute woman who shall be comforted in [her] mourning', and Jerusalem is frequently portrayed in the Bible as a female and, combined with the reference to the extermination of the nations and God's comforting Jerusalem, the theme in this Qumran prayer may be the city of Jerusalem. Such texts are represented by 4Q179 and 4Q501, both reminiscent of Lamentations.

Jeremiah lamenting the destruction of Jerusalem, painted by Rembrandt in 1630.

Poetry, Psalms and Prayers

'You remembered your covenant, for you redeemed us in the eyes of the nations, and did not abandon us among the nations. You showed favour to your people Israel, in all the lands to which you exiled them, to induce in their heart a return to you and a listening to your voice, as you had commanded through your servant Moses.' (4Q504 5:9–14)

The Dead Sea Scrolls greatly expand the number and variety of psalms, prayers and poetic pieces beyond what is found in the biblical canon. These range from liturgical pieces for national festivals to daily prayers, sabbath prayers, psalms for the community and the individual, and items for special occasions. Many of the texts imply a solar calendar, and many (though not all) have a probable sectarian character. (Self?)-exile from the Temple may have resulted in the creation of new liturgical occasions and poems, though since the Temple was the source and site of a great deal of Jewish liturgy, its own practices strongly influence the liturgical forms and patterns observable in the scrolls.

Hymns in the broadest sense are so prevalent among the scrolls that they cannot all be dealt with here. The Hodayoth and the Psalms Scrolls from Cave 11 are treated elsewhere (p. 160), as are the Blessings (1QSb, p. 90) and the Songs of the Sabbath Sacrifice (p. 146) Here we consider a miscellaneous collection of poems including Apocryphal Psalms (11Q11; 4Q88), prayers against demons (including the Songs of the Maskil and

German Jewish soldiers praying during Yom Kippur (the Hebrew name for the Day of Atonement) in 1870.

4Q560), Daily and Festival Prayers (4Q503; 4Q507–09, 1Q34), Words of the Luminaries (4Q504–06; see also 4Q393), Blessings (not to be confused with 1QSb: 4Q280, 286–87, 4Q434, 436; 11Q14) and miscellaneous poems for special occasions, such as grace after meals (4Q434a), purification (4Q512), immersion (4Q414) and, possibly, marriage (4Q502). There are other pieces (such as 4Q392) with no indicated function or setting.

Apocryphal Psalms are, strictly, non-biblical compositions but known from outside Qumran, such as Psalms 151 (in the Greek Psalter) and 154–55 (Psalms 1–3 in the Syriac Psalter) which are included in 11Q11. But they also cover non-biblical (and in some cases clearly sectarian) psalms found in Psalms Scrolls. The Cave 11 scroll has three of these that are legible, plus several others; and the Cave 4 Psalms Scrolls (4Q88) include three others.

From the Community Rule we know of a covenant renewal ceremony (col. 2) and the War Scroll (p. 92) contains a large number of hymns set during the course of the battle and the ensuing campaigns. These two instances show that liturgical pieces may be firmly rooted in practice or composed for a future occasion. In some cases they are perhaps not intended to be performed at all. But there is direct evidence of intense liturgical activity among the groups responsible for the scrolls. A fragment of one text (4Q334) seems to contain a list of hymns to be sung day and night, on consecutive days of each month, though the text of the hymns is not stipulated. 4Q408 and 4Q503 also refer to blessings at sunrise and in the evenings on certain numbered days of the week. Other manuscripts (4Q507–09) provide prayers for festivals, including the Day of Atonement and the Festival of Firstfruits. Hymns that have a national context are the Words of the Luminaries (4QDibHam, or 4Q504–06), which refer to Israel's exile, caused by its own sins:

'For you have shed your holy spirit upon us, bringing upon us your blessings, so that we can seek you in our distress, in the ordeal of your chastisement. We have come into distress, have been struck and been tested by the oppressor's wrath. We have also tested God with our iniquity.' (4QDibHam 5:15–19)

Another example of a communal confession is 4Q393, and there are also several communal blessings, which include curses on Belial and Melchiresha', similar to those found in 1QS col. 2.

A number of prayers, presumably not written for performance, are also assigned to historical figures: 4Q381 is attributed to a humbled Manasseh, king of Judah, when the King of Assyria imprisoned him (this is not the same as the Greek 'Prayer of Manasses in the Apocrypha). The Prayer of Nabonidus (4Q242) speaks of the ulcerous condition of the Babylonian king Nabonidus, who called

Examples from the Spiritual Writings in the Scrolls

National Festival

Prayer for the day of first-fruits.

'Remember, o Lord, the festival […] and the pleasant free-will offerings that you have commanded […] to present before you the first-fruits of your works […] upon the earth…' (Festival Prayers (4Q509), frags 131–32, 2:5–7)

Daily Prayers

'At the rising of the [sun…] to the vault of the heavens they shall bless. They shall lift up their voice, [and say], "Blessed be the God [of Israel]. This day he re[news…] in the fourth [gate of light…] for us…" On the fifth [day of the month, in the] evening, they shall bless. They shall lift up their voice and say, "Blessed be the God [of Israel] who hides before him in each part of his glory"'. (Daily Prayers (4Q503), frags 1–6, 3:1–7)

Psalm for the Community

'The princess of all the nations is desolate, like a forsaken woman; and all her [daug]hters are abando[ned, like] a forsaken woman. Like a woman hurt and abandoned by her [husband]. All her palaces and walls are like a barren woman; and like a cloistered woman are [her] ways…like a woman of bitterness, and all her daughters like women mourning for [their] husbands.' (4Q179, frag. 2, 5–8)

Songs for Special Occasions

'And you will purify him for your holy laws…for the first, third and sixth…in the truth of your covenant…to purify from uncleanness…And afterwards he shall enter the water…And he will answer saying, "Blessed are you…because what comes from your mouth…"' (Baptismal Liturgy (4Q414), frag. 2, 2:1–70)

Individual Psalm

'Your name is my salvation, my rock, my fortress, and [my] refuge [is my God]. I will call upon the Lord and he will answer me, my help…those who hate me. And he will say, …My plea to him comes to his ears; from his temple he will hear my voice. And the earth will tremble and sway, and the foundations of the hills will shake…because of his anger.' (Non-Canonical Psalms B (4Q381), frag. 24, 7–10)

in a Judaean exorcist to heal him. Once Nabonidus praises the Most High God he becomes well.

This last example leads us into a group of prayers of exorcism, such as the Songs of the Maskil:

'And I, the *maskil*, proclaim the splendour of his beauty to frighten and ter[rify] all the spirits of the destructive angels and the spirits of the bastards, the demons, Lilith…those who strike suddenly to lead astray the spirit of understanding…' (4Q510, 4–5)

Among other prayers for special occasions are 4Q512, for purification of an individual, where a blessing precedes the physical actions of cleansing the body and the clothes, and a similar blessing concludes the ritual. 4Q414 also contains blessings before and after an immersion, and one fragment (24:4) of the so-called 'marriage ritual' (4Q502, see p. 124) reads 'and she will take her place in the assembly of elderly men and women'.

One highly unusual and provocative manuscript, beginning with a praise of God for redeeming his poor ones from their oppressors and electing Jerusalem (4Q448), continues by speaking of a King Jonathan and God's people Israel in the four corners of the earth. Presumably this king functions as God's representative and perhaps his instrument for war on earth. But who is this king, and why is he praised in a collection of scrolls that generally opposes the rulers of Judah? The majority interpretation is that the honoree is Alexander Jannaeus (who opposed the Pharisees), but another candidate is Jonathan Maccabee (thought also by some to be the recipient of the 'Halakhic Letter', 4QMMT).

A stela representing King Nabonidus, who is the subject of one of the prayer scrolls found in Cave 4 (4Q242, see p. 129).

The Songs of the Sabbath Sacrifice

'The [cheru]bim prostrate themselves before him and bless. When they rise, a soft divine sound [is heard], and there is a roar of praise. When they drop their wings, there is a [sof]t divine sound. The cherubim bless the image of the throne-chariot above the firmament…there is what appears to be a fiery vision of the most holy spirits.' (4Q405)

Eight fragmentary manuscripts of this work were discovered in Cave 4, another in Cave 11, and still another turned up at Masada. This last discovery seemed to have established a connection between the two sites, with some scholars arguing that an Essene-turned-Zealot had fled Qumran in 69 CE with his sacred literature, while others believe that the appearance of this work at presumably unrelated sites suggests that this work was not exclusively 'Qumranic' at all. Palaeography suggests that this work was copied at least 10 times from the early 1st century BCE up to the fall of Masada in 73 CE.

John Strugnell, its first editor, dubbed it 'The Angelic Liturgy'. His student, Carol Newsom, who edited all the extant fragments from Qumran and Masada (along with Yigael Yadin), renamed it 'Songs of the Sabbath Sacrifice'. Both titles are apt. The fragments command and describe divine praise for the King of Glory. With the help of Hartmut Stegemann of the University of Göttingen, Newsom was able to reconstruct a running series of 13 songs of praise clearly assigned to the first 13 sabbaths (quarter) of a liturgical year. The first sabbath begins on the fourth day of the first month, indicating that the author assumes

Two columns from one of the fragmentary manuscript copies (4Q403) of the Songs of the Sabbath Sacrifice.

Factfile

Manuscripts:
4QShirShabb
(4Q400–07),
11QShirShabb (11Q17),
MasadaShirShabb
Editor: C.A. Newsom
(*DJD* 11)
Commentary: J. Davila
Script: Late Hasmonaean
to Late Herodian

Like many Jews in antiquity, the writers of the Songs of the Sabbath Sacrifice believed that God was worshipped in heaven by his angels, as shown in this painting by Guariento of the mid-14th century.

the 364-day solar year, in which the year begins on the fourth day, when the sun was created. Each song begins with a formulaic expression preserved best in the seventh song:

'for/by the *maskil*. Song of the Holocaust of the seventh sabbath on the sixteenth of the month (the second). Praise the most high among all the gods of knowledge. May the Holy ones of God sanctify the King of Glory…' (4Q403, 1:30–31)

Although not all the introductory formulae have been entirely preserved, they are clearly stereotypical. But the content of the praise, or description of praise, that follows is quite unpredictable. These songs, however, all command the angelic priesthood in the heavenly temple to praise the author of holiness. 4Q400 (frag. 1, 1:15–16) reads:

'There is [n]othing impure in their holy gifts. He engraved for them [precepts, by which] all the eternally holy ones

keep themselves holy…Their expiations shall obtain his good will for all those who repent from sin.'

Experts have often noted that these songs were designed to provide the image of the ideal heavenly priesthood after which the earthly priesthood should be modelled. The worship in the 'camps of the divine beings' is so marvellous that the priests of Israel's God can only ask:

'…for how shall we be counted among them? For how shall our priesthood be counted in their dwellings? [How shall our] ho[liness compare with their supreme] holiness? How does the offering of our tongue of dust compare with the knowledge of the divine [ones…]' (4Q400, 2:6–10)

In this text, human, priestly praise of God approximates to that of the angels who surround God in the heavenly temple and exalt him perfectly. Yet the writer is not lamenting the futility of it all, but

147

The Structure of the Angelic Sabbath Songs

The Songs of the Sabbath Sacrifice are, according to their editor Carol Newsom, well-crafted literary pieces that functioned within a context of worship over a period of 13 sabbaths, occupying the first quarter of each year. They also exhibit a chiastic (mirror-pattern) structure, as follows, with the first six balancing the last six in reverse order. In such structures the central element (here the 7th sabbath song) usually provides the clue to the meaning of the whole.

7th sabbath: *angels called to praise*

6th sabbath: 7 chief princes and their blessings

8th sabbath: seven angelic priesthoods

5th sabbath: heavenly war mustering of troops

9th sabbath: vestibule of temple and its images

4th sabbath: call to praise

10th sabbath: temple veil and chariot-throne

3rd sabbath: ?

11th sabbath: praise of wall images and movements of chariot throne

2nd sabbath: description of heaven and its sanctuary

12th sabbath: one divine chariot throne, angelic procession, praise of gates

1st sabbath: establishment of angelic priesthood

13th sabbath: sacrifice, angelic high priests in vestments, God's mercy, contents and structure of heavenly temple

Biblical sources mentioning the existence of a heavenly temple/palace and perhaps influencing this text are:

Exodus 24:10–11:	Moses, Aaron, Nadab, and Abihu see in a vision Israel's God and the sapphire pavement under his feet
Isaiah 6:3	Isaiah has a vision of himself in the temple with angels ministering to God
Ezekiel 1, 3, and 10	Detailed description of the heavenly throne and angels around it
Daniel 7:9–14	Daniel has a vision of heaven with two thrones

rather emphasizing the beauty of understanding, and trying to reproduce, angelic praise.

The sabbath songs include priestly and princely angelic praise of the divine king as well as praise issuing from the vestibules and walls of his temple. In one fragment several extant letters suggest that Melchizedek may have been the chief angelic priest. In the twelfth song the cherubim, almost indistinguishable from the wheels of God's throne-chariot (see Ezekiel 1), worship God silently. One cannot hear this praise, but it is evident in the brass-like flashes of light emerging from his throne.

What was the function of this cycle of songs? Newsom thinks they may originally have been used in a Qumran communal sabbath ritual to legitimate their Zadokite priesthood. Schiffman sees these songs as descriptive in nature and not necessarily tied to communal worship. It is most peculiar that this work extends only through the first quarter of the religious year. Was it repeated? Did the priesthood of a sect separated from the Temple replicate the worship of the heavenly sanctuary instead? Or is it to be seen rather as a mystical text, describing a vision of glory?

The most obvious biblical antecedents to the sabbath songs are Ezekiel 1 and 10 and Isaiah 6:1–5. Revelation 8–11 also stands in this general tradition of visions of the heavenly courts. Another possible literary analogue is in 1 Enoch 14, where Enoch dreams he is taken up into the heavens and sees a building constructed of crystalline walls and tongues of fire. In this house there was a throne upon which sat the Great Glory. But this liturgy lacks a narrative framework. Nevertheless, whether or not it is sectarian, this Qumran text stands within a tradition that extends from the Bible to the so-called *Heikalot* (heavenly temples) texts of the early rabbinic period.

Fragments of the Damascus Document

'Whoever interrupts a fellow member shall be isolated and [punished for ten] days. Whoever falls asleep during the m[eeting of the Assembly]…shall be isolated for thirty days and be punished for ten days.' (4Q267 frag. 18, col. 4:4–6)

While the fragments from Caves 5 and 6 contain a portion of the known Damascus Document (4:19–21; 5:13–14, 5:18–6:2; 6:20–7:1), the Cave 4 manuscripts carry additional material, and sometimes in a different order. The two-part structure of Admonition and Laws appears to be in place, but there is additional material at the beginning, and a major additional section of Laws, compared to Cairo manuscript A (see p. 18).

J.T. Milik, the first editor of these fragments, therefore suggested that originally the document

Factfile

Manuscripts: 4QD[a-h] (4Q266–73), 5Q512, 6Q15
Editors: J.T. Milik and J. Baumgarten (*DJD* 18)
Commentary: J. Baumgarten
Script: Hasmonaean to Late Herodian

4QTherapeia

4QTherapeia was the provisional name that John Allegro gave to a small, nearly triangular (77 x 35 x 58 mm) fragment of text. Allegro called its script 'late Qumranic', which today would mean probably 50 CE or later. He described its language as 'an extraordinary mixture of transliterated Greek, Aramaic, and a grammatically irregular Hebrew, giving the inescapable impression of deliberate obscurantism, not entirely unfamiliar in medical writing.' In Allegro's view this text was the medical report of a travelling medicine man named Caiaphas. His translation mentions treatment for the ulcer of Hyrcanus Yannai; someone named Peter Yosai is also mentioned and one Zacharai Yannai is diagnosed as 'colicky'; a witness named Eli was present and Omriel dictated the text.

More recently James Charlesworth advocated a similar reading of the text. Joseph Naveh, however, decided it was nothing more than a scribe's writing practice, perhaps someone doodling in preparation for real writing. He observed that at points the scribe seemed to be practising certain letters of the alphabet, partly in alphabetical order, as a list of proper names.

Since Naveh's views were published, scholars (including Charlesworth) have tended to agree with him that 4QTherapeia constituted a writing exercise. And although Naveh noted that it was penned by a skilled scribe, no one has ever identified his script with any of those used to record the Dead Sea Scrolls.

Is Naveh's the last word or a failure to make sense of a peculiar Qumran text? Further attempts to understand this fragment may well be made.

The sabbath is strictly observed by the modern Jewish community; here a shop in Jerusalem is closed on a Friday afternoon in preparation.

Fragments of the Damascus Document from Cave 4.

consisted of an Admonition, a lengthy list of laws (greatly expanded in the Cave 4 fragments), and a concluding liturgy for the Feast of the Covenant Renewal. Philip R. Davies later studied the Damascus Document as a text modelled on the Covenant Renewal form, but the Cave 4 fragments were not then available to him or to other scholars. On the whole the text of the Cairo manuscripts is almost the same as those in Cave 4, but it remains uncertain whether there was one definitive version of this document (there certainly was not in the case of the Community Rule). It is not even certain that all the Cave 4 manuscripts contained an identical edition, and neither Milik nor Baumgarten, who took over the task of producing the official edition, has offered a definitive reconstruction of the original Damascus Document. The most significant variations from the Cairo texts in some of the Cave 4 manuscripts is an introductory discourse suggestive of the Two Spirits dualism of 1QS, and a Penal Code (also similar to the disciplinary rules in 1QS). These additions may confirm, as was already suspected by Davies from the Cairo manuscripts, that the Damascus Document had been edited within the *yahad*, which had made small but important additions. This in turn implies that in some way

the *yahad* developed from the 'Damascus' community. The suggestion remains disputed, but the differences between the D and S (as the 'Damascus' and Community Rule manuscripts are collectively termed) remain sufficiently distinct to require some kind of explanation.

Praise for Jerusalem and King Jonathan

The first column of one Cave 4 fragment (4Q448) contains a psalm, at first unrecognized but now identified as a Hebrew version of Psalm 154 in the Syriac Old Testament, which is also found in 11QPs[a].

But this discovery is as nothing compared with the next two columns, which contain a new hymn, written by a different scribe. Although it is in a fragmentary state, it has been deciphered by Ada Yardeni, with the main part as follows:

'…holy city for King Jonathan and for all the congregation of your people Israel, who are in the four corners of heaven. May their peace be on your kingdom. Blessed be your name.' (col. B)

'I will glo[ry] in your love…by day and until evening…to approach, to be…to visit them with

Documentary Texts

When the new editor-in-chief of the scrolls, Emanuel Tov, presented a list of still-unpublished scrolls from Cave 4 in 1992, he included a group of texts in Aramaic, Hebrew and Nabataean comprising letters, records of debts, property conveyances and accounts for grains. Lack of such everyday records had long puzzled scholars, and it was hoped that these texts would elucidate daily life at Qumran.

But are these texts actually from Qumran? In her edition of texts from the Wadi Seiyal, otherwise known as Nahal Hever, Ada Yardeni includes the so-called Cave 4 documentary texts only as an appendix, and expresses doubts over their origin. She does not claim to know where they came from, but for some she proposes Nahal Hever itself, 20 km (12 miles) south of Khirbet Qumran. This is because the so-called Cave 4 fragments include one from a manuscript found at Nahal Hever. She also notes that this kind of text is unlike the vast majority of materials in Cave 4. The cursive script is also quite different, and, finally, recent Carbon-14 dates for the manuscripts 4Q342 and 4Q344 date them 'long after the settlement at Khirbet Qumran was abandoned' (p. 74).

Twelve of these manuscripts were written on leather and seven on papyrus. 4Q342 is a letter, datable by its script to the 1st century CE (Carbon-14: 14–115 CE). It mentions the names Yehudah, Eleazar and Elishua. 4Q343, datable to *c*. 50 BCE, refers to Shimon, S'dlhy and Beit 'Aphek. 4Q344, which Carbon-14 has dated 72–127 CE, is a promissory note mentioning a certain Eleazar bar Joseph.

But palaeography and Carbon-14 do not always agree. 4Q345 is dated by its script to the middle to late 1st century BCE; but Carbon-14 gives the range 373–171 BCE. This fragment mentions the month of Elul, 30 silver denarii, and the names Yeshua', Hosha'yah, and Yishma'el ben Shimon. 4Q346 and 4Q348 are also deeds, containing personal names; 4Q351–58 are accounts dealing with grain; 4Q359 is a papyrus deed and Yardeni suggests that 4Q360a must have been a literary text that referred to sacrifices.

But are none of these from Qumran? Cross and Eshel claim to have deciphered a deed of a gift, written on two ostraca that were discovered in 1996 at Khirbet Qumran and contained the names of individuals from Jericho and perhaps Engedi. They even claimed that it includes the word *yahad*, though this has since been contradicted. Nevertheless, it is not impossible that some of these texts came from Qumran. Indeed, since the site was certainly occupied for at least 150 years in the Graeco-Roman period, it would be surprising for no such texts to be found at all.

Factfile

Manuscripts: 4Q342–60
Editors: H. Cotton and A. Yardeni (*DJD* 27)
Script: Early Herodian to post-Herodian

blessing…on your name which we call…kingdom to bless…day war…King Jonathan (?)' (col. C)

The question upon which all scholars seized is: who is King Jonathan? The editors, Hanan and Esther Eshel, followed by most scholars, identify him as the Hasmonaean king Alexander Jannaeus (Hebrew Yannai, an abbreviation of Yehonatan), who ruled from 103 to 76 BCE, and who is possibly alluded to in the Commentary on Nahum (see p. 98). The difficulty that this posed was that according to the received theory the writers of the scrolls were opposed to the Hasmonaeans. Hence the Eshels suggest that this hymn is not 'sectarian' (though they do not explain how or why it was used at Qumran). Geza Vermes has suggested an earlier Jonathan, the brother of Judas Maccabee and ruler of Judah from 160–142 BCE (well before the settlement at Qumran). Vermes regards this Jonathan as having first been in favour with the groups that finally went to Qumran (hence this text) but later as having been their arch-enemy, the 'Wicked Priest' of the Habakkuk Commentary (which hardly explains why the text was preserved at Qumran!).

While it was once thought that the scrolls are consistently anti-Hasmonaean, such a bias is not really evident, and Robert Eisenman is one Qumran scholar who has always maintained that the scrolls writers were strongly *pro*-Hasmonaean. In fact, there are no obvious sectarian features to this hymn, but its presence in a Qumran cave is not especially problematic. The mention of historical persons, however, is so rare in the scrolls that this text is important, whoever it refers to.

4Q448 contains a psalm, and a hymn praising King Jonathan. This king cannot be identified with certainty.

Caves 5 to 10

Cave 5 was discovered in 1952 just to the west of the ruins and near Wadi Qumran. It was on the edge of the plateau and Cave 6 (the only one of this group found by the Bedouin) was less than 1 km (0.6 miles) from the ruins. Caves 7 to 10, located to the south of the ruins, followed in 1955. Two of these caves, 5 and 10, seemed to have provided shelter. There were no traces of jars in Caves 5 and 9.

Cave 5 preserved the remains of rotted fragments from approximately 25–50 scrolls. These include portions of Deuteronomy, Kings, Isaiah, Amos, Psalms, Lamentations, the Damascus Document, the Community Rule, New Jerusalem and a text containing curses.

The fragments in Cave 6 include Genesis and Exodus in palaeo-Hebrew, Deuteronomy, Kings, Psalms, Song of Songs, Daniel, the Book of Giants, the Damascus Document, blessings, unknown apocrypha and calendrical materials.

Cave 7 is particularly interesting, for it contained four jars and the remains of 12 scrolls, all written in Greek, plus seven small scraps of papyrus. Two of the scrolls contained the Greek text of Exodus and the Letter of Jeremiah (an apocryphal work). Some of the other texts were sensationally claimed to have contained parts of the New Testament, but this was unsubstantiated, and a more likely identification is a Greek translation of 1 Enoch. But

the presence of only Greek texts in a single cave (there are also a very few in Cave 4) has naturally raised questions about the likely depositor.

Cave 8 preserves fragments of Genesis, the Psalms, a phylactery, and a mezuzah, while in Cave 9 there was just one unidentifiable papyrus fragment. Cave 10 contained only an ostracon inscribed with ten letters of the Hebrew alphabet, but indecipherable.

Although these caves, along with Caves 2 and 3, are usually considered 'minor caves', they are by no means insignificant. Most of them preserve portions of some biblical works. The presence of works such as the Damascus Document, the Community Rule and New Jerusalem shows, too, that the caves in the marl terrace and the cliffs close to the site were somehow connected with each other.

An important discovery in Cave 8 is a collection of leather tabs, of the kind that would be attached to the end of a scroll for opening it. Such a collection may add plausibility to the idea that Qumran was a scroll-making centre. Their presence in the cave strengthens the suggestion that the inhabitants of the site generally inhabited some of the caves rather than the buildings, because in the summer months artificial caves hewn in the marl terrace were considerably cooler.

Aerial view of the southern end of the Qumran terrace, with Caves 4, 5 and 6 shown on the promontory in the foreground (see map, p. 11, for their exact locations). The Qumran site is top left.

Cave 11

The last discovery of a manuscript cave was, fittingly, made by the Ta'amireh, the Bedouin tribe that had found the first cave. Thus, they rounded off a successful contest with the archaeologists, for although they discovered five, and the archaeologists six, the Bedouin hits included Caves 1, 4 and 11 – the three richest in scrolls.

Cave 11 was found in 1956, a year after Caves 7–10. It is just south of Cave 3 (the farthest from Qumran), and about 2 km (1.25 miles) north of the settlement. This cave contained 21 texts, some of them relatively complete, and the editing of these was entrusted to various parties. The first edition to appear was the Psalms Scroll (1965), edited by James Sanders, now of Claremont, California. A scroll of Leviticus written in palaeo-Hebrew was edited by D.N. Freedman and K.A. Mathews. Most of the remaining texts were assigned to the Netherlands; fragments of four other Psalms manuscripts and an apocryphal psalm were entrusted to J. van der Ploeg (appearing as journal articles between 1967 and 1987). Van der Ploeg also edited, with A.S. van der Woude, the Job Targum, and separately these two also published six other texts, while their colleague B. Jongeling published the 'New Jerusalem' manuscript. The complete edition of texts assigned to scholars in the Netherlands was published in *DJD* 23.

The most celebrated scroll from Cave 11 came to light much later than the initial discovery. Immediately following the occupation of the West Bank by Israelis in 1967, Yigael Yadin acquired from a dealer's shop in Bethlehem the longest non-biblical scroll preserved among the Qumran texts – the Temple Scroll. In an exemplary feat, Yadin published a three-volume edition in Hebrew in 1977, and an English translation appeared in 1983.

The entrance to Qumran Cave 11.

Factfile

Manuscripts: 11QT
(11Q20–21)
Editor: Y. Yadin
Commentary: J. Maier,
M.O. Wise
Length: c. 9 m (30 ft)
Script: Herodian

The Temple Scroll

'I will dwell with them for ever and will sanctify my sanctuary by my glory. I will cause my glory to rest on it until the day of creation on which I shall create my sanctuary, establishing it for myself for all time, according to the covenant which I made with Jacob at Bethel.' (11QT 29:7–9)

Rumours of large and as yet still hidden scrolls were circulating in Jerusalem throughout the 1960s. These were heightened when an American citizen approached Yigael Yadin, archaeologist and general, acting as a negotiator between the same Bethlehem dealer earlier involved with the Cave 1 manuscripts ('Kando'), and the State of Israel, in a deal for the sale of such a scroll. For seven years Yadin was waiting for his prize, but the negotiations came to nothing. However, in 1967 the dream was realized as the Israeli forces swept into the West Bank. Within days what was to be called the Temple Scroll, the largest of all non-biblical Dead Sea Scrolls, was in Yadin's hands rather than in the shoebox where it had lain previously, and within 10 years Yadin had produced a very full commentary. Kando was also considerably richer as a result of this transaction.

This beautifully written scroll is a rearrangement of biblical laws, with some additions, that appears to follow a pattern: the depiction starts in the inner Temple court of the priests and radiates outwards through Temple and city to the land itself, which provides the crops, animals and materials for the sacrifices over the festival cycle. The name 'Temple Scroll' reflects the fact that most of what is preserved covers the Jerusalem sanctuary. Nevertheless, the title may be a misnomer: its subject matter is more comprehensive.

In this text, God speaks almost continually in the first person, even when the biblical sources ascribe the words to Moses. He commands Israel to obey the laws that he dictates as soon as they settle in the Promised Land. Scriptural law clearly serves as the major source and inspiration, but there is a great deal of additional information about the architecture of the Temple, which is not mentioned in the Pentateuch. Behind this composition, in fact, lies a further scriptural tradition, for both 1 Kings 6–7 and Ezekiel 40–43 contain detailed descriptions of the building and furnishings of the Temple. The Temple Scroll then goes on to describe in detail the liturgical practices to be carried out here (again there are biblical precedents in Ezekiel 44–46 and in 1 Chronicles 23–26, not to mention the book of Leviticus). Laid out are the religious calendar, the sacrifices, purity rules; but also legislation for the military and political behaviour of the Jewish king, including how to deal with cases of treason – none of this latter legislation being scriptural in origin, nor known from any ancient Jewish source before the discovery of the scrolls.

(Above) This silver coin may depict the façade of the Jerusalem Temple. It was minted during the Second Jewish Revolt.

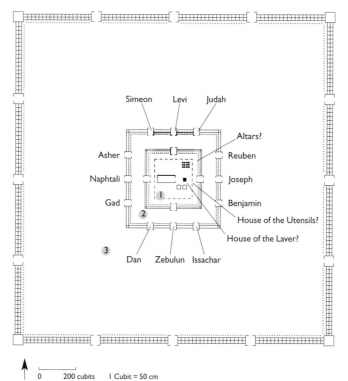

(Left) A diagram of the square Temple precinct as depicted in the Temple Scroll, with 12 gates, one for each tribe, and three courts.

Simeon   Levi   Judah

Altars?

Asher   Reuben

Naphtali   Joseph

Gad   Benjamin

House of the Utensils?

House of the Laver?

Dan   Zebulun   Issachar

1 Inner court (priests)
2 Middle court (males)
3 Outer court (Israelites)

0   200 cubits   1 Cubit = 50 cm

The scroll devotes 17 of its 65 columns (13–29) to describing meat, grain and liquid offerings to be brought to the Temple at the appropriate festivals. The ritual function of the High Priest, his fellow priests and the Levites are also spelled out in detail. Some festivals not included in the scriptures are also added, such as a wood-offering, and first-fruits of (olive) oil, and of wine:

'You shall count seven weeks from the day when you bring the new grain offering to the Lord…seven full sabbaths…until you have counted fifty days to the day after the seventh sabbath. You shall bring new wine for a drink-offering, four *hins* from all the tribes of Israel, one third of a *hin* [a *hin* was perhaps about 6 litres] for each tribe.' (col. 19)

The pattern of 50-day (7-week) intervals suggests to some scholars an ancient liturgical calendar, perhaps based on seven festivals a year. But if so, this cannot now be reliably reconstructed as a whole. What can be seen is that while these regulations are, strictly speaking, additions to scriptural law, they represent an extension of the scriptural principle of offering first-fruits of all harvests. They also, as we might expect from such a Qumran text, add details to a liturgical year that is based on a solar calendar.

The Temple itself is constructed with three courtyards, the inner one for the priests (descendants of Aaron), and for the Levites, descended from the families of Kohath, Gershom and Merari (Numbers 3:14–19). The middle court provides space for the ritually pure (males), non-priests and non-Levites to participate in Temple service. On each of the four walls of this court are three gates, each bearing a name of one of the 12 tribes of Israel. The walls of the outer court form a square space for women and foreigners, those not ritually qualified to enter the middle court.

The architectural and theological conception of this structure does not follow that of the desert tabernacle, nor either Solomon's (1 Kings 7) or Ezekiel's (Ezekiel 40–44) Temple. Its inspiration comes from the Israelite desert camp depicted in Exodus and Numbers. It represents concentric areas of increasing holiness, from the city of Jerusalem itself (represented by the 'camp'), through the three courts to the Holy of Holies. Outside the city ('camp') lies the area for impure persons such as lepers and those defiled by impure emissions.

'The city which I will sanctify, causing my name and my sanctuary to abide in it, shall be holy and pure of any impurity with which they can become impure.' (col. 47)

In the remaining columns of 11QT, the author follows closely the laws of Deuteronomy, though he presents a more systematic arrangement. The 'law of the king' in Deuteronomy 17:12–19 is modified considerably to fit more stringent holiness requirements. The king may not marry more than one wife (who must be Jewish), nor acquire too much wealth, and must obey the instruction of the priests.

(Following pages) Columns 56–57 of the Temple Scroll.

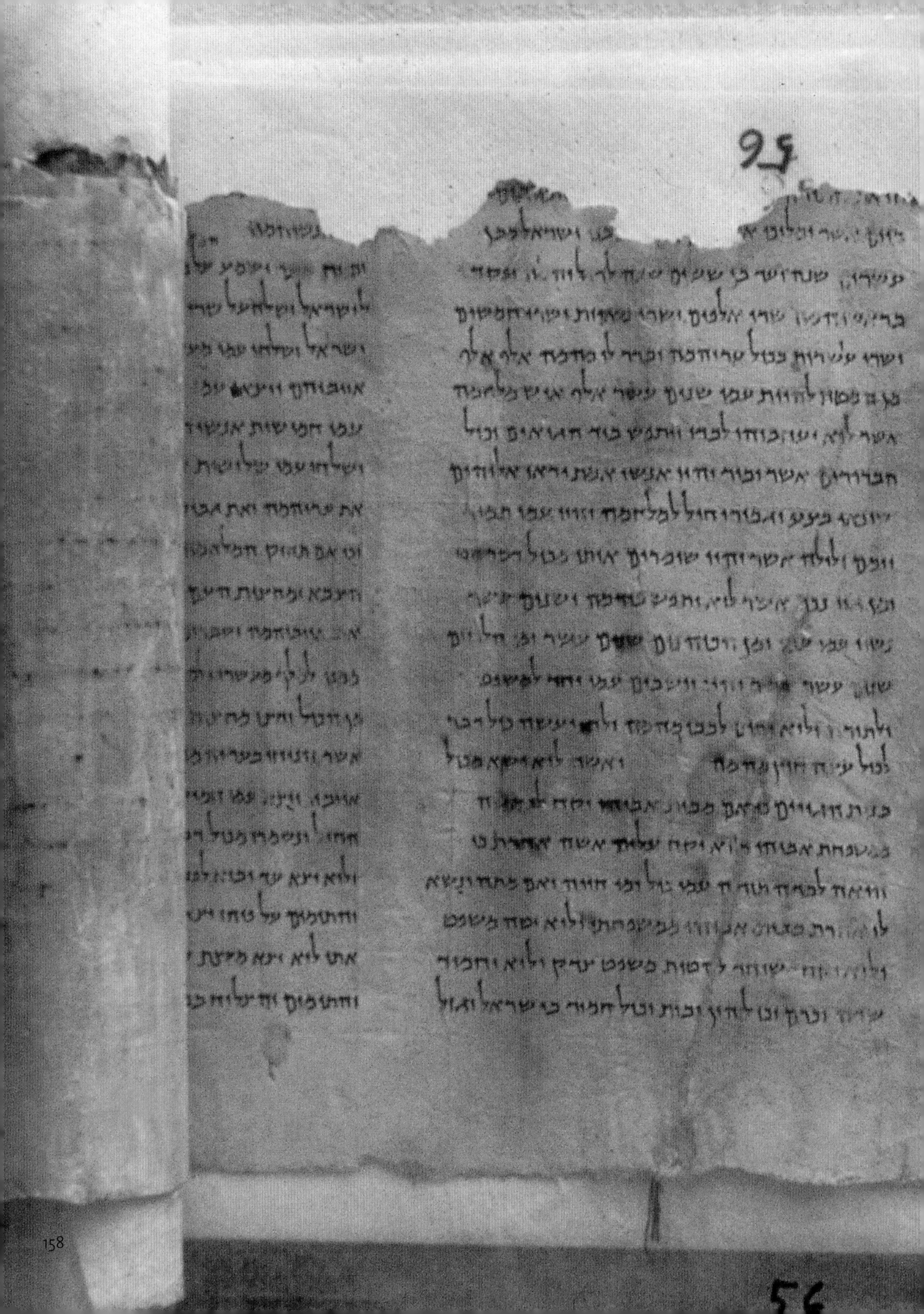

הדבר אשר על ...

ועשיתה על פי התורא אשר יגידו לכה ועל פי הדבר

אשר יאמרו לכה מספר התורא ויגידו לכה באמת

מן המקום אשר אב... לשכן שמי עלו ושמרתה לעשות

ככול אשר יורוכה ועל פי המשפט אשר יואמרו לכה

תעשה לוא תסור מן התורה אשר יגידו לכה ימין

ושמאול והאיש אשר לוא ישמע ויעש בזדון לבלתי

שמוע אל הכוהן העומד לשרת לפני או אל

השופט ומת האיש ההוא ובערתה הרע מישראל וכול

העם ישמעו ויראו ולוא ילידו שוד בישראל

כי תבוא אל הארץ אשר אנוכי נותן לכה וירשתה וישבתה

בה ואמרתה אשימה עלי מלך ככול הגואים אשר סביבותי

שום תשים עלוכה מלך מקרב אחיכה תשים עלוך מלך

לוא תתן עלוכה איש נוכרי אשר לוא אחיכה הוא רק לוא

ירבה לו סוס ולוא ישיב את העם מצריים למלחמה למען

הרבות לו סוס וכסף וזהב ואנוכי אמרתי לכה לוא

תוסיף לשוב בדרך הזואת עוד ולוא ירבה לו נשים ולוא

יסורו לבבו מאחרי וכסף וזהב לוא ירבה לו מואדה

והיה כשבתו על כסא ממלכתו וכתבו

לו את התורה הזואת על ספר מלפני הכוהנים חנק

Military officers he chooses must be of the highest calibre, and his bodyguard of 12,000 will be God-fearing warriors. His 36-man council of advisors will assist him in his decision-making:

'He [the king] shall select from them one thousand per tribe to be with him; twelve thousand warriors who shall not leave him alone to be captured by the nations…men of truth, God-fearers, haters of unjust gain and mighty warriors…The twelve princes of his people shall be with him, and twelve priests, and twelve levites…' (col. 57)

All these provisions serve to protect the king from impurity and violence, while the idea that he is to be subject to written laws and priestly guidance is already prescribed in the Bible (Deuteronomy 17:18, 'And when he sits on the throne of his kingdom, he shall have a copy of this law written for him in the presence of the levitical priests').

But what is the status of the law, and the Temple, presented in the Temple Scroll? One sentence in the scroll reads: '…until the day of creation (?) on which I [God] shall create my sanctuary…for all time'. Is the scroll, then, a blueprint for a future Temple, and for an Israel to be reconstituted? Or is it a vision of how things *should have been*? Perhaps these two alternatives, much debated by scholars, are not entirely contradictory. The author of the Temple Scroll has indeed presented an idealized priesthood, people and Temple, one which never existed in history, but perhaps one that it was thought would soon be brought into existence. The dimensions of the Temple itself are nevertheless quite fantastic, unlike any known Jewish temple. Its 1,600 cubits square (a cubit is about 45 cm or 18 ins) would have spread across the entire Herodian city of Jerusalem. How realistic is such a scheme?

Another vexing question is: how does this scroll relate to other Qumran scrolls? Yadin was convinced that it was a product of the 'Qumran sect' (i.e. the *yahad*). It was even suggested (by B.Z. Wacholder) that its contents were the Torah for the community, written by its founder, the Teacher of Righteousness. Some other scholars were initially not sure of a connection, because the contents of this scroll seemed then so different from the character of the other sectarian compositions. Yet its calendar is also shown by other scrolls, based on a year of 364 days made up of 12 30-day months plus four 'quarter days'. Moreover, other subsequently published texts, such as the Halakhic Letter (4QMMT), provide clear connections with its purity laws. The picture now emerging seems to be that, while there is little that links the Temple Scroll specifically to the *yahad*, it has clear overlaps with the book of Jubilees and the Damascus Document. There seems little doubt that it can be regarded as a 'sectarian' composition from the same circles as several other Qumran scrolls.

The Psalms Scroll

'David, Jesse's son, was wise and brilliant like the sun's light, a scribe both intelligent and perfect in all his ways before God and men. The Lord imbued him with an intelligent and brilliant spirit, whereby he composed 3,600 psalms and 364 songs for singing before the altar for the continual daily sacrifice, for every day of the year, and 52 songs for the sabbath offerings, and 30 songs for the new moons, for festivals and for the Day of Atonement. Together, the songs that he spoke were 446 and 4 songs for entertainment for those who were stricken [by evil].' (11QPs 27)

It is customary in Qumran studies to divide scrolls into 'biblical' and 'non-biblical'. Although the word 'biblical' is rather anachronistic, it is convenient. But this major Psalms Scroll, one of several found in Cave 11, is a disputed case.

The editing task was eventually entrusted in 1962 to James A. Sanders, who was then serving as Annual Professor at the American Schools in Jerusalem. Within about 13 months, and helped by many discussion partners, Sanders completed his work late in 1963, and it was published in 1965 – another case, like Yadin's Temple Scroll edition, of editorial efficiency. The scroll itself, with 27 columns and five fragments, contains about 51 items, but these are not arranged in the traditional scriptural order, while some psalms never before known to exist in Hebrew are included. The contents com-

prise – in their scroll order, but identified by scriptural numbering where relevant – Psalms 101–03, 109, 105, 146, 148, 121–32, 119, 135–36, 118, 145 with a superscription, 154, a 'Plea for Deliverance', 139, 137–38, Ben Sira or Sirach (now in the Apocrypha) 51:13–20 and 30, an 'Apostrophe to Zion', 93, 141, 133, 144, 155, 142–43, 149–50, a 'Hymn to the Creator', 2 Samuel 23:7, a prose piece about David's compositions, 140, 134 and 151.

Some of the additional psalms are known: 151 is in the Greek and 154–55 in the Syriac Old Testament. The extracts from 2 Samuel and Ben Sira are also known, but not in a book of Psalms. The rest are previously unknown, and one intriguing item (as quoted at the beginning of this section) is a prose account of David's compositional activity, suggesting that all the contents were ascribed to him. If this scroll is a Psalter, then, it represents a different order of contents – at least for the last two sections of the biblical book of Psalms (90–150). With the more recent release of information about Cave 4 texts, it is now known that there are more manuscripts of Psalms than of any other scriptural book (a total of 36), and these seem to fall broadly into two different recensions, one following the biblical order entirely, another following a different order (as here). An earlier suggestion that this Psalms Scroll did not represent a 'scriptural' collection but a private, individual edition, now seems improbable. More probably, we simply have two different editions of a canonized Psalm collection.

Two other general features of this manuscript are worth mentioning. One is that the catalogue of

the increased number of superscriptions to these psalms, linking them to events in David's life. That these increased over time can be seen by comparing this scroll with the Hebrew and the Greek Psalters (the Greek also has more superscriptions than the Hebrew). The ascription of psalms to David can thus be seen as a developing tradition in the Graeco-Roman period rather than an original assumption, far less a historical fact.

The strong Davidic character of this Psalter is reflected in Psalm 151, which is in reality two poems, recounting God's choice of David the shepherd, Samuel's anointing of him, and David's first display of divine strength against Goliath after the anointing. The Davidic climax to the Psalms collection is probably intentional, and contrasts with the structure of the biblical Psalter. (In the Syriac Psalter, this Psalm is the first, achieving a similar effect.)

Although the catalogue of David's compositions reflects a solar calendar (364 songs for daily sacrifice) it is not clear that any actual Psalms are sectarian. They may, nevertheless, display themes and interests shared by the writers of the scrolls: the psalms are prophetically inspired, there is an emphasis on revealed wisdom (Psalm 154, Hymn to

Factfile

Manuscript: 11QPs^a (11Q5)
Editor: J.A. Sanders
(*DJD* 4)
Length: 27 columns and 5 fragments (4.2 m, 13 ft)
Script: Middle to Late Herodian

(Left) This terracotta plaque probably shows the young David playing the harp.

(Below) A sheet from the Cave 11 Psalms Scroll. The divine name is written in palaeo-Hebrew.

Davidic compositions shows him credited with a complete cycle of sacrificial poems as well as songs against evil spirits (presumably inspired by the case of Saul). David is also said here to have been perfect in his ways and to have composed under prophetic inspiration (both the *pesharim* and the New Testament, e.g. Acts 2:30, treat the Psalms as prophetic). The other feature of the collection is

the Creator, the Davidic prose section), and also a reference to four Davidic compositions in aid of those stricken by evil spirits – in keeping with other exorcistic hymns at Qumran, such as the 'Songs of the Maskil' (see p. 145). The possibility that these Psalms were used in a sectarian liturgy must therefore be considered.

Factfile

Manuscript: 11QMelch
(11Q13)
Editor: A.S. van der
Woude (*DJD* 23)
Commentary: P. Kobelski
Length: 3 columns (c. 42
cm, 18 in)
Script: Late Hasmonaean

Melchizedek

'…this will (occur) in the first week of the Jubilee that
follows the nine Jubilees. And the Day of Atonement is
the e[nd of the] tenth [Ju]bilee, when all the sons of [light]
and the men of the lot of Mel[chi]zedek will be atoned
for.' (11QMelch, 2:7–8)

Melchizedek appears three times in the Bible.
In Genesis 14:18, he is a mysterious 'King of Salem'
and priest of 'God Most High', to whom Abraham
gives a tithe. In Psalm 110:4 the king is addressed
as 'a priest forever according to the order of
Melchizedek', while in Hebrews 5–7 Melchizedek
and his rank form the basis for the author's
presentation of Jesus as a
high priest. A king-priest, this
figure was an important proto-
type for the Hasmonaean
priest-kings and for those looking for a messiah to combine
both the anointed offices.

The text of the document is
unfortunately only partially
preserved, and in 10 fragments.
Only the second of the three
columns that can be made out
preserves any readable text
(col. 3 has odd words in about
eight lines) – a total of roughly
two-dozen incomplete lines.
Many of the fragments contain
biblical texts, which makes it
easier to reconstruct the flow. It
is, like the Florilegium (see p.
129), a 'thematic' commentary,
interpreting texts from different parts of the scriptures on
the basis of a topical link, not
interpreting texts from a single book and in
sequence, as in the Commentaries on Habakkuk or
Nahum. Here it differs from the *pesharim*, although
it includes some passages that begin with the word
pesher and introduce *pesher*-like equations of
biblical words or phrases with people or objects.
The overall theme of the composition (or at least of
what has been preserved of it) is the final deliverance of Israel from its sin through a Day of
Atonement sacrifice by the heavenly high priest
Melchizedek, which will be accompanied by the
destruction of the wicked.

The argument is built up through the association
of texts from different scriptural books, starting
with Leviticus 25:13 and Deuteronomy 15:2, which
legislate for the sabbatical and Jubilee years (7th
and 49th/50th). Deuteronomy calls this a 'year of
release', and Isaiah 61:1 is the next text cited
because it speaks of proclamation of freedom for

captives in the 'year of the Lord's favour' (hence
'year of release' is identified as 'year of favour'). A
piece of *pesher* exegesis explains that the captives
will join the 'children of Heaven' and the 'party of
Melchizedek', and that this will occur in the first
week after the end of the ninth Jubilee. Then at the
end of the tenth Jubilee, the 'children of light' and
the party of Melchizedek will be atoned for.
Melchizedek, in fact, is being identified in places
where the biblical texts speak of 'God', and this is
justified by citing Psalm 82, where 'God' judges in
the divine assembly. This judgment by 'God' is
interpreted (a *pesher* again) as a judgment against
'Belial and the spirits of his lot' who rebelled
against God's precepts. Hence 'God' (as in 'sons of
God', e.g. Genesis 6:2) can be taken to refer to any
divine being.

*The view to the east
from the inside of
Cave 11.*

The argument moves on: 'this is the day…of
which Isaiah the prophet spoke: "How beautiful
upon the mountains are the feet of the messenger…"' (Isaiah 52:7). Isaiah's mountains are
interpreted (another *pesher* section) as the prophets,
while the 'messenger' is the 'one anointed by the
spirit', a prince foretold in Daniel 9:25. The 'bearer
of good tidings' in Isaiah 52:7 is then identified with
the 'comforter' of Isaiah 61:2–3, bringing the interpretation full circle back to the 'year of favour'.

The task of this anointed 'comforter' is to give
solace by helping the 'afflicted' to understand the
course of history. For eventually, God will reign in
'Zion', which is interpreted as referring to those who
'abandon the ways of the people'. The column ends

with a return to Leviticus 25:9, which mentions the blowing of a horn on the year of Jubilee, and probably associates this with the blowing of the horn to announce warfare, for the scraps of text in col. 3 mention 'devouring Belial with fire' and the 'ramparts of Jer[usalem?]'.

This text offers not only an ingenious argument from scripture but a number of very interesting features besides. First, we have a *heavenly* deliverer (not an earthly messiah) in the form of a high priest. Melchizedek, as priest and king, and without a genealogy, who blessed Abraham, is an obvious figure to whom to assign a role such as this. Also significant is the calculation of world history as 10 jubilees (490 or 500 years) such as is found in 1 Enoch and in Daniel 9 (which calculates the total by 70 x 7). A common tradition regarding the imminent end of the world order seems to underlie all these texts. Finally, the emphasis on salvation for the 'children of light' through an act in the heavenly temple suggests some connection with the Songs of the Sabbath Sacrifice (4Q400–07, 11Q17 – see p. 146), in which Melchidezek (as High Priest) probably also plays a role.

The Letter to the Hebrews uses Melchizedek in a slightly different way, as an archetype of a different order of priesthood (i.e. not Levitical); that there is any *direct* connection between the two texts is possible, though doubtful. But there are strong links between the Qumran text and Luke 4:18–19, where Jesus stands up after the reading of the Law, unrolls Isaiah almost to the end, quotes 61:1–2, and announces its present fulfilment. This is a more emphatic statement of the same claim as in our text, that the end of Israel's 'captivity' was over. That the act of salvation was understood in the same way by either Jesus or Luke (whoever the author of this statement) is unlikely. But divine release would have to be preceded by atonement for the sins that had caused the captivity, and the Qumran scrolls seem to be almost if not entirely in support of this position.

This painting by Rubens (c. 1616–17) shows the meeting between Melchizedek, the priest and king, and Abraham.

Biblical Manuscripts from the Qumran Caves

It is clearly anachronistic to use the term 'biblical' without some qualification. The groups and individuals who owned and used the scrolls did not consistently follow a strict list of 'biblical' works. Such an exclusive canon of scriptures is

Their relationship to other varying contemporary forms of the scriptural books, such as those that became the 'received' Hebrew text of the Bible (known as the 'Masoretic text'), the text underlying the ancient Greek version, and the text (of the Pentateuch) preserved by the Samaritans, enables us to reconstruct to some extent a complicated history of the evolution of the scriptural text. Although the Qumran authors clearly did not have (or apparently care about) a standard text of the scriptures, the process of standardization of the Hebrew text was perhaps by this time already beginning, since new Greek translations were starting to conform to this new standard, for example the text of the Minor Prophets found in the Judaean desert at Murabba'at (and published in *DJD* 8).

The Isaiahᵃ Scroll from Qumran Cave 1.

never spelled out. Although all (except Esther and Nehemiah, which may be accidental) the books in the Hebrew Bible/Old Testament are represented in the Qumran caves, it seems that other texts were regarded as having equal status. Jubilees and an (unknown to us) work of Levi are also cited as authoritative. Testimonia seems to quote the Apocryphon of Joshua (see p. 122) as an authority. Other influential texts such as the Enoch books were quite probably regarded similarly, and some now in the Apocrypha, such as Tobit (Cave 4) and Ben Sira (Cave 2) may also have been included in what the writers of the scrolls took as their scriptures.

There is a wide variety of textual forms and editions of most of the Qumran biblical manuscripts.

The most famous of the Qumran biblical scrolls is the 'Great Isaiah Scroll' from Cave 1. It is the longest of the biblical scrolls, containing the entire book of Isaiah. It is very similar to the standard Hebrew 'Masoretic' text but there are occasional differences in wording and in spelling. Several of its readings have even been incorporated into modern English Bible translations, such as the Revised Standard Version (RSV). Here is one example: in Isaiah 49:24, where the traditional Hebrew text runs: 'Can prey be taken from a powerful man, or can the captive of a righteous man escape?'. 'Righteous' looks so wrong that the King James Version alters it to: 'Shall the prey be taken from the mighty, or the lawful captive delivered?' The Isaiah Scroll reads 'tyrant' instead of 'righteous', which is the translation given in the RSV.

Manuscripts and Caves

	1	2	3	4	5	6	7	8	11
Genesis	*	*		*		*		*	*!
Exodus	*	*		*			*		
Leviticus	*	*		*		*			
Numbers				*					
Deuteronomy	*	*		*	*	*			
Joshua				*					
Judges	*			*					
Samuel	*								
Kings				*	*	*			
Isaiah	*			*					
Jeremiah		*		*					
Ezekiel	*		*	*					
Hosea				*					
Amos				*	*				
Obadiah				*					
Jonah				*					
Micah				*					
Nahum				*					
Habakkuk				*					
Zephaniah				*					
Haggai				*					
Zechariah				*					
Malachi				*					
Psalms		*	*	*!	*	*		*!	
Job		*		*					
Proverbs				*?					
Ruth		*							
Song of Songs						*			
Ecclesiastes									
Lamentations			*		*				
Esther									
Daniel	*					*			
Ezra				*					
Chronicles									

Above is a table indicating the presence of the traditional biblical books in the Qumran caves. An asterisk (*) indicates the presence of some portion of the book. An exclamation mark (!) indicates the presence of the book but with clear deviations from the traditional order. A question mark (?) indicates there is some doubt about the identity of the manuscript.

But is the Qumran Isaiah Scroll the most reliable version of the book of Isaiah that we have, just because it is the oldest (from about 100 BCE)? Not necessarily: there are places where differences from our traditional text may be due to error or even deliberate alteration and it is often impossible to be sure.

Did any 'sectarian' works, or other works found at Qumran, enjoy a similarly authoritative status to known scriptural texts within certain communities? Were they part of the 'scriptures' for some Jews? The Damascus Document also quotes, apparently as an authoritative source, the book of Jubilees. It also puts the 'words of the Teacher' on a similar footing with the 'Law of Moses' and so it seems in principle likely that some of the *yahad*'s own writings, or some of their favourite writings, were given a scriptural or quasi-scriptural status (such as, for instance, the letters of Paul acquired before a formal New Testament canon was recognized). The Temple Scroll (whether or not it stems from the *yahad*) is thought by some scholars to belong to such a category.

The table (right) shows the number of manuscripts of each biblical book discovered in the caves. The numbers do not necessarily reflect the original quantities that may have belonged to the archive, of course, but possibly give some idea of the relative popularity of the books among the writers and original readers of the scrolls. Even a brief glance will show that the Pentateuch (and especially Deuteronomy), Isaiah and Psalms were clear favourites.

The table below shows the number of Hebrew manuscripts of biblical books discovered in the caves.

Genesis	19
Exodus	17
Leviticus	13
Numbers	7
Deuteronomy	30
Joshua	2
Judges	3
1–2 Samuel	4
1–2 Kings	3
Isaiah	21
Jeremiah	6
Ezekiel	6
Minor Prophets	8
Psalms	36
Proverbs	2
Job	4
Song of Songs	4
Ruth	4
Lamentations	4
Ecclesiastes	2
Esther	0
Daniel	8
Ezra	1
Nehemiah	0
1–2 Chronicles	1

Although the ruins at Qumran had long been known by the time Cave 1 was discovered, the two sites were not at first connected by de Vaux and his colleagues. However, once the connection had been made, and the ruins excavated, it became clear that an ancient settlement, contemporary with the writing of the scrolls, had once stood close to the manuscript caves. It became commonplace to regard this settlement as the home of the writers of the scrolls, the residence of the 'Qumran sect'.

The manuscript connection probably influenced even the excavations themselves, and certainly dominated the next 40 years of scholarship. Nevertheless, over this time a number of little problems continued to niggle. Basically, the settlement itself does not necessarily suggest a religious, sectarian community unless the contents of the scrolls are read into the interpretation. More particularly, the place of the Copper Scroll in this scheme remains problematic. And why were the scrolls written in so many different hands (and often in different versions) if they were the product of a small group? How is the different manner of deposit (from the careful storage in Cave 1 to the apparently careless abandonment in Cave 4) to be explained? And what are female skeletons doing in the cemetery adjacent to a supposedly celibate male commune?

These questions, together with the publication of further reflections, interpretations and even excavations of the Qumran site itself in recent years, have led to some doubts about the nature of the connections between the settlement and the scrolls. While most scholars continue to accept a close relationship, it is doubted by many that all (or perhaps any) of the scrolls were actually written here. That they belonged to the inhabitants remains the majority view, however.

In the following pages we shall explore the ruins themselves and then trace their probable history as reconstructed by de Vaux. We conclude with a review of more recent work and of the various options currently under consideration.

Aerial view of the settlement of Qumran, clearly showing the aqueduct system and cisterns.

IV The Qumran Settlement

The Qumran Settlement

The setting

The ruins known as Khirbet Qumran ('Khirbet' means 'ruin' in Arabic) lie roughly 20 km (13 miles) east of Jerusalem, about 15 km (9 miles) south of Jericho, 32 km (20 miles) north of Engedi, and just over a kilometre (less than a mile) inland from the Dead Sea. Today a modern road runs along the western shore of the Dead Sea, with a spur to the plateau at the foot of the cliffs, just beside the Wadi Qumran, on which the ruins stand, protected by ravines on three sides and fed with water by an aqueduct from the wadi. In ancient times one would have walked along the shore to Jericho, the main city of the province in which Qumran lay, but to Jerusalem the route lay up the Wadi Qumran, across the Buqei'a (a shallow plain above the cliffs) and through the Judaean desert. Another possible access route lay by boat across the Dead Sea.

Many writers insist on the splendid isolation of Qumran, but it is doubtful that its settlers were completely isolated from Jewish civilization, and in recent years more and more ancient settlements in the region have been uncovered. Jerusalem could easily have been visited for festivals, while Jericho may have provided a major market for the goods produced at Qumran, such as pottery or perhaps date honey, balsam, leather or even scrolls. The Hasmonaean-Herodian fortress of Hyrcanion was visible from the top of the Wadi Qumran. A number of Iron Age sites, found during the Qumran excavations in the Buqei'a (and including Qumran itself), suggest that the area had formerly been developed for agriculture (unless, as some scholars think, these were fortresses). Two recently published ostraca (potsherds with writing on them – see p. 186) found on the surface next to the eastern wall of the main settlement at Khirbet Qumran refer to individuals from Jericho and possibly Engedi. If these readings are correct, they at least prove that the inhabitants of Khirbet Qumran were in touch with these two towns.

The area was not as inhospitable as is sometimes claimed. The mean annual rainfall in the region rarely exceeds 75 mm, compared to 550 mm for Jerusalem. But rains from the Judaean desert highlands to the west run off to the Dead Sea through wadis (seasonal watercourses), one of which lies adjacent to the site. A couple of miles to the south at Ain Feshkha fresh water was also constantly available. For centuries Bedouin and others have watered (and fed) their herds in this vicinity. Early in the 20th century expeditions carried out by E.W.G. Masterman on behalf of the Palestine Exploration Fund noted the abundant presence at Ain Feshkha of wild game, including boars, conies, partridges, quails, pigeons and wild ducks, not to mention snakes, gazelle and hares. The caves

View over the Qumran ruins looking west. An aqueduct (visible remains link the site to the foothills) brought water from the hills on the few occasions when it rained each year.

around Khirbet Qumran yielded reed mats and some woven cloth, leather pieces, nails and wooden pegs, while above the cliffs, on the Buqei'a, it was possible to grow cereal crops. The inhabitants of Qumran, then, were neither isolated nor unable to sustain themselves.

Thus, while some scholars (and the popular imagination) picture a desolate life at Khirbet Qumran, others see a connection between this settlement, the immediate physical context, and the larger world. The original excavators, prompted by the scrolls, were influenced by the ideology of the Cave 1 texts. They did not, as archaeologists do now, ask about the ecology or the economic or social context of this settlement, but focused on it as a *segregated* settlement. For this was a place to which people, it was thought, had fled from elsewhere. The following report by the 1st-century CE traveller Pliny of a monastic community 'above Engedi' led the excavators to focus on the site itself, whose function and inhabitants they thought they already knew:

'On the west side of the Dead Sea, but out of range of the noxious exhalations on the coast, is the solitary tribe of the Essenes, which is remarkable beyond all the other tribes in the whole world, as it has no women and has renounced all sexual desire, has no money, and has only palm trees for company. Day by day the throng of refugees is recruited to an equal number by numerous accessions of persons tired of life and driven thither by the ways of fortune to adopt their manners. Thus through thousands of ages – incredible to relate – a race in which no one is born lives on forever. So prolific for their advantage is other men's weariness of life!

Lying below them was formerly the town of Engedi, second only to Jerusalem in the fertility of the land and in its groves of palm trees, but now, like Jerusalem, a heap of ashes.' (*Natural History* 5:73)

Even if Pliny means 'Jericho' and not 'Jerusalem', it was his report that directly led to the identification of Qumran as an Essene settlement. But recently renewed scrutiny of the archaeology of the site has led to uncertainty about its use, and other candidates for Pliny's site have been found further south along the shore, nearer (and even above) Engedi. So was Qumran such an isolated settlement? Did it perhaps belong with other similar settlements near the Dead Sea? What *were* the connections between Qumran and Ain Feshkha (which is widely thought to have been part of the Qumran complex) and other settlements such as Ain el Ghuweir a little further south? To what degree was Qumran economically linked with the outside world? And what sort of economy did the Qumran inhabitants practise?

Pliny's statements suggested, rather romantically, a place cut off from the world, and resorted to for that purpose. But his account, it has to be said, conflicts with certain data. Skeletons of women and children are included in the large cemetery complex at Khirbet Qumran. The presence of carved pillar bases, and the significance of several hoards of coins, apparently buried at the site, also raises questions about his description of the poverty of the inhabitants.

If the 'monastery' theory has generally held sway since de Vaux's excavations, the longest-standing theory about the nature of Khirbet Qumran is that it was a fort. When the explorer F. de Saulcy ventured upon Khirbet Qumran in 1861, he thought he had found biblical Gomorrah. Amazingly, the name Qumran sounds quite similar. The biblical scholar F.-M. Abel later thought he had found the cemetery of a Muslim-type sect before Mohammed. At the time of the First World War Gustav Dalman, the German orientalist, again characterized the ruins as those of a Roman fort. The chief archaeologist of the site, Roland de Vaux, even dubbed it a sort of fortress or military outpost at first. It certainly exhibits some defensive architecture, including a tower, perimeter walls and a site atop a plateau accessible from one side only. And the Romans used it as an outpost during and just after they captured it during the Jewish revolt of 66–73/74 CE. But in this part of the world, any settlement might require such precautions.

How many persons did this settlement accommodate? In the three or four cemeteries lying approximately 50 m (165 ft) east of the settlement, it has been estimated that more than 1,100 people were buried. Estimates of the population actually vary from about 100 to several hundred. If, as seems likely, the core buildings themselves were used only for working and not habitation (for which some of the nearby caves, and possibly also tents, were used) it is difficult to be certain. It is also difficult to calculate the population from the water provision, because evaporation rates, and the amount of water provided for ritual washing, cannot be accurately measured. And, most important of all, who were these inhabitants? Of their beliefs the site tells us very little. That is why the nature of the connection between the site and the scrolls is a crucial issue.

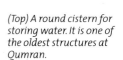

(Top) A round cistern for storing water. It is one of the oldest structures at Qumran.

(Above) A water channel runs through the Qumran site carrying water to several large cisterns and ritual baths.

(Above) View over Qumran to the north-east
from the hills above the Wadi Qumran, with
the Dead Sea in the distance.

(Below) Line drawing of the photograph
above identifying key places in the
topography.

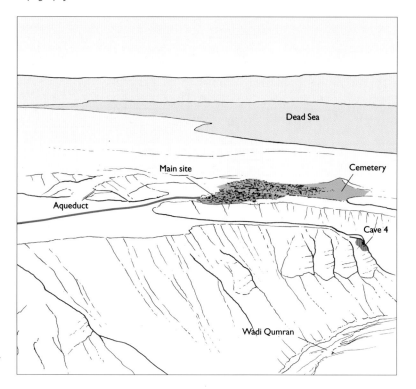

Dead Sea

Main site

Cemetery

Aqueduct

Cave 4

Wadi Qumran

(Opposite) Aerial view over
the Qumran site towards
the Dead Sea, which is a few
hundred metres to the east.

Excavating Qumran

The scrolls and scroll fragments discovered in Cave 1, less than a mile north-northwest of Khirbet Qumran, focused attention upon this previously uninteresting site. After the Israeli-Jordanian war of 1948–49, Cave 1 was rediscovered, and then excavated, by de Vaux of the French École Biblique and Lankester Harding of the Department of Antiquities of Jordan. After initially ignoring it, de Vaux then quickly linked the site to the scrolls, and began to interpret the settlement at Khirbet Qumran in the light of the contents of the scrolls that were being published even as the excavations began.

After an initial survey of the site in 1951, excavations were conducted from 1953–56, under the auspices of the Department of Antiquities of Jordan and the École Biblique in Jerusalem. Although he published reports in the École's own journal (the *Revue Biblique*) and a popular account of the excavations entitled *Archaeology and the Dead Sea Scrolls*, de Vaux's detailed notes are only now being published, many years after his death in 1971. His excavation journals show that from locus 1 (which he excavated in December 1951) onwards, he had already recognized a series of occupation layers. The earliest dated from the time of the Judaean monarchy (Iron II), when it was a small outpost with a walled courtyard, cistern and a few rooms. A key piece of evidence for this settlement period was a stamp on a jar handle reading *lmlk* ('royal property'). Some possible biblical evidence for the site may lie in Joshua 15:16, mentioning towns 'in the Arabah [the Dead Sea depression], including the "City of Salt"'. There is also a note in 2 Chronicles 26:10 that Uzziah king of Judah 'built towers in the Arabah (Dead Sea Valley) and hewed cisterns'. Although this so-called 'Israelite' occupation had no connection with the scrolls at all, it is instructive in showing the possible uses for a site in this location, whether for military or economic purposes, while the fact that a previous occupation had taken place here presumably prompted the later settlers to choose this spot.

(Above and left) Scenes from excavations at Qumran.

Ain Feshkha

The settlement at Khirbet Qumran needs to be seen in its broader context, which includes the nearby site of Ain Feshkha, situated 3 km (2 miles) south, and excavated by de Vaux in the last season of his Qumran campaign (1956). Remains of a wall, previously observed, running south from Qumran and north from Ain Feshkha, suggested a connection between the two sites, and the periods of occupation were found to correspond. Ain Feshkha is famous for its freshwater springs, and today it is known for its swimming beach. The remains of the main excavated structure measure 25 by 20 m (82 by 66 ft) and comprise a central courtyard with corner structures, one perhaps a storage area and the other a drainage system. Archaeologists discovered cupboards and paved floors to what was definitely a two-storey building.

De Vaux came to see Khirbet Qumran and Ain Feshkha as sections of a single agricultural and economic complex. The wall may have enclosed the property of the occupants of the sites. The pottery at Feshkha corresponds to Qumran Periods Ib and II, and the site was apparently destroyed by fire at the end of Period II, though coins recovered from later layers suggest it was reoccupied by Jews during the 1st and 2nd centuries CE.

De Vaux rather tentatively interpreted a system of water channels northeast of the main structure as a tannery, producing the leather for scrolls, but this theory is now discarded. However, Feshkha may have served the Qumran

inhabitants in other ways. Herdsmen and shepherds could feed flocks on dried reeds, and the date-palms were no doubt part of the human diet.

Several years after de Vaux's excavations, the possibility of other related sites on the Dead Sea shore was raised by the discovery of another huge building (c. 20 by 45 m, 66 by 148 ft) about 12 km (7.5 miles) south of Qumran, at Ain el Ghuweir in 1977. This site also had a cemetery with graves of the same distinctive kind as at Qumran. Possibly, then, the western shore of the Dead Sea was inhabited by related religious groups, even perhaps other Essene communities?

The remains of Ain Feshkha shortly after the completion of the excavations there.

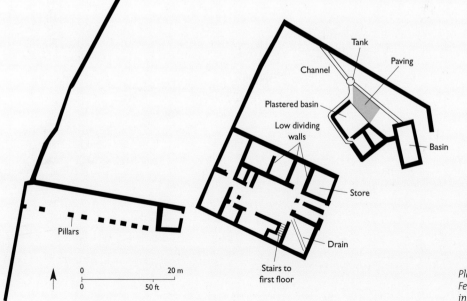

Plan of the site at Ain Feshkha. Notice the water installation.

Outline of the site

The plans of the site show its occupation in three phases, as de Vaux interpreted its settlement history. After the ancient occupation in the days of monarchic Judah (possibly the 8th century BCE), it saw a very restricted re-occupation (Period Ia) in the form of a round cistern, courtyard, a few rooms and possibly a tower. Soon afterwards it was expanded and assumed the form it was to retain (in Periods Ib–II), with a central corridor running north-south and dividing two blocks. The western block was understood to be devoted to industrial and economic activity, with workshops and storerooms, while the eastern block contained meeting rooms and kitchens. A solid tower guarded the site entrance.

To the south was a large room, possibly for meeting or eating (or both), and further east a potter's workshop, with a wheel and kilns. A wall then formed the eastern boundary, beyond which lay the cemetery. Entering the northwest corner, an aqueduct brought water, transported from the wadi, into a large pool and thence through the settlement, filling numerous cisterns.

On first impressions, the strategic location of the site, on a plateau overlooking the Dead Sea, with walls and a tower, favours a military use and the site ended its occupation as the home of a Roman garrison in the wake of the First Jewish Revolt (66–73/74 CE).

(Below and opposite) Plans of Qumran at different stages in the settlement's history.

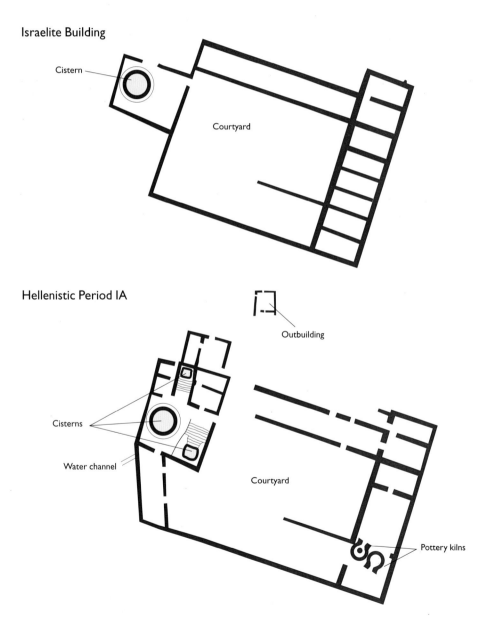

Israelite Building

Cistern

Courtyard

Hellenistic Period IA

Outbuilding

Cisterns

Water channel

Courtyard

Pottery kilns

Hellenistic Period 1B and Herodian Period

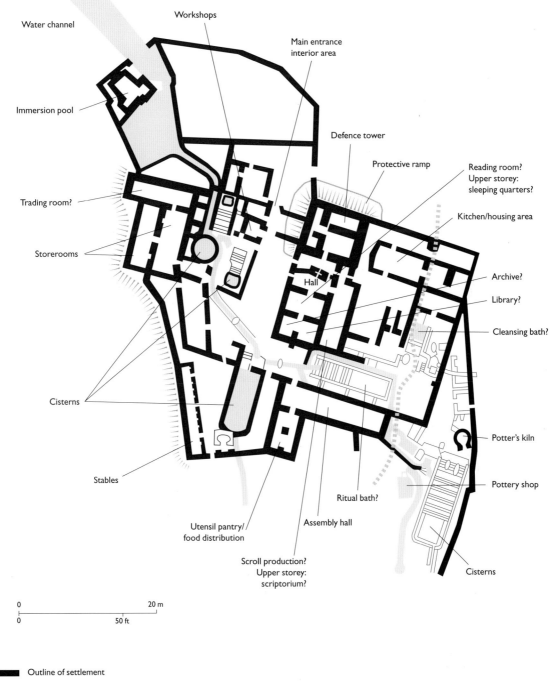

Water channel

Workshops

Main entrance
interior area

Immersion pool

Defence tower

Protective ramp

Reading room?
Upper storey:
sleeping quarters?

Trading room?

Kitchen/housing area

Storerooms

Archive?

Library?

Hall

Cleansing bath?

Cisterns

Potter's kiln

Stables

Pottery shop

Ritual bath?

Cisterns

Utensil pantry/
food distribution

Assembly hall

Scroll production?
Upper storey:
scriptorium?

0   20 m

0   50 ft

Outline of settlement

Water system

Split possibly caused by earthquake of 31 BCE.

Main phases of occupation

The first phase of settlement in the Graeco-Roman period, which de Vaux called Period Ia (and for which he had no direct evidence), was conjectured to have lasted for a few years during the last third of the 2nd century BCE. It was erected on the earlier remains from the time of the old Judaean monarchy, and the original (round) cistern was provided with a water channel, while two more rectangular cisterns were added. Extra rooms and two pottery kilns were also built.

Only with Period Ib, the so-called definitive phase in the settlement history of Khirbet Qumran, can dating be attempted, and here pottery and coins provide the evidence. Now the settlement was enlarged to the west and south, its water system vastly expanded to include an aqueduct from the wadi and a two-storey defensive tower on the north. The site was now divided into two parts, with a central passage between them; the smaller western block was the industrial area, the eastern for cooking, meeting and (possibly) sleeping. Several more large cisterns were also attached to the water channel, many with steps provided.

Few of the buildings, apart from the storerooms (whose walls were coated with lime) can actually be identified as to their use, though some conjectures were made in line with the supposed daily life of the inhabitants. For example, in one room at the south end the ceiling had collapsed in Period Ib, trapping over 1,000 pieces of pottery, including 210 plates and 708 bowls, all stacked and piled into rectangular batches. In front of these bowls de Vaux uncovered approximately 75 beakers. The largest room in the complex, which lay next door, was interpreted as the dining/assembly room ('refectory'), and this pottery room as the crockery store. However, the pottery workshop was quite near, and the room may have been a store for finished products. And was the room next door a 'refectory'? A more prominent example of de Vaux's scrolls-inspired interpretation was a second-storey chamber identified as a writing room ('scriptorium'), because of some pieces of plaster that were later famously 'reconstructed' as a writing-table 5 m (16.4 ft) long. A couple of inkwells were also found – all this having fallen down to ground level at some point. But locus 30 is probably no scriptorium: writing was not done on tables in this era.

What are the dates of the Ib period of settlement? In some locations de Vaux discovered a destruction layer and above this accumulated sediment. This suggested to him a fire and some flooding of the water system. But the pottery both below and above these layers is not sufficiently distinctive to give a date for the end of Ib. The coins are a different matter, especially bronze coins, which have a life of a few decades at most. The coins on top of this sediment dated from the time of Agrippa I (37–44 CE). The coins below included Seleucid silver pieces (i.e. from the Greek/Syrian Hellenistic kingdom that ruled Judaea in the early 2nd century BCE). Silver coins have a longer life, and these dated from 145–125 BCE. But Seleucid bronze coins from 223–129 BCE were also found. Some 143 coins come from the time of King Alexander Jannaeus (*c.* 103–76 BCE) and single coins represent the reigns of his widow and successor Salome Alexandra (*c.* 76–67 BCE) and her son Hyrcanus II (*c.* 63–40 BCE). Four belong to the time of Antigonus Mattathias (*c.* 40–37 BCE). De Vaux also discovered undated coins from the reign of the next ruler, Herod the Great, but decided that these had been dropped during the later Period II. This reasoning led him to suggest a date around the beginning of the 1st century BCE for Period Ib.

Was this cistern damaged by an earthquake or by a fault in the marl plateau? Was it used for drinking-water or for ritual bathing?

But when did this period of occupation end? For a clue, de Vaux turned to a large crack along the eastern side of the settlement, which he attributed to the major earthquake reported by Flavius Josephus for the year 31 BCE (*War* 1:270–72; *Antiquities* 15:121–22). The earthquake, he surmised, caused a fire, and the fire led to abandonment of the site, which then silted up. The thickness of the silt led de Vaux to surmise that the site was deserted for a long period, with the aqueduct and channel overflowing on several occasions.

De Vaux assigned the following Period II to the same people who had lived there in Period Ib. His reasons were that the site was used for the same purpose as before. However, the debris was not removed completely, and there was no attempt to reconstruct the site as it had been. The elongated cistern to the south of the main building was split in two, and two cisterns in the east block were left unused. Several rooms were left derelict, others were divided. To the south of the round cistern, locus 101 was paved and a brick furnace and a smaller oven were installed. There were also carved-out troughs and basalt millstones from this period. Whether it can be determined that the site was reoccupied by the same group is dubious.

To date Period II de Vaux again used coins. Digging a trench on a slope north of the ruins, he found coins dated to between 6 BCE and 4 CE. The trench, in de Vaux's view, contained debris removed from the ruins by the settlers coming back in Period II, and these coins belonged to them: so Period II must have started around the turn of the era. The coins found elsewhere between the destruction layer of Period Ib and the end of Period II date from the time of Herod Archelaeus (4 BCE –6 CE) to the third year of the First Jewish Revolt against the Romans (68 CE). Ninety-one coins come from the age of the procurators (6–66 CE), one of them from the time of Agrippa I (37–44 CE). Ninety-four bronze coins are Jewish coins of the First Revolt, 83 from the second year and only five from the third year. These coins thus span the extent of Period II.

The absence of coins from the fourth year of the revolt, 69 CE, indicated to de Vaux that the Jewish settlement at Qumran was destroyed by Roman troops marching from Jericho in June 68 CE. Some

(Top) Locus 30, the room beneath the so-called 'Scriptorium'. Inkwells and plaster 'tables' from the upper storey were found here.

(Above) Part of the hoard of Tyrian shekels unearthed at Qumran; these enable fairly precise dating of some phases of occupation.

(Above and right) As well as pottery, stone vessels were also found at Qumran. According to Jewish purity laws pottery can contract impurity while stone cannot.

arrowheads were found at this level, and Frank M. Cross, one of the excavators, claimed that the foundations of the settlement had also been mined through. The equation was neat, and the depositing of the scrolls in the caves could also, on this evidence, be placed around this time, caused by the desire to protect them from the advancing Romans. Thus the archaeology of Qumran also offered a latest date for the writing of the scrolls.

The inhabitants of the brief Period III were the victorious Romans, de Vaux surmised, who used Qumran as a temporary outpost. The evidence for this is several coins, most of which post-date the year 68 CE, including coins of Nero and his family from Caesarea and Antioch, Vespasian or Titus as late as 73 CE, four celebrating the defeat of Judaea, and one of Agrippa II (87 CE). The Romans reinforced the tower and walls, jumbled some of the rooms together and abandoned others. The water system was simplified, only one large cistern in the southeast being used. After the Romans departed, other visitors or brief inhabitants left odd coins, from the reigns of Vespasian (69–79 CE), Trajan (98–117 CE), and the Second Jewish Revolt (Year 2, 133 CE).

Challenges to De Vaux's interpretation

De Vaux's connection of the ruins and the caves seems with hindsight to have been a little over-enthusiastic, and may have led to an over-interpretation or even misinterpretation of the site. Apart from the earlier

Judaean occupation, most scholars would agree that the site was settled by 100 BCE. Using clues from the allusions in the Habakkuk commentary from Cave 1, de Vaux was inclined to push the date of occupation back into the 130s BCE, but there is no archaeological evidence for this. There have also been challenges to his view that the site was abandoned for about 30 years between Periods Ib and II. The supposed 'earthquake damage' could equally well have been caused by a landslip (the plateau is known to be quite unstable), and the nearby site at Ain Feshkha, which de Vaux thought was inhabited by the same people as Qumran, shows continuous occupation through this period. His interpretation of the coin hoard, which involved some complicated calculation, is also debated. (Unfortunately, many of the coins retrieved from the site have subsequently been mislaid.)

De Vaux's interpretations were in fact fundamentally challenged, first by E.-M. Laperrousaz, later by Philip R. Davies, and more recently still by the archaeologist and pottery expert Jodi Magness who has offered a revision that seems to be better in line with the evidence. Her view is that the hoard of coins found in locus 120 was probably buried in a time of crisis at the end of Period Ib and the owner never returned to retrieve it. Since the latest coin in the hoard dates to 9/8 BCE, the burial occurred after that time. The earthquake of 31 BCE and the lengthy abandonment therefore disappear as key dating indicators. Resettlement would have occurred, she thinks, within five years, and, according to the accumulated sediment, Magness proposes it may even have come after a single winter hiatus spent elsewhere. She therefore dates the reoccupation of the site (Period II) to 4 BCE.

Magness also believes that bowls and lamps can be distinguished as between Period Ib and Period II. If the new settlers were in fact previous inhabitants, they certainly would have wanted to continue their old way of life. But the archaeological record suggests that their clean-up of the settlement was less than thorough. There was no attempt to recreate the water system as it had existed in Period Ib. It is therefore entirely possible that a different kind of group occupied Qumran in Period II.

Finally, most scholars have accepted de Vaux's belief that the Romans destroyed and reoccupied Khirbet Qumran in June 68 CE, which he based on the absence of Jewish coins from the year 69 CE and the proximity of a Roman legion. But one would not necessarily expect the last represented coins to have circulated so quickly after minting. It would be equally plausible to assign the destruction of Qumran to 74 CE, when Masada was captured, and to assign the Roman occupation to the years following that.

Clues to the inhabitants

Apart from some tenuous and speculative identifications already mentioned, prompted by a prior identification of the site of Qumran with the home of the scrolls writers, there are some specific areas in which correspondences have been suggested. One is the similarity of the pottery at the site and in the caves, on which de Vaux laid great stress. Another is evidence of leather tabs in one cave (Cave 8), and tracks supposedly leading from the site to some nearby caves (but not the manuscript caves). Apart from these, there are two specific areas in which the relationship between the scrolls and the ruins have been explored: the cemetery and the ritual baths. A look at the recently discovered ostraca will also extend the discussion in this vein.

The cemetery

Few archaeological clues point to the kind of people who once lived at Qumran. Here we can focus on two areas that have usually been thought to help. The most important indicator at a site of the identity of its inhabitants is often the cemetery, since the manner of burial (and often the kinds of goods buried with the dead) can indicate the ethnic identity and religious beliefs of the group. There is a large cemetery (de Vaux thought rather of several cemeteries) 50 m (165 ft) east of the Qumran settlement. A few of the 1,100–1,200 individual graves

View over the cemetery at Qumran. The graves were covered by piles of stones.

179

had been opened in 1873, and an unusual burial procedure noted. The bodies lay upon their backs in a niche, and the graves were covered with low mounds. De Vaux had a further 26 graves opened and later H. Steckoll unofficially investigated another dozen. Those graves so far opened amount to 43, 30 of which have been identified as containing men, seven women and four children. De Vaux interpret the burial area as comprising a 'main' cemetery, in which the graves were neatly arranged in rows, and contained only male skeletons, and 'secondary' cemeteries, in which there was less order; here the unusual manner of burial was not followed, and women and children were included. There has been considerable recent interest in the cemetery area, and it is now questioned whether such a division is warranted. Also challenged is the reliability of indicating the gender of the skeletons.

But perhaps the most significant new data has been the discovery of similar burials elsewhere. In the 1960s P. Bar-Adon discovered a graveyard south at Ain el Ghuweir (about 7 miles south of Khirbet Qumran) of a similar kind. Twenty graves were opened revealing the skeletons of 12 men, seven women and one child. Since then, more similar burials have been unearthed: 20 graves south of Ain el Ghuweir, others in Jericho, Jerusalem and in Transjordan. If all these reports are accurate, the Qumran type of burial, namely with the body on its back, with the feet towards the north, is no longer

Plan of Qumran showing the location of the cemeteries and Caves 4–5 and 7–10.

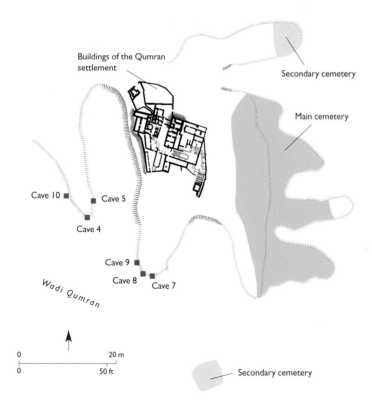

Buildings of the Qumran settlement

Secondary cemetery

Main cemetery

Cave 10
Cave 5
Cave 4
Cave 9
Cave 8
Cave 7
Wadi Qumran

0   20 m
0   50 ft

Secondary cemetery

What Did Hananiah Do?

Few of the Qumran texts are what are called 'documentary' (i.e. serving a practical everyday purpose). 4Q477 may be a precious one of these. It includes the names of several individuals and their character or behavioural defects. A certain Yohanan ben Ar[…] is characterized as short-tempered. Hananiah Notos is accused of disturbing the spirit of the community. Another person is singled out for something unclear, which scholars have hotly debated since the unusual Hebrew phrase can be translated in a number of ways: 'He loves his bodily nature'; 'he loves the carnal foundation of his flesh'; 'he shows preference to his family members'; even 'he drank his urine' and 'he liked his bodily emissions'. The best translation of what is certainly an odd Hebrew expression is still debated.

The Community Rule (5–6, 8) and the Damascus Document (13–14) both speak of keeping records of those who are joining the community and 'weighing their spirits' as they progress towards full membership or towards denial of membership. These manuscripts also list various punishments to be exacted for misconduct. 4Q477 seems to provide an actual record of such administrative activity; its preservation in Cave 4 alongside the literary texts may be a happy accident.

so distinctive. Perhaps it still points to a certain kind of 'sectarian' Jewish practice; perhaps not.

Norman Golb of Chicago University, who believes that the site and the scrolls are entirely unrelated, holds that Qumran was a Jewish fort and that the graves were all dug at one time after a battle. However, this is unlikely: the graves are all individual, which is most improbable in such an event, even if the victors bothered to bury the dead at all. But whatever more the cemetery at Qumran may be able to tell us, the ban on excavation of burial sites in Israel rules out further research here.

In an important recent development, it has emerged that a number of bones from the Qumran cemetery are now in Bavaria. Gottfried Kurth, whom de Vaux had invited to analyze them at Qumran, had sent them in the late 1950s to Germany where, unable to work on them, they were transferred to his successor Olav Röhrer-Ertl. He examined the bones, and an exhibition and conference was organized in Eichstätt in 2000. According to Röhrer-Ertl's analysis, and the notes left by Kurth, the manner of burial throughout the cemetery was much less regular than de Vaux represented (some north–south burials had heads to the north, while half of the tombs had a niche for the body in the pit, and half did not); there were also some double burials, while a number of bones

Many of the burials at Qumran follow the pattern in the sectional diagram below.

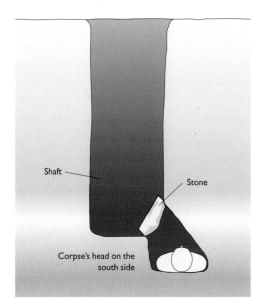

Shaft

Stone

Corpse's head on the south side

were 'resexed' from male to female. Unfortunately, Carbon-14 analysis is not possible on these bones, whose collagen (registered in these tests) has been removed by chemicals in the soil.

The remaining bones collected in the excavations lie in Paris, where they are being analyzed by Susan Sheridan of Notre Dame University. Until we can learn more, the cemetery will throw doubt on de Vaux's theory of a celibate community at Qumran.

In an even more intriguing development, it has been claimed that the skeletons in the cemetery that do not conform to the regular type of north-south orientation are actually of Bedouin corpses and thus unrelated to the settlement. The outcome of this claim remains to be seen.

Purity, ritual baths and bathing

The most impressive feature of practically every photograph of Khirbet Qumran is its system of canals, cisterns, and perhaps baths. Qumran was not a fresh-water location like its southern neighbour, Ain Feshkha. For practical reasons, whatever they may have been, the settlement required immense amounts of water. The aqueduct bringing rainwater began on the hillside northwest of the site and fed into it, traversing it diagonally from the northwest to the southeast. There are six massive reservoirs within the settlement and a square-shaped cistern near the northwestern entrance. Following calculations by Israel Eph'al, Qumran's cisterns could have held 1,200 cubic m (42,000 cubic ft) of water, which could have provided 750 people with drinking water during the eight dry months after the spring rains.

But de Vaux, and most interpreters since, associated the water system with the ritual baths of the purity-loving brotherhood described in some Qumran scrolls. In particular, those reservoirs that have steps extending across the breadth of the baths are also commonly thought to be for ritual bathing.

Indeed, many of the scrolls betray a high concern for purity, which would suggest strict attention to the requirements of bathing. However, despite what is often claimed, the scrolls do not refer to a rite of ritual initiation by washing, or regular rites beyond the prescriptions of the law. Many Jews of the period observed ritual washing and several such baths have been found in houses and palaces and public places. Do the provisions for bathing at Qumran indicate any more than that the inhabitants were Jewish?

A stepped cistern near the entrance to the settlement; it might have served as a ritual immersion pool.

How Were the Qumran Caves Used?

Although the caves near Qumran were used to store scrolls, this was not their only function. Natural caves in the Judaean wilderness had long been used for refuge (David hid in one, according to 1 Samuel 22); in the summer, especially, they offered cool as well as protection. In 1952 a survey in the wilderness of Judaea located nearly 300 caves, many of which showed signs of having been used as (at least temporary) shelters. Their occupants were probably goatherds, shepherds, travellers, or even fugitives.

It is generally agreed, following de Vaux, that the Qumran dwellers did not live in the settlement buildings, but only worked there. They probably lived in the caves (and possibly some in tents). So the caves have to be regarded as part of the settlement. Indeed, it has recently been claimed that remains of ancient tracks from the buildings to some of the caves can still be seen. But while the caves in the cliffs are natural, those in the Qumran plateau (e.g. 4, 5, 7–10) are artificial. Why were they created, when there

were so many natural caves nearby? Cave 10, because of its size, has been identified as possible living quarters. Cave 4 could also have housed a few individuals at some time, while Caves 7, 8, and 9 may have functioned as workshops of some sort. Cave 8 shows evidence of having been used for the manufacture of tabs used for tying scrolls. Pieces of tefillin (phylactery) cases found in Caves 4, 7 and 8 may suggest habitation or work use.

A minor mystery of Qumran relates to the storage of the scrolls. While Caves 1 and 11 lie at least 2 km (just over a mile) from the Qumran buildings, several closer caves contain no hints of previous occupation. Again, while some of the scrolls were carefully preserved in storage jars, such as in Cave 1, those in Cave 4, on the Qumran plateau, were not, being found scattered in fragments across the floor. No single explanation covers all these facts, and the relationship between (different kinds of) caves, scrolls and settlement remains a complicated one.

The ruling of the rabbis (which may well reflect earlier practice) says that a *miqveh* (pool for ritual bathing) must hold at least 40 seahs of water, roughly the equivalent of 80 gallons, and the water must be flowing (which meant that stored rainwater was permissible, since it had originally 'flowed'). Washing was a regular requirement after a state of ritual uncleanness was incurred, but this should not be confused in any way with Christian baptism, though Gentile proselytes were required to wash as part of their conversion (whether this was the significance of John the Baptist's baptism is keenly disputed).

If the people at Qumran modelled themselves on the requirements of the Jerusalem priesthood, which required a permanent state of purity while on service, and is hinted at by many of the Qumran texts, they would have required ritual purification after nocturnal emissions, sexual intercourse and contact with a corpse or other ritually defined objects. A fragment from Cave 4, entitled Aramaic Levi[d], has been reconstructed using the Greek Testament of Levi and reveals how the purification ritual may have been carried out (4Q213a, frag. 1, 11:6–14). Levi says that he has laundered his garments with pure water, and washed himself in living water, making his paths right. Then he lifts his eyes and fingers towards heaven, praying that God may protect him and his children from the unrighteous spirit, evil thoughts, fornication and pride, and give him a holy spirit, wisdom and knowledge.

Ritual purity laws known from the Jewish Bible and scrolls such as the Temple Scroll prescribe washing one's garments and body at given inter-

vals in order to remove layers of defilement and restore oneself to ritual purity:

'No man who has had a nocturnal emission shall enter the sanctuary at all until three days have passed. He shall wash his garments and bathe on the first day and on the third day he shall wash his garments and bathe, and after sunset he shall enter the sanctuary.' (Temple Scroll, 44:8–10)

The preparation of ritually clean vessels such as bowls, cups, chalices or even animal skins, necessitated a continuously available supply of water:

'No skin of clean animals slaughtered in their cities shall be brought there [the city of the temple]. But in their cities they may use them for any work they need.' (Temple Scroll, 46:8–10)

For this reason, the preferred material for ritual vessels was stone, which did not convey uncleanness; several stone vessels have been found at Qumran (see p. 178).

In any discussion of ritual bathing at Qumran, it matters whether or not we identify the inhabitants with the Essenes. The ancient historian Josephus writes that the Essenes of his time bathe at the fifth hour (11 am), assemble in the refectory for the common meal, pray and eat (*War* 2:158). Certainly, they bathed at other times as well. Josephus also points out that members who had attained higher degrees of obedience participated in corresponding purificatory baths. Essenes who married required purification at certain times, as did their wives. With regard to temple sacrifice, Josephus claims that the Essenes follow their own rules of sacrifice and purification (*Antiquities* 18:18–20). The Community Rule notes, however, that purifying waters were not automatically efficacious:

'He shall not be counted among the perfect, nor by atonement, nor cleansed by purifying waters, nor sanctified by seas and rivers, nor washed with any ablution. Unclean, unclean shall he be…

Once his flesh is sprinkled with purifying water and made holy by cleansing water, it shall be made clean by the humble submission of his soul to all God's laws.' (1QS 3:7–10)

Thus, in the *yahad*, while regular washing was surely practised, it was *obedience to the Law* that rendered one clean. The contrast with Christian baptism, which cleansed one from the *yoke* of the law, is vivid. Was the elaborate water system at Qumran aimed at purification as much as sustenance? Not certainly, but quite possibly.

Recent excavations

Further archaeological work in and around Qumran has intensified. Radar groundscanning has been conducted over the area, and the caves themselves have been re-examined. Israeli archaeologists Magen Broshi and Hanan Eshel, and also Joseph Patrich, have been examining other nearby caves (not the scroll caves) for signs of ancient use. So far their conclusions are diametrically opposed: Broshi and Eshel believe there are such clues, including traces of ancient paths between caves and settlement. Patrich does not. Some years ago a balsam jar was found in a nearby

(Above right) Excavations are even today continuing in caves near Qumran to resolve the many unanswered questions about the context of the site.

(Right) Do these nails from the Roman period, recently discovered between the ruins and the caves, come from sandals worn by the ancient inhabitants of Qumran?

cave that might have been connected with Qumran.

On the site itself, Yitzhak Magen has been discovering more extensive remains from the Iron Age settlement period, suggesting a more substantial site than once thought; and among other things the course of the aqueduct has been exposed closer to the site. During the summer of 2001 a reinvestigation of the water cisterns began, to try to establish for certain whether they were really used for ritual bathing or for storing drinking water. An especially interesting new discovery, made during the same excavation season, is a coffin covered in zinc (a unique construction) found within the cemetery area at Qumran. A few metres away, an ancient mausoleum, surrounded by a wall and possibly containing more than one skeleton, has also been found. Whether these two finds are linked to the Qumran settlement, or perhaps tell us more about the habitation and use of the region in antiquity, remains to be seen.

A number of bones taken from the Qumran cemetery at the original excavations have now been examined in Germany, and may help to resolve questions of dating and of the gender distribution in the cemetery. Unfortunately, despite recent controversy over the interpretation of the contents of the cemetery area, under Israeli law no further excavation of human bones is permitted. Broshi and Eshel claim to have found coffins and coffin nails, concluding that the corpses of women were brought to Qumran from elsewhere.

These new ventures are all a direct result of the wide-ranging doubts expressed about the original interpretations of the use and history of the site, but a good deal of uncertainty still remains.

Recent excavations of artificial caves near Qumran. This might be the location where some of the site's inhabitants slept.

The Qumran Water System

One of the most distinctive features of the Qumran settlement is its extensive water system. Its source was the nearby Wadi Qumran, a seasonal watercourse. A dam high in the wadi, which cascades steeply over the cliffs, forced water into a basin and thence into an aqueduct, through a tunnel in the cliff face and down to the settlement at its northwestern corner, along a channel that can still be seen. After settling in a large pool, it flowed through the settlement, filling numerous large cisterns on the way, before ending up on the southern end of the settlement.

Bryant G. Wood (in *Bulletin of the American Schools of Oriental Research*, 1984) believes that each inhabitant of Qumran would have needed about 3 litres (6 pints) of water per day in winter and perhaps 5 litres (10 pints) in the other seasons. The unstepped cisterns were most likely used purely for water storage, on the argument that steps would diminish the volume of water collected. Hence the stepped cisterns, as most scholars believe, served as ritual baths, *miqva'ot*. Some of these even had ridges down the steps, possibly to act as separators between those entering and leaving. According to Wood, the small baths were reserved for special ceremonies for individuals, 'such as initiation rites or the purification of a member who had fallen from grace' (p. 58).

The Israeli archaeologist Yitzhar Hirschfeld estimates that these cisterns and baths would

have held approximately 1,200 cubic m (42,400 cubic ft) of water and Jodi Magness calculates that a single flash flood during winter would have filled up all the Qumran pools. Wood guesses that about 200 people used the water at Qumran during its heyday (Period Ib).

One of the best-known sights at Qumran is the huge cracked cistern (locus 49). It was long believed that the earthquake of 31 BCE, reported by Josephus and held responsible for the end of Qumran Period Ib, caused this and other damage to the settlement. But more recently it has been suggested that the brittle limestone of the Qumran plateau might have been cracked by the huge weight of water in the cisterns.

The remains of the aqueduct bringing water from the Wadi Qumran to the settlement.

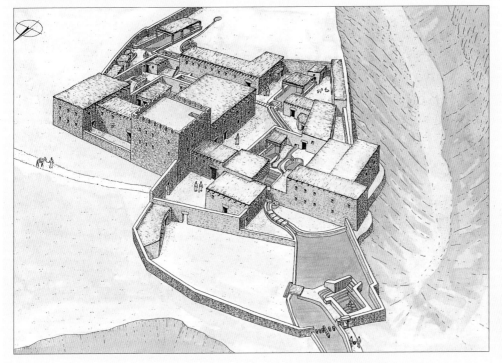

Artist's reconstruction of the Qumran site showing the elaborate water system.

Recently Discovered Ostraca from Khirbet Qumran

Factfile

Name: Ostracon 1, 2
Editors: F.M. Cross, E. Eshel (*DJD* 36)
Commentary: A. Yardeni
Script: Late Herodian to post-Herodian

'In year two of…in Jericho, Honi son of…gave to 'Eleazar son of Nahamani…Hisday from Holon…from this day to perpetui[ty] and the boundaries of the house and…the fig trees, the ol[ive trees, and] when he completes…?'

It took over 40 years from the initial discovery of Cave 1 for a written text to be uncovered among the ruins of Khirbet Qumran itself. In the winter of 1996, James Strange of the University of South Florida was conducting a small expedition investigating the limestone terrace on which the Khirbet Qumran settlement stood. Some volunteers cleaning up the eastern boundary wall came across two inscribed potsherds (ostraca) 'at the base of the eastern face of the wall' in an unstratified context. Strange assigned the publication of these ostraca to Frank M. Cross and Esther Eshel, who believe they can date them by their presumably Late Herodian script (50–68 CE). It is ostracon 1 that has attracted attention. The editors interpret its contents as witnessing an individual joining the Qumran community, and transferring his assets to its members: a new member named Honi transfers his slave, Hisday, his house, his fig and olive trees to Eleazar, the community's bursar, upon completing some initiatory stage into the *yahad* (community). The editors present this scenario as a fact, but their reading has been challenged by other scholars. Although the editors compare the script with the Copper Scroll, the two texts are only generally similar. While the Copper Scroll, if difficult to decipher at times, is more consistently executed, ostracon 1 is unskilled and clumsily written (which would seem strange in an obviously literate community). Subsequently, the accomplished Israeli palaeographer and epigrapher Ada Yardeni has published a different reading and translation in which no connection to the *yahad* is evident.

Indeed, the text is missing typical parts of a deed of property transfer: it lacks a first-person statement of transfer, any description of the property, and any clear reference to witnesses. One would also expect legal documents to be in Aramaic rather than Hebrew (as is the case with all other legal transactions from the period). The central controversy surrounds Cross's and Eshel's reading of line 8: 'when he fulfils [his oath] to the Community'. Certainly, the beginning of this clause refers to the completion of some activity, but the word 'oath' was inserted by the editors and not present in the original Hebrew, while the crucial word *lyhd* ('to the *yahad*') is actually a highly improbable reconstruction of some illegible letters. After line 8 practically no context can be comfortably reconstructed. Honi and Eleazar were indeed involved in a property transfer at Jericho at some point in the past, but that is all we know.

Ostracon 2, penned with a different hand, preserves the names [Jehose]ph son of Nathan and someone's sons from 'En [?]'. The editors suggest 'Engedi'. Whether that is correct or not, the point is that both ostraca concern people who originated from elsewhere. The editors have eagerly fabricated a Qumranic context, and yet the script bears no resemblance to the beautiful and usually skilled hands known from the manuscripts in the caves.

The absence of such records about community life at Qumran has often been remarked upon, but unfortunately this initially promising discovery is unlikely to point us there. Again, optimistic links between theories and data have overinterpreted the evidence. We remain without an unchallengeable textual link between the ruins and the scrolls.

Ostracon 1 from the eastern wall leading south from Qumran.

Differing Interpretations of the Ostracon

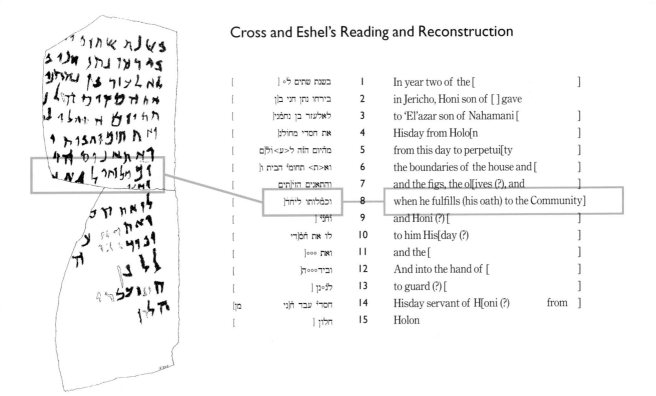

Yardeni's Reading and Reconstruction

בשנת שתים לן	1	On the second year of […]
ביריחו נתן חֹנֹי בֹן	2	in Jericho, *Hny* s[on of …] (?) gave
לאלעזר בן נ....]	3	to 'El'azar son of *N*… […]
את הסקים הלוֹן	4	the …[…] sacks/sackcloths […]
מ/ת./מ/ת./יֹם ה..לי/ו.ן	5	… …[…]
ואת ח/תֹם/פותבי/ות ר/ין	6	and the walls (?)/coverings (?) of the house (?) of …[…]
וה/אתאנים הב/י.ן	7	and the fig-(tree)s, the p[alms (?), …(?)]
וכולאילנ אֹחֹן.	8	and every oth[er(?)] tree[…]
וֹנֹגֹ .ן	9	…[…]
לי./ואת ח.ן	10	to me/him the …[…]
ואת ....צֹן	11	and …[…]
וֹבֹידעֹ.. יהן	12	and in the hand (?) of …[…]
ל.]?[ג.ן	13	…[…]
ה..עב..ן	14	the […]
הל..ן	15	the …[…]
.לן	16	…[…]

Cross and Eshel's Reading and Reconstruction

[	בשנת שתים ל◦]	1	In year two of the [	]
[	ביריחו נתן חני בֹן	2	in Jericho, Honi son of [ ] gave	
[	לאלעזר בן נחמֹנֹן	3	to 'El'azar son of Nahamani [	]
[	את חסדי מחולֹנן	4	Hisday from Holo[n	]
[	מהֹיום הזה ל<ע>ולֹם	5	from this day to perpetui[ty	]
[	וא<ת> תחומֹי הבית הֹ	6	the boundaries of the house and [	]
[	והתאנים הזֹיֹתֹים	7	and the figs, the ol[ives (?), and	]
[	וכמֹלֹותו ליחֹדֹן	8	when he fulfills (his oath) to the Community]	
[	וחֹנֹי]	9	and Honi (?) [	]
[	לו את חֹסֹדֹי	10	to him His[day (?)	]
[	ואת]◦◦◦	11	and the [	]
[	ובידֹ◦◦◦◦הֹן	12	And into the hand of [	]
[	לֹגֹ◦נֹן]	13	to guard (?) [	]
מֹן]	חסדֹי עבד חֹנֹי	14	Hisday servant of H[oni (?) from]	
[	חלון]	15	Holon	

187

Scrolls, Caves and Ruins: Are They Connected?

Now that the ruins of Qumran and some of the issues they raise have been introduced, we can widen the picture to consider the broader question: do the ruins and the scrolls mutually illuminate each other? We can review this question by showing how Qumran scholarship in general has evolved its answers over time, beginning with a fairly widespread affirmation and ending, as things now stand, in a wide range of answers and a good deal less overall certainty.

The traditional explanation

The approach that dominated from the time of the Qumran excavations until the mid-1980s is presented in de Vaux's excavation reports, and rehearsed by the once-standard textbooks of Milik and Cross (both participators in the dig and members of the Cave 4 editorial team), as well as most other scholars. It holds that the scrolls were either written or owned by the residents of Qumran, and stored in the caves, probably under the threat of impending Roman attack. The caves were used, however, not only to store the scrolls, but also as habitations for the members of the Qumran community.

Basic to this hypothesis are the texts found in Cave 1. The Community Rule (1QS), the War Scroll (1QM), and the Thanksgiving Hymns (1QH), together with the already well-known Damascus Document (CD), were taken, even before the site of Qumran was excavated, to describe the structure and beliefs of a religious community that was identified with the Essenes. The mention of Essenes in this vicinity by Pliny (see p. 169) and Josephus' account of their practices, which closely resemble those in the Community Rule, offered a firm basis for this identification.

With the link between scrolls and ruins apparently secure, the history of the site was therefore adjusted to reflect the allusions in the Habakkuk Commentary (held to reveal the origins of the 'Qumran sect'). This scroll's 'Wicked Priest' was identified as the Hasmonaean ruler Jonathan (or, by Cross, as his brother Simon) from whom the Teacher fled. It was thus obvious that the settlement must have been inhabited by the 130s BCE, despite the lack of archaeological evidence. The inhabitants were also reckoned by many early commentators to have derived from a group called *Hasidim* ('pious') who fought with the Maccabees against the forces of the evil Seleucid king Antiochus IV who was trying to exterminate Judaism and who had defiled the Temple. These Hasidim had then split into two factions: Pharisees and Essenes. The reasons for the settlement were thought, therefore, to be persecution, together with an underlying dislike of Hellenistic influences on Judaism (of which there is a little, but not much, trace in the sectarian writings). The various stages of occupation were linked to other known

(Right) Inside Cave 1. The entrance has been greatly enlarged since the cave's first discovery.

(Opposite) Timeline comparing the proposals of de Vaux and Magness for the likely periods of occupation at Qumran.

historical events, such as the persecution of Pharisees by Alexander Jannaeus, leading to a sudden rise in population at Qumran (Period Ib). More conjecturally, a period of abandonment coincided with the reign of Herod the Great, either because he liked them (as Josephus records) or he did *not* like them, or perhaps because of increased aggression at this time from the Parthians whose empire extended to the eastern bank of the Jordan.

Occupation by Essenes was also invoked to explain the elaborate water system, the communal dining room and the lack of females, since, as described by Josephus, and with his account supplemented by that of the Alexandrian Jewish philosopher Philo (1st century CE), the celibate Essenes ate, studied, worshipped and worked together, holding all things in common, washing frequently and accepting new members under very rigid conditions. To this Qumran scholars, following de Vaux and his colleagues, added new data: they also wrote and copied scrolls in their scriptorium, living mostly in the caves, to which they occasionally took back scrolls with them for private study. When the Romans came in the summer of 68 CE, they laid to waste the buildings of the Qumran community. But by that time the scrolls had been brought to safety in the nearby caves. The inhabitants either fled or were killed in the fighting, and the Essenes disappeared from history.

Alternative suggestions

The standard 'Essene hypothesis' is far from dead, and it will continue to influence future interpretations of Khirbet Qumran, partly because much of the archaeological data cannot now be checked, partly because of the simplicity of the explanation, and largely because de Vaux was willing to tell the story with lots of details and was immediately supported by his colleagues and many of the scholarly community. It is also, up to a point, very plausible. But alternative views have always been expressed: G.R. Driver of Oxford University argued for linking the 'Covenanters' with the Zealot movement, which combined religious conservativism with political action. This identification would hardly explain the daily life of the inhabitants (active opposition to the establishment is not easy from a commune based on the Dead Sea shore), but it could be the reason that the Romans decided to demolish the site. Driver and another English scholar of similar views, Cecil Roth, both drew on the War Scroll from Cave 1 for literary support of their views. The fragmentary manuscript of the Songs of the Sabbath Sacrifice discovered at Masada, the Zealots' last stand, as well as in Caves 4 and 11, provides another piece of circumstantial evidence for a revolutionary enclave located at Qumran.

In more recent years several new hypotheses have emerged. Jean-Baptiste Humbert of the École

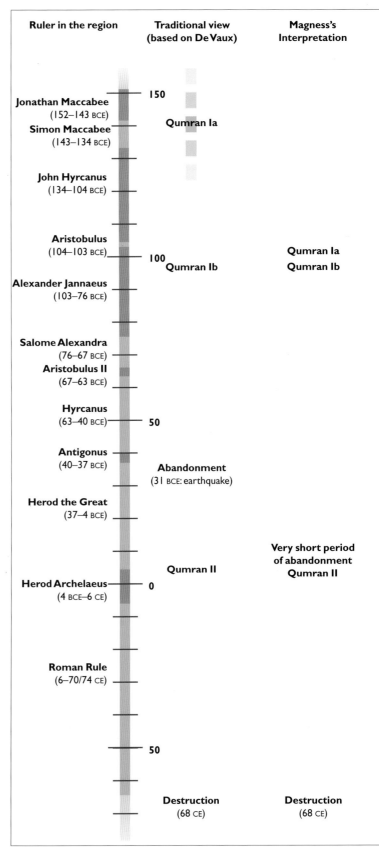

Biblique also links the scrolls with Qumran and with the Essenes, but thinks that the site was originally built up by the Hasmonaeans as a sort of patrician estate – evidenced by some of the finer materials that de Vaux failed to note in his presentation. Only in the time of Herod the Great does Humbert think that the Essenes, whom Herod is said to have favoured, moved to Khirbet Qumran. Once established there, the Essenes practised their own sacrificial cult, breaking the Jerusalem monopoly. After several decades the beliefs of the Essenes evolved to a more spiritual level, and they no longer sacrificed animals. Instead, they prayed together, studied scripture together, and shared ritual meals involving grains, wine and fruits. Humbert emphasizes the presence of one curious feature of the site noted by de Vaux but with some puzzlement: jars filled with animal bones were buried under the floor. Humbert stresses that they belonged to the early period of Essene occupation only.

Did Cave 7 Contain Fragments of the New Testament?

Just under two-dozen tiny fragments with Greek writing were the only texts to come from Cave 7. One scholar claimed sensationally that these belonged to books of the New Testament, notably the Gospel of Mark. But it is impossible to make such an identification from tiny scraps bearing only a few letters each. For instance, 7Q3 preserves only 26 Greek characters, while 7Q10 has only two. Altogether 7Q3–19 contain about 130 letters. Of all the fragments 7Q19 alone preserves as much as two consecutive lines with some context: 'of the creation…in the writings'.

Other more intrinsically plausible suggestions are that 7Q1 is from a Greek translation of Exodus 28:4–6, 7; 7Q2, the Letter of Jeremiah 43–44; 7Q4 Numbers 14:23–24, Job 34:12–15, Enoch 103:3–4; 7Q5 (identified with Mark 6:52–53) is perhaps 2 Samuel 4:12–5:1, 5:13–14, Zechariah 7:3–5, or Enoch 15:9–10; 7Q6 frag. 1 could be Psalm 9:32, 34; 28; 50; or 17–18, or Proverb 7:12–13; 7Q6 frag. 2, Isaiah 18:2; 7Q8, Zechariah 8:8–9 or Enoch 103:7–8, Numbers 1:3–4, 22:38; 2 Kings 7:28, Psalm 18:14–15, Daniel 2:43, or Ecclesiastes 6:3. But any such identifications must remain guesses.

A much more fruitful question is: why are there any texts in Greek here at all? And why only Greek ones in this cave? Should we assume there was anyone at all among the owners of the scrolls who was unable to read Hebrew or Aramaic? That *would* be strange. Here lies a minor, but intriguing, Qumran mystery.

The Israeli archaeologist Yitzhak Magen also brings the Hasmonaeans into the picture, but unlike Humbert, he leaves the scrolls out of it. He suggests that Qumran was constructed in the style of a typical fortress or fortified villa of the period, and housed supporters of the dynasty, whether former soldiers or others. Similar fortresses were located to the north, south, east and west. Magen is continuing to excavate all of these settlements and is chiefly concerned with understanding more about Qumran in the Iron Age (1200–c. 600 BCE), not in the Graeco-Roman period. Another Israeli archaeologist, Yitzhar Hirschfeld, has recently also argued that Qumran was a fortified estate similar in design to an estate at Khirbet el-Musaq. The Essene settlement described by Pliny he places on the heights above Engedi.

The views of Magen and Hirschfeld to some extent support the thesis of Norman Golb, who also dissociates the scrolls and caves on the one hand from the settlement on the other. In Golb's view the scrolls from the caves derived from libraries in Jerusalem, and their owners brought them to the Qumran area to hide them. Qumran was a Jewish fortress, and possibly not even occupied when the scrolls were deposited. Golb's thesis has met with a strong response, since he emphatically denies any 'Qumran sect' and makes of the site of Qumran something that is not in any way extraordinary. The scrolls represent a wide range of Jewish writings from different sources and thus tell us more about the Judaism of the period than is usually thought.

Many other views are currently being expressed on the purpose of the Qumran buildings. Pauline Donceel-Voûte suggests the site was a villa, quite comfortably furnished; Alan Crown and Lena Cansdale of Australia have emphasized the strategic position of the site and propose that it was a trading post, with accommodation for travellers, especially those crossing the Dead Sea. They have suggested that herbs and aromatic plants were macerated in shallow basins. Like Hirschfeld, Crown and Cansdale locate the Essene colony closer to Engedi. Qumran has even been viewed as a sort of hospice for lepers. Persons with even more chronic skin diseases may have lived on and worked there until their deaths. The laws on skin diseases and purity in the Halakhic Letter, the Temple Scroll and the Damascus Document are said to lend credence to such a view.

There are, then, many approaches to Qumran that seek to understand it apart fom the scrolls. But the majority continue to base their interpretation of the ruins on the scrolls, as does Lawrence Schiffman. Schiffman interprets legal texts like the Halakhic Letter, the Temple Scroll and the Damascus Document as pointing to a Sadducean purity cult that constituted the first members of the Qumran community. A special focus on the

What are the Plastered Objects in the 'Scriptorium'?

The modern visitor to Qumran will see among the ruins a room marked 'Scriptorium'. What most visitors do not realize is that the sign should refer to the original first-floor room, and not the ground floor, into which the remains of the so-called 'Scriptorium' had fallen (locus 30).

The major exhibit from this room was a table reconstructed at the Rockefeller Museum (originally the Palestine Archaeological Museum) in Jerusalem from the pieces of plaster found on the ground below. It measured 5 m by 40 cm (16 ft by 17 ins), and was a mere 50 cm (20 ins) high. And although de Vaux himself realised that scribes at this time did not sit at tables to copy manuscripts, the 'Scriptorium' and the 'table' remained largely unchallenged. Two inkwells, one still containing ink, were also found among the debris.

Yet were the scrolls even written at Qumran? Were de Vaux and his team guilty of finding just what they wanted to find to link the scrolls and the site? De Vaux's interpretation of the entire site as a 'monastery' has come under increasing attack in recent years, and his reconstruction of the plaster pieces from locus 30 has been challenged by the Belgian scholar Pauline Donceel-Voûte. In her opinion, the plastered furniture consisted of couches with podiums, banked along the walls, as found in eastern Mediterranean dining rooms.

Interestingly, de Vaux's account states, 'This [the table] might have suggested the furniture of a dining-room except for the fact that we had already identified this in another part of the buildings,

which did not contain a table. In any case it would have been most surprising for the refectory to be situated on an upper storey' (*Archaeology and the Dead Sea Scrolls*, p. 29). Donceel-Voûte's interpretation has found few supporters, for the pieces of plaster are rather narrow and unsturdy and could hardly have withstood the weight of reclining or sitting adults. Scholars are now left without an entirely satisfactory explanation of the function of this 'upper room' and the purpose of the plaster pieces. For the time being the sign 'Scriptorium' will doubtless remain at Qumran.

Reconstructed tables and a plastered basin or stand from the 'upper room'.

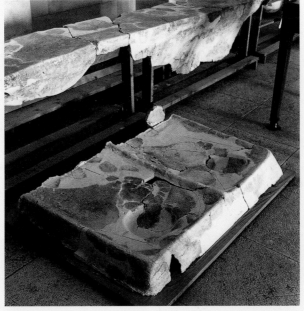

practice of Sadducean purity laws necessitated the construction of so many cisterns and baths at Qumran. These Sadducees came to differ from other Sadducees who remained in touch with Jerusalem and the Temple, and gained power there; these secessionist Sadducees perhaps acquired the name 'Essenes'. A distinctive view of Qumran that starts with the scrolls is that of Hartmut Stegemann, for whom the Essenes were a mainstream Jewish movement that built Qumran as a centre for book production, and a place to which Essenes would go for spiritual refreshment.

There are more views than can be mentioned here, but it should already be clear that at present

no consensus about the relationship between the scrolls and ruins exists. It still seems reasonable to suggest that the scrolls and caves and the site are connected, even if the evidence is not conclusive. But does it matter? Qumran tells us nothing about the scrolls that we cannot read in them; nor do the scrolls tell us anything about Qumran. In the end, the link might not necessarily mean very much, for the importance of the scrolls, it can be argued, goes well beyond any one group or community of Jews and actually gives us a first-hand picture of a Jewish religious culture that is richer, and perhaps more broadly based, than we had ever imagined.

If the place of the scrolls in the history of the Qumran settlement and in the life of ancient Judaism remains sometimes unclear and often disputed, we can say something of their importance to our understanding of both ancient Judaism and Christianity. Shortly after their discovery (see p. 000) the contents of Cave 1 were already being divided between Jewish and Christian owners, and due to the quirks of history the contents of the other caves were for a long while kept from the eyes of Jewish scholars. Since 1967 the scrolls have been reunited under Israeli jurisdiction, and Israeli and Jewish scholarship has reasserted its own interest in the manuscripts.

To argue about whether the scrolls are more important for Judaism or for Christianity, however, is to miss not only the fact that they are important for both, but to forget that they are *older* than both, if by 'Judaism' we mean the religion of the last 2,000 years, the Judaism of the rabbis, of the synagogue, the Law and the family. The incredibly rich religious current that the scrolls reveal enables us to understand better the

V The Meaning of the Scrolls

The Dead Sea Scrolls and Judaism

A civilization cannot be defined strictly by its literary remains, but the contours of Judaism and even Christianity have always been drawn on their great literary monuments. The primary body of written material for understanding Judaism and its progenitors is of course the Bible. But in the case of Judaism, if not Christianity, the scriptures formed Judaism as much as the other way round. The books of Ezra, Nehemiah, Maccabees and Ben Sira show that groups and individuals repeatedly attempted to create a Jewish life in accordance with the inspired writings of the past. Yet not only fresh interpretation of these writings, but also continued divine revelation, was claimed. The ongoing life of the scriptures is widely attested in the scrolls. Fresh perspectives are reflected in original compositions in the scriptural tradition, such as wisdom sayings and psalms. Sometimes the contents of the books of Moses are reorganized to harmonize them with each other and make them more logical, as in the Temple Scroll. Or the words of the prophets are interpreted as cryptic predictions of the interpreter's own day, as in the *pesharim* (commentaries). Or even passages from several different scriptural books are drawn together to fashion a new plot, as in the Melchizedek midrash or the Florilegium. Behind all these techniques lies a conviction that scripture condemns certain contemporary practices rejected by the writers of the scrolls, foretells the imminent destruction of the wicked and reveals the will of God and the secrets of salvation to the righteous few. The scriptures, in short, are being moulded into a world-view constituted by the beliefs and practices of a particular form, or forms, of Judaism.

A Torah scroll, the scroll of the Law.

Was there a 'normative' Judaism?
Before the discovery of the Dead Sea Scrolls most of our pictures of Early Judaism (the last few centuries BCE) were created out of the narratives in the

Ancient Witnesses to an Emerging Canon

During the period when the scrolls were written, some of the Jewish scriptures were formally canonized into a fixed list (probably by the initiative of the Hasmonaeans). These books were also divided into Law, Prophets, and usually other writings (such as those attributed to David) were additionally mentioned. The scrolls seem largely to reflect this canon, but we cannot be sure how quickly a firmly fixed list became the norm for them or for all other Jews. A sample of Jewish writers from the period illustrate the degree of fixity of the scriptural canon:

Ben Sira ('Ecclesiasticus'; 2nd century BCE, Jerusalem):
'Since many things and great have been delivered unto us through the Law and the Prophets and the others who followed after them...' (prologue)

2 Maccabees (2nd–1st century BCE, Alexandria):
'These things [a story about Solomon] were narrated also in the archives or memoirs of Nehemiah; as well as how he founded a library and collected the books about the kings and the prophets, and the books of David and letters of kings about sacred gifts.' (1:13–15)

Halakhic Letter (4QMMT)(1st century BCE?) :
'...you must understand the book of Moses [and the words of the pro]phets and of David...' (C 98)

*Philo (*1st century CE, Alexandria)
'...laws and oracles delivered through the mouth of prophets, and psalms and other books by which knowledge and piety may be increased and perfected.' (*On the Contemplative Life* 25)

Gospel of Matthew (end of 1st century CE, Antioch? Alexandria?)
'In everything do to others as you would have them do to you: this is the law and the prophets.' (7:12)

Josephus (end of 1st century CE, Rome)
'...we do not possess myriads of inconsistent books, conflicting with each other. Our books, those which are justly accredited, are but twenty-two, and contain the record of all time.' (*Against Apion* I 37–39)

But there were books outside the public canon, too:
4 Ezra (*2 Esdras*) (end of 1st century CE, Jerusalem?)
'Make public the twenty-four books that you wrote first and let the worthy and the unworthy read them; but keep the seventy that were written last, in order to give them to the wise among your people. For in them is the spring of understanding, the fountain of wisdom, and the river of knowledge.' (14:44–48)

A Jewish scribe checks over
a biblical scroll.

books of Maccabees, the writings of Josephus, a
few of the apocryphal books preserved in some
Christian canons and some pseudepigraphical
Jewish writings. The picture formed of this 'early
Judaism' was largely of a monolithic, normative
religion, divided into four groups – Pharisees,
Sadducees, Essenes and Zealots – with Pharisees
and Sadducees of major interest, since we possessed no ancient writings clearly attributable to
the other two groups. Moreover, both the extent of
the scriptures and the Jewish way of life were
assumed to have been broadly agreed by all Jews,
and, despite the loss of the Temple in 70 CE, a high
degree of continuity in Judaism from the time of
Ezra to that of the rabbis was assumed.

The Dead Sea Scrolls have revolutionized our
perception of Early Judaism. Unlike most of our
other sources, they are (mostly) in Hebrew, they
engage in direct controversy, they interact closely
with scripture, and they offer first-hand evidence of
some quite unusual doctrines. They expose bitter
controversy over law and temple, and over the
meaning of the scriptures; and they are permeated
by a belief in the imminent end of the world order.
They witness the ongoing production of religious
literature at a time when most scholars claimed
prophecy had ended, canonization had taken place,
and an official Judaism had established itself at
least within the area directly influenced and affected by the Jerusalem power brokers.

Until recently most scholars agreed in understanding the scrolls to be the library of an Essene
group living at Khirbet Qumran, an organized but
sectarian community to be contrasted with the
'official' Judaism that they opposed. Other scholars
agreed that some of the scrolls derived from a solitary sectarian community, but recognized that
other texts must have come from affiliated groups,
perhaps also Essene in name, located throughout
the countryside. Recent voices have announced that
the scrolls came from no single group, and indeed
not from sectarians at all, but from libraries in
Jerusalem containing writings reflecting a range of
Jewish beliefs and practices. Increasingly scholars
are beginning to read the scrolls as the religious
outpourings of the broader spectrum of diverse
but related Judaisms in the late Hellenistic and
Roman periods, revealing a much more diverse and
dynamic pattern of religious beliefs and practices.
If this assessment is true, then the scrolls even
more radically alter our understanding of Judaism.

One of the areas, for example, in which Judaism
can be seen as both united and diverse, is in its attitude towards the Law. The scrolls depict a Judaism
involved in developing from the scriptures not only
a law for all Israel (on which other Jews would not
have agreed) but also for their own group, during
its period of isolation from the rest of doomed
Israel. And the dominant principle behind this concern for law was the divine requirement of Israel to
be holy. Many of the legal works found in the
Qumran caves, especially in Cave 4, reflect an inten-
sive preoccupation with the problem of impurity
and purification through specific rituals. If Israel
had to be holy, even more so had the true, sectarian
Israel to be holy.

(Following pages) Jews
wearing phylacteries
praying at the Western
Wall in Jerusalem.

195

The scrolls writers were not the only group in their day to extend a concern for holiness beyond the priesthood. It is portrayed in the New Testament gospels as characteristic of the Pharisaic opponents of Jesus. We know from other sources, too, that the Pharisees were concerned with developing the scriptural law to cover details of everyday life to enable not just priests but other Jews to live in a state of holiness (i.e. purity). The difference between the scrolls writers and the Pharisees seems to be that while both groups despised unholy Jews, the Pharisees did not deny that those Jews who did not recognize or follow Pharisaic rulings (whom they called the 'people of the land') were still members of 'Israel'. Nor did the Pharisees cut themselves off from other Jews. However, their successors, the rabbis, were later to create a wide-ranging and detailed system of Jewish law (*halakhah*) that would govern the life of every true member of Israel. In this exercise, however, they had been anticipated by sectarian communities, who, because of their ideology and their physical exclusion, had already used the concept of holiness and the rigorous application of the law to establish their own social and religious boundaries and assert their claim to be the only true Israel.

On other issues, the scrolls also present us with a bigger and more colourful picture of Early Judaism. Expectation of the end of history was clearly more widespread than other ancient Jewish sources suggest, as was belief in the arrival of a Messiah. But the scrolls do not suggest a uniform Jewish belief in one sort of Messiah, a Davidic figure (as the Gospels tend to imply). Instead, we have angelic redeemers, priestly messiahs, teaching messiahs – and sometimes no Messiah at all. It was widely agreed that the righteous were soon to be vindicated and the wicked punished. But who the righteous were, and how and by whom this salvation would come: on this even the scrolls do not agree, and, presumably, neither did other Jews.

The most dramatic evidence in the scrolls of a split within Jewish society is surely the calendar. For the calendar affected law, purity and eschatology. Not only were people and places holy, but times. Observing the festivals on the wrong dates invalidated these holy times, and rendered the Temple ineffective if not actually profaned. Observing the wrong dates broke the divine law and incurred the wrath of God. And, of course, only the correct calculation of time could estimate the arrival of the end of history.

At first, scholars took the 364-day calendar based on the sun (as opposed to the 354-day, or so, based on the moon) of the scrolls to be a sectarian invention. Now it is widely conceded that the 'solar' calendar may have enjoyed a continuous history in Judah, whether or not alongside the other. Was it ever possible for Jews to tolerate more than one calendar, with separate festivals? Most scholars still think not, but perhaps we are still defective in our understanding of Judaism. One of the lessons of the scrolls is that different versions of Judaism coexisted in the last centuries of the pre-Christian era. We now have to ask: was there ever a single and agreed Judaism before that?

(Right) A 15th-century view of Jerusalem from the manuscript of Burchard of Mt Sion.

(Below) Part of the central mosaic in the 4th-century CE synagogue at Beit Alpha in southern Galilee depicting the sun in his chariot surrounded by the signs of the Zodiac.

Origins of sectarian Judaism

It seems clearer than ever that the 'sectarian' features of the scrolls – their dualistic theology, in which God created the good and the evil and predestined their ways, their intense cultivation of mantic (i.e. divinatory, predictive) reading of heavenly signs and holy books, their adherence to the sun as the proper marker of time, and their close familiarity with, imitation and rewriting of, the holy books – these are not the *results* of a sectarian rift: they are, in large measure, among the *reasons* for it. Whatever the historical processes that generated the formation of sectarian communities like the Damascus groups or the *yahad*, their traditions, or many of them, belong within a broader Judaism, as the books of Enoch or Jubilees, for example, show us. Of this diverse Judaism the scrolls now show us a picture we could not see before. And our understanding of the history and nature of Early Judaism will not be the same again.

But do the scrolls describe any kind of dramatic revolution in Jewish thought or practice? Clearly, disenchantment with the Temple and its authorities reached in some cases an extreme level (though we must beware, as always, of imposing complete uniformity on the scrolls). Whether or not as the result, rather than a cause, of the sectarianism of the *yahad*, we find the role of the Jerusalem Temple being transfigured as the community itself becomes the 'holy house'. Solidarity in that community and obedience to its authorities (characteristic of all sectarian communities) constitute the way of salvation, and inner purity (including true belief) assumes a place alongside outward ritual:

'He shall not be counted among the perfect. He shall neither be purified by atonement, nor cleansed by purifying waters, nor sanctified by seas and rivers, nor washed clean with any ablution. Unclean, unclean shall he be. For as long as he despises the precepts of God he shall receive no instruction in the community of his counsel.' (1QS 3:3–6)

Along with this belief may come a conviction that one is in communion with the heavenly cult and the angels. The Songs of the Sabbath Sacrifice may reflect a tradition or a practice born of physical separation from the Jerusalem cult. But they also continue elements of a tradition of communion with a heavenly cult found in Ezekiel, and continued well beyond the time of the scrolls into the mystical traditions of Judaism. Here again, what may be expressed in a sectarian form is not necessarily alien to the mainstream.

The last important observation about the scrolls and Judaism comes from one of the first of the scrolls scholars, Millar Burrows:

'The religious vocabulary of Judaism in these periods is richly illustrated by the texts. One of the most significant aspects of pre-Christian Judaism which finds expression in them is its devotional spirit. Everything that is important for Judaism in the last two or three centuries before Christ is also important for Christianity.' (*Burrows on the Dead Sea Scrolls* pp. 326–27)

Those brought up on the New Testament may easily come to regard the Judaism of that period as concerned with external rituals and lacking in true religious feeling. What is clear from the scrolls is that beneath the controversy over the proper observance of ritual acts, over the observation of correct times, and performance of the details of the law, lies a stratum of spirituality which is both communal and personal, and can be highly intense. In the Hodayoth there is an almost tangible revulsion on the part of the poet of his own humanity which can hardly bring itself to address the purity and might of God; yet breaking through this is a conviction of grace, of infinite goodness and mercy that constantly refreshes and restores the unworthy human. With whatever else the scrolls confront us, they do reveal a deep religious sensibility and sensitivity that tells us not only about their writers but also about the nature of the Judaism just prior to the age of the rabbis.

A Jewish rabbi, painted by Rembrandt (1606–69).

The Dead Sea Scrolls and Early Christianity

According to a long-standing hypothesis the Dead Sea Scrolls were hidden in the Qumran caves about 40 years after the crucifixion of Jesus. Many of the New Testament writings had not yet been composed by 70 CE, when the Romans destroyed the Jerusalem Temple. The early Jesus movement was well underway by the middle of the 1st century CE. Archaeologically speaking, the activities of John the Baptist, Jesus, Paul and others were contemporary with the last phase of Qumran occupation.

Is it likely that the people associated with Khirbet Qumran and certain figures of the Jesus movement crossed paths in Jerusalem, at Khirbet Qumran, or elsewhere? While the Jesus movement rapidly expanded into the Christ cult, finding supporters inside and outside Judaea, what happened to those who once lived at Qumran, or those who wrote the scrolls? We have no idea. Scholars have long speculated about the Essene origins of John the Baptist (and even Jesus), but the New Testament makes no mention of Essenes. Equally, despite some claims over tiny Greek fragments from Cave 7, none of the New Testament writings nor their sources have been found in the Qumran caves.

There are important similarities, nevertheless, between the Qumran scrolls and the New Testament. But rather than pointing to a direct relationship, they suggest an indirect one, mediated through a shared Jewish culture. This does not minimize the importance of such similarities, for they demonstrate that the differences between Christianity and Judaism, at least in their beginnings, are less dramatic and more subtle than a facile contrast allows.

Expectation of the Messiah

To begin, within the scrolls we find a description of a messianic sect (probably one both founded by, and waiting for, one or two messiahs) that cannot help inviting comparisons with the immediate followers of Jesus. Both communities conceived of their groups as representations of the ideal Israel. The Damascus Document refers to its community as the 'New Covenant', a phrase also used in the account of the Last Supper. Again, the Community Rule advocates a communal lifestyle whereby some resources are pooled. Acts 2:4–5 also refers to surrendering one's property to the community. According to the Damascus Document, the leader of the community has the Hebrew title of *mebaqqer*, the exact equivalent of the Greek *episkopos*, used by the early Church.

The interpretation of certain biblical passages as referring to eschatological events is also common to both movements. Texts like the one featuring Melchizedek (see p. 162) weave ancient scripture from the Qumran caves in a way that is reminiscent of the techniques of similar thematic sections in the New Testament writings. The most recognizable is the 'reference to making a way in the wilderness' in Isaiah 40. In the Community Rule it is made to refer to the birth of an elect community, but in the Gospel of Mark (1:2–4) it applies to John the Baptist. The Melchizedek text also draws on Isaiah 61 to proclaim the ultimate future redemption from evil. In Luke 4:16–21 Jesus quotes this chapter in order to announce that the scripture had already been fulfilled. As in Acts 2:15–17,

(Below left) 'The Good Shepherd' as depicted in a mosaic above the entrance to the mausoleum of Galla Placidia in Ravenna, dating to the 5th century CE. This is one of the many Christian (and Jewish) images of the Messiah.

(Below right) John the Baptist, who is seen by some scholars as a link between the Essenes of Qumran and Jesus, is shown here in this painting by Titian of the 1540s.

(Opposite) The traditional location of the Tomb of Christ in the Church of the Holy Sepulchre, Jerusalem. It is still debated whether or not the scrolls express a belief in resurrection.

some of the scrolls reveal that prophecy was again a relevant activity in the last days. This statement seems to be based on a view like that found in the book of Joel. The Teacher of Righteousness, the presumed founder of the *yahad*, is given authority in matters of teaching and the law (in the Damascus Document) and in the proper understanding of prophetic texts (in the Habakkuk Commentary); these functions are also, among others, assigned to Jesus in the Gospels.

The notion of a messianic banquet in 1QS 6 and 1QSa 2 is similar to the meals mentioned in Matthew 26:26–29 (parallels in Mark 14:22–25, Luke 22: 17–20) and 1 Corinthians 11:27–30. Moreover, the Damascus Document permitted, perhaps even encouraged, celibacy; and the *yahad* possibly required it, while celibacy also played an important role in early Christianity.

Those who press the connection between the Dead Sea Scrolls and the early Jesus movement particularly emphasize shared language. Certain texts from both groups speak of the 'children of light', the righteousness of God, works of the Law, lawlessness, light and darkness, Belial, and the human temple of God. The Community Rule uses the expression 'the many' to refer to one of its assembled bodies. Matthew 26:27–28 and Mark 14:23–24 employ similar language. The dualism of light and darkness is found in the Community Rule (col. 3), the War Rule (col. 4), and Galatians 5 and 2 Corinthians 6. Also striking is the identical attitude towards divorce, which both the Damascus Document (CD 4:20–5:6) and Jesus (Mark 10:2–9) reject (against common Jewish practice).

Major differences in outlook

The similarities just mentioned show at the very least that the groups behind the scrolls and the early Jesus movement both grew out of a radical expression of communal and individual Jewish piety. But differences must also be allowed for. One of the most obvious and significant is that the Qumran communities were highly organized, and with clear boundaries, excluding or controlling access to outsiders. The Jesus movement apparently mixed freely with outsiders. Thus, Christianity moved in an entirely opposite direction from the

yahad, turning towards non-Jews. Another difference is that at Qumran obedience to the Mosaic law was intensified, while in the New Testament it is qualified. Here a specific difference is the law about helping animals on the sabbath, which the Damascus Document forbids (CD 11:13–14) and Jesus implicitly allows (Matthew 12:11).

Finally, the Teacher of Righteousness did not come to be regarded as divine. However, this issue brings us to the text 4Q246 (4QAramaic Apocalypse). This small fragment includes the phrases 'he shall be proclaimed the son of God, and the son of the Most High they shall call him'. The context does not allow us to determine whether the words refer to a messianic figure or to an enemy, such as a foreign king. But the language is strikingly similar to that in Luke's account of the annunciation of the birth of Jesus (Luke 1:32–35):

'He will be great, and will be called the Son of the Most High: and the Lord God will give unto him the throne of his father David…therefore the child to be born will be holy; he will be called Son of God.'

This Qumran text does not necessarily describe a divine figure. As in Psalm 2 or 110, the king of the Davidic dynasty could be addressed as the (adopted) son of God. If this figure is in any way messianic, the application of such a title does not necessarily imply divinity in the way that it was ascribed to Jesus by his followers. If this text refers to a non-Jewish king, however, the context may rather be that of Hellenistic monarchs who, like some later Roman emperors, claimed divinity for themselves, and would, in this text, be criticized for such arrogance.

Further parallels?

Dramatic parallels between the scrolls and the New Testament have been pointed out from the beginning. But it is the overall picture that matters. If there were no agreement at all between the literature of two Jewish movements such as these, that would, after all, be quite surprising. Equally, the contrasts between the two bodies of literature can also be too quickly drawn. For example, many scholars maintain that the Jesus movement was not

It is questionable whether the description of a communal meal in the Rule of the Congregation can be compared to the Christian eucharist, depicted here in the Priscilla catacomb, Rome.

interested in purity as a cultic issue. But given the importance of such an issue in the scrolls, we need to reassess whether this is really so. It may well be that Jesus participated in the debate about purity laws that we see both within the Qumran documents and among the Pharisees themselves (for example, between the followers of Hillel and Shammai). Also unclear is how far the scrolls and the early Christians agreed in their attitude towards Roman occupation. Most likely, neither had a monolithic attitude, while both clearly expected an imminent end to history and were minded to see the Romans as agents of Satan.

Was there a different attitude towards the Temple? Both the scrolls and the New Testament seem critical of the Temple, and the Community Rule has been interpreted as expressing the doctrine of a 'spiritual temple'. In fact, both literatures simultaneously venerate the Temple and criticize it. Certainly the statement in 1QS 8:1–4 that the practice of justice and suffering of affliction can work atonement, and in 3:6–8 that one is cleansed by the Holy Spirit and atones for sin through 'uprightness and humility', suggest a displacement of the Temple cult. But how far was the Christian attitude influenced by the fall of the Temple in 70 CE? And does 1QS envisage a permanent replacement of the Temple or a temporary expediency, confined to its own community? Superficial parallels, however dramatic, must reflect systematic similarities if they are to rank as true parallels. Thus, the book of Revelation (chapter 21) speaks of the holy city Jerusalem coming down out of heaven from God, painting a picture not unlike that of the New Jerusalem text from Caves 4 and 11. It also describes the heavenly worship there, corresponding somewhat to the angelic worship in The Songs of the Sabbath Sacrifice. Here is a parallel; but while the Jerusalem Temple remains the focus of concern at Qumran, in the New Testament it is already destroyed and superseded.

Finally, two further examples of dubious parallels. One is so-called 'baptism'. It has often been asserted that the *yahad* was a baptizing community, because of the many cisterns, and the reference to purification by water in many of the texts (especially 1QS 3:4). Such a parallel has also been used to support the notion that John the Baptist was an Essene. But the use of water in the scrolls seems to have followed Jewish practice generally, if more strictly: it was regular, and intended to remove impurity. Christian baptism is an initiation rite. What is common is the use of water as an agent of cleansing. But that is so general a phenomenon as to be useless for comparison.

The second dubious parallel is 'eucharist'. There is a description in 1QSa, the Rule of the Congregation, of a meal attended by two messiahs, in which bread and wine are eaten after being blessed. This passage is very difficult to interpret, since it seems to reflect both an eschatological meal and a regular one. Josephus' description of the Essenes has them eating bread and 'new wine' at their meals. But regular meals of bread and wine are not unusual, and blessing of food is a regular Jewish custom. The Christian eucharist seems to have originated in a Passover meal, and has a specific cultic significance. It is not a regular, daily meal. Whether eating bread and wine in a communal setting can really be called 'eucharist' is very questionable.

Christian and Jewish interpretations

Have the parallels between the New Testament and Qumran overdominated Qumran research? Lawrence Schiffman's *Reclaiming the Dead Sea Scrolls* argues that modern interpreters of the scrolls have imposed Christian interpretations onto them. He was especially concerned about themes that presented the Teacher of Righteousness as a figure like Jesus, that equated the Hebrew term *mebaqqer* with the Christian *episkopos* (bishop), and that treated the *yahad* as a monastic community. He also dislikes Christianized language, such as 'baptismal rites', 'refectory', 'eucharist', 'monks', 'ascetics', and a 'scriptorium' where monks copied manuscripts. He recommends, instead, that one speak of observant Jews, led by their rabbi, practising ritual purity and taking food in their dining room after immersion in a *mikveh*. They said the prayer '*ha-motzi*' before their meal and offered a *berakhah* for their wine. Their scribes copied the most important texts of the group.

It is true that the scrolls were largely worked on, and the site of Qumran excavated, by Christians. The immediate reason had to do with the politics of Palestine and the Arab-Israeli war. But it is also true that Christian interest in the scrolls has been centred on understanding the origins of Christianity, recognizing that the inhabitants of Qumran, at least in its later phase, were contemporaries of Jesus and his followers. Jewish readers have not recognized, until perhaps recently, the relevance of the scrolls for Judaism. Nevertheless, the unification of the collections of scrolls after 1967 and the more recent introduction of Jewish scholars into the official process of editing, together with the prominence of legal texts like the Temple Scroll and the Halakhic Letter, have resulted in a more balanced appreciation of the scrolls as in many respects closer to rabbinic Judaism than to Christianity. The fact is that the scrolls are what one might expect from a time before either Christianity or rabbinic Judaism emerged. They preserve a variety of Jewish perspectives from a time before certain events and groups led to the elimination of much of that variety. The scrolls, in short, contain the seeds of both religious systems – and, indeed, help us to understand much better the relationships between the two.

Who Wrote the Scrolls?

Essenes

Almost from the time of their discovery the majority of scholars have maintained that the owners and composers of the scrolls were Essenes. Many believe that the settlers at Qumran wrote and copied the scrolls for their own use in study and worship. In the evenings, on sabbaths and other holy days, the Qumran Essenes buried their heads in the writings of the ancients in order to understand better God's will. Often texts were copied for group sessions so that several specialists might study and discuss passages of keen interest or perhaps even for Bible study away from the premises of Khirbet Qumran. In this view the settlement itself was a retreat for a coterie of pietists who, by virtue of losing their political dominance in Jerusalem, were forced to abandon the wicked city and its leaders and volunteered to serve as a human atoning sacrifice for Israel's past, present and future sins.

But although this theory relied on Josephus, among other ancient writers, Josephus never presented the Essenes as a radical reformist party, nor even as a small sectarian group. On the contrary, for him the Essenes were a major group who lived in colonies throughout Palestine. If the Qumran settlers were Essenes, then, they were not the only ones. It was widely held, however, that Khirbet Qumran was the Essene headquarters which contained either an elite group or served as a centre which Essenes could visit.

While the Essene theory is still widely held, it now embraces a range of options. The presence of skeletons of women and children, and even references to wives and mothers in some Cave 4 texts, have led to the view in some quarters that the settlement was not inhabited by celibates, as Pliny's description, perhaps the strongest evidence for the identification, stated. The most developed Essene thesis is that of Hartmut Stegemann of Göttingen, who believes that the Essenes were a major, mainstream Jewish movement, for whom Qumran served as a publishing house, but not merely for Essene literature. Traditional writings, such as the canonical Bible, were revered and copied here. Besides these authoritative texts, others, also considered worthy of study and exposition, were copied. Many of them were legal texts, sometimes mixed with narrative sections, edifying accounts of biblical figures and testaments of famous fathers, prayers, prophetic revelations and calendrical works.

Stegemann's view accommodates the fact that there is a great variety in the literature within the caves. This variety means, without a doubt, that it is impossible to use all the non-biblical scrolls indiscriminately in compiling an account of

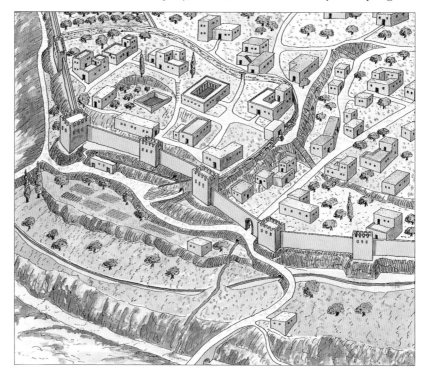

Reconstruction of what might have been the Essene quarter in Jerusalem before the capture of the city by the Romans in 70 CE.

'Essene beliefs'. It raises the problem, in fact, of working out which scrolls might be Essene, or even 'sectarian', and which not. That problem remains to be solved, if it can be solved. But Stegemann's theory does not explain why the handwriting and spelling, and the conventions of preparing and inscribing the scrolls, are so varied. Nor is there any convincing evidence of major scroll-production at the site, or in nearby Ain Feshkha.

Others who sustain the Essene theory suggest rather that the site was visited by other Essenes who brought their own scrolls, not all of which were necessarily of Essene composition. This would explain the variety of contents and techniques of writing, and perhaps the female skeletons. It also explains, up to a point, the differences between the communities in the Damascus Document and the Community Rule. The former are led by a *mebaqqer* ('overseer, guardian'), live in several 'camps' and 'cities', include families as well as celibate males (and females?), have some dealings with the Temple, live by their own interpretations of the law and apparently look forward to a messianic teacher. The latter are apparently celibate, are ruled by *maskilim* ('wise teachers') and by Zadokite priests, and have turned their backs on the Temple. Several other differences between the two could be enumerated. The question remains: what is the relationship between the two groups? Broadly, two theories exist: one is that the *yahad* was a splinter group of a wider movement, described in the Damascus Document; the other is that the *yahad* was the original group and over time extended to form other groups. In either case, the word 'Essene' applies to all of these communities.

Other identifications

Other proposals as to the authors of the scrolls have been offered. Pharisees, Zealots and Sadducees have all at one time or another been nominated as candidates. The Pharisee theory, offered by Louis Ginzberg and supported by Chaim Rabin, is no longer advocated, and indeed there is now general agreement that the Pharisees are criticized in the scrolls. The Sadducee theory, first attached to the Damascus Document when it was initially discovered in Cairo, has been revived recently by a number of scholars, including Schiffman, who equate legal positions adopted in the Halakhic Letter and the Temple Scroll with views assigned to *zadduqim* in rabbinic literature. But the picture of the Sadducees offered in Josephus and the New Testament fits so badly that it is necessary to theorize a split in the Sadducee movement in order to sustain the identification.

The Zealot identification, once held by Roth and Driver, persists in a certain way in the thesis of Robert Eisenman, who maintains that a Jewish movement, nationalistic, messianic, devoted to the law and above all attached to the notion of 'righteousness' (Hebrew *zedaqah*, hence the names 'Zadok', 'Zadokite' and 'Sadducee') can be identified in turn with Maccabees, Zealots, Sadducees and the early Christian community led by James, the brother of Jesus.

Norman Golb has recently contested the idea that the scrolls are either Essenic, Saducean, or Pharisaic, or for that matter even Qumranic in origin. The great diversity of these writings – from widespread traditional works to partly known and used traditional pieces to insider sectarian texts – lead him to believe that the collection called the Dead Sea Scrolls came from a number of libraries of those fleeing Jerusalem as it was under siege from the Romans. Although some scholars think Golb has disregarded the overwhelming array of Essene motifs in the collection, he is convinced that the collection is not completely unified by themes and ownership. What they do have in common is their Jewishness.

It seems that despite major problems with Golb's overall position, more and more scholars are beginning to state explicitly that the majority of scrolls in the Dead Sea caves came from somewhere other than Qumran. Against Golb's theory would seem to be the obvious antagonism in the writings towards the Jerusalem priesthood. But at the time the majority of the scrolls were apparently hidden, namely during the war with Rome, the Temple had fallen into the hands of rebelling priestly groups, who also opposed the previous Temple authorities and who, accordingly, may have been sympathetic to the views of the dwellers at Qumran. Whether the writers of the scrolls and/or the Qumran residents participated in the war against Rome is, however, a separate issue.

In considering all these scholarly views, it is necessary to bear in mind that we are dealing with about 150 years of Qumran settlement, and in some cases with documents that have been revised, perhaps several times. We also have to bear in mind that the ancestry of the scrolls may go back well beyond the settlement at Qumran, and well beyond any sectarian groups that the writings portray. The books of Enoch and Jubilees, sharing many features with the scrolls, suggest that behind these manuscripts lies a long history. The invitation to reconsider the nature of late Second Temple Judaism is strong. Is it true, for instance, as Gabriele Boccaccini has recently suggested, that Qumran represents a late phase in a struggle between two different kinds of Judaism, an Enochic and a Mosaic? The question of the origin of the Qumran scrolls, once confined to the history of the settlement itself, now sets a much broader and more radical agenda than was once envisaged.

Norman Golb of Chicago University addresses the 1997 scrolls conference in Jerusalem.

Epilogue

In *Our Bible and the Ancient Manuscripts* (1939), Frederick Kenyon wrote: 'There is, indeed, no probability that we shall ever find manuscripts of the Hebrew texts going back to a period before the formation of the text which we know as Massoretic' (p. 48). Less than a decade later Kenyon's claim was disproved.

Fifty-year commemorations of the discovery of the first Dead Sea Scrolls were held at several venues in 1997. What was said there will certainly be different from what the centenary will witness. Had the new and improved editorial team, consisting of about five-dozen or so scholars from around the globe, not been set up in the early 1990s, these celebrations would have amounted to a litany of denunciation.

An unhappy legacy

Yes, the best-preserved scrolls were all published by about 20 years ago. But until recently guerrilla warfare, character defamation and public litigation continued to plague the scholarly discussion about the editing and publication of the remaining thousands of scroll fragments. Certain scholars tried to jolt lethargic colleagues and opponents into more rapid disclosure of their goods by making public the bitter correspondence and childish name-calling that was going on. The chief editor of the scrolls, a Harvard professor, was dismissed from his position. A bevy of scrolls 'insiders' researching the scrolls in America petitioned to condemn and denounce two outsiders who had published a book of translations of scrolls to which they had no rights. One of the 'guilty' scholars pleaded *mea culpa* and was quickly forgiven. An Israeli scholar chose to advance publicly his 'ownership' of the reconstruction of certain fragmentary Hebrew manuscripts in a court of law over the scientific and public 'right-to-know'.

The scrolls melodrama is certainly not boring. Just before the 50th anniversary jamboree, two inscribed pieces of pottery (ostraca) were found at Khirbet Qumran (see p. 186). One bears several Jewish names and a possible reference to Engedi. The other, which was broken in half, seems to refer to a property transfer executed between a man named Honi and a man named Eleazar in the area of Jericho. Continuing the controversy typical of Qumran and scrolls scholarship, the editors of the inscriptions, Esther Eshel and Frank Cross, claimed that Honi was joining the Qumran Essene community and adding his property to the community's holdings in the time close to the First Jewish Revolt against the Romans. They even read the word *yahad* on the main ostracon. Subsequently, their reading has been challenged, and it now seems to have been largely abandoned by scrolls scholars. Meanwhile, the charge of conspiracy against individuals, institutions and the Vatican are being quietly forgotten in a new atmosphere of congeniality.

The value of the scrolls

What, then, has scrolls research contributed to human knowledge? First, in a broad sense, it has reunited in a new way the study of the Hebrew Bible and the New Testament and brought Jewish and Christian scholarship into a fruitful dialogue. As the previous chapter has shown, a host of new questions about the nature of Judaism and the emergence of Christianity have been posed.

Thus, scrolls research has generated a revolution in several fields of Jewish history. Among the scrolls were found the oldest known manuscripts of the Jewish Bible in Hebrew and Aramaic. Besides that, the scrolls truly upset lots of apple carts. Terms like 'Bible', 'Pseudepigrapha', and 'sectarian Judaism' will require serious rethinking in the light of the revolutionary new paradigm established by the scrolls. Imagine that the scrolls reflect what

was typical in the time of John the Baptist, Jesus and Paul. A number of truisms find themselves being tested. Was the biblical canon closed? Had prophecy ended? What exactly did define 'Judaism'?

Our appreciation of the background of Christianity has also been affected. No new 'Life of Jesus' can be plausibly written without these manuscripts. Jesus has not been found in the Dead Sea Scrolls, despite the claims of at least one scholar. Nor has John the Baptist or Paul. But the scrolls came from the time of these pioneering figures of early Christianity, and they destroy for ever any simplistic opposition of 'Jesus' and 'Judaism'. Do they demonstrate that Christianity is older than Jesus? Strictly, no: but they expose very strong continuities.

The scrolls have also afforded the opportunity for several new scientific techniques to be deployed and developed. They have shown concretely how ancient Jewish parchment and papyrus scrolls were produced, scored, corrected, patched and preserved, and allowed us to measure the evolution of Jewish scripts over more than two centuries. Carbon-14 (AMS) analysis has also been applied to some of the scrolls in order to prove their great antiquity, and, most recently, DNA analysis of the uninscribed portions of inscribed parchment manuscripts has begun in order to determine the origin of the herds from which the hides came.

But despite the impression given by many books on the subject, the riddles of the scrolls are not all solved. There is much yet to be done, and much to be understood. With the texts already completely available in translation and the official *DJD* series virtually complete, the saga of Qumran publication is effectively over. But understanding these texts will remain an urgent task. Despite an earlier confidence in our answers, we now have to admit that we do not know for sure who wrote these scrolls, or the origins or history of the communities they describe. We do not know what, if any, is the link between Qumran and the manuscript caves; who occupied the settlement and why the scrolls were left where, and as, they were.

We do know, however, that the scrolls underline the ongoing religious imagination and the desire of Jews to become attuned to the words and the will of God in the final days of the Second Temple. They represent the religious matrix of both rabbinic Judaism and Christianity. Therefore, they belong to the intellectual history of all humanity, and, after 50 years of less than decorous behaviour, humanity can read them all.

Replicas and Qumran memorabilia produced for sale at exhibitions held around the world and permanently at the Shrine of the Book at the Israel Museum, Jerusalem.

Where to See the Scrolls

At the Israel Museum, in the centre of Jerusalem, is the Shrine of the Book, specially built for housing the scrolls. Here the seven major scrolls from Cave 1 are conserved and some of them can be seen.

The Rockefeller Museum was the repository for fragments from all 11 caves; these are mostly not on public display. Also in Jerusalem, at the Museum of the Flagellation, can be found a fragment (no. 1) of 4Q379, a copy of the Apocryphon of Joshua.

The Archaeological Museum in Amman houses the Copper Scroll, as well as some fragments from Caves 1 and 4.

Some scrolls can be found in the United States: the Oriental Museum at the University of Chicago has a fragment of 4Q484 (identified as a Rule for a Menstruating Woman); some fragments possessed by Mar Samuel are also held in New Jersey by the Syrian community.

Elsewhere, the Bibliothèque National in Paris has some Cave 1 fragments. Nearly 100 uninscribed fragments are housed at the John Rylands University Library in Manchester, England. Professor Georges Roux, the distinguished ancient historian, has a fragment (L) of 11QpalaeoLeviticus. Another private owner is the scholar M. Testuz, who has a fragment of 4Q537 (part of an Aramaic 'Apocryphon of Jacob'). K.G. Kuhn, one of the pioneers of Qumran research, also acquired some phylacteries (fragments of 4Q128, 129, 135 and 137), which remain in Heidelberg. The Norwegian antiquarian collector Martin Schøyen possesses a number of Qumran fragments, mostly uninscribed, but one of which belongs to 1QSb (he also possesses a scrolls jar and an inkwell from Qumran).

Other fragments of scrolls undoubtedly exist in other private collections. A detailed listing is available in Stephen A. Reed's

The Dead Sea Scrolls Catalogue: Documents, Photographs and Museum Inventory Numbers (2nd edition, revised and edited by Marilyn J. Lundberg with the collaboration of Michael B. Phelps, Atlanta, 1994).

Political conflict means that the future of the Dead Sea Scrolls and Qumran remains, to an extent, uncertain. The scrolls were found in what was Jordan and Qumran remains outside the internationally defined legal borders of the State of Israel. Regardless of the fact that the scrolls are obviously Jewish, can the State of Israel claim legal ownership of them? Might the new Palestinian Authority assume jurisdiction over Qumran, and wish to repossess the scrolls housed in the Rockefeller Museum in East Jerusalem? It is uncertain whether any such move is seriously contemplated at present by the Palestinian authorities, but some kind of negotiation on both issues may one day be undertaken.

Further Reading

Translations of the Dead Sea Scrolls
Garcia Martinez, F., *The Dead Sea Scrolls Translated* (2nd ed., Leiden, 1996)
García Martinez, F. and E.J.C. Tigchelaar, *The Dead Sea Scrolls Study Edition* (Leiden and Grand Rapids, 2000) (Hebrew and English)
Vermes, G., *The Complete Dead Sea Scolls in English* (5th ed., New York and London, 1997)
Wise, M.O., M. Abegg Jr. and E. Cook, *The Dead Sea Scrolls: A New Translation* (San Francisco, 1996)

The Further Reading does not include the *Discoveries in the Judaean Desert* series, a list of which can be found on p. 29.

Journals devoted to the Dead Sea Scrolls
Dead Sea Discoveries, Leiden
The Qumran Chronicle, Cracow
Revue de Qumrân, Paris

Introduction
Allegro, J. M., *The Dead Sea Scrolls. A Reappraisal* (2nd ed., London, 1966)
Flint, P.W. and J.C. VanderKam (eds), *The Dead Sea Scrolls after Fifty Years*, 2 vols (Leiden, 1998, 1999)
Golb, N., *Who Wrote the Dead Sea Scrolls?* (New York and London, 1995)
Schiffman, L. H., *Reclaiming the Dead Sea Scrolls* (Philadelphia and Jerusalem, 1994)
Schiffman, L.H. and J.C. VanderKam (eds), *The Encyclopedia of the Dead Sea Scrolls* (New York, 2000)

VanderKam, J. C., *The Dead Sea Scrolls Today* (London and Grand Rapids, 1994)

I THE SCROLLS REVEALED

Early Dead Sea Discoveries
Allegro, J. M., *The Shapira Affair* (London and Garden City, New York, 1964)
Driver, G.R., *The Judaean Scrolls* (Oxford, 1964)
Stegemann, H., *The Library of Qumran. On the Essenes, Qumran, John the Baptist and Jesus* (Grand Rapids and Leiden, 1998)

The Damascus Document
(including Cave 4 texts)
Baumgarten, J., E.G. Chazon and A. Pinnick (eds), *The Damascus Document: A Centennial of Discovery* (Leiden, 2000)
Baumgarten, J. and M.T. Davis, 'Cave IV, V, VI Fragments'. In J.H. Charlesworth (ed.), *The Dead Sea Scrolls*, vol. 2 (Tübingen and Louisville, 1995) pp. 59–79
Baumgarten, J. and D.R. Schwarz, 'Damascus Document (CD)'. In J.H. Charlesworth (ed.), *The Dead Sea Scrolls*, vol. 2 (Tübingen and Louisville, 1995), pp. 4–57
Davies, P.R., *The Damascus Covenant: An Interpretation of the 'Damascus Document'* (Sheffield, 1983)
Ginzberg, L., *An Unknown Jewish Sect* (reprinted New York, 1976)
Hempel, C., *The Damascus Texts* (Sheffield, 2000)

Rabin, C., *The Zadokite Documents* (Oxford, 1958)
Schechter, S., *Documents of Jewish Sectaries: Fragments of a Zadokite Work* (reprinted New York, 1970)

Editing the Scrolls: The First Fifty Years
Trever, J., *The Dead Sea Scrolls. A Personal Account* (Grand Rapids, 1977)

II THE ANCIENT WORLD OF THE SCROLLS

The Historical Framework
Grabbe, L.L., *Judaism from Cyrus to Hadrian*, 2 vols (Minneapolis, 1992)
Sacchi, P., *The History of the Second Temple Period* (Sheffield, 2000)

Jewish Parties and Sects
Boccaccini, G., *Beyond the Essene Hypothesis* (Grand Rapids, 1998)
Coggins, R.J., *Samaritans and Jews* (Atlanta, 1975)
Eisenman, R., *The Dead Sea Scrolls and the First Christians* (Shaftesbury, 1996)
Farmer, W. R., *Maccabees, Zealots and Josephus* (New York, 1956)
Neusner, J., *Formative Judaism (3rd series): Torah, Pharisees, and Rabbis* (Chico, 1983)
Rivkin, E., *The Hidden Revolution: The Pharisees' Search for the Kingdom Within* (Nashville, 1978)
Saldarini, A. J., *Pharisees, Scribes and Sadducees in Palestinian Society* (Wilmington, 1988)

Stemberger, G., *Jewish Contemporaries of Jesus: Pharisees, Sadducees, Essenes* (Minneapolis, 1995)

Vermes, G. and M. Goodman, *The Essenes according to the Classical Sources* (Sheffield, 1989)

III   INSIDE THE SCROLLS

Scripts and Writing Styles

Cross, F. M., Jr, 'The Development of the Jewish Scripts'. In G.E. Wright (ed.), *The Bible and the Ancient Near East. Essays in Honor of William Foxwell Albright* (Garden City, New York, 1965), pp. 170–264

Reconstructing a Scroll

Stegemann, H., 'Methods for Reconstruction of Scrolls from Scattered Fragments'. In L. H. Schiffman (ed.), *Archaeology and History in the Dead Sea Scrolls* (Sheffield, 1990), pp. 189–220

List of Scrolls by Cave

Fitzmyer, J A., *The Dead Sea Scrolls. Major Publications and Tools for Study* (rev. ed., Atlanta, 1990)

Cave 1

The Rules Scroll

(Community Rule, Rule of the Congregation, Rule of Blessings)

Burrows M., (ed.), *The Dead Sea Scrolls of St. Mark's Monastery*, vol. 2, fasc. 2: *The Manual of Discipline* (New Haven, 1951)

Charlesworth, J.H., *Rule of the Community and Related Documents* (Tübingen and Louisville, 1994)

Leaney, A.R.C., *The Rule of Qumran and its Meaning* (London and Philadelphia, 1966)

Metso, S., *The Textual Development of the Qumran Community Rule* (Leiden, 1997)

Pouilly, J., *La Règle de la Communauté: son évolution littéraire* (Paris, 1976)

Schiffman, L.H., *The Eschatological Community of the Dead Sea Scrolls: A Study of the Rule of the Congregation* (Atlanta, 1989)

Wernberg-Møller, P., *The Manual of Discipline* (Leiden, 1956)

The War Scroll

Davies, P. R., *1QM, The War Scroll from Qumran* (Rome, 1977)

Duhaime, J., 'War Scroll'. In J.H. Charlesworth (ed.), *The Dead Sea Scrolls*, vol. 2 (Tübingen and Louisville, 1995), pp. 80–203

Yadin, Y., *The War of the Sons of Light Against the Sons of Darkness*, English translation by B. and C. Rabin (Oxford, 1962)

The Thanksgiving Hymns

Holm-Nielsen, S., *Hodayot. Psalms from Qumran* (Aarhus, 1961)

Kittel, B., *The Hymns of Qumran* (Chico, California, 1981)

Licht, J., *The Thanksgiving Hymns* (Jerusalem, 1957) (Hebrew)

Puech, É., 'Quelques aspects de la restauration du Rouleau des Hymnes', *Journal of Jewish Studies* 39 (1988), pp. 38–55

Sukenik, E.L., *The Dead Sea Scrolls of the Hebrew University* (Jerusalem, 1954–55) (Hebrew)

The Biblical Commentaries

Brownlee, W. H., *The Midrash Pesher of Habakkuk* (Missoula, 1979)

Doudna, G., *4Q Pesher Nahum* (Sheffield, 2001)

Horgan, M. P., *The Pesharim* (Washington, 1979)

Lim, T. H., *Pesharim* (Sheffield, 2002)

The Genesis Apocryphon

Avigad, N. and Y. Yadin, *A Genesis Apocryphon* (Jerusalem, 1956)

Fitzmyer, J., *The Genesis Apocryphon from Cave 1: A Commentary* (2nd ed., Washington, 1971)

Morgenstern, M., E. Qimron and D. Sivan, 'The Hitherto Unpublished Columns of the Genesis Apocryphon', *Abr-Nahrain* 23 (1995), pp. 30–54

The Book of Jubilees

Charles, R.H., *The Book of Jubilees or the Little Genesis* (London, 1902)

Hempel, C., 'The Place of the Book of Jubilees at Qumran and Beyond'. In T.H. Lim *et al.* (eds, *The Dead Sea Scrolls in Their Historical Context* (Edinburgh, 2000)

Wintermute, O.S., 'The Book of Jubilees'. In J.H. Charlesworth (ed.), *The Old Testament Pseudepigrapha*, vol. 2 (Garden City, New York and Cambridge 1985), pp. 35–142

Cave 2

New Jerusalem

Chyutin, M., *The New Jerusalem Scroll from Qumran, A Comprehensive Reconstruction* (Sheffield, 1997)

Jongeling, B., 'Publication provisoire d'un fragment provenant du grotte 11 de Qumrân', *Journal for the Study of Judaism* 1 (1970), pp. 58–64

Licht, J., 'The Ideal Town Plan from Qumran: The Description of the New Jerusalem', *Israel Exploration Journal* 29 (1979), pp. 47–59

Cave 3

The Copper Scroll

Allegro, J.M., *The Treasure of the Copper Scroll* (London, 1960)

Goranson, S., 'Sectarianism, Geography, and the Copper Scroll', *Journal of Jewish Studies* 43 (1992), pp. 282–87

Lefkovits, J., *The Copper Scroll (3Q15): A Reevaluation* (Leiden and Boston, 1999)

McCarter, P.K., 'The Mysterious Copper Scroll: Clues to Hidden Temple Treasure?" *Bible Review* 8 (1992), pp. 34–41, 63–64

Pixner, B., 'Unravelling the Copper Scroll Code', *Revue de Qumrân* 11 (1983), pp. 323–65

Wolters, A., *The Copper Scroll: Overview, Text and Translation* (Sheffield, 1996)

Cave 4

The Commentaries on Genesis

Allegro, J.M., 'Further Messianic References in Qumran Literature', *Journal of Biblical Literature* 75 (1956), pp. 174–76

Bernstein, M., 'From Re-Written Bible to Biblical Commentary', *Journal of Jewish Studies* 45 (1994), pp. 1–27

Targums to Leviticus and Job

van der Ploeg, J.P.M. and A.S. van der Woude, *Le Targum de Job de la grotte XI de Qumrân* (Leiden, 1971)

The 'Reworked Pentateuch'

Segal, M., '4QReworked Pentateuch or 4QPentateuch?'. In L.H. Schiffman, E. Tov and J.C. VanderKam (eds), *The Dead Sea Scrolls: Fifty Years after Their Discovery 1947–1997* (Jerusalem, 2000), pp. 391–99

Tov, E., 'Biblical Texts as Reworked'. In E. Ulrich and J.C. VanderKam, *The Community of the Renewed Covenant* (Notre Dame, 1994), pp. 123–39

The Books of Enoch

Black, M., *The Book of Enoch or I Enoch* (Leiden, 1985)

Milik, J.T., *The Books of Enoch* (Oxford, 1976)

Stuckenbruck, L., *The Book of Giants from Qumran* (Tübingen, 1997)

VanderKam, J.C., *Enoch and the Growth of an Apocalyptic Tradition* (Washington, 1984)

The Florilegium

Brooke, G.J., *Exegesis at Qumran. 4QFlorilegium in its Jewish Context* (Sheffield, 1985)

Steudel, A., *Der Midrasch zur Eschatologie aus der Qumrangemeinde (4QMidrEschat^{a,b})* (Leiden, 1994)

The Testimonia

Brooke, G.J., 'Testimonia'. In *Anchor Bible Dictionary* (New York, 1992), pp. 391–92

Ordinances

Schiffman, L. H., 'Ordinances'. In J.H. Charlesworth, *Rule of the Community and Related Documents* (Tübingen and Louisville, 1994), pp. 145–57

The Calendar Texts

Callaway, P. R., 'The 364-Day Calendar Traditions at Qumran', *Mogilany 1989, I* (Cracow, 1993), pp. 19–29

Greenfield J.C. and M. Sokoloff, 'An Astrological Text from Qumran (4Q318) and Reflections on Some Zodiacal Names', *Revue de Qumrân* (1995), pp. 507–25

VanderKam, J.C., *Calendars in the Dead Sea Scrolls* (London and New York, 1998)

Wise, M.O., *Thunder in Gemini* (Sheffield, 1994), pp. 186–221

The Halakhic Letter

Kampen, J. and M. J. Bernstein (eds), *Reading 4QMMT: New Perspectives on Qumran Law and History* (Atlanta, 1996)

Lim, T.H., H.L. McQueen and C. Carmichael (eds), *On Scrolls, Artefacts and Intellectual Property* (Sheffield, 2001)

The Wisdom Texts

Harrington, D., *The Wisdom Texts from Qumran* (London and New York, 1996)

Poetry, Psalms and Prayers

Charlesworth, J.H. (ed.), *The Dead Sea Scrolls*, vol. 4A: Pseudepigraphic and Non-Masoretic Psalms and Prayers (Tübingen and Louisville, 1997)

Nitzan, B., *Qumran Prayer and Religious Poetry* (Leiden, 1994)

The Songs of the Sabbath Sacrifice

Newsom, C.A., *The Songs of the Sabbath Sacrifice* (Atlanta, 1985)

Newsom, C.A., 'Angelic Liturgy: Songs of the Sabbath Sacrifice'. In J.H. Charlesworth (ed.), *The Dead Sea Scrolls*, vol. 4B (Tübingen and Louisville, 1999)

Cave 11

The Temple Scroll

Brooke G., J. (ed.), *Temple Scroll Studies. Papers Presented at the International Symposium on the Temple Scroll, Manchester, December 1987* (Sheffield, 1989)

Maier, J., *The Temple Scroll* (Sheffield, 1983)

Swanson, D.D., *The Temple Scroll and the Bible. The Methodology of 11QT* (Leiden, 1995)

Wacholder, B.Z., *The Dawn of Qumran: The Sectarian Torah and the Teacher of Righteousness* (Cincinnati, 1983)

White Crawford, S., *The Temple Scroll and Related Texts* (Sheffield, 2000)

Wise, M.O., *A Critical Study of the Temple Scroll from Qumran Cave 11* (Chicago, 1990)

Yadin, Y., *The Temple Scroll* (Jerusalem, 1983)

The Psalms Scroll

Flint, P. W., *The Dead Sea Psalms Scrolls and the Book of Psalms* (Leiden, 1997)

Melchizedek

de Jonge, M. and A.S. van der Woude, '11QMelchizedek and the New Testament', *New Testament Studies* 12 (1966), pp. 301–26

Kobelski, P., *Melchizedek and Melchireša^c* (Washington, 1981)

van der Woude, A.S., 'Melchisedek als himmlische Erlösergestalt in den neugefundenen eschatologischen Midraschim aus Qumran Höhle XI', *Oudtestamentische Studiën* 14 (1965), pp. 354–73

Biblical Manuscripts from the Qumran Caves

Cross, F.M., Jr. and S. Talmon (eds), *Qumran and the History of the Biblical Text* (Cambridge, Mass., 1975)

Flint, P.W. (ed.), *The Bible at Qumran* (Cambridge and Grand Rapids, 2001)

Tov, E., *Textual Criticism of the Hebrew Bible* (2nd ed., Minneapolis and Assen, 2001)

Ulrich, E., *The Dead Sea Scrolls and the Origins of the Bible* (Leiden, 1999)

IV THE QUMRAN SETTLEMENT

The Settlement

Davies, P.R., *Qumran* (Guildford and Grand Rapids, 1982)

Davies, P.R., 'How Not to Do Archaeology: the Story of Qumran', *Biblical Archaeologist* (1988), pp. 203–07.

de Vaux, R., *Archaeology and the Dead Sea Scrolls* (Oxford, 1973)

Humbert, J.-B. and A. Chambon, *Fouilles de Khirbet Qumrân et de Aïn Feshkha,* vol. I (Fribourg and Göttingen, 1994)

Laperrousaz, E.-M., *Qoumrân, l'établissement essénien des bords de la Mer Morte: Histoire et archéologie du site* (Paris, 1976)

Magness, J., 'Qumran Archaeology: Past Perspectives and Future Prospects'. In P. Flint and J. VanderKam (eds), *The Dead Sea Scrolls After Fifty Years*, Vol. I (Leiden, 1998), pp. 47–77

Recently Discovered Ostraca from Qumran

Cross, F.M., Jr, and Esther Eshel, 'Ostraca from Khirbet Qumran', *Israel Exploration Journal* 47 (1997), pp. 17–28

Cryer, F.M., 'The Qumran Conveyance', *Scandinavian Journal of the Old Testament* Vol. 11 No. 2 (1997), pp. 232–40

Yardeni, A., 'A Draft of a Deed on an Ostracon from Khirbet Qumran', *Israel Exploration Journal* 47 (1997), pp. 233–37

Yardeni, A., 'Breaking the Missing Link', *Biblical Archaeology Review* 24 (1998), pp. 44–47

Scrolls, Caves and Ruins

Driver, G.R., *The Judaean Scrolls. The Problem and a Solution* (Oxford, 1965), pp. 1–15

Humbert, J.-B. and A. Chambon, *Fouilles de Khirbet Qumrân et de Aïn Feshkha, I* (Fribourg, 1994)

Stegemann, H., *The Library of Qumran: On the Essenes, Qumran, John the Baptist and Jesus* (Grand Rapids and Leiden, 1998)

V THE MEANING OF THE SCROLLS

Books relating to this section are listed under Jewish Parties and Sects (see p. 208).

Epilogue

Baigent, M. and R. Leigh, *The Dead Sea Scrolls Deception* (London, 1991)

Kenyon, F., *Our Bible and the Ancient Manuscripts* (London, 1939)

Silberman, N.A., *The Hidden Scrolls* (New York, 1994)

Bibliographies

Burchard, C., *Bibliographie zu den Handschriften vom Toten Meer* (Berlin, 1959)

Burchard, C., *Bibliographie zu den Handschriften vom Toten Meer II* (Berlin, 1965)

Garcia Martínez, F. and D. W. Parry, *A Bibliography of the Finds in the Desert of Judah 1970–95* (Leiden, 1996)

Jongeling, B., *A Classified Bibliography of the Finds in the Desert of Judah 1958–69* (Leiden, 1971)

LaSor, W.S., *Bibliography of the Dead Sea Scrolls* (Pasadena, 1958)

The Orion Dead Sea Scrolls website: http://orion.mscc.huji.ac.il/resources/bib/bib.shtml

Illustration Credits

Index

Page numbers in *italics* refer to illustrations

Aaron 38, 137, 148, 157
Abegg, Martin 13, 26, 27
Abel, Felix Marie 169
Abihu 148
Abraham 100–01, *101*, 122, 128, 162, 163, *163*
Abyssinian (Ethiopic) church 102
Achor, Vale of 111
Acts, book of 59, 61, 62, 119, 161, 200
Adah 100
Admonition 150
Admonitory Parable 143
Agrippa I 10, 42, 176, 177
Agrippa II 42, 178
Ahura Mazda 88, *88*
Ain el Ghuweir 173, 180
Ain Feshkha 12, 67, 168, 169, 173, *173,* 178, 181, 205
Albright, William F. 7, 68
Alexander Jannaeus, King 10, 41, 42, 96, *99*, 130, 135, 145, 151, 176, 189
Alexander the Great 10, *38*, 39, 61
Alexander, Philip 34, 83, 84
Alexandria 194
Allegro, John M. *7,* 12, 13, 17, 22, 23, 24, 30, 31, *31, 32, 32, 33, 34, 99,* 109, 110, 111, 116, 120, 121, 132, *142,* 149
Al-Qirqisani 16
Amalek 117
American Schools of Oriental Research (ASOR) 7, 9, 12, 22, 24, 28, 31, 82
Ammonites 92
Amos, book of 50, 129, 152, 165
AMS *see* Carbon-14 dating
Anan 16
Ananias 59
Angelic Liturgy, The *see* Songs of the Sabbath Sacrifice
angels 138, *147,* 148; myth of the fallen *126*
Angra Mainyu 88
Annenberg Research Center, Philadelphia 26
Annual of the Department of Antiquities of Jordan 30
Antigonus Mattathias 42, 58, 176, 189
Antioch 178, 194

Antiochus III, King 10, 39, *39*
Antiochus IV, King 10, 39–40, *39*
Apocrypha 124, 144, 160, 164
Apocryphal Psalms *67*, 144, 145, *151*
Apostrophe to Zion 160
Arabah (Dead Sea Valley) 172
Aramaic 7, 9, 22, 28, 33, 49, 100, 114, 118, 124, 126, 129, 149, 186, 190, 206
Aramaic Levi Document 128, 182
Archelaus 10, 58
Aristobulus 10, 42, 130, 134, 189
Aristobulus II 10, 42, 134, 135, 189
Aroer 122
Arsenal Bible *102*
Asmodeus 124
Assyria 38, 61, 144
astrology 133–34, *198*; see also Zodiac; horoscopes
Atonement, Day of 144
Attridge, Harold W. 13, 34
Avigad, Nahman 12, 22, 28, 34, 100

Babylon 10, 38, 129
Babylonia 10, 38, 39, 42, 133
Baden-Württemberg 12
Baillet, Maurice 12, 13, 22, 23, 24, 32, *32*, 33, 34, 92, 124, 132
baptism 63, *63*, 182, 203; as initiation rite 203
Bar Kokhba, Simon 10, 38, 44, 68, 113, 132
Bar Kosiba, Simon *see* Bar Kokhba, Simon
Bar-Adon, Pesach 180
Barthélemy, Dominique 33, 89
Baruch 49
Batanaea 110
Bathenosh 100
baths *see* miqva'ot
Baumgarten, Joseph M. 13, 18, 23, 34, 82, 124, 149, 150
Bedouin 2, 6, *6*, 14, 108, 114, 152, 154, 168, 181
Beersheva University 25
Beit Alpha *198*
Belial 85, 88, 92, 103, 139, 144, 162, 163, 202
Ben Gurion, David 12
Ben Jair, Eleazar 62
Ben Sira, book of 49, 77, 126, 160, 161, 164, 194
Ben-Dov, Jonathan 34, 133

Benedictions 9
Benoit, Pierre 13, 24, 26, 31, 32, *32*
Bernstein, Moshe 34, 116
Bet-Eshdatain 111
Bethel 122
Bethlehem 6, 7, 12, 14, 38, 108, 154, 156
Betz, Otto 130
Bible 6, 8, 16, *16*, 17, 22, 31, 38, 43, 50, 59, 61, 62, 73, 77, 114, 120, 126, 143, 149, 160, 162, 164, 194, 204, 206; Arsenal Bible *102*; modern English translations of 164; order of books in Jewish 50; Syriac Old Testament 150, Old Testament 161; *see also* named books of the Bible
Biblical Archaeologist 25
Biblical Archaeology conference, Jerusalem (1984) 136
Biblical Archaeology Review (*BAR*) 24, *24*, 25, 26, 27
Biblical Archaeology Society (BAS) 26, 27, 28, 139
Biblical Commentaries (*pesharim*) 96–99; *see also* named Commentaries
Biblical Paraphrases 120
Black, Matthew 126
Blessings 144
Boccaccini, Gabriele 205
Book of Astronomical Secrets (1 Enoch) 126, 133
Book of Giants 126, 152
Book of Parables (1 Enoch) 126
Book of Watchers (1 Enoch) 126
books, invention of 66
British Museum, London 17
Brooke, George J. 13, 34, 116
Broshi, Magen 13, 34, 183, 184
Brown, Raymond 23, 27
Brownlee, William 7, 9, *33*, 83, 85
Bulletin of the American Schools of Oriental Research 185
Buqei'a 168
Burgmann, Hans 123
burials 180
Burrows, Millar 7, 83, 199

Caesar 42
Caesarea *41*, 42, 178
Caiaphas 149
Cairo 13, 14, 16, 18, 205; Genizah 18

calendars 46, 64, 85, 102, 133, 134–35, 144, 152, 156, 161, 198, 204; Gezer Calendar *71*; World Calendar of Jubilees 104–05
Calendar Texts 133–35
Calendrical Document/Mishmarot B *135*
California State University, Long Beach 26
Cambridge University 18
Canaan 116
Cansdale, Lena 190
Caracalla, Emperor 16
Carbon-14 dating (AMS) 12, 13, 70, 74–75, 181, 207
Carmignac, Jean 12, 13
Castiglione, Giovanni Benedetto *116–17*
Catholic University of America, Washington, D.C. 33
Cave 1 7, 8, 12, 14, 22, 25, 30, *31*, 34, 64, 67, 68, 82–105, 108, 130, 141, 154, 156, 164, 166, 169, 172, 178, 182, 186, *188*, 189, 192
Cave 2 13, 33, 102, 108, 164
Cave 3 12, 13, 16, *16*, 18, 33, 62, 64, 102, 108–12, *108*, 110, 112, 154
Cave 4 7, 8, *8*, 12, 13, 22, 23, 25, 26, 27, 30, 31, 32, 34–35, 41, 72, 75, 76, 83, 84, 92, 102, *114–15*, 114–51, 134, 136, 137, 138, 141, 143, 144, 146, 154, 164, 166, 180, 182, 188, 189, 195, 203, 204; location of *180*
Cave 5 12, 13, 18, 33, 149, 152; location of *180*
Cave 6 9, 12, 13, 18, 33, 149, 152
Cave 7 12, 13, 33, 152, 154, 182, 200; location of *180*; possible fragments of New Testament in 190
Cave 8 12, 13, 33, 152, 154, 179, 182; location of *180*
Cave 9 12, 13, 33, 152, 154, 182; location of *180*
Cave 10 12, 13, 33, 154, 182; location of *180*
Cave 11 12, 13, 24, 25, 28, 33, 34, 35, 63, 64, 73, 75, 102, 110, 119, 129, 144, 146, 154, *154–55*, 160, *162*, 182, 189, 203
cemeteries, Ain el Ghuweir 173; Qumran 169, 179–81, *179, 180*, 184; *see also* burials
Centre National de la Recherche Scientifique, Paris 23, 30
Chaldeans 97
Charles, Robert Henry 102
Charlesworth, James H. 28, 83, 89, 149
Chazon, Esther 34
Chicago University 180, 205
Christianity 8, 36, 44, 51, 62, 130, 192, 194, 199, 200, 203, 207; early 7, 61, 62–63
Chronicles, book of 10, 11, 50, 129, 135, 156, 165, 172
Church of the Holy Sepulchre, Jerusalem *201*
Cincinnati 26
Claremont Graduate School 26
Claremont School of Theology, Ancient Biblical Manuscript Center 33
coins *39*, 44, *44*, *85*, *132*, *156*, 176, 177, *177*, 178, 179
College of Science and Technology, Manchester 108
Collins, John J. 34
Commentaries *see* named Commentaries; *see also pesharim*
Commentaries on Genesis 116–17, 133
Communal Confession 144
Community Rule 8, 12, 18, 22, 46, 54, 55, 58, 59, 67, 71, 72, 73, 82–85, *83*, *86–87*, 88, 89, *89*, 92, 129, 130, 142, 143, 144, 150, 152, 180, 183, 188, 200, 202, 203, 205; analysis by Sarianna Metso 84
Composition on Divine Providence 142
Copper Scroll 12, 23, 30, 31, 63, 64, 109, *109, 110–12*, *110, 111, 112, 113*, 166, 186
Corinthians, Letter to the 202

Cotton, Hannah M. 34, 151
Crawford, Sidnie A. White 35, 121 (*see also* White, Sidnie A.)
Cross Jr., Frank M. 12, 13, 22, 23, 25, 28, 31, *31*, *33*, 34, 68, 70, 71, 72, 114, 130, 178, 186, 188, 206
Crown, Alan 190
crucifixion 96, *96*
Cyrus of Persia 38

Daily Prayers 144
Dalman, Gustav 169
Damascus 18, 90, 199
Damascus Document 13, 18, *19*, 27, 31, 38, 54, 59, 61, 63, 71, 85, 88, 98, 102, 127, 132, 133, 140, 142, 152, 160, 165, 180, 188, 190, 200, 202, 205; Cairo manuscripts of 149, 150 ; fragments of in Cave 4 149–50, 150
Daniel, Apocryphon of 202
Daniel, book of 38, 43, 50, 88, 92, 97, 126, 129, 140, 148, 152, 162, 163, 165, 190
David, King 41, 50, 128, 130, 139, 143, 161, *161*, 182, 194
Davidic dynasty 202
Davies, Philip R. 18, 26, 27, 92, 150, 178
Davila, James 34, 147
de Saulcy, Ferdinand 169
de Vaux, Roland 7, 12, 13, 22, 23, 24, 30, *30*, 31, 32, *32*, 67, 111, 114, 119, 166, 169, 172, 173, 174, 176–77, 178, 179, 180, 181, 182, 188, 191
Dead Sea 7, 16, 54, 88, 110, 168, 169, *170,* 171, 173, 174, 189, 190
Dead Sea Discoveries 13
Dead Sea Scrolls, and Christianity 206; and early Christianity 200–03; and early Jesus movement 202; and Judaism 194–99, 206; and relevance for Judaism 203; authorship of 204–05; battles over ownership 7; battles over proper interpretation 7; biblical manuscripts 164–65; brontologia in 50; campaign for publication 25–27; Christian and Jewish interpretations 203; chronology of discoveries and publications 12–13; classification of 77, *77*; computer reconstruction of documents 27; connection with caves and ruins 188–91; Daniel and 129; delay in publication 25, 27, 139; early discoveries 16–17; editing of 22–27, 30–33; editors 30–35, *32*; English translations of 28; historical framework 38–44; horoscopes in 50; importance for Judaism and Christianity 192; list of by cave 78–81; origin of 105; palaeography of 70–72; plates of 28; poetry, psalms and prayers in 144–49; production of 66–67; publications 28; reconstruction of 76–77; replicas and memorabilia *206–07*; scripts and writing styles in 68; similarities with New Testament 200, 202, 203; spelling in 73, *73*; tabs and fastenings in *67*; Teacher of Righteousness in 25, 63, 77, 95, 97, 98, 137, 139, 160, 202, 203; tools and materials in production of 66–67, *66*; Wicked Priest in 77, 97, 98, 137, 188; Zoroastrianism and 88
Dead Sea Valley (Arabah) 172
Demetrius III, King 61, 98
Department of Antiquities of Jordan 30, 172
Deuteronomy, book of 9, 13, 16, *16*, 17, 22, 50, 62, 68, 85, 89, 96, 117, 120, 121, 122, 129, 130, 132, 133, 140, 152, 157, 160, 162, 165
Deutsche Forschungsgemeinschaft 23, 33
dietary regulation 50
Diloa 111
Dimant, Devorah 34

Discoveries in the Judaean Desert (DJD) 13 , 22, 27, 28, 30, 31, 32, 33, 82, 154, 164, 207; contents of 29
divorce 63
DNA analysis 207
Donceel-Voûte, Pauline 190, 191
Doq 111, 130
Dorner, Dalia 139
Dream Book (1 Enoch) 126
Driver, Godfrey R. 189, 205
Duhaime, Jean 92
Duncan, Julie 34

Ecclesiastes, book of 50, 71, 140, 165, 190
École Biblique et Archéologique Française, Jerusalem 7, 12, 13, 22, 23, 24, 30, 32, *32*, 33, 172, 189
Edfu Papyri 68, 71
Edom 38, 41, 92
Egypt 10, 18, 36, 39, 40, 121, 122
Eichstätt 180
Eisenman, Robert 13, 26, 28, 139, 151, 205
Eleazar 186, 187, 206
Elephantine Papyri 68, 71
Elgvin, Torleif 34
Eli 149
Elisha, Apocryphon of 128
Emmaus 58
Encyclopedia of the Dead Sea Scrolls 13
Engedi 54, 168, 169, 186, 190, 206
Enoch, books of 38, 77, 103, 126–27, *126–27*, 128, 129, 133, 149, 152, 163, 164, 190, 199, 205
Eph'al, Israel 181
Ernst, Dorothee 34
Esau 117
Eschatological Midrash 129
Eshel, Esther 34, 71, 151, 186, 206
Eshel, Hanan 34, 151, 183
Essenes 10, 54–55, 58, 63, 77, 85, 146, 169, 173, 182, 188, 189, 190, 191, 195, 200, 203, 206; and celibacy 54, 58; as possible authors of Dead Sea Scrolls 204–05; hierarchy of 58; John 58; Judas 58; Menahem 58; Simon 58
Esther, book of 8, 48, 50, 62, 164, 165
Ethiopic 126
eucharist *202*, 203
Eusebius of Caesarea 16
Exodus, book of 17, 22, 50, 89, 102, 121, 130, 148, 152, 157, 190; Song of the Sea 120, 132
Exodus, the *120*, 122
Ezekiel 48
Ezekiel, book of 129, 148, 149, 156, 157, 165, 199
Ezra, book of 10, 38, 50, 61, 165, 194, 195

Falk, Daniel 34
fasting 50
Feast of the Covenant Renewal 150
festivals 137, 157; Booths (Tabernacles) 46, 121; Festival of First-fruits 144 ; Festival Prayers 144; Hanukkah 62; Passover 46, 203; Purim 62; Weeks (Pentecost) 46, 85, 88
First Jewish Revolt 10, 58, 174, 177, 206
Fitzmyer, Joseph A. 12, 23, 27, *32*, 34, 100, 124
Flint, Peter 34
flood story 116–17, *116–17*, 133; *see also* Noah
Florilegium 129, 162, 194
food, ritual preparation of 61; ritually pure 138; *see also* dietary regulation

Fouquet, Jean *130*
Fourth Philosophy 54, 62
fragments 9, 23, 27, 31, 33, 66, 76–77, 119, 143, 152, 162, 182, 200; Cave 4 23; damage pattern of 76; reconstructing a manuscript from 75
Freedman, David Noel 13, 25, 35, 154
Fribourg, University of 33
Fuller, Russell 34

Galatians, Letter to the 202
Galilee 41, 42, 62, *198*; Sea of 42
Gamaliel, Rabban 61, 119
Gamul 135
García Martínez, Florentino 34, 35
Genesis Apocryphon 12, 22, 34, 74, 75, 100–01, *100*, 128
Genesis, book of 50, 61, 100–01, 102, 117, 120, 121, 126, 133, 140, 152, 162, 165
Genesis Pesher *see* Commentaries on Genesis
Gerizim, Mt 10, 38, 39, 61, 62, 110, 111
Gershom 157
Gezer Calendar *71*
Ginsburg, Christian David 17
Ginzberg, Louis 18, 205
Glessmer, Uwe 34, 133
Golb, Norman 180, 190, 205, *205*
Goliath 161
Gomorrah 169
Gottesman, Samuel 12
Göttingen, University of 16, 33, 146, 204
grace after meals 143, 144
Greek 7, 16, 22, 33, 41, 49, 88, 102, 112, 149, 161, 164, 182, 190, 200
Greeks 39, 43
Greenfield, Jonas 34, 133
Guariento *147*

Habakkuk 8, 50, 97, *97*, 165
Habakkuk Commentary 8, 12, 22, 43, 50, 61, 82, 95, 96–98, *97*, 151, 162, 165, 178, 188, 202
Hadrian 10
Hagar 101, *101*
Haggai 10, 50, 165
halakhah 198
Halakhic Letter 13, 25, 27, 32, 59, 82, 98, 103, 136–39, *136, 138*, 142, 145, 160, 190, 194, 203, 205; copyright of 139
Ham 116
Hananiah 180
Harding, Gerald Lankester 7, 12, 22, 30, *30*, 172
Harrington, Daniel 34
Harvard University 13, 31, 114, 206
Hasidim 188
Hasmonaean dynasty 18, 40, 41, 42, 43, 48, 58, 71, 103, 130, 139, 151, 162, 176, 188, 190, 194; growth of Jewish territory under *39*
Hazor 34
Hebrew 7, 9, 16, 22, 25, 28, 33, 34, 46, 49, 59, 73, 82, 98, 108, 114, 118, 119, 123, 124, *125*, 143, 149, 151, 152, 154, 160, 164, 180, 186, 190, 195, 200, 203, 206; *see also* palaeo-Hebrew
Hebrew Union College, Cincinnati 27
Hebrew University, Jerusalem 6, 12, 13, 22, 82, 92; Institute of Archaeology 34
Hebrews, Letter to the 63, 162, 163
Heidelberg, University of 23, 76
Heikalot texts 149
Herbert, Edward 35

Herod Antipas 10, 42
Herod Archelaeus 42, 177, 189
Herod Philip 42
Herod the Great 7, 10, 41, 42, 43, 44, 58, 61, 62, 88, 189, 190; extent of the kingdom of *43*
Hillel 203
Hirschfeld, Yitzhar 185, 190
Hisday 186, 187, 196
Hodayoth 73, 144, 199
Holm-Nielsen, Svend 94
Holon 186, 187
Honi 186, 187, 206
Horoscope text 72
horoscopes 50, 72
Hosea, book of 50,165
Hosea Commentary 99
Humbert, Jean-Baptiste 189, 190
Hunt, Holman *60*
Huntington Library, San Marino, California 13, 26
Hunzinger, Claus-Hunno 12, 22, 23, *32*, 33, *33*, 114
Hurarat, mountains of 100
Hymn to the Creator 160, 161
Hymns Scroll *see* Thanksgiving Hymns
Hyrcanion 168
Hyrcanus 134, 189
Hyrcanus II 10, 135, 176
Hyrcanus, Prince 101

Idumaea 41, 42, 44
immersion 144
Iran *88*
Iraq 16
Isaiah, book of 8, 9, 48, 50, 66, 82, 129, 148, 149, 152, 162, 164, 165, 190, 200
Isaiah, George 6, *9*
Isaiah Scroll *9*, 22, 34, 68, 74, 75, 82, 164–65
Israel 7, 8, 12, 18, 26, 27, 38, 46, 55, 62, 84, 85, 88, 89, 92, 93, 96, 128, 130, 144, 145, 146, 156, 157, 160, 162, 163, 180, 195, 198, 204; War of Independence 12
Israel Antiquities Authority (IAA) 13, 26
Israel Museum, Jerusalem, Shrine of the Book 7, 12, 207
Israel Department of Antiquities 26
Israeli-Jordanian war (1948–49) 172

Jacob 62, 103, 128
James, brother of Jesus 205
Japheth 100
Jastram, Nathan 34
Jehoiachin, King 38
Jeremiah 38, 39, 48, *143*
Jeremiah, Apocryphon of 128
Jeremiah, book of 50, 117, 165
Jeremiah, Letter of 152, 190
Jericho 16, 43, 110, 111, 122, *122–23*, 123, 130, 143, 169, 180, 186, 187, 206; burials in 180; destruction of 130, *130*
Jerusalem 7, 10, 13, 16, 18, 25, 26, 31, 33, *36*, 38, 39, 40, 41, 42, 44, 46, 58, 61, 62, 68, 96, 97, 98, 108, 110, 130, 137, 138, 139, 143, 145, *149*, 150–51, 156, 157, 162, 168, 169, 180, 182, 190, 195, *198*, 204, 205; American Schools in 160; burials in 180; Church of the Holy Sepulchre in *201*; Essene quarter in *204*; fall of 10, 62; reconstructed as Aelia Capitolina 10; topography of *32*; treasure presumed hidden in and around 110, *110*; Western ('Wailing') Wall *47, 52–53, 196–97*

Jerusalem Temple 8, 10, 18, 36, 38, 39, 41, 43, 44, *44*, 46, *48–49*, 50, 51, 58, 59, 61, 62, 64, 84, 93, 109, 110, 112, 112, 132, 134, 135, 137, 138, 144, *156*, 160, 188, 191, 195, 198, 199, 200, 203, 205; destruction of 10; Tomb of Christ *201*; *see also* Temple cult; Temple tax
Jesus 7, 61, 63, 88, 162, 163, 198, 200, 202, 203, 205, 207; crucifixion of 200
Job, book of 50, 88, 119, 140, 165
Job Targum 13, 25, 118–19, *119,* 154
Joel 50, 202
Johanàn 134
John (Essene) 58
John Hyrcanus 10, 41, 42, 61, 130, 189
John Paul II, Pope *193*
John the Baptist 63, 182, 200, *200*, 203, 207; as Essene 200, 203
John, Gospel of 62
Jonah 48, 50, 165
Jonathan Maccabee 10, 42, 145, 188, 189
Jonathan, King 145, 150–51
Jones, Vendyl 110, 112
Jongeling, Bastiaan 13, 154
Joppa 58
Jordan 7, 30
Jordan, River 17, 38, 42, 122, 189
Jordanian Antiquities exploration team 82
Joseph 97, 116
Josephus, Flavius 38, 39, 44, 54, 55, 58, 59, 61, 62, 96, 138, 177, 182, 188, 189, 194, 195, 203, 204, 205
Joshua *123*, 130
Joshua, Apocryphon of 122–23, 128, 130, 164
Joshua, book of 13, 50, 66, 122, 130, 165, 172
Joshua Roll *123*
Journal of Biblical Literature 143
Journal of Jewish Studies 122
Jubilees, book of 27, 31, 61, 62, 77, 102–03, 121, 122, 126, 127, 128, 129, 133, 164, 165, 199, 205
Jubilees, World Calendar of 104–05
Judaea 10, 23, 36, 41, 42, 43, 46, 58, 111, 164, 168, 176, 178, 182, 200
Judah 38, 39, 40, 42, 96, 97, 117, 144, 145, 151, 172, 174, 198
Judaism 18, 32, 36, 38, 39, 46–51, 58, 61, 62, 88, 137, 139, 188, 190, 192, 194, 200, 207; ancient 7, 8; Dead Sea Scrolls and 194; Enochic 127, 205; Jewish parties and sects 54–63; Jewish religious life/practices 46–49, 50–51; Mosaic 205; Rabbinic 44, 50, 139, 143, 199, 203, 207; relevance of the scrolls for 203; ritual purity in 46, 50, 58, 63, 133, 181–83; sectarian 199, 206; superstitious practices attached to 50
Judas (Essene) 58
Judas Maccabee 7, 10, 58, 62, 102, 130, 151
Jude, Letter of 126
Judges, book of 13, 50, 165
Judith, book of 49 , 61
Jum'a Muhammad *6*

Kando (Khalil Iskander Shahin) 6, *7*, 12, 13, 156
Kapera, Zdzisław J. 26, 27, 139
Kaufman, Stephen 34
Kenyon, Frederick 206
Khirbet el-Musaq 190
Khirbet Qumran *see* Qumran
Kidron Valley *36*
Kings, book of 10, 13, 18, 38, 50, 61, 66, 152, 156, 157, 165, 190
Kiraz, Anton 12

Kister, Menahem 34
'Kittim' 43, 92, 97, 98
Knohl, Israel 34
Kobelski, Paul 162
Kohath 157
Kuhn, Karl Georg 12, 110
Kurth, Gottfried 180

Lachish 30; capture of *97*
Lady Folly 143
Lamech 100
Lamentations 50, 143, 152, 165
Lange, Armin 34
languages *see* named languages
Laperrousaz, Ernest-Marie 178
Larson, Erik 34
Last Supper 200
Latin 102
Law *see* Moses, Law of
Leaney, Robert 83
leather 76, 108, 168, 169; tabs 152, 179
Lebanon 12
Lefkovits, Judah 109
Lehmann, Manfred 34
leprosy 18, 137, 190
Levi 128, 130, 164
Levi, Testament of 182
Levites 85, 88, 89, 130, 157
Leviticus, book of 25, 50, *118–19*, 119, 120, 133,
    154, 156, 162, 163, 165
Licht, Jacob 94
Lim, Timothy 34
Lippens, Philippe 12
List of Proper Names 149
London 16, 26
Lot 101
Lubar, Mount 100
Luke, Gospel of 88, 163, 200, 202
Lydda 58

Maccabean wars 93
Maccabees 40, 42, 68, 188, 205; battle of the *102*;
    book of 10, 49, 194, 195
Macedonians 88
Machaerus 42
Madrid 13
Magen, Yitzhak 184, 190
Magness, Jodi 178–79, 185, 189
Maier, Johann 156
Malachi 50, 165
Malachi Commentary 99
Manasseh, King 144
Manchester 108, 111; University of 23, 31
Mark, Gospel of 190, 200, 202
marriage 144, 145; forbidden 137
Masada 12, 34, 42, 44, *45*, 62, 68, 93, 122, 146, 179;
    fall of 10
maskil 82, 84, 90, 95, 141
maskilim 129, 205
Masoretic text 73, 121, 164, 206
Masterman, Ernest W. Gurney 168
Mathews, Kenneth 13, 35, 154
Matthew, Gospel of 10, 18, 59, 61, 194, 202
McCarter, P. Kyle 109
McCormick Theological Seminary, Chicago 23, 31
McGill University, Montreal 23

mebaqqer 200, 205
Media 124
Meditations of Creation 142
Megiddo 34
Melchiresha 144
Melchizedek 63, 149, 162–63, *163*
Melchizedek midrash 128, 194, 200
Menahem (Essene) 58
Merari 157
messiah 62, 90, 130, 198; Christian and Jewish
    images of *200*; expectation of 200; of Aaron 90;
    of Israel 90
Methuselah 100
Metso, Sarianna 34, 83, 84
mezuzot 13, 22, 50, 152
Micah 50, 165
Micah Commentary 99
Michigan, University of 25
Milgrom, Jacob 34
Milik, Jozef T. 12, 13, 18, 22, 23, 24, 25, *25*, *30*,
    30–31, *32*, *33*, 34, 90, 109, 111, 114, 119, 126,
    149, 150, 188
miqva'ot (ritual baths) 46, 182, 185; *see also* purity,
    ritual baths and bathing
Miriam 118, *118*
mishmarot 27
Mishmarot texts 41, 134, 135
Mishnah 59, 108, 137, 138
Moab 92
Moffett, William 26
Mogilany Papers 26
Moses 102, 103, 122, 128, *128*, 130, 139, 148, 156,
    194; books of 140, 194; Law of 18, 38, 50, 58, 62,
    63, 89, 102, *103*, 104, 121, *128*, 139, 163, 165, 195,
    202; *see also* named books of Moses
Muhammad eb-Dib *6*, *6*, 7, 12, 16
Murabba'at 32, 51, 71, 164
Murphy, Catherine M. 34
Mystery texts 141

Nabataean 33, 134
Nabonidus, King 129, 144–45, *145*
Nadab 148
Nahal Hever 33
Nahamani 186, 187
Nahum 98; book of 41, 50, 165
Nahum Commentary 96, *98–99*, 151, 162;
nails *183*, 184
Nash Papyrus 9, 68, *68*
Nathan 186
National Archaeological Museum, Amman 30, 90
National Centre for Scientific Research, Paris *see*
    Centre National de la Recherche Scientifique
Naveh, Joseph 34, 149
Nebuchadnezzar 10, 38, 39, 129
Nehemiah 10, 194; book of 8, 10, 38, 61, 164,
    165, 194
Nero 68, 178
Netherlands, the 154
New Covenant 200
New Jerusalem 152, 154
New Testament 31, 32, 33, 50, 58, 59, 61, 62, 63, 88,
    92, 140, 152, 161, 165, 190, 198, 199, 200, 202, 205,
    206; similarities between Dead Sea Scrolls and
    200; *see also* named Gospels and books
New York 26; All Souls Church 23; University 25
Newsom, Carol A. 13, 26, 34, 35, 75, 76, 114, 122,
    123, 46, 147, 148, 149
Niccum, Curt 34

Niehoff, Maren 34
Nineveh 124
Nitzan, Bilhah 34
Noah 100, 116, 117, 128
Non-Biblical Psalms 114
Non-Canonical Psalms 13, 144
Notre Dame, University of 25, 26, 181
Numbers, book of 17, 50, 90, 93, 110, 120, 121, 130,
    137, 157, 165, 190

Obadiah 50, 165
offerings 18, 157
Olyan, Saul 34
Omriel 149
Onias III 10, 40
Ordinances 132–33, *132, 133*
Ordo 144
Origen 16
ostraca 13, 152, 168, 179, 186–87, 206
Oxford University 23, 189
Oxtoby, William 27

palaeography 28, 68, 70–72, 74, 83, 124, 130, 146
palaeo-Hebrew 25, 33, 152, 154, *161*
Palaeo-Hebrew Leviticus Scroll 13
Palestine 7, 10, 12, 14, 39, 41, 43, 44, 58, 71, 93, 203,
    204
Palestine Archaeological Museum (now Rockefeller
    Museum), Jerusalem 13, *32*, *69*, 136, 191
    'scrollery' *22*, 23, *25*; *see also* Rockefeller
    Museum
Palestine Exploration Fund 168
Palmyrene 33
Panion, Battle of 39
papyrus 9, 67, 76, 108, 152, 207; Edfu Papyri 68, 71;
    Elephantine Papyri 68, 71; Nash Papyrus 68, *68*
Parables 126
parchment 66, 67, 207
Parry, Donald 34
Parthians 42, 88, 189
Patrich, Joseph 110, 112, 183
Paul of Tarsus 61, 62, 119, 200, 207; letters of 165
Penal Code 150
Pentateuch 50, 61, 62, 66, 156, 164, 165; Enochic
    126; Samaritan 120, 121, 130
Pentateuchal Paraphrase *see* Reworked Pentateuch
Peraea 41, 42
Persepolis, palace *88*
Persian Empire 10, 36, 38, 39, 46, 48, 88
pesharim 9, 72, 73, 95, 96–99, *161*, 162, 194; *see also*
    Commentaries
Peter, Second Letter of 126
Petrie, Flinders 30
Pfann, Stephen 34
Pharisees 48, 54, 58, 59, 61, 98, 123, 136, 138, 145,
    188, 189, 195, 198, 203; as possible authors of
    Dead Sea Scrolls 205
Phasael 42
Philip the Tetrarch 10, 42
Philistines 92
Philo of Alexandria 54, 58, 118, 189, 194
phylacteries (tefillin) 13, 22, 50, *51*, 82, 152, 182,
    196–97
Pike, Dana 34
Pilate, Pontius 10
Pixner, Bargil 110
Plea for Deliverance 160
Pliny 54, 169, 188, 190, 204

Poland 26
Pollaiuolo *125*
Pompey 10, 41, 42
pottery *30*, 82, 108, 114, 168, 174, 176, 178, 206
Pouilly, Jean 83
Prayer of Manasses 144
Prayer of Nabonidus 144
Princeton Theological Seminary 28
Priscilla catacomb *202*
Proverbs 48, 50, 140, 143, 165, 190
Psalms, book of 16, 33, 48, 50, 95, 96, 129, 140, 150, 152, 160, 161, 162, 165, 190, 202
Psalms Commentary 98, 99
Psalms of Joshua *see* Joshua, Apocryphon of
Psalms Scroll 13, 24, 33, 72, 73, 133, 144, 154, 160–61, *161*
Psalter, Greek 144, 161; Hebrew 161; Syriac 144, 161
Pseudepigrapha 22, 206
Pseudo-Daniel text 128, 129
Pseudo-Ezekiel text 128, *128*
Ptolemies 39
Ptolemy 10
Puech, Émile 13, 26, 33, 34, *76*
purification 63, *63*, 144; by water 203; rituals 138, 195, 199
purity 190, 198, 199; cult 190–91; laws 61, 156, 178; of poured liquids 136–37, *137*, 138; of the priesthood 137; of vessels 136–37, *137*; ritual baths and bathing 181–83, *181*; *see also miqva'ot*

Qaraites 16
Qimrom, Elisha 13, 25, 27, 35, 136, 137, 139, *139*
Qumran 7, 8, *8*, 10, 12, 13, 14, 16, 17, 18, 22, 25, 27, 30, 31, *31*, 33, 34, 36, 41, 44, 46, 50, 54, *55*, 58, 59, 62, 63, 64, 67, 70, 71, 72, 73, 74, 76, 77, 82, 85, 88, 90, 92, 96, 97, 101, 102, 108, 110, 111, 112, 114, 121, 122, 124, 125, 126, 129, 130, 133, 135, 138, 140, 143, 144, 146, 149, 151, *152–53*, 154, 157, 160, 161, 163, 164, *166–67*, 167–85, *168, 169, 170, 171, 183, 184*, 186, 188, 200, 202, 203, 204, 206, 207; abandonment 189; as a scroll-making centre 152; biblical manuscripts from 164–65; cemetery 169, 179–81, *179, 180*, 184; community/sect 25, 55–56, 66, 82, 98, 108, 127, 137, 188, 190; destruction 189; excavations 172, *172*, 183–84; Qumran, likely periods of occupation at *189*; manuscript production at *68–69*; non-biblical scrolls 127; ostraca from 186–87; outline of *174–75*; pattern of burials at *181*; Roman Rule in 189; scriptorium 67, 177, 191; viewed as a hospice for lepers 190; water system 185, *185*
Qumran Chronicle 26

Rabbinic Judaism 8, 44, 50, 139, 143, 199, 203, 207
rabbis 199, *199*
Rabin, Chaim 18, 205
ram's horn *135*
Raphael 124
Ravenna, Galla Placidia *200*
Rebukes Reported by the Overseer 180
Reclaiming the Dead Sea Scrolls 26
red heifer, ceremony of the 137, 138
Reed, Stephen A. 13, *119*
Rembrandt *143*
resurrection of the dead 61, 200
Revelation, book of 149, 203
Revue Biblique 33, 172

Revue de Qumrân 12, 13
'Reworked Pentateuch' 74, 75, 118, 120–21, *121*
ritual bathing *see* purity; *miqva'ot*
Ritual of Purification text 145
ritual purity *see* purity
Robinson, James 26, 28, 139
Rockefeller Museum, Jerusalem (formerly Palestine Archaeological Museum) 23, *23*, 76, 191; *see also* Palestine Archaeological Museum
Rockefeller, John D. 12, 13, 23
Rohrer-Ertl, Olav 180
Roman empire 36, 46, 92
Romans 43, 44, 97, 98, 112, 178, 179, 200, 203, 205
Rome 36, 40, 42, 44, 58, 61, 62, 88, 93, 194, 205; Arch of Titus *43*
Roth, Cecil 189, 205
Rotterdam 16
Royal Netherlands Academy of Sciences 24
Rubens, Peter Paul 126, *163*
Rule of Blessings 82, 90
Rule of the Congregation 54, 82, 89–90, *90–91*, 203
Rules Scroll 82, *83*, 85
Ruth, book of 48, 50, 165

Saad, Joseph *32*, *69*
Sabbath, observance of 18, 50, 61, 137, *138, 149*
sacrifice 50, 51, 54, 121, 156, 162, 183
Sadducees 54, 58–59, 136, 137, 139, 190, 195; as possible authors of Dead Sea scrolls 205; opinions of the 138
Salahi, Feidi 12
Salome Alexandra 10, 42, 134, 176, 189
Samaria 10, 38, 41, 42, 61
Samaritans 39, *61*, 61–62, 161, 164
Samuel, Apocryphon of 128
Samuel, books of 50, 74, 75, 117, 129, 130, 160, 165, 182, 190
Samuel, Mar Athanasius Yeshua 6–7, *9*, 12, 22
Sanders, James A. 13, 24, 28, 33, *33*, 35, 154, 160, 161
Sanderson, Judith E. 13, 33, 35
Sarah 100–01, *101*
Saul 117, 161
Scaurus, Marcus Aemilius 41, 134, 135
Schechter, Solomon 18, *20–21*
Schiffman, Lawrence H. 26, 35, 59, 89, 149, 190, 203, 205
Schönfeld, Johann *59*
Schuller, Eileen M. 13, 26, 35, 76, 94, 114
Schwarz, Daniel 18
scribes 46, 66, 67, 70, 72, *72*, 149, *195*, 203
script 68; Aramaic 68; Archaic 68, 70, 71; Hasmonaean 18, 68, 70, *70*, 71, 83, 92, 94, 102, 116, 119, 120, 124, 126, 132, 133, 136, 147, 149, 162; Hebrew 68, 70; Hebrew/Phoenician 17; Herodian 18, 68, 70, *70*, 71, 83, 92, 94, 100, 102, 119, 122, 124, 126, 133, 136, 147, 149, 151, 156, 161, 186; late Qumranic 149; Medieval 18, *70*; Moabite 17; palaeo-Hebrew *70*, 71, 72, 97, 114
scroll jars *6*, 108
Sebaste 62; *see also* Samaria
Second Jewish Revolt 10, 118, 156, 178
Second Temple period 17, 39, 46, 50, 70, 205, 207
'Secrets of the Dead Sea Scrolls' documentary 13
Seductress, the (Lady Folly) 143
Seely, David 35
Sekakah, Valley of 111
Seleucia 16
Seleucids 36, 39, 40, 98, 102, 176

Semitic 41
Sennacherib 96
Septuagint 32
sexual intercourse, permitted and forbidden 18
Shammai 203
Shanks, Hershel *24*, 25, 27, 139
Shapira, Moses William 16–17
Shechem 39, 61, 62, 110
Sheffield University 26, 27
Shelamzion (Salome) 134
Sheridan, Susan 181
Shrine of the Book *see* Israel Museum
Simon (Essene) 58
Simon Bar Kokhba 10
Simon Maccabee 10, 188, 189
Sinai, Mt 102, 103, 121, 128
Six-Day War 13
Skehan, Patrick W. 12, 13, 22, 23, 25, 33, *33*, 35, 114
Skinner, Andrew C. 35
Smith, Mark S. 35
Sodom 101
Sokoloff, Michael 35, 133
Solomon 38, *59*, *140*, 157, 194
Song of Miriam 118
Song of Songs 50, 152, 165
Song of the Sea (Exodus) 120
Songs of the Maskil (Songs of the Sage) 76, 144, 145, 161
Songs of the Sabbath Sacrifice 13, 26, 44, 51, 72, 75, 76, 90, 114, 133, 144, 146–49, *146*, 163, 189, 199, 203; structure of 148
South Florida, University of 186
Starcky, Jean 12, 22, 23, *32*, 33, *33*, 114
Starkey, James L. 30
Steckoll, Solomon H. 180
Stegemann, Hartmut 16, 27, 35, 67, 76, 120, 129, 146, 191, 204–05
Steudel, Annette 35, 129
stone *178*, 182
Stone, Michael 35
Strange, James 186
Strugnell, John 12, 13, *22*, 22, 23, 24, 25, 26, 27, 28, 31–32, *31*, *33*, 35, 114, 136, 139, 146
Stuckenbruck, Loren 35
Sukenik, Eleazar 6, 12, 22, 28, 34, *34*, 68, 92, 94
Sussman, Jacob 27
Syria 10, 36, 39, 61
Syriac 33
Syriac Old Testament *see* Bible

Ta'amireh tribe 154
tabs, leather 152, 179
Talmon, Shemaryahu 35, 122, 133
Talmud 59
Tamna 58
Tanzer, Sarah 35
Targum to Job 13, 25, 118, *119*, 154
Targum to Leviticus 118–19
tefillin *see* phylacteries
Teiman 129
Teixidor, Javier 27
Tell ed-Duweir 30
Tell el-Far'ah 30
Temple cult 46, 63, 92, 203
Temple Scroll 13, 25, 35, 46, 54, 59, 62, 66, 74, 75, 88, 96, 98, 121, 132, 133, 154, 156–60, *157, 158–59*, 165, 182, 190, 194, 203, 205; English translation of 154
Temple tax 46, 132, 133

Testament, of Judah 128; of Naphtali 128; of Amram 128; of Joseph 128; of Kohath (Qahat) 74, 75, 128; of Levi 74, 75, 182; as literary form 128
Testaments of the Patriarchs 128
Testimonia 72, 122, 123, 130–31, *131*, 164
Thanksgiving Hymns 12, 22, 34, 68, 74, 75, 76, *76*, 94–95, *94–95*, 188
The Dead Sea Scrolls series 28
The Times, London 12
Therapeutae 118
Tigchelaar, Eibert 35
Tigris, River 124
Timotheus I 16
Titian *200*
Titus 178
Tobias (Tobiah) 124, *125*
Tobit, book of 49, 77, 124–25, *124–25*, 164
Torah 17, 50, *72*, 83, 102, 140, *194*
Toseftah 138
Tov, Emanuel 13, 26, 27, 34, *34*, 35, 73, 114, 120, 121
Trebolle Barrera, Julio 35
Trajan 178
Transjordan 41, 180; burials in 180
Trever, John C. 7, 9, *9*, *33*, 68, 83
Tufnell, Olga 30

Ulrich, Eugene 13, 25, 26, 35
Uzziah, King 172

van der Ploeg, Johannes P.M. 13, 35, 119, 154
van der Werff, Adriaen *101*
van der Woude, Adam S. 13, 25, 35, 102, 119, 154, 162

VanderKam, James C. 26, 27, 35, 102, 126
Vatican 12, 23, 206
Vermes, Geza 25, 26, 35, 151
Vespasian 62, 178
vessels, purity/impurity of 136–37, *13*; stone *178*, 182
vows, making of 50

Wacholder, Ben Zion 13, 26, 27, *27*, 160
Wadi Murabba'at 68
Wadi Qumran 7, *14–15*, 114, 152, 168, 185
Wall Street Journal 7, *7*, 12
War of the Sons of Light against the Sons of Darkness 34
War Scroll 12, 22, 33, 35, 43, 44, 62, *64–65*, 71, 72, 73, 88, 90, 92–93, *92, 93*, 144, 189, 202; 4Q285 9
Ways of Righteousness 143
Weinfeld, Moshe 35, 143
Wernberg-Møller, Preben 83
West Bank, Israeli occupation of 154, 156
West Semitic Research 77
White, S.A. 120; *see also* Crawford, Sidnie A. White
Wiles of the Wicked Woman *see* Seductress, the
Wisdom Texts 140–43, *141, 142*
Wise, Michael O. 13, 26, 121, 156
Wolters, Al 109
Wood, Bryant G. 185
Words of the Heavenly Lights 129
Words of the Luminaries 144
Works of the Law 77
Wright Baker, Henry 108

Yadin, Yigael 12, 13, 22, 25, 28, 34, 35, *35*, 92, 93, 100, 121, 146, 154, 156, *157*, 160
yahad 18, 82, 84, *88*, 89, 90, 95, 102, 103, 139, 143, 150, 165, 183, 186, 199, 202, 203, 206
Yannai, Hyrcanus 149
Yannai, Zacharai 149
Yardeni, Ada 27, 35, 70–71, 150, 151, 186
Yarmuk, River 110
Yom Kippur/Ramadan War 13
Yosai, Peter 149

zadduqim 59, 137, 205
Zadok 38, *59*, 62, 88; dynasty of 58–59
Zadokite Fragments *see* Damascus Document
Zadokite priesthood/priests 83, 90, 149, 205
Zealots 62–63, 146, 189, 195; as possible authors of Dead Sea Scrolls 205
Zechariah 10, 50, 165, 190
Zedekiah 38; Apocryphon of 128
Zephaniah 50, 165
Zephaniah Commentary 99
Zillah 100
Zion, Mt 110
Zoan 100
Zodiac *198*
Zoroaster (Zarathustra) 88
Zoroastrianism 38, 84; and the scrolls 88
Zuckerman, Bruce 77, *89*, *119*